WITHDRAWN

Stafford Library
Columbia College
1001 Rogers Street
Columbia, Missouri 65216

Talcott Parsons
An Intellectual Biography

Talcott Parsons (1902–1979) has been called the most influential of American sociologists for his theoretical work on social systems and for his important role in delineating the field of sociology as a distinct discipline. He is credited with introducing to the United States and further refining and applying the social theories of European thinkers Max Weber and Émile Durkheim. He is best known for his classic works *The Structure of Social Action* (1937), once called a "charter for sociology," and *The Social System* (1951), which laid the building blocks for what was to become known as the "functionalist perspective" in sociology.

As a pivotal figure in the history of the field of sociology, Parsons has been the subject of a long line of writing seeking to explain and interpret, or critique his theories. Parsons was often accused, among other things, of being an overly abstract, even apolitical thinker, remote in Harvard's ivory tower. As this book argues cogently, however, this accusation is false. The controversial Parsons, in fact, emulated his mentor, the venerable Max Weber, in at least two respects: As a scholar, he practiced *Wertfreiheit* (scientific professionalism) and as a political activist he worked for the preservation and expansion of democracy. In this unique, intellectual biography, Uta Gerhardt traces this double commitment and links Parsons's scholarship to his politics.

Utilizing rich archival material, Gerhardt examines four periods in Parsons's intellectual life in the context of American history and society. From the New Deal and the rise of German fascism to World War II, through the McCarthy era and the Civil Rights movement, Parsons's overriding agenda was to develop both a sociological understanding and a defense of the development of modern democracy. By taking into account the larger, intellectual context of these years, Gerhardt offers a valuable and vibrant account of Parsons and the political aspects of his work. Those concerned with the historical development and contributions of the field of sociology more broadly will find Gerhardt's portrayal of Parsons richly informed and illuminating.

Uta Gerhardt holds a chair and professorship in sociology at the University of Heidelberg. She is the editor of *Talcott Parsons on National Socialism* (1993) and *German Sociology* (1998), among many other published titles. She is a member of the advisory board of the *Journal of Classical Sociology* and *American Sociologist* and other journals.

Talcott Parsons
An Intellectual Biography

UTA GERHARDT
University of Heidelberg

PUBLISHED BY THE PRESS SYNDICATE OF THE UNIVERSITY OF CAMBRIDGE
The Pitt Building, Trumpington Street, Cambridge, United Kingdom

CAMBRIDGE UNIVERSITY PRESS
The Edinburgh Building, Cambridge CB2 2RU, UK
40 West 20th Street, New York, NY 10011-4211, USA
477 Williamstown Road, Port Melbourne, VIC 3207, Australia
Ruiz de Alarcón 13, 28014 Madrid, Spain
Dock House, The Waterfront, Cape Town 8001, South Africa

http://www.cambridge.org

© Uta Gerhardt 2002

This book is in copyright. Subject to statutory exception
and to the provisions of relevant collective licensing agreements,
no reproduction of any part may take place without
the written permission of Cambridge University Press.

First published 2002

Printed in the United Kingdom at the University Press, Cambridge

Typeface Times Roman 10/12 pt.   *System* LATEX 2_ε [TB]

A catalog record for this book is available from the British Library.

Library of Congress Cataloging in Publication Data
Gerhardt, Uta, 1938–
Talcott Parsons : an intellectual biography / Uta Gerhardt.
  p. cm.
Includes bibliographical references and index.
ISBN 0-521-81022-1
1. Parsons, Talcott, 1902–1979   2. Sociology – United States – History.
3. Political sociology.   I. Title.
HM477.U6 P37   2002
301'.0973–dc21   2001052776

ISBN 0 521 81022 1 hardback

For permission to reproduce the photographs, I wish to thank Amherst College Library,
Archives and Special Collections (No. 5), Stadt- und Universitätsbibliothek Frankfurt
am Main (No. 8), Harvard University Archives (Nos. 1, 2, 3, and 4), Lois Lord,
New York (No. 10), and Charles Parsons, Cambridge, Massachusetts (Nos. 6 and 9).

If you think you understand some of these things at first reading, let this be a warning. You will get something, but to really understand you must go back and back and back.

—*Parsons,* A Short Account of
My Intellectual Development

Contents

	Preface	*page* ix
1	Understanding *The Structure of Social Action*	1
	Introduction	1
	The Long Shadow of Darwinism	12
	The Matter of Facts	32
	Summary	51
	Postscript: What about Cultural Pessimism?	53
2	Parsons's Sociology of National Socialism, 1938–1945	58
	Introduction	58
	The Pre-War Period	61
	Before Pearl Harbor	72
	The Year 1942	89
	Toward VE-Day	105
	Beyond Victory	120
	Summary	126
3	The Harvard Social-Science War Effort and *The Social System*	129
	Introduction	129
	Some Scenarios in the War Effort of the Social Sciences at Harvard	130
	Parsons's Themes Connected with Harvard's War Effort	137
	The War Effort Realized by Three of Parsons's Harvard Colleagues	144
	Parsons's Reaction to the Deployment of the Atom Bomb	149
	The Fate of Parsons's Memorandum Analyzing the War Effort of the Social Sciences	153
	The Second Memorandum, an Unpublished Book	160
	The Third Attempt	167

	Summary	177
	Postscript: Becoming Politically Embattled Personally	178
4	A New Agenda for Citizenship: Parsons's Theory and American Society in the 1960s	184
	Introduction	184
	The New Perspective on Power and the Polity	188
	Understanding Value-Commitments	210
	The Generalized Symbolic Media and the Theory of Society	215
	The New Perspective on Integration and Democracy	225
	Introducing Societal Community	231
	Theory of Integration	245
	Summary	260
	Postscript: The Three Arenas for Change and Crisis	261
	Epilogue A Life of Scholarship for Democracy	276
	Bibliography	281
	Name Index	289
	Subject Index	299

Photo gallery appears after Chapter 2.

Preface

Talcott Parsons may be one of the truly tragic figures in the history of sociology in the twentieth century. Although he struggled all his life to make sociological theory more concrete when it went beyond mere description of apparent social facts, he was charged to remain unable to incorporate reflexivity into social thought. Although he aimed vigorously to account for the dynamics of meaning orientation in the increasingly pluralist modern society, he was accused of mechanistic systems thinking fitting a hermetic *Brave New World*. Although he personally contributed to political program planning for democratization in post–Nazi Germany, he was suspected of shepherding a Nazi sympathizer into the United States. Although he remained a Weberian all his life subsequent to his encounter with Max Weber's intellectual genius during work on his doctoral dissertation, he had to defend himself against attempts, by younger colleagues, to rescue Weber (and also Durkheim) from the prongs of an allegedly false Parsonian interpretation.

My purpose in writing this book has been to make Parsons's sociological work more accessible, by documenting three things. For one, I wish to show how a recognizable knowledge interest in sociological understanding of modern democracy, understood as both a methodological desideratum and an analytical-empirical program, pervaded Parsons's oeuvre from the 1930s to the 1960s (and beyond).

Second, I want to document how this focus on democracy had different forms of expression in the succession of periods of American history. As political agendas changed, reaching from the New Deal through World War II and McCarthyism to the Civil Rights movement in the 1960s, and eventually Watergate in the 1970s, he revised his concern for democracy accordingly.

Third, I want to argue that despite his constant openness for the problems and solutions of the society of the day in his various analyses, two basic tenets remained unchanged throughout his life. One was that he warned of utilitarianism (ranging from social Darwinism to exchange theory and rational-choice theory). The other was that his conceptual framework for sociology, emulating Weber, endorsed society as it was to be, not only as it could be observed. The conceptual scheme envisaged a two-pronged system for social action varying between a favored pole of integration (denoting potential for democracy) and a dreaded one of anomie (denoting danger of authoritarianism).

Parsons's writings comprised seventeen books, among them the world classics *The Structure of Social Action* (1937) and *The Social System* (1951), and more than two hundred articles in scholarly journals and contributions to books, frequently translated into foreign languages and reprinted in collections of essays worldwide. In addition, the Harvard University Archives contain a wealth of book reviews, lecture notes, memoranda, memoirs, research proposals and reports, and speeches, as well as an immense collection of letters and other material.

This vast oeuvre is difficult to penetrate, even for American scholars. Apparently, Parsons's style of thought was adopted from the German when he read Weber in the original as he first discovered sociology during his sojourn in Heidelberg. Students at Harvard in the 1950s who were required to know two foreign languages as an entrance requirement for sociology are said to have inquired whether "Parsonese" could be one of the two. His Weberian style made him proceed, in his published works, from the highly generalized aspects of a phenomenon or problem to its empirical forms (often complicated by an outline of methodological presuppositions). As can be learned from the material preserved in the Harvard Archives, however, his style of work when he familiarized himself with a topic was different from the procedure in the finished product. He studied historical records and empirical as well as analytical accounts characteristic of the phenomenon concerned, before giving it a tentative analytical shape in his lecture notes or draft paper(s), to be revised time and again.

Working from the published texts only, as most secondary accounts have done, tends to de-emphasize the background and sometimes miss out on the baseline of his analyses. Even as outstanding an author as Jürgen Habermas, in *Theory of Communicative Action*, misinterprets Parsons's knowledge aim and overlooks his political engagement.[1] My book takes notice of preparatory material, lecture notes, or draft versions of Parsons's works, to assure that their interpretation be (more) adequate. Incorporating archival materials into the database used in this book, I focus on four central phases of his oeuvre. My venture is to ascertain the cumulative

---

[1] The literature used in this preface is Jeffrey Alexander, *The Modern Reconstruction of Classical Thought: Talcott Parsons* (Berkeley: University of California Press, 1983); Bernard Barber and Uta Gerhardt, eds., *Agenda for Sociology: Classic Sources and Current Uses of Talcott Parsons's Work* (Baden-Baden: Nomos, 1999); Max Black, ed., *The Social Theories of Talcott Parsons* (Englewood Cliffs, N.J.: Prentice Hall, 1961); Charles Camic, ed., *Talcott Parsons: The Early Essays* (Chicago: University of Chicago Press, 1991); Uta Gerhardt, ed., *Talcott Parsons on National Socialism* (New York: Aldine de Gruyter, 1993); Uta Gerhardt, "From Brave to New: Talcott Parsons and the War Effort at Harvard University," *Journal of the History of Behavioral Sciences*, Vol. 25, 1999, pp. 257–289; Jürgen Habermas, *Theory of Communicative Action* (Boston: Houghton Mifflin, 1987); Robert S. Holton and Bryan S. Turner, *Talcott Parsons on Economy and Society* (Englewood Cliffs, N.J.: Prentice Hall, 1986); William C. Mitchell, *Sociological Analysis and Politics: The Theories of Talcott Parsons* (Englewood Cliffs, N.J.: Prentice Hall, 1967); Fritz Stern, *The Politics of Cultural Despair: A Study in the Rise of the Germanic Ideology* (Berkeley: University of California Press, 1961); and Bruce Wearne, *The Theories and Scholarship of Talcott Parsons to 1951* (New York: Cambridge University Press, 1989).

achievement in his analysis of a sociology of democracy, predominantly in the time period between the 1930s and the 1960s. My hope is to elucidate – in our age of globalization – the greatness of this American sociologist, making a contribution to renewed understanding of his exceedingly contemporaneous sociological theory.

This book, to be sure, is written from what may be a European standpoint. Such effort might emulate Parsons's endeavor as he endorsed, in *The Structure of Social Action*, the theories of four then-recent European writers and rejected Spencerian liberalism, which still prevailed in mainstream American sociology, in the 1930s. In this vein, my book may add another perspective to contemporary views on Parsons, supplementing the many existing accounts that seek an understanding of his oeuvre with an intellectual biography. From a presumably European standpoint, I undertake to rearrange some hitherto known as well as unknown sources, proving how Parsons's scholarship benefited from and was related to his politics, passionately pro-democracy.

Since the early 1960s, in a succession of appreciations, he has been pictured mainly as a theorist whose knowledge interest was systems theory, distinct from politics in contemporary society. To name but a very few, *The Social Theories of Talcott Parsons* (1961) reconstructed and, in some of its contributions, criticized his then innovative schemes of systems analysis; *Sociological Analysis and Politics: The Theories of Talcott Parsons* (1967) reconstructed his general theory of action and systems strictly from the standpoint of political science (not allowing for anything but the sociology of an "incurable theorist"); *The Modern Reconstruction of Classical Thought: Talcott Parsons* (1983) recognized phases of his oeuvre leading up to the "later period" featuring "multidimensional theory," but could not see contemporary connotations in the paradigm, when four out of ten chapters discussed what allegedly were Parsons's errors.

That Parsons was far from apolitical when he proclaimed social theory was recognized, in the late 1980s, in the much-undervalued *The Theory and Scholarship of Talcott Parsons to 1951* (1989), an account of how value-neutrality and political consciousness constituted the Weberian heritage in structural-functional theory-building. Also, *Talcott Parsons on Economy and Society* (1986) recollected the Weberian side as well as various accomplishments in special fields such as medical sociology. Eventually, *Talcott Parsons: The Early Essays* (1991) and *Talcott Parsons on National Socialism* (1993) proved the depth and breadth of some of his hitherto unpublished or little known texts on economic and political themes in the 1930s and 1940s.

My book links Parsons's scholarship and his politics. The endeavor can be reconciled as it should, for one, with Max Weber's principle of *Wertfreiheit* ("ethical neutrality"), in the light of American intellectual history. However, another perspective may also apply in my understanding that relates politics with scholarship. In his seminal *The Politics of Cultural Despair: A Study in the Rise of the Germanic Ideology*, cultural historian Fritz Stern elucidated an often-neglected aspect of intellectual criticism. This aspect may be applicable for social-science approaches as well. German religionist, popular philosophical, etc., writings in the late nineteenth and early twentieth centuries, of their culture as declining in an age of ever-more-accelaterating modernization, Stern argues, promoted nationalism as it foreshadowed acquiescence with the charismatic authoritarianism of Nazism. Cultural pessimism, in this vein, meant politics implicit in quasi-scientific manifestations of *Zeitgeist*. As the opposite end in a continuum of thought, no doubt, negating such politics of cultural despair must also be a route to take. A politics of societal progress must exist as well. Such politics would mean a pro-democracy stance, lodged with social-science analysis. Rejecting the antidemocratic message of skepticism as implied in the world view à la "Germanic ideology," such politics must favor an understanding of evolution of democracy in the history of modern society. Such politics carry the torch of democracy, even in sociological theory. Such politics, for Parsons, I venture, showed in his scholarship. Furthermore, as will be amply documented, he never hesitated to defend the cause of democracy as an activist, if need be.

When he was in his twenties, still a student at Amherst, Parsons expressed this ambitious aim of reconciling scholarship and politics quite clearly. He opted for a relationship between theory and facts in sociology committed to the latter when the issue was to link behavior and morality. He wrote, in an essay for his philosophy class using terminology that mirrored his having read Charles Darwin and William Graham Sumner:

> All theories have to explain facts, otherwise they are entirely useless. The theory is valuable just in so far as it explains facts which are comprehensive and significant. If new facts turn up which do not fit the theory, the theory must be modified, not the facts. It is the universal inertia of the mores which so often accomplishes the latter result. So it is with our theories of societal and moral evolution. Since the time of Morgan and Darwin a great many facts have come to light which have necessitated a radical revision of the then current theories of evolution in biology and in sociology and ethnology. We do not blame the earlier men for their mistakes and we recognize the value of their work, but we do not accept it as final. We know more than they did, hence our generalizations can be more comprehensive and more accurate than theirs, and it is our manifest duty to make them as much so as we can with the facts we have, and to get as many more facts as we can. It means painstaking research, but the end is worth while if anything is worth while and that is as much as we can say.[2]

In the published version of his doctoral dissertation, in the first of the two articles in the *Journal of Political Economy*, he had this to say about the conception of a society fitting theories strictly (if undogmatically) based on fact: "There seems to be little reason to believe that it is not possible on the basis which we now have to build by a continuous process something more nearly approaching an ideal society.... In the transition from capitalism to a different social system surely many elements of the present would be built into the new order."[3]

---

[2] Talcott Parsons, "Philosophy III. Professor Ayres. March 27, 1923. A Behaviorist Conception of the Nature of Morals," p. 23. See Harvard University Archives, Parsons papers, call number 42.8.2, box 2 (hereafter, archival material will be identified as "Parsons papers," and call number).

[3] Parsons, "'Capitalism' in Recent German Literature: Sombart and Weber," *Journal of Political Economy*, vol. 36, 1928, p. 653.

This book elucidates how Parsons followed these ideas all his life. The narrative is organized in four chapters, which contribute toward an intellectual biography of this greatest of American sociologists. Each of the four scenarios highlights one particularly innovative stage in the emergence and development of his social theory, spanning a time period of more than forty years.

The first scenario, Chapter 1, depicts his first world classic, *The Structure of Social Action*, in light of two developments which he opposed. One was positivism and utilitarianism in the development of (social) science, rejecting Herbert Spencer's social Darwinism, which he contrasted with voluntarism derived from, among others, Max Weber and Émile Durkheim. The other oppositional impetus targeted antidemocratic régimes in Europe (particularly Nazism in Germany) at the time, against which he endorsed both the theories of three (four) "recent European writers," and New Deal liberalism in the United States, which was a political reality countering Nazism.

The scenario in Chapter 2 epitomizes how Parsons opposed National Socialism, openly mainly in the years 1938–45, as both citizen and sociologist. He analyzed comparatively the régimes in Germany and the United States, highlighting their structural elements. He also explained the dynamics of how a rational-legal type society (in Weberian terms) turned charismatic-coercive, and how a charismatic-traditional became a *Rechtsstaat* democracy. Then, more than at any other time in his life, I argue, his predominant focus was totalitarian dictatorship. He analyzed how it functioned, and he held it against its obverse, integrated society (American democracy).

The third scenario, in Chapter 3, takes his second world classic, *The Social System*, as its anchor, elucidating how it related to two concrete settings of American history. One was the war effort of social science at Harvard University, and the other was a Social Science Research Council initiative in connection with the emergent National Science Foundation, through the memoranda "Social Science – A Basic National Resource," and "Social Science – A National Resource." In *The Social System*, Parsons discussed a broad range of topics undeniably related to issues of the war and its aftermath, including deployment of the atom bomb – a topic which he addressed in the guise of the role of science (symbolization) for modern society. In this phase of his life, he was clearly oriented to make understood how the democratic system functioned, if only as a model for the transformation of former dictatorships, as he saw it, as had occurred in the 1940s in Germany and Italy and might one day be likely for Soviet Russia.

The fourth scenario, Chapter 4, deals with another transformation which Parsons diagnosed – the 1960s, when American society became a full-fledged democracy offering full citizenship to all classes, races (ethnic groups), and so on. His new theory started entirely fresh, taking into account what he deemed seminal achievements in the most recent past. He developed two theoretical models explaining democracy. One was through generalized symbolic interaction media whose cumulative-expansive nature necessitated that a novel concept of power be coined – together with that of three other generalized symbolization media. The other model focused on the societal community, a formation epitomizing democracy in fully developed modern societies. He felt that this new approach required the theory to adopt a new name – "evolutionary-cybernetic." It was the culmination of his concern for democracy.

In all four phases of this oeuvre, starting from *Structure* and extending into the 1960s and beyond, Parsons's defense of democracy implied that he saw two opposite possibilities of societal development: anomie was the one extreme, integration the other. Only the latter meant democracy, to be sure, although it was permanently threatened by relapse into some kind of anomie (such as McCarthyism). This double focus rendered the integration–anomie divide a variable. The theme that emerged in the four phases in his intellectual biography signaled loss and (re)gain of democratization, which spurred his dynamic theory of modern society.

This book uses some previously published material that has been thoroughly reworked. Chapter 1 is a reformulation of the argument made in my contribution to *Agenda for Sociology: Classic Sources and Current Uses of Talcott Parsons's Work* (1999). Chapter 2 is based on the introductory essay in *Talcott Parsons on National Socialism* (1993). Chapter 3 extends the argument made in "From Brave to New: Talcott Parsons and the War Effort at Harvard University" (1999). Chapter 4 is entirely original. All four chapters were replenished with archival material that welds them together into a new unity of interpretation, though three of them resume an argument previously published in one way or another.

This book has benefited greatly from help from many quarters. For one, staff at the Harvard University Archives and the Harvard Imaging Services have been of memorable help. Harvard's Center for European Studies granted me successive visits as a research associate, which were invaluable for the completion of the study. I particularly wish to thank Abby Collins and Charles Maier for their support. I owe thanks for discussion, comment, criticism, and encouragement to Jeffrey Alexander, Daniel Bell, Guenter Endruweit, Thomas Ertman, Mark Gould, Dieter Henrich, Susannah Herschel, Barbara Heyl, Alex Inkeles, Eva Kahana, Klaus-Peter Koepping, Edward Lehman, Christiane Lemke, Donald Levine, Victor Lidz, Renate Mayntz, Robert K. Merton, Sven Papcke, Charles Parsons, Anne Rawls, Neil Smelser, Justin Stagl, Edward Tiryakian, Xavier Trevino, Bryan Turner, and Bruce Wearne, among many others.

Mary Child of Cambridge University Press was a model editor, in more than one way.

My most profound thanks go to Bernard Barber. Throughout the five years when my understanding of Parsons's sociology in defense of democracy gradually took shape, he has been not only a spirited critic but a devoted good friend.

This book is dedicated to him with gratitude.

1
Understanding *The Structure of Social Action*

Introduction

Parsons's first major opus, *The Structure of Social Action*, did not become a classic of sociology when it first appeared in 1937.[1] Although it was reviewed in both *The American Journal of Sociology* and the newly established *American Sociological Review*, and even featured in the widely read *The Saturday Review of Literature*, such recognition did not produce much acclaim for the book.

The review in *The Saturday Review of Literature* entitled "Is Homo Sapient?" an essay by Robert Bierstedt, who was then based at Columbia University's Department of Philosophy, addressed Parsons as "a young Heidelberg-trained sociologist at Harvard."[2] Bierstedt found the book opposed to an objective empiricist approach, which, he said, presumably made it unlikely that "such hard-headed empiricists as the authors of 'Middletown in Transition' would bother to read *The Structure of Social Action*." In his view, it proposed a subjective approach which was "the 'voluntaristic theory of action' growing out of . . . theoretical convergence" that claimed to be able to "give sociology a well-defined field of its own."

Bierstedt did not recommend Parsons's book. He could not see in it an answer to the problems of sociology, let alone a "charter for sociology" as it would be hailed

---

[1] Talcott Parsons, *The Structure of Social Action. A Study in Social Theory with Special Reference to a Group of Recent European Writers* (New York: MacGraw Hill, 1937). The first part of the advertisement text ran: "This book...presents an analysis of the theory of the structure of social systems so far as they can be analyzed in terms of the 'theory of action,' taking the relation of means and ends as a starting point. The approach to the subject is new in that no one has previously attempted a comparable general analysis of this particular theoretical structure in its relation to empirical problems, nor has brought together the work of recent European writers in relation to this structure." See Parsons papers, HUG(FP) – 42.8.2, box 2. The book's second edition was published by The Free Press, Glencoe, IL, in 1949, and its paperback edition by The Free Press/Collier Macmillan, New York, in 1968. The latter edition will be used throughout here, henceforth referred to as *Structure*.

[2] "Is Homo Sapient? THE STRUCTURE OF SOCIAL ACTION. By Talcott Parsons. Reviewed by Robert Bierstedt," *The Saturday Review of Literature*, March 12, 1938, p. 18; the next three quotes are from the same page.

1

at the end of the 1980s, on the occasion of the fiftieth anniversary of its publication.[3] In the late 1930s, *Structure* appeared to Bierstedt, who himself had studied with Parsons, a far from satisfactory solution. "A sociology of the subjective" in the guise of Parsons's voluntarism, Bierstedt commented in 1938, "is about as scientifically useful as a sonnet to a skylark, and the 'voluntaristic theory of action' would make William James – and probably Pareto – turn in his grave."[4]

In his far more scholarly criticism, Louis Wirth, in the *American Sociological Review*, acknowledged that "the book goes beyond the scope of a mere commentary by treating each writer in the light of all of the others"[5] and thus found it "highly interesting and helpful in the diagnosis of our present-day battle of theories – which, it may be added, is more than a battle of words." But Wirth would not go along with Parsons any further. Albeit unconvinced, he realized that Parsons sought a synthesis derived from elements of the four oeuvres to delineate a realm for sociology beyond that of the economy or politics. But he charged that there were no grounds to envisage a sociology that would analyze a field of reality beyond other social sciences. Although Parsons's "distinction between pure economics and sociology" made sense, he judged, Parsons's conception of division of labor between, above all, politics and sociology could at best be "a crude formulation of differential emphasis."[6] In all, Wirth believed that the book offered least where it aimed to accomplish most. That is, in regard to the "better understanding of the meaning of rationality or of the role of rationality in society,"[7] he saw no worthwhile contribution from the book.

A third reviewer, Floyd N. House, eventually reviewed both editions of *Structure*. In both reviews, however, he failed to understand the importance of the work. In 1939, he praised it for "the contribution it makes to the elucidation of the persistent and difficult problem of the place of values in social behavior."[8] In 1950, however, he was even less on the mark. He reminded his readers that he had reviewed the previous edition of which "the present edition ... is simply an identical new printing, except for a new Preface of five and one-third pages."[9] Insisting that he was "in pretty thoroughgoing agreement with practically the whole of the author's reasoning," he also ventured a hypothesis to explain why the first edition of the book had had little influence on American sociology: "The reason for this seeming neglect of an important work is, I suspect, just what I anticipated in 1939: 'It is unfortunate that it is so long and so abstruse in style; many American students of sociology who would profit by it will be deterred from reading it.'"

---

[3] See, for instance, Charles Camic, "*Structure* After 50 Years. The Anatomy of a Charter," *American Journal of Sociology*, vol. 95, 1989, pp. 38–107.

[4] "Is Homo Sapient?," p. 19.

[5] "The Structure of Social Action. Review by Louis Wirth," *American Sociological Review*, vol. 4, 1939, p. 400; the next quote is from the same page.

[6] Ibid., p. 404.

[7] Ibid., p. 402.

[8] "The Structure of Social Action. Review by Floyd N. House," *American Journal of Sociology*, vol. 45, 1939/40, p. 129.

[9] "The Structure of Social Action. Review by Floyd N. House," *American Journal of Sociology*, vol. 55, 1949/50, p. 505; the next two quotes are from the same page.

Ironically, House erred in his prediction not in 1939 but in 1950. Though remaining unchanged and thus presumably still being "long" and "abstruse in style," the book became an important source of sociological theory. In the 1950s and beyond, students apparently were no longer "deterred from reading it," despite House's verdict. Obviously, between the first and second editions of *Structure*, a majority of sociologists experienced a change of mind or heart. House was right in 1950 when he pointed out that the 1937 edition of *Structure* had reached only a small audience of American scholars. But House was wrong when he assumed that this would not change with the book's reissue. The 1949 second edition became a success – despite the fact that the book, in 1949, was an "identical new printing, except for a Preface of five and one-third pages." Indeed, it became mandatory reading in sociology courses during the next decade. By the 1970s, the book advanced to become a classic. It has been analyzed in a long stream of elaborate secondary accounts.[10] The paperback edition, published in 1968, eventually spread the work around the globe. It became a milestone of sociology's development as an academic discipline.

The Point of Politics

The difference in impact of the first and second editions of *Structure* raises the question hitherto unasked: What explains the conspicuously different reception of *Structure* before and after World War II?

This question, to be sure, presupposes that the reception of a book of social theory is related to the reception in the scientific community in sociology, or the social sciences in general. Are classics in a discipline related in some identifiable way to the historical or societal situation of the time in which they are appreciated for what they are? Do scholars make sense of social theory according to the perspective of the society of their day? My thesis is: Behind sociologists' becoming fascinated with *Structure* after but not before World War II, lay a change in the historical situation in the decade between *Structure*'s two editions.

One salient aspect of the historical situation that was only emerging in 1937, or 1939, but had become flagrantly obvious in the late 1940s, was the defeat of fascism in Europe, especially National Socialism in Germany, through an alliance of fifty-two states in a war of historically unparalleled dimensions. Moreover, by the late 1940s, Nazi Germany had become a subject for analytical accounts concerning crimes unparalleled in the history of mankind. At the end of World War II, unspeakable crimes against humanity committed under the Nazi regime had been revealed to a horrified world public.[11] As of 1944–45, Nazi atrocities had

---

[10] To name but two out of many such appreciations: Robert Bierstedt, *American Sociological Theory* (New York: Academic Press, 1981), and Donald Levine, *Visions of the Sociological Tradition* (Chicago: University of Chicago Press, 1995), devoted an entire chapter to *Structure*.

[11] The American public was made aware of the atrocities committed in Nazi Germany through an extensive press campaign invited by Supreme Commander of the Allied Expeditionary Forces in Europe, Dwight D. Eisenhower, in the spring of 1945. See Norbert Frei, "'Wir waren blind, ungläubig und langsam'. Buchenwald, Dachau und die amerikanischen Medien im Frühjahr 1945." *Vierteljahreshefte für Zeitgeschichte*, vol. 35, 1987, pp. 385–401.

become a verified truth that the postwar world had set out to explain in a long series of scholarly and literary accounts, extending until today.[12]

As of the latter half of the 1940s, I believe, an undeniably urgent need arose for a majority of contemporaries – including sociologists – to analyze National Socialism as a régime of terror. Although a steady flow of work since the 1930s had focused on the German dictatorship, I argue that the driving force behind *Structure's* reception after but not before World War II had to do with the political side of the book. My suggestion is: Not when it first appeared, but when it became a success after 1949, was the aim of *Structure* recognized, if indirectly. Parsons's intent in this book, I wish to maintain, was to make understandable why, from a scientific point of view, National Socialism was the obverse of democratic structure of social action.

Structure, written between 1933 and 1937 and continued through lectures, memoranda, and, eventually, articles on topics concerning Germany and the war, was a work related to the troubled times of the 1930s. When its second edition became successful, it provided sociologists in the post–World War II era with an answer to the question how a regime of terror could be conceptualized within a theory of the structure of social action.

My suggestion may appear to contradict Parsons's own concern with Max Weber's principle of *Wertfreiheit* separating politics from sociology. To be sure, Parsons himself was conscious of the apparent dilemma. When he replied to Louis Wirth's book review in an eight-page letter commenting on the latter's views on *Structure*, he made it clear that he fully agreed with Weber. To observe Weber's quest for value neutrality of social science did not mean that sociology should refrain from recognizing the undemocratic nature of authoritarian regimes. He asserted: "By distinguishing politics from sociology, I do not mean to imply that concrete power relationships have no relation to values."[13] Despite the fact, in the tradition of Max Weber, that a political stance could not be taken by sociology, he felt that *Structure* involved a particular brand of politics. Recognition of the undeniably political nature of social relations in any historical or contemporary society could not be taken as outside the realm of sociology. That is, he followed Weber when he felt that the structure of social action was situated in the world of its day, either coercive control systems as in authoritarian regimes, or the voluntary curtailment of state power and establishment of citizens' rights in a *Rechtsstaat* enabling democracy in a modern societal community.

However, in his letter to Wirth, he explained what he saw his book achieving, in a language of caution against an all too facile positivism or empiricism:

---

[12] German accounts published shortly after the end of World War II included: Eugen Kogon, *Der SS-Staat. Das System der deutschen Konzentrationslager* (Frankfurt: Fischer 1946), translated *The Theory and Practice of Hell. The German Concentration Camps and the System Behind Them* (New York: Farrar, Straus & Co., 1950), and Alexander Mitscherlich and Fred Mielke, *Das Diktat der Menschenverachtung* (Heidelberg: Lambert Schneider, 1947), translated *Doctors of Infamy* (New York, 1949). American accounts included, for instance, Morris Janowitz, "German Reactions to Nazi Atrocities," *American Sociological Review*, Vol. 52, 1946, pp. 141–146.

[13] Letter, Parsons to Louis Wirth, dated Oct. 6, 1939, p. 7; Parsons papers, HUG(FP) – 42.8.2, box 2; the next quote is from the same page.

The distinction is analytical and not a classification of concrete social structures. It is crucial to the methodological problem which I have followed through in terms of the status of economic theory that analytical systems such as economic theory or the corresponding type of sociology not only are not but cannot be adequate schemes for the analysis of classes of concrete phenomena for all purposes. On the contrary, there are sociological elements not only in the political world as we ordinarily understand it but in the economic world and vice versa.

The position in his book involved two ways in which methodology was a guide to the analysis of substantive tenets. On the one hand, the conceptual model of what constituted a fact and therefore apparently was taken for granted in an economic or social theory evidently had to be scrutinized. (In this vein, positivist utilitarianism failed the test of methodological modernity.) On the other hand, through theories that already had partly done the work of analyzing the contemporary world, the theories of "recent European writers" that required adopting rather than criticizing their conceptual achievements, an analytical perspective of voluntarism emerged.

In *Structure*, Parsons reconstructed insights taken from the four theories, arriving at two concluding chapters, one on substantive findings and the other on "tentative methodological implications."[14] His argument was factual when he emphasized that it was methodological. He refuted positivism as he proposed voluntarism. Particularly in the guise of social Darwinism, which he pronounced "dead" although it was far from dead in his time, he opposed utilitarian positivism. He addressed the thought of his time, in the guise of something "dead," when he meant to destroy it thoroughly. He castigated the type of regime associated with "dead" social Darwinism (racism) when he meant to opt for its obverse, democracy in modern society. His own theory, termed voluntarism, claimed recognition, in Weberian terms, of the constructed nature of scientific concepts.

In the later years of his life, Parsons would admit to this knowledge interest of his earlier work. At the end of the 1960s, he admitted in two separate biographical accounts that he had been concerned about Germany when he wrote *Structure*. In the introductory notes to Part II of his *Politics and Social Structure*, a book that assembled his four most important articles on National Socialism published between 1942 and 1945, he recalled what had been his motives for concern:

> I took my Ph.D. degree in 1927. This study in Germany was a crucial experience in my life.... At Heidelberg I came into contact with what most would regard as the very best of German culture.... By the time of my last visit to Germany prior to World War II, in the summer of 1930, much had changed. The Nazi movement was in full swing.... For all observers of social and political processes in the Western world of the time, the Nazi movement presented not only intellectual, but also profoundly moral, problems. Perhaps I can say that these were somewhat more poignant for me than for most other American intellectuals, not only because of my German experience, owing to the fact that I had come to love and respect that aspect of Germany which I had known. The critical question was, Why and how could this happen in what from so many points of view should be evaluated as a "good society"?[15]

---

[14] This is the title of Chapter XIX.
[15] Parsons, "Historical Interpretations (Introduction, Part II)," *Politics and Social Structure* (New York: Free Press, 1969), pp. 59–60.

In 1969, when contributing to a conference organized by *Daedalus*, the journal of the American Academy of Arts and Sciences, recollecting his intellectual biography, and revealing his motives to write *Structure* in this memoir on his building social system theory, Parsons admitted that fascism in Germany had been a strong factual ground for him to study the structure of social action (he also referred to communism in Russia as another dictatorial regime which had been his target):

> *The Structure of Social Action* marked a turning point in my professional career. Its major accomplishment, the demonstration of the convergence among the four authors with which it dealt, was accompanied by a clarification and development of my own thought about the problems of the state of Western society with which the authors were concerned. The state of Western society which might be designated as either capitalism or free enterprise – and on the political side as democracy – was clearly then in some kind of state of crisis. The Russian Revolution and the emergence of the first socialist state as controlled by the Communist party had been crucial to my thinking since undergraduate days. The Fascist movements affected friendships in Germany. Less than two years after the publication of the book the Second World War was to begin, and, finally, came the Great Depression with its ramifications throughout the world.[16]

On the note of real types of society, the modern welfare state could be contrasted with the then contemporary regime of National Socialism. The former, for Parsons, meant an integrated society, the latter anomie.

The Meaning of "Civics"

The text of the advertisement announcing the book in 1937 characterized it as "'civics' in the highest sense" – a theme not recognized in the book reviews on the occasion of the three editions. Interestingly, the characterization was made in the advertisement through a quote attributed to Joseph Schumpeter, whose comment was reproduced verbatim: "Whoever cares for the philosophy of social processes will find this volume... very stimulating reading. It contributes not only to a branch of scientific sociology but also to 'civics' in the highest sense."[17]

Schumpeter, it appears, did indeed read the manuscript, if only in a previous version entitled *Sociology and the Elements of Human Action*. In a memorandum addressed to the Committee on Research in the Social Sciences at Harvard, praising

---

[16] Parsons, "On Building Social System Theory: A Personal History," *Daedalus*, vol. 99, 1970, pp. 826–882, cit. 831.

[17] The full wording of the second half of the text of the advertisement was: "Professor Joseph Schumpeter of Harvard, commenting on this book, says: 'The men who created that important body of ideas which lie at the back of modern political thought are, with the possible exception of Pareto, very imperfectly known to American readers. Professor Parsons presents the messages of some of them in a series of scholarly analyses, and winds up by welding them into a structure of his own. Whoever cares for the philosophy of social processes will find this volume... very stimulating reading. It contributes not only to a branch of scientific sociology but also to 'civics' in the highest sense.'" Parsons papers, HUG(FP) – 42.8.2, box 2.

the book's ability to make accessible with "scholarly care"[18] to an American audience German sources such as Weber's thought, Schumpeter pointed out that Parsons, by adding Durkheim to his exposition of Pareto and Marshall, rejected positivism, even in the original, Comtean, tradition.[19] He added the comment that "both his introduction and his concluding chapters are eminently sensible and scholarly although I do not put them as high as those which are devoted to critical exposition."[20] Schumpeter, it seems, preferred Parsons's argument proposing voluntarism through convergence of the four theories to the latter's rebuttal of positivism. Parsons's "analytical realism,"[21] to Schumpeter,[22] obviously appeared less compelling than Parsons's "synthetic" conception of social action.[23]

In 1936, Schumpeter noticed the book's antipositivism, although he did not find that to be its strongest achievement. Parsons, introducing his opposition to positivism in the guise of rejecting Herbert Spencer's sociology, adopted the stance vis-à-vis Spencer which he took from a then recent book written by a colleague of both Schumpeter's and Parsons's, Harvard historian Crane Brinton.

Parsons's opening paragraph expressed his rejection of positivist utilitarianism dismissing Spencer, through a quote from Brinton's *English Political Thought in the Nineteenth Century*, first published in 1933.[24] The message was not only that Spencer's sociology was obsolete but indeed his political thought was dead.[25] Through Brinton's words, at the very beginning of the nearly eight hundred pages of *Structure*, Parsons stated not only that Spencer's work contained a political

---

[18] "In re: Mr. Talcott Parsons's manuscript: *Sociology and the Elements of Human Action*. To the Committee on Research in the Social Sciences." Memorandum by J. A. Schumpeter, Department of Economics, Cambridge, Massachusetts, dated December 23, 1936, p. 1. The memorandum was kindly made available to me by Nico Stehr.

[19] Ibid., p. 2; the two relevant sentences were: "The laborious disquisitions about Durkheim have, to me, opened many nooks and crannies in a system which I did not notice or understand before. It should be added that understanding Durkheim involves understanding the Comtest tradition from which much of his work arose and that Mr. Parsons seems to me to meet that test successfully."

[20] Ibid.

[21] See Parsons, *Structure*, p. 757.

[22] Schumpeter might have had doubts about Parsons's "analytical realism" because Parsons insisted that "the employment of analytical categories drawn from more than one ... system (of analytical categories), perhaps from several" might be required for "the adequate understanding of many concrete phenomena." Schumpeter, however, might have preferred that "only *one* system of analytical categories could be applicable to the understanding of any given concrete class of phenomena."

[23] Camic, who, in his commemorative essay written on the occasion of the fiftieth anniversary of the publication of *Structure*, made reference to Parsons's self-characterization of his approach as "analytical realism," cited three locations where he thought this was being discussed. These were said to be indicated in the index. On closer inspection, however, two of these were not applicable. On the other hand, Camic failed to notice that Parsons himself in the index of *Structure* pointed out three locations as relevant for analytic realism; two of these were not recognized by Camic. See Camic, "*Structure* After 50 Years," p. 53; Parsons, "*Structure*," p. lv.

[24] Crane Brinton, *English Political Thought in the Nineteenth Century* (Cambridge, Mass.: Harvard University Press, 1949); (originally, 1933).

[25] Parsons's quote from Brinton read: "'Who now reads Spencer? It is difficult for us to realize how great a stir he made in the world.... He was the intimate confidant of a strange and rather unsatisfactory God, whom he called the principle of Evolution. His God betrayed him. We have evolved beyond Spencer.'" Parsons, *Structure*, p. 3; the next eight quotations are from the same page.

conception of the structure of social action but also that this conception could be judged dead in the 1930s. He meant to imply that religious or even ritualistic forces were involved in the political philosophy of Spencer, which had to be proclaimed dead. He thus stated, through Brinton, that although Spencer previously, in the nineteenth century, had "made . . . a stir," he now, in the 1930s, was obsolete and untimely. Parsons expressed interest in the "crime" that he assumed to have occurred as Spencer's political philosophy ostentatiously was "dead." By virtue of Brinton's verdict assuming the air of a coroner inspecting a corpse, he dismissed the quality of Spencer's political thought for the 1930s, though it had been adequate, presumably, in the latter part of the nineteenth century. Appropriating the dismissal of a whole tradition of political thought which Brinton had argued, Parsons gained a platform from which to analyze the deadly flaws of "the positivistic-utilitarian tradition."

In the two opening paragraphs, he did two things. First, he diagnosed the undeniable demise of quasi-religious doctrine as in Spencer's political philosophy – which, as he presumed, belonged to the wider field of positivistic utilitarianism. He clad this statement rather whimsically in the words, regarding Spencer, that "a strange and rather unsatisfactory God, whom he called the principle of Evolution, . . . has betrayed him." He then introduced his own program, using a reference to evolution but not Evolution. Upon the death of Spencer's political philosophy following that of the latter's "God," Evolutionism, he pronounced, a nonpositivist, nonmechanistic theory of action had evolved. The latter, product of "the evolution of scientific theory," was his own explanation of the structure of social action that would be shown in the book. At this early stage of his argument, he phrased his program in the language of a thriller: "We must agree with the verdict. Spencer is dead. But who killed him and how? This is the problem. . . . Spencer was . . . a typical representative of . . . the positivistic-utilitarian tradition. What has happened to it? Why has it died? The thesis of this study will be that it is the victim of the vengeance of the jealous god, Evolution, in this case the evolution of scientific theory."

In a version of the preface written in September 1937 but abandoned at the request of his publisher, McGraw Hill, Parsons clarified that, originally, he had only been "interested in the empirical problems of economic individualism as they were treated by various authors."[26] Only in the course of this work, he reported, had he discovered that the "four European writers" had independently come up with the same solution, which in turn made him examine their convergence. Whereas the primary emphasis of his study was now on "the emergence of the theoretical system," he said, "it is, however, worth while noting that this was not the original emphasis." He went on to remark, "Indeed it could not have been, for in the earlier stages of genesis of the study the author was not conscious that there was any such logically integrated system as the voluntaristic theory of action, least of all

---

[26] "Preface," marked "Alstead, N.H. Sept. 15, 1937." Parsons papers, HUG(FP) – 42.41, box 2, p. 5; the next two quotes are from the same page.

that the three principal writers treated in this study had converged on its main outline."

In the published preface, he omitted this reference to his original view. He no longer mentioned that originally he had not suspected that there was a unifying reality behind the various views on economic individualism of the four authors. At the same time, in the published preface dated "October, 1937 Cambridge Mass.," he emphasized more fully than in the unpublished version that what concerned him were empirical problems. These, he now knew, occupied him as well as the writers whose work he interpreted.

> True scientific theory is not the product of idle "speculation," of spinning out the logical implications of assumptions, but of observation, reasoning and verification, starting with the facts and continually returning to the facts. Hence at every crucial point explicit treatment of the empirical problems which occupied the writers concerned is included. Only by treating theory in this close interrelation with empirical problems and facts is any kind of an adequate understanding either of how the theory came to develop, or of its significance to science, possible.[27]

He knew that such allegiance to facts meant that the scientific nature of the theory as it related to the facts had to be ascertained carefully.

In neither version of the preface, however, did he spell out the facts whose taking into account was to be the litmus test for the quality of the theory. He named some empirical problems relevant for himself as well as the authors he dealt with,[28] but he failed to concretize sufficiently the relevant empirical issues. He was rather parsimonious in sharing with the reader what were the empirically concrete structures of, for one, economic individualism in his time.

Hitherto unrecognized materials that have been preserved in the Harvard University Archives, however, may give a clearer picture of the empirical facts that his theory of the structure of social action aimed to fit. In a lecture presumably delivered at Yale University, New Haven, Connecticut, in March 1938, he apparently had contemporary structure(s) of social action in mind. His handwritten lecture notes carried subheadings such as "anomie," "values," "force," among others, when he also dealt with German (Nazi) society.[29] He jotted down keywords that emulated *Structure* which had been recently published. These denoted clearly that Germany under National Socialism was on his mind when he used the key concepts of his voluntaristic theory. For the purpose of explicit sociological understanding, he contrasted Nazi Germany and the United States.

"Anomie," for example, was a subheading on pages 1 as well as 3 of his lecture notes, which are here reproduced in the way in which he arranged the words on

---

[27] *Structure*, p. xxii.
[28] That is, "capitalism," "free enterprise," "economic individualism," p. xxii.
[29] The lecture notes carry the headline "New Haven," accompanied by the date "March 1938." They are in the Parsons papers, HUG(FP) – 42.45.4, box 1. Other relevant lecture notes are marked "Gov 16, May 3 1938," "Soc A May 3rd 1938," or "Shop Club Feb. 16th 1938," all preserved in Parsons papers, HUG (FP) – 42.45.4, box 1.

his note sheet:

> Anomie:
> Rapid industrialization
> Changing class structure
> Nationalism[30]
> Jews
> Defeat & Humiliation
> Goals and Means[31]
> Anomie – a breakdown of institutional integration:
> Individualization
> Mobility – industrialization
> Nationalism as obverse
> Class structure – never entirely integrated
> Plan of Jews – Liberation not assimilation
> Rapid rise to national power. Defeat and humiliation.[32]

In similar fashion, he listed "values" twice in his notes, detailing under two separate headings the following different themes:

> Value – emotional-ideological side of Nazi Movement:
> A re-integration phenomenon
> Confusion – probably true to some extent of all revolutionary movements
> Obsessiveness – Jews. Communists – Foreign enemies – tendency to coalesce all.
> Paranoid tendency
> Ambivalence – esp. in attitudes to science + learning
> Mass neurosis? Abnormality reaction of normal people to abnormal situation.[33]
> Values –
> In Germany always more opposition to liberalism than elsewhere
> Authoritarian structures much undermined but little to replace.[34]

One subheading referred to "force" where he noted:

> Force – Pareto –
> Both internal and external applications. Success despite lack of unity.[35]

Eventually, at the end of his notes, he included a summary:

> *Modern* dictatorship largely a product of social disorganization.
> Consequences:
> Shift from universalistic to particularistic basis –
> Führerprinzip
> Race

---

[30] On the note sheet, this word was actually written on the margin in a way indicating where its place would be in the sequence of themes.
[31] Unpublished notes entitled "New Haven," p. 1. The capital letters in some of the words which would usually not be capitalized in English are Parsons's own.
[32] Ibid., p. 3.
[33] Ibid., p. 1.
[34] Ibid., p. 4.
[35] Ibid., p. 2.

> Science – Weisse Juden
> Law – Attack on Romanism
> Importance of universalism to Western Civilization
> Roman heritage + Christianity
> Specificity to diffuseness
> Breakdown of concept of office
> (two words unreadable) danger of immobile traditionalism.[36]

These notes, interestingly, used concepts such as anomie, values, force, and so on, and referred to Pareto explicitly, and Durkheim and Weber implicitly, when the topic obviously involved Nazi Germany.

Parsons again used concepts taken from *Structure*, in a lecture entitled "Gov 16," delivered May 3, 1938. There, he phrased his topic in his lecture notes thus:

> A single comprehensive conceptual scheme for analysis of "man in society" the theory of social action. . . .
> Problem of order. . . .
> 2 Primary sources of problem
>
> 1) Lack of perfect value-integration. Hobbes posited random ends – rationality – hence problem dominated his thought. . . .
> 2) Availability of means of attaining ends which do not take full account of
>   a) value system b) rights of others under it.
>   a) Without presupposing limitations on rationality of "victim": bargaining power and coercion
>   b) Involving such limitations
>   fraud + propaganda
>   Taken together "power." . . .[37]

This suggests that politics were a background for *Structure*. Parsons not only opposed German fascism but also, from about 1930 onward – even before the beginning of Roosevelt's presidency – was a supporter of institutions of the welfare state,[38] putting sociology on the agenda of politics. Through sociological categories such as universalism, the concept of office, avoidance of immobile traditionalism, and so on, he voiced his credo for New Deal liberalism.[39] He

---

[36] Ibid., pp. 4–5.
[37] Lecture notes, "Gov 16," dated May 3, 1938, pp. 1–2; Parsons papers, HUG(FP) – 42.45.4, box 1.
[38] Some evidence on his pre-1932 political stance was in an autobiographical essay published in 1964. He revealed that before becoming a medical sociologist in the mid-1930s, he had participated in research in medical economics meant as a precursor to introducing, in 1930 or subsequent years, general health insurance. See Parsons, "Some Theoretical Considerations Bearing on the Field of Medical Sociology," in *Social Structure and Personality* (London: Free Press, 1964), esp. p. 326. Opposition to the idea of health insurance by the AMA, to Parsons's chagrin, destroyed the prospect for realization of this welfare program. See, for some background information, Gerhardt, "Models of Illness and the Theory of Society," *International Sociology*, vol. 5, 1990, esp. pp. 340–342.
[39] Howard Brick convincingly argues Parsons's pro-Roosevelt politics, in the 1930s and also subsequently. He sees in him a progressive liberal, which he proves. See Howard Brick, "The Reformist Dimension of Talcott Parsons's Early Social Theory," in Thomas L. Haskell and Richard F. Teichgraeber III, eds., *The Culture of the Market* (New York: Cambridge University Press, 1993), pp. 357–396.

perceived the egalitarian welfare state (which promoted universal public education) a thoroughly humanist road to equality of opportunity in modern society. In contradistinction, he opposed the social theory of Herbert Spencer, William Graham Sumner, and others who opposed the emerging welfare state. Both National Socialist racism and its less conspicuous version, the evolutionism in social theory hooked on the late nineteenth century world view of Darwinism, were to be overcome. Through voluntarism embracing the modern welfare state, he knew, sociology could help understand the structure of social action as it benefited the integrated society.

My argument recalls in some detail the teachings of social Darwinism. I wish to elucidate the doctrine against which *Structure* set an agenda of modern sociology in the 1930s. Only on the background of how then mostly contemporary sociology matched the ideologies of then (still) contemporaneous society, including National Socialism in Europe, could the need be expressed for sociology to understand the society of the day.

In order to show the degree to which sociology was involved in the social Darwinism, even racism, of the 1930s, I must go back as far as the 1850s.

The Long Shadow of Darwinism

Parsons's quote from Brinton's *English Political Thought in the Nineteenth Century* dismissed Spencer as utterly forgotten.[40] Like a crime novel pronouncing Spencer dead at the beginning of *Structure*, Parsons phrased his problem as "who killed him and how"[41] and went on to speculate that it had been "the vengeance of...Evolution" which led to the "evolution of scientific theory" which was, no doubt, what in his mind had "killed" Spencer. "Scientific theory," evidently, had emerged through converging elements in, as the subtitle of *Structure* read, the theories of "the group of recent European writers." Such clever formulations helped Parsons to avoid reconstructing Spencer's theories. He proceeded to explicate his own ideas as he might presume that Spencer's were sufficiently known. All the same, he condemned the political and social thought of positivist utilitarianism which he identified with Spencer.

---

[40] Brinton's chapter on Spencer started with the paragraph from which Parsons quoted, "Who now reads Spencer? It is difficult for us to realize how great a stir he made in the world. The *Synthetic Philosophy* penetrated to many a bookshelf which held nothing else quite so heavy. It lay beside the works of Buckle and Mill on the shelf of every Englishman of a radical turn of mind. It was read, discussed, fought over. And now it is a drug on the second-hand market, and hardly stirs the interest of the German or American aspirant to the doctorate in philosophy." Brinton briefly considered whether Spencer was worth bothering with at all, and decided, "Spencer himself was never merciful, not merciful intellectually at least. He seems never to have harboured any kind of doubt. In a century surely not predisposed to scepticism, few thinkers surpass him in cock-sureness and intolerance. He was the intimate confidant of a strange and rather unsatisfactory God, whom he called the principle of Evolution. His God has betrayed him. We have evolved beyond Spencer." Crane Brinton, *English Political Thought in the Nineteenth Century* (Cambridge: Harvard University Press, 1949), p. 226–227.

[41] *Structure*, p. 3; the next four quotations are from the same page.

Today, little seems to be known about Spencer as a source of social Darwinism. It is barely remembered that Spencer's sociology spurred elitism in American thought and, eventually, racism in German universities, even politics. The story needs to be told which, I presume, is between the lines of *Structure*.

Spencer and the History of Social Darwinist Sociology in the United States

In 1893 in a new introduction for his re-issued *Principles of Ethics*, Spencer complained that Darwin was credited with the idea of struggle for existence when originally he had promoted it. "Of course it yields me no small satisfaction to find that these ideas which fell dead in 1850, have now become generally diffused,"[42] Spencer admitted. Detailing that it was "the evolutionary view of Ethics" and also "the doctrine of 'Natural Selection'" whose authorship he claimed, he reported that these had been established before 1859 when Darwin's first major opus propagated them. Spencer held that the public image in the 1890s wrongly harbored "the impression that they are sequences of those of Mr. Darwin." He clarified that "the doctrine of organic evolution in its application to human character and intelligence, and, by implication, to society, is of earlier date than *The Origin of Species*."[43]

Spencer was right. It had been he who, in 1852,[44] explained the growth of population in animals as well as humans as the outcome of laws governing natural selection of the most disciplined or best adapted. The principle which he introduced was characteristic, Spencer explained, of life in general, ranging from single-cell organisms to homo sapiens. He argued that in nature one and the same contradiction prevailed throughout, namely between individuation and multiplication. Whereas individuation allowed for singularity but also meant vulnerability and even risk of untimely death, multiplication guaranteed race survival but curtailed intelligence in the individual being. In the perennial antagonism between the two principles, Spencer explicated, individuals above all attempted to cultivate their innate intelligence which helped them conquer adversities and dominate rivals in the hostile world of nature and men. At the same time, populations of animals and humans predominantly aimed at the highest number of offspring, thereby preserving the survival prospects of their respective races.

In the interplay between individuation and multiplication, Spencer maintained, intelligence was instrumental for survival of the fittest. That intelligence benefited those better able to outdo others in the struggle for existence, he knew, in turn, secured progress. Racial improvement depended on the higher chance for survival of those fitter than others, who, above all, conquered environmental obstacles and

---

[42] Herbert Spencer, *The Principles of Ethics*, Vol. I (originally, 1879). Reprint of the 1892 edition in its 1904 version (with an introductory essay dated 1893), Osnabrück: Otto Zeller, 1966, p. vii; the next three quotes are from the same page.

[43] Ibid., p. viii.

[44] Spencer, *A New Theory of Population Deduced from the General Law of Animal Fertility*, republished from the *Westminster Review* for April 1852. With an introduction by R. T. Trall, M.D. (New York: Fowler and Wells, 1852).

combatted animals and men more intelligently. Spencer substantiated his thesis using, among other similar data, experiential evidence that "the mean capacities of the crania" measured 75 cubit inches in Australian aborigines but 96 cubit inches in Englishmen.[45] Consequently, he argued, the most advanced races having proved fittest for survival were also the most skilled, intelligent, self-controlled – in one word, they were the most disciplined. Invoking the disastrous so-called potato famines in Ireland in the late 1840s, he maintained that death from starvation meant lack of effort to get ahead of others, denoting lack of self-control. He reasoned:

> All mankind . . . subject themselves more or less to the discipline . . . ; they either may or may not advance under it; but, in the nature of things, only those who *do* advance under it eventually survive. . . . This truth we have recently seen exemplified in Ireland. . . . For as those prematurely carried off must, in the average of cases, be those in whom the power of self-preservation is the least, it unavoidably follows, that those left behind to continue the race are those in whom the power of self-preservation is the greatest – are the select of their generation.[46]

Premature death, he thus claimed, extinguished "those in whom the power of self-preservation is the least," thus assuring that such power of self-preservation was greatest in those who actually survived. The two dangers thus banned were surplus population and idleness. Surplus population developed, he warned, due to "excess of fertility" which tended to aggravate an already severe scarcity of needed goods and resources. Idleness, especially on a mass scale, indicated lack of discipline which, in turn, jeopardized struggle which was the only way to guarantee survival of the fittest. The road to happiness that meant progress, he knew, necessitated extinction of those unfit for the harsh conditions of life. In this vein, survival cultivated aggressive intelligence on which it largely depended. He stressed

> that, whether the dangers to existence be of the kind produced by excess of fertility, or of any other kind, it is clear, that by the ceaseless exercise of the faculties needed to contend with them, and by the death of all men who fail to contend with them successfully, there is insured a constant progress toward a higher degree of skill, intelligence, and self-regulation – a better co-ordination of action – a more complete life.

Two years prior to the two articles in *Westminster Review*,[47] Spencer had published a book extolling similar ideas, entitled *Social Statics: or, the Conditions essential to Human Happiness specified, and the first of them developed*.[48] There he had developed in abundant detail his philosophy that rugged individualism meant ethics compatible with David Ricardo's political economy, as the latter was conducive to racial betterment.[49] He aimed to prove that supremacy of intelligence

---

[45] Ibid., p. 40.
[46] Ibid., p. 42. The next three quotations are from the same page.
[47] The booklet held by Harvard College Library appears to be the reprint of an article that was one of a pair.
[48] Spencer, *Social Statics; or: the Conditions essential to Human Happiness specified, and the first of them developed*. Abridged and revised (originally, London, 1850) (together with *The Man Versus the State*; New York: Appleton, 1904).
[49] The classic, David Ricardo, *The Principles of Political Economy and Taxation* (originally, London

over fertility could only be achieved, as he documented with reference to animal as well as human evolution, through practices such as Sparta's selective infanticide of weaklings, or bedouin nomads' abandoning their aged to a lonely death from starvation.

Behind this, he stressed, was the principle that "every man may claim the fullest liberty"[50] limited only by another's "like liberty." In this vein, the civilized, free individual was to remain unaffected by naive compassion for the unfit, a contemporary weakness which Spencer saw prevail in philanthropy or social-reform legislation in his time.[51] He wrote condemning the then recent poor laws:

> Blind to the fact that under the natural order of things society is constantly excreting its unhealthy, imbecile, slow, vacillating, faithless members, these unthinking, though well-meaning, men advocate an interference which not only stops the purifying process, but even increases the vitiation – absolutely encourages the multiplication of the reckless and incompetent by offering them an unfailing provision, and discourages the multiplication of the competent and provident by heightening the difficulty of maintaining a family. And thus, in their eagerness to prevent the salutary sufferings that surround us, these sigh-wise and groan-foolish people bequeath to posterity a continually increasing curse.[52]

As it happened, Darwin accounted for evolution in *The Origin of Species* by adopting Spencer's principle of struggle for existence. Using Spencer's idea, Darwin could trace progress to natural selection. The book's subtitle clarified this: *The Preservation of Favoured Races in the Struggle for Life*.[53] Indeed, Spencer was the original source of the idea that struggle for existence caused natural selection with which Darwin was credited from then on. Spencer continued to refer to the principle of natural selection, and when he became widely known and indeed rose to celebrity status in the 1870s and early 1880s, Spencer's embracing the allegedly Darwinian paradigm of natural selection boosted recognition of Spencer's philosophy. This situation was not then commented on by either of the two men.

Darwin, in his second major opus, *The Descent of Man*, acknowledged his intellectual debt to Spencer, though in a somewhat dismissive manner:[54] He granted

---

1817), in the 1850s became the target for criticism raised by German emigré Karl Marx who had settled in London. His *Kritik der politischen Ökonomie* which argued against Ricardo as well as Adam Smith, Jean Baptiste Say, and others, was left unfinished in 1859.

[50] Spencer, *Social Statics*, p. 36; the next quote is from the same page.
[51] Brinton in his description of Spencer's political philosophy explained: "He denied to the State any right to interfere with the freedom of play of supply and demand, and carried his allegiance to *laissez-faire* so far as to attack sanitary legislation." This said, Brinton could not help remarking: "But he was subject to insomnia, and we find him asserting the right of the State to prevent by law the unnecessary blowing of locomotive whistles." Brinton, *English Political Thought in Nineteenth Century*, p. 228, citing Spencer's *Principles of Ethics*, section 296.
[52] Spencer, *Social Statics*, p. 151.
[53] Charles Darwin, *On the Origin of Species by Means of Natural Selection or the Preservation of Favoured Races in the Struggle for Life* (London: J. Murray, Albemarle Street, 1859); reprinted London: William Pickering, 1988.
[54] Charles Darwin, *The Descent of Man, and the Selection in Relation to Sex* (London: J. Murray, 1871); reprinted from the 2d, revised and augmented edition of 1877, London: Pickering, 1989, p. 71; the next quotation is also from this page.

to Spencer's *The Principles of Psychology* the idea which he, Darwin, endorsed, namely that "the first dawnings of intelligence...have been developed through the multiplication and coordination of reflex actions."[55] But Darwin also invoked against Spencer two insights from his own, Darwin's, then recent studies on mutation. There, he had argued that cultivation through domestification of animals and plants needed to be taken into account.[56] He now ventured against Spencer's theories of inheritance of moral traits, that "some intelligent actions, after being performed during several generations, become converted into instincts and are inherited,"[57] and, second and more importantly, "the greater number of the more complex instincts appear to have been gained...through Natural Selection of variations of simpler instinctive actions." These clarifications, Darwin felt, supplemented the views of "our great philosopher, Herbert Spencer,"[58] especially his "views on the moral sense." Nevertheless, he credited Spencer with the insight, quoting from one of Spencer's published letters,[59] laying out Spencer's words verbatim, that "the experiences of utility organised and consolidated through all past generations of the human race, have been producing corresponding modifications which, by continuous transmission and accumulation, have become in us certain faculties of moral intuition – certain emotions responding to right and wrong conduct, which have no apparent basis in the individual experiences of utility."

Darwin, therefore, went along with Spencer when it came to explaining society, especially morality and culture in civilized populations, through the principles of inheritance. From this vantage point, he was prepared to acknowledge that evolution extended to "social faculties." To prove it, he contended:

> There is not the least inherent improbability, it seems to me, in virtuous tendencies being more or less strongly inherited; for, not to mention the various dispositions and habits transmitted by many of our domestic animals to their offspring, I have heard of authentic cases in which a desire to steal and a tendency to lie appeared to run in families of the upper ranks; and as stealing is a rare crime in the wealthy classes, we can hardly account by accidental coincidence for the tendency occurred in two or three members of the same family.... Insanity is notoriously inherited.... Except through the transmission of moral tendencies, we cannot understand the differences believed to exist in this respect between the various races of mankind.[60]

Spencer's project, despite the fact that it may have inspired Darwin's evolutionism, went beyond Darwin's naturalism, however. Spencer's *The Study of Sociology*,

---

[55] Darwin referred to Herbert Spencer, *The Principles of Psychology* (London: Longman, Brown, Green, and Longmans, 1855), as a reference in a footnote. Rather sweepingly (in the second edition of his book), he cited Spencer's book's second edition of 1875, page numbers 418–443 without further specifications.

[56] Darwin, *Variations of Animals and Plants Under Domestification* (London: J. Murray, 1868); reprinted New York: New York University Press, 1988.

[57] Darwin, *Descent of Man*, p. 72; the next quote is from the same page.

[58] Ibid., p. 127; the next three quotes are from the same page.

[59] Darwin referenced a "letter [from Spencer] to Mr. Mill in Bain's *Mental and Moral Science*, 1868, p. 722."

[60] Darwin, *Descent of Man*, pp. 127–128.

first published in 1873,[61] made no mention of Darwin. The book aimed to establish a science of sociology superseding biology. Its first chapters dealt with three types of difficulties which were the reason of frequent blindness to the obvious fact that laws of social organisms explained "the phenomena of conduct."[62] These difficulties, Spencer held, were either objective (e.g., due to lack of suitability of behavioral phenomena for measurement), or subjective (i.e., due to random variation in the relationship between intellect and emotions). A third difficulty entangled the observer of social life in "his relationships of race, and country, and citizenship."[63] This latter difficulty, Spencer explained, resulted from a variety of biases which, he suggested, had to do with education, patriotism, class, or religion. All of these were ideological origins of egalitarianism. They derived from what he called noxious philosophies. They often became arenas for social reform, he complained, which meant that they would inadvertently interfere with societal evolution and progress.

In his chapter on educational bias, he denied categorically that availability of education for everybody could lead to equality of capacity to excel. Instead, he praised the efficiency of war in more primitive societies, which sharpened the struggle for existence. He likened war to competition in our modern world whose function was to weed out those incapable or unfit. Aggression, he emphasized, was the key to moral evolution in the race, although in civilized communities egoistic selfishness, as in crimes of violence, had to be checked. Pre-industrial societies, he found, might have favored extirpation of inferior races as a suitable outlet for aggressiveness, but modern industrialism called for selection in the interest of the race by what he termed "industrial war": "After this stage has been reached, the purifying process, continuing still an important one, remains to be carried on by industrial war – by a competition of societies during which the best, physically, emotionally, and intellectually, spread most, and leave the least capable to disappear gradually, from failing to leave a sufficiently-numerous posterity."[64]

It is common knowledge that William Graham Sumner's sociology, widely successful in the 1880s and later, was undeniably social Darwinist.[65] Sumner's *What Social Classes Owe To Each Other* was first published in 1883 and republished in 1925, with a second printing in 1934.[66] Its main thrust opposed social legislation: "The notion of civil liberty which we have inherited is that of a status

---

[61] Herbert Spencer, *The Study of Sociology* (originally, 1873), reprinted, Ann Arbor: University of Michigan Press, 1961. On the occasion of the book's republication in 1961, Parsons wrote an introduction which judged Spencer from the vantage point of modern sociology in the 1960s, no longer that of the 1930s. But one thing did not change, compared with the 1930s, namely that Parsons criticized Spencer for having denied the value of general education, one of the most basic values of modern democratic society.

[62] Ibid., p. 52.

[63] Ibid., p. 67.

[64] Ibid., p. 180.

[65] On Sumner, see Richard Hofstadter, *Social Darwinism in American Thought* (originally, 1944), revised edition, New York: Braziller, 1959, esp. chapter 3; see also Hofstadter, "William Graham Sumner, Social Darwinist," *New England Quarterly*, vol. 14, 1941, pp. 457–477.

[66] William Graham Sumner, *What Social Classes Owe To Each Other* (New York: Harper and Brothers, 1883); republished New Haven: Yale University Press, 1925, 2d printing 1934; republished 1947; 9th printing, Caldwell, Idaho: Caxton Printers, 1982.

created for the individual by laws and institutions, the effect of which is that each man is guaranteed the use of all his own powers exclusively for his own welfare."[67]

This meant, as the book's title suggested, that the social classes owed nothing to each other except being left to their own devices. In no way did the upper classes ("the rich") owe anything to the lower classes ("the poor"). In this vein, the modern welfare state had no right to legitimately compel the better-off to pay for the maintenance or even advancement of the disadvantaged, lest the very essence of civilization were endangered. Only if natural selection was allowed to take its toll could modern society live up to its responsibility of ensuring humankind's progress. Accordingly, Chapter V was entitled, "That We Must Have Few Men, If We Want Strong Men." Emulating Spencer, Sumner declared industrialism the new credo, emulating Malthusianism: "The maxim...is, Get capital....That it requires energy, courage, perseverance, and prudence is not to be denied. Any one who believes that any good thing on this earth can be got without those virtues may believe in the philosopher's stone."[68]

To accomplish such vitally required industrialism through the means of unfettered individualism, society had to follow the maxim, Back to Nature. This meant abandoning any interference with natural selection. Sumner suggested ridding social life of social legislation when he recommended disavowing the naive albeit well-intentioned advocates of such legislation in political economy and social science: "A vast number of social ills which never came from Nature...are the complicated products of...social quackery...now buttressed by habit, fashion, prejudice, platitudinarian thinking, and new quackery in political economy and social science....Society, therefore, does not need any care or supervision."[69]

Only without such interference, at last, would prevail the virtue of the "Forgotten Man."[70] The latter was destined to "minding one's own business"[71] which, in turn, assured continuous progress in civilization. The struggles and sufferings of past generations, Sumner maintained, had made modern civilization possible. Now the duty of our time was not to break the cycle of Nature. Because solely through heredity, based on competitive adaptation to environment, could racial survival be secured. Further improvement of civilization hinged on the more productive and intelligent population outnumbering and outliving the less industrious and able. "The struggles of the race as a whole produce the possessions of the race as a whole," Sumner concluded, adding a warning against egalitarianism: "Something for nothing is not to be found on earth."[72]

---

[67] Ibid., p. 30.
[68] Ibid., p. 68.
[69] Ibid., pp. 102–103.
[70] Ibid., p. 107. See pp. 107–131, chapters IX–X, namely chapter IX, "On the Case of a Certain Man Who Is Never Thought of," and chapter X, "The Case of the Forgotten Man Further Considered," pp. 107–131.
[71] Ibid., p. 106.
[72] Ibid., p. 116.

Sumner remained a Darwinist thoughout his academic career.[73] His *Folkways*, first published in 1906,[74] understood folkways and mores, the cultural habits and customs in primitive as well as civilized societies, as the outcome of the struggle for existence. In chapters on the themes of the struggle for existence, the legitimacy of wealth that purified fitness for survival when it helped cultivate lifestyle, and societal selection, he explicated the principles and vast array of forms of manipulation of the environment.[75] The latter, he claimed, was the purpose of institutions whose scope ranged from marriage to warfare, including practices such as infanticide, and under which also came "industrial organization"[76] that served the supremacy of the stongest.

As an advocate of social selection, Sumner was opposed to the modern welfare state, which he condemned throughout his book. For instance, the pension system appeared to him but a symptom of decay of the vital forces of progress for mankind: "The pension system in the United States is an abuse which has escaped from control. There is no longer any attempt to cope with it. It is the share of the 'common man' in the great system of public plunder. 'Graft' is only a proof of the wide extent to which this lesson to get into the steal is learned. It only shows that the corrupt use of legislation and political power has affected the mores."[77]

Sumner was vigorously opposed to public education, which he condemned as a myth and panacea for every unwanted problem in modern America. The main defect of such "superstition of the age," he charged, was that "book learning is addressed to the intellect, not the feelings, but the feelings are the spring of action."[78]

Hofstadter, in his treatise on social Darwinism in American social thought, reported that Sumner's early philosophy of moral superiority of the successful in the upper classes was effectively challenged by Thorstein Veblen's *Theory of the Leisure Class*, first published in 1899.[79] However, Veblen was rather ineffective as a challenger of Sumner or Spencer. Veblen evidently was a controversial figure in American academe in the early part of the century, whereas Sumner was considered a serious scholar.

Sumner continued to publish until his death, although his fame faded in the last decade of his life. At the time of the end of World War I, his essay entitled "The Forgotten Man" was reprinted, which gave the title to an entire collection of his writings, extolling the topic of warning against social reform.[80] The metaphor of

---

[73] Robert Bierstedt, *American Sociological Theory: A Critical History* (1981), who has a chapter on Sumner, reports that Sumner had a portrait of Darwin hung over his desk, p. 11.

[74] William Graham Sumner, *Folkways. A Study of the Sociological Importance of Usages, Manners, Customs, Mores, and Morals* (Boston: Ginn and Company, 1906).

[75] Chapters III–V, pp. 119–260.

[76] Ibid., p. 157.

[77] Ibid., p. 170.

[78] Ibid., p. 629.

[79] Thorstein Veblen, *Theory of the Leisure Class. An Economic Study of Institutions* (New York: Macmillan, 1899). See Hofstadter, *Social Darwinism in American Thought*, pp. 151–156.

[80] Sumner, *The Forgotten Man and Other Essays*, edited by Albert Galloway Keller (New Haven, Conn.: Yale University Press, 1918); it contained the essay, "The Forgotten Man," originally written in the early 1880s, pp. 465–495.

"Forgotten Man," which Sumner had used (twice) in the 1880s, referred to the hard-working citizen whose industriousness was punished rather than rewarded when his profit was taxed away by the state. The latter, in turn, wasted tax money for programs of support for the poor who, Sumner maintained, were thus spared having to work hard for their living.[81]

Another opponent of social Darwinism whom Hofstadter mentioned as an active writer on social theory in the 1890s was Lester Ward.[82] To be sure, Ward's notion of "effort" denoting an important force in social life might well have inspired Parsons in *Structure* when he introduced effort into the theory of the structure of social action at a crucial point.[83] Nonetheless, Ward in his later years appears to have become more and more fascinated with the sociology of Ludwig Gumplowicz, an influential Austrian, who advocated race as a sociological principle. In the 1890s, though Ward's *Outlines of Sociology* proclaimed mutual interest and community forces as basic elements of social life,[84] Ward had Gumplowicz's *Grundriss der Soziologie*[85] translated and saw it published under the same title as his own book, *Outlines of Sociology*, in 1899.[86]

Gumplowicz insisted that power and knowledge originated in and were biologically tied to social collectivities, among them prominently race. Consequently, freedom of thought or will or even individuality were all mere illusions. Absolute priority lay in "the life of the species" throughout evolution, he stated, which undeniably suggested destruction of individuals unable to submit to or serve the forces of history. "Historical events are not brought about by men any more than natural events by God," he wrote in defense of his view,[87] apparently alluding to Darwin's eventual victory over theological bigotry when he, Gumplowicz, wished to find evidence supportive of his own historical determinism.

In the 1930s, evidently, these thoughts were far from forgotten. In the spring of 1933, a collection of letters from Gumplowicz to Ward filled the annual supplement of the German journal *Sociologicus*, whose co-editor was Sorokin.[88]

---

[81] Even after Parsons's *Structure* had been published, in 1940, a volume entitled *Sumner Today* paid tribute to this prophet of social Darwinism. The book, subtitled *Selected Essays with Comments by American Leaders*, reprinted a number of essays by Sumner; its second part contained laudatory comments on his works and person by public figures such as, among others, Harold Moulton, president of the Brookings Institution, William Green, president of AF of L, and Charles Seymour, president of Yale University. Cf. Maurice R. Davie, ed., *Sumner Today. Selected Essays of William Graham Sumner With Comments by American Leaders* (New Haven, Conn.: Yale University Press, 1940).

[82] Hofstadter, *Social Darwinism in American Thought*, chapter IV.

[83] On the notion of effort in *Structure*, see below.

[84] Lester Ward, *Outlines of Sociology* (New York: Macmillan, 1898).

[85] Ludwig Gumplowicz, *Grundriss der Soziologie* (Vienna: Manz, 1885).

[86] Ludwig Gumplowicz, *Outlines of Sociology* (Philadelphia: American Academy of Arts and Sciences, 1899); reprinted, edited, and with an introduction by Irving L. Horowitz, New York: Paine Whitman, 1963.

[87] Ibid., p. 31.

[88] See, Bernhard J. Stern, ed., "The Letters of Ludwig Gumplowicz to Lester Ward," *Sociologicus*, vol. 9, Beiheft 1, 1933, pp. 5–32.

Racism in Germany

This American sociological scene, however, was only one arena entered into in *Structure* advocating, to cite Weber, an "ethics of responsibility" (*Verantwortungsethik*). The other was European. When *Structure* started off on Brinton's formula declaring Spencer "dead" and long overcome, contemporaneous Nazi pseudoscience was in its prime. Its influence pervaded German social as well as natural science.

Racial biology, termed eugenics, had originated in the 1850s and spread in Europe as well as the United States during subsequent decades. In Germany, eugenics had become a respected branch of biological as well as medical science; it was taught at universities from the late nineteenth century onward. In 1928, a *Kaiser Wilhelm Institute for Anthropology, Human Genetics, and Eugenics* had been established, of which Otmar von Verschuer became first director after the Nazi takeover in 1933. On the occasion of the Institute's establishment, von Verschuer, who was a biologist specializing in public health, had published a small book that became notorious when it invoked sociology to represent social politics as it advocated racial hygiene, which meant Nazi racism.[89]

The topic of race, however, haunted sociology in Germany from the late nineteenth century onward. The earliest writings on race in German-language sociology dated back as far as the 1880s, as did one by Gumplowicz[90] and others by authors such as Gustav Ratzenhofer or Adam Schäffle. A more important figure than these was Alfred Ploetz, who prided himself on creating an academic discipline devoted to (racist) biology applied to (preferably, future) society (*Gesellschaftsbiologie*). In 1910, on the occasion of the First Conference of the newly founded German Sociological Society, Max Weber suggested that Ploetz be invited as one of the keynote speakers, only to vigorously attack Ploetz's teachings. Speaking from the floor, commenting on Ploetz's lecture stressing the importance of racial categories for sociological analysis, Weber denied all semblance of its scientific appeal.[91] Ploetz, who apparently coined the term "racial hygiene," had a remarkable career, finding followers in German sociology after 1895 when he published an influential treatise.

The book's title was *The Fitness of Our Race and the Protection of the Weak*; it carried the subtitle, *A Study of Racial Hygiene and Its Relationship to Humane*

---

[89] Otmar Freiherr von Verschuer, *Sozialpolitik und Rassenhygiene* (Langensalza: Beyer, 1928).

[90] Gumplowicz's earlist work, predating his *Grundriss der Soziologie* by two years, had been his *Der Rassenkampf* (The Race Struggle), originally published in 1883 and republished in l909 and again in 1928. In its introduction to the 1909 edition, Gumplowicz claimed that a booming tradition of sociology focusing on race had emerged since the 1880s; he praised such success as one of positivist, evolutionist sociology. See Ludwig Gumplowicz, *Der Rassenkampf*. Zweite Auflage, 1909. Mit einem Vorwort von Gottfried Salomon. Ausgewählte Werke, Bd. III (Innsbruck: Universitätsverlag Wagner, 1928), p. ix.

[91] See, for comment, Detlef Peukert, "Weber contra Ploetz," in *Max Webers Begriff der Moderne* (Göttingen: Vandenhoek und Ruprecht, 1990), pp. 92–101; Weber's original statement was republished in his *Gesammelte Aufsätze zur Soziologie und Sozialpolitik*, 2d edition (Tübingen: Mohr, 1988), pp. 456–462.

Ideals, Especially Socialism.[92] Ploetz's problem was whether the most recent social-policy programs of sanitary improvements, social insurance, support of the poor, and indeed general medical care that frequently saved children despite their weaknesses or defects, jeopardized "constitutionary" fitness of the Germanic race(s). Natural selection, he claimed, led to elimination of the less fit in the course of "normally" either economic or noneconomic "weeding-out" (*Ausjäten*). Inasmuch as modern social policy protected the weak from dying early and childless, he insisted, compensatory measures stalling its consequences through policies of racial hygiene were imperative. In his terminology of convariates and devariates, defined as approximations of or deviations from a utopian idealized race, Ploetz phrased his problem thus: "For every part of the weeding-out struggle for existence which we do away with through hygiene, therapy, social and economic protection of the weak, and socialist reforms in general, we must by necessity establish an equivalent in the form of related improvement of the devariants, as otherwise deterioration of the species is certain."[93]

The solution, as he saw it, combined two strategies securing so-called *Auslese*.[94] Racial hygiene had to fulfill the two obvious tasks. One was education for self-discipline that was to harden the person, thus bringing out the best in racial potentialities as inherited. The other was to permit only persons or couples to have children who represented optimal racial stock. Long passages in Ploetz's work discussed how the racially fit could be denied birth control and how the unfit be prevented from having children. On the part of the latter, the idealized, pure race was to be accomplished through self-restraint, enforced abortion, or possibly even mass sterilization – although the latter topic was barely mentioned.

Racial hygiene, as he outlined it, was social policy serving two opposite ends. On the one hand, Ploetz suggested explicitly benefiting multiplication of the racially best, and, on the other, discouraging or preventing from conception racially doubtful populations. These ends meant to improve overall racial quality, he claimed, were to be achieved through policies that gave individuals no say in whether their fate was procreation or its opposite, sterilization.

Ploetz endorsed "race-hygienic demands for perfection of type and increase of number"[95] of the Aryan and especially Germanic race(s). He divided the Aryans (Germans) into many different national races, estimating the overall number of such

---

[92] Alfred Ploetz, *Die Tüchtigkeit unserer Rasse und der Schutz der Schwachen. Ein Versuch über Rassenhygiene und ihr Verhältnis zu den humanen Idealen, besonders zum Sozialismus* (Berlin: S. Fischer, 1895).

[93] Ibid., p. 229. In German: "Für jedes Stück des ausjätenden Kampfes um's Dasein, das wir durch Hygiene, durch Therapeutik, durch socialen und wirthschaftlichen Schutz der Schwachen, durch socialistische Reformen im Allgemeinen beiseite schaffen, müssen wir nothgedrungen ein Äquivalent bieten in Form von entsprechender Verbesserung der Devarianten, sonst ist eine Entartung sicher."

[94] *Auslese* is the German word for selection that would be conducted actively, which became a keyword in Nazi racial politics. The other strategy was called *Ausmerze*, deliberate destruction of populations not deemed worthy of survival. See, for instance, Gisela Bock, *Die Politik und Praxis der Sterilisierung im Dritten Reich* (Göttingen: Vandenhoek und Ruprecht, 1986), and Robert Procter, *Racial Hygiene. Medicine Under the Nazis* (Cambridge, Mass.: Harvard University Press, 1988).

[95] Ploetz, *Die Tüchtigkeit unserer Rasse*, p. 114.

Aryans (Germans) at some 160–200 million in (Western) Europe, the United States, and Australia taken together. (As Ploetz explicitly mentioned, to him Jews were a cultured race and deserved to mix or even merge with German-Aryans, for mutual benefit to racial substance.)

Ploetz, a physician (general practitioner), was widely recognized for his contribution to sociology in his time. In 1904, he founded a journal *Archiv für Rassen- und Gesellschaftsbiologie* (Archives for Racial and Social Biology), possibly the first forum and soon to become one of a number of journals in a field now named racial hygiene or, its other theme, social biology. (The journal ceased publication in 1944.)

Such academic discussion no doubt marked the beginning of Nazi-type thought even before the seizure of power of National Socialism. In his pamphlet entitled *Social Politics and Racial Hygiene*, von Verschuer linked racial hygiene to racist social politics. The two sides in his theme of *Social Politics and Racial Hygiene*, von Verschuer felt, were related to two types of sciences. One was "Gesellschaftslehre oder Soziologie" that provided the source of social politics, and the other was "Rassenbiologie oder Anthropologie" to be applied in racial hygiene. These two fields, he stated, could be as much as merged into one: "Social-political arrangements and measures have racial-hygienic consequences, and race-hygienic demands and wishes often involve social politics. These various interactions can be understood and judged adequately only if the *tasks* both of social politics and racial hygiene are clearly shown, and especially if their *common purpose* is clearly kept in mind."[96] This common purpose, he went on to say, related to "the people – that is, not...the individuals."[97] The issues were both the state and the race. The idea was that both state and race represented collectivities in which individuals were only parts of an all-encompassing whole. Von Verschuer took this idea from the sociology of Othmar Spann.[98]

To illustrate inspiration from Spann's sociology in von Verschuer's short book, Spann's two works may be cited briefly. His *Gesellschaftslehre* postulated that society, as an entity of holistic force, embraced and incorporated individuals as elementary units. He saw two tendencies in social thinking: universalism and individualism. He opted for their integration, espousing a view in which society meant an organic whole with a life beyond that of its elements. He thus reduced individuals to members in an all-encompassing collectivity. These member-elements were

---

[96] von Verschuer, *Sozialpolitik und Rassenhygiene*, p. 7. The German original reads: "Sozialpolitische Einrichtungen und Massnahmen haben rassenhygienische Folgen, und rassenhygienische Forderungen und Wünsche liegen vielfach auf sozialpolitischem Gebiet. Diese verschiedenartigen Wechselwirkungen kann man nur dann einheitlich betrachten und beurteilen, wenn man die *Aufgaben* von Sozialpolitik und Rassenhygiene, vor allem aber ihr *gemeinsames Ziel* klar vor Augen hat" (emphasis original).

[97] Ibid., p. 8. In German: "Volkstum – also nicht...Einzelmenschen." A literal translation of "Volkstum" might be peoplehood, if such a word existed in English.

[98] The sociology of Spann to which von Verschuer referred were the two works, *Gesellschaftslehre* (originally, 1914) in its second edition (Leipzig: Quelle & Meyer, 1923), and *Kategorienlehre* (Jena: Gustav Fischer, 1924). Parsons, in *Structure*, referred to Spann in the index, cf. p. lviii (misspelling the latter's first name, however).

to be welded together into a dominant totality of *Gesellschaft*, through a process of compulsive community formation (*Vergemeinschaftung*). Such community formation, he demanded, had to be based on race as well as hereditary endowment in its members.[99]

The basic tenets in his doctrine as they appealed to von Verschuer (but might have antagonized Parsons) were expressed in *Gesellschaftslehre* in passages like the following:

> Every historical and living society is based on the principle that it holds down the morally bad and tames all value systems hostile to it. It exists only through unending victory, through, as Schelling says about the divine order in the cosmos, sitting on a throne above constant terror. To be sure, this is not a scene of peace and love, as pacifists and utopians dream about. Without value-authority and therefore real power-authority and dominating force, no society is possible; but this authority must be based on certain dominant valuations, the rank order of cultural [geistige] superiority.[100]

In his other book mentioned by von Verschuer, *Kategorienlehre*, Spann elaborated on how the individual in society (constituting a member in the way of a member in a chain) had to be seen "bound back" by necessity into the archetypical whole. He proclaimed the overarching unity and undivided essence of an all-encompassing entity. The somewhat mystifying terminology in which he addressed categories of thinking not as cognitive but intuitive concepts anticipated some of the philosophical ruminations which a decade later became the kind of philosophy the Nazis welcomed. (Spann, to be sure, was complimented by Hitler personally in the 1920s, publicly honored by the regime in the early years of Nazi rule, but later in the 1930s excluded from party favors and had his works banned from public libraries due to their alleged conservative viewpoint.)

In his programmatic book, embracing Spann's sociology, von Verschuer arrived at a formula-like conclusion, namely: Social politics benefited the state, racial hygiene benefited the race, and both together benefited the *Volk* (or, rather, "Volkstum").[101] All three, although primarily state and race, he warned, were in constant danger of deterioration: "If race degenerates, culture dies.... If the state withers, viz. if the environment becomes unfavorable, race becomes silent in its cultural productivity."[102] Such reasoning led him to warn that racial substance was compromised, or indeed severely harmed, by the modern welfare state (i.e., as he

---

[99] Spann, *Gesellschaftslehre*, p. 267.

[100] Ibid., p. 254 (my translation). In German: "Jede geschichtliche und lebendige Gesellschaft beruht darauf, daß sie sittlich Schlechtes niederhält und darüber hinaus noch alle ihr feindlichen Wertsysteme bändigt, daß sie nur durch unaufhörlichen Sieg besteht, indem sie, wie Schelling einmal von der göttlichen Ordnung im Weltall sagte, über Schrecken thront. Auch hier ist also nichts mit eitel Friede und Liebe, wie Pazifisten und Schwärmer träumen. Ohne Wert-Herrschaft und darum ohne wirkliche Macht-Herrschaft und Herrschergewalt ist keine Gesellschaft möglich; aber diese Herrschaft muß sich auf bestimmte vorherrschende Wertungsweisen, geistige Rangordnungen gründen."

[101] See above, fn. 97.

[102] Von Verschuer, *Sozialpolitik und Rassenhygiene*, p. 12. In German: "(E)ntartet die Rasse, so stirbt die Kultur.... Verfällt der Staat, beziehungsweise wird die Umwelt ungünstig, dann verstummt die Rasse in ihrer geistigen Produktivität."

explicitly stated, programs such as unemployment insurance, minimum wages, or sickness insurance). Evaluating one after another a number of Weimar Republic welfare programs, von Verschuer insisted that measures had to be taken to assuage the damage resulting from welfare programs. Considering that no lessening of racial perfection should result from any welfare measure, he suggested counter-action. To this end, he made explicit what Ploetz had only hinted at: "Abuse of social insurance by the inferior leads to economic support and multiplication of the inferior. The natural health-restoration process of the race is obstructed. Recommended counter-measures against such race-hygienically dangerous damages caused by social insurance are: stricter repressive measures by physicians in state-controlled public health agencies, deliberate sterilization of the mentally ill and feeble-minded."[103]

Another measure, which he also suggested, might exclude those unwilling to work from eligibility for insurance, which by the same token would increase a sense of in-group cohesion among those proved fittest for survival (i.e., who were actually working). In no uncertain terms, therefore, he rejected the democratic welfare state on the account that it presumably destroyed the racially purifying impact of inequality.

Citing Spann as an ideological ally yet again, von Verschuer embraced Spann's universalism as he wrote: "The advocate of race hygiene, therefore, feels close to all those who participate in the spiritual stuggle of idealism against materialism, of universalism against individualism."[104] Incidentally, shortly after publication of *Sozialpolitik und Rassenhygiene*, in his contribution to a Handbook on Social Hygiene and Preventive Health, von Verschuer made it clear that both heredity *and* environment were deterministic.[105] He stated that human development consisted of "hereditary endowment, on the one hand, and environment or peristasis, on the other hand."[106] He clarified that heredity meant biological characteristics lodged with race or family, the latter instead of individual endorsement being crucial. The environment, which helped develop inborn racial potential, was in constant interchange with holistic forces that governed race (family)-prone heredity. This meant that "the essence of influences impinging on the hereditary endowment, the genotype, [were] 'from without', i.e. from outside the morphological substratum of the genes."[107] In this vein, both heredity and environment were mechanistic forces.

---

[103] Ibid., p. 21. In German: "Dieser Missbrauch der sozialen Versicherungen durch die Minderwertigen führt zur wirtschaftlichen Unterstützung und zur Mehrung der Minderwertigen. Der natürliche Gesundungsprozess der Rasse wird gehemmt. Als Gegenmaßregeln gegen diese rassenhygienischen Schäden der sozialen Versicherungen kommen in Frage: verschärftes Durchgreifen beamteter Ärzte, künstliche Unfruchtbarmachung von Geisteskranken und Schwachsinnigen."

[104] Ibid., p. 32. In German: "Der Rassenhygieniker fühlt sich deshalb als Bundesgenosse von all denjenigen, die im geistigen Kampf des Idealismus gegen den Materialismus, des Universalismus gegen den Individualismus ... stehen."

[105] Von Verschuer, "Soziale Umwelt und Vererbung." In *Ergebnisse der Sozialen Hygiene und Gesundheitsfürsorge*, edited by A. Grotjahn, L. Langstein and F. Rott, Vol. II (Leipzig: Georg Thieme, 1930), pp. 1–33.

[106] Ibid., p. 1.

[107] Ibid., p. 2. He saw environmental impact, which he called peristasis, as (in the original German) "den Inbegriff der Einflüsse, die das Erbgefüge, den Genotypus, 'von außen,' d.h. von außerhalb des morphologischen Substrats der Gene treffen."

They could not be influenced by individual effort when they impinged directly on the *Volk* (i.e., race, or family as an ethnic clan): Not that the individual was the elementary unit for the dynamics of heredity and environment, but influences from the environment impinged on the racial substance in the genes of the *Volk*, or a similar wholesome entity, from whence derived everything individual.

Using statistical inference, von Verschuer took as an example hereditary diseases such as mental retardation and goiter, to calculate the effect of disease on the racial constitution of entire populations. Using statistics in a strictly mechanistic fashion, he demonstrated that, due to the dominant inheritance of a gene causing hereditary disease, an entire population could within a relatively small number of future generations be affected by pathology, with no prospect of ever regaining racial health.

Since environmental influences, for him, meant causal forces impinging on the racial substratum in the genes, they could produce defects in hereditary genetic endowment. Photographs of twins, some naked in military-like posture, were to document that environment-identical monozygotic or bizygotic twins could help understand heredity and environment. Von Verschuer proved his point through information on these individuals' (twins') occupations, height, shape of skull, and so on.

At the end of his text he summed up that "social environment and heredity together in close interaction determine the development of man and the fate of groups of men."[108] Whereas he meant to forecast danger of racial degeneration, he also pointed at ways of avoiding such impending disaster. He concluded with a plea for politics: "These findings serve the purpose of helping to find ways to influence the biological life of men and peoples, through *measures* of some kind."[109] The latter, he suggested, were twofold. For one, "social hygiene" could influence environments so as to improve on hereditary endowment. Furthermore, through what he called *eugenics*, "the fact of being born of men of particular groups"[110] could be influenced. The aim of such measures, he stated, was "(1) protection and nurturing of the bearers of healthy, valuable genes, and (2) struggle against environmental influences causing genetic damage."[111]

---

[108] Ibid., p. 30.
[109] Ibid. In German: "Unsere Ausführungen haben ergeben, daß soziale Umwelt und Vererbung in innigem Wechselspiel die Entwicklung des Menschen und das Schicksal von Menschengruppen bestimmen. Diese ursächlichen Erkenntnisse dienen dem Zweck, Wege zu finden, um durch *Maßnahmen* irgendwelcher Art das biologische Geschehen im Leben der Menschen und Völker zu beeinflussen."
[110] Ibid., p. 31. The practical possibilities were, he summarized (in German), "1. Die Entwicklung der geborenen Menschen beeinflussen wir durch die Gestaltung der Umwelt (Individuelle, Soziale Hygiene). 2. Die Entwicklung einer Menschengruppe in der Abfolge der Generationen, d.h. das Geborenwerden von Menschen in bestimmten Gruppen, beeinflussen wir durch die Gestaltung der Auslese (Eugenik). Die Richtung der Auslese wird bestimmt durch die Umwelt."
[111] Ibid. In German: "Hier ergeben sich als praktische Folgerungen: 1. Behütung und Förderung der Träger von gesunden, wertvollen Erbanlagen, und 2. Bekämpfung der Erbschädigungen hervorrufenden Umwelteinflüsse." To recollect, it was von Verschuer, as Procter documents, whose research projects on the potential changeability of biological endowment, such as the color of the iris in monozygotic twins, were being carried out in the Auschwitz concentration camp by von Verschuer's former assistant at the *Kaiser Wilhelm Institute*, the infamous Nazi doctor Mengele. See Procter, *Racial Hygiene*, pp. 44, 349.

Anti-Darwinism in Structure

Parsons, to be sure, did not cite von Verschuer when he rejected as sociologically irrational the principle(s) of heredity and environment. He did, however, if only in the bibliography, refer to authors who had aligned their sociology with Nazi doctrine, such as Spann and also Hans Freyer. He also mentioned the doctrine of Nordic blood, in the shape of a reference to "Nordic" man. In Chapter I of *Structure*, where he discussed various types of concepts, Parsons referred as presumptively scientific concept to that of "Nordic" man.[112] Allowing for hypothetical empirical usefulness of the concept, he pointed out that here was an example of typological thinking that could epitomize what was a "pure type."[113] He asserted that "we can well conceive meeting a purely 'Nordic' man (however the type may be defined) and need not assume a priori that he *by definition* has Mediterranian or any other non-Nordic blood."[114]

Mocking Nazi quasi-scientific doctrine, Parsons here expressed skepticism against "pure type" concepts when he also mocked unscientific thinking. Against the background of contemporary social Darwinism that dominated even professedly scientific thought in Germany, this mention of Parsons of the Nazi concept demonstrated his strong objection. He also evidenced the fact that he took notice of the pseudoscience practiced in Germany in the 1930s. Parsons made direct mention of Nazism in two footnotes. These were placed in the parts on Pareto and Durkheim. One dealt with Nazi anti-Semitism, and the other with practices of manipulation and control of knowledge and public opinion.[115]

In the latter of the two footnotes, the sentence upon which it hinged invoked the "fact that social existence depends to a large extent on a moral consensus of its members and that the penalty of its too radical breakdown is social extinction"[116] – a fact, Parsons remarked, that "the type of liberal whose theoretical background is essentially utilitarian is all too apt to ignore – with unfortunate practical as well as theoretical consequences." In the footnote, defending Durkheim against ill-grounded critics who might charge him, Durkheim, with a hermetic image of social integration, Parsons clarified: "It does not in the least follow from this that such a consensus must, should or except in a very limited degree *can* be maintained by coercion. Durkheim himself continually reiterated the importance of spontaneity for truly moral action. From this position it is illegitimate to deduce a facile

---

[112] Parsons, *Structure*, p. 31.

[113] A brief comment: Parsons's dismissing the idea of "pure type" should be reconciled with his criticism, in chapter XVI of *Structure* dealing with Weber, of ideal type as in Weber's works. Parsons obviously misunderstood Weber's idea of ideal type (including the construction of "pure types"). He followed, in his understanding Weber's methodology, an apparently authoritative view in the 1930s, namely Alexander von Schelting, *Max Webers Wissenschaftslehre* (Tübingen: Mohr [Siebeck], 1934). (He published an extensive book review in *American Sociological Review* in 1936.) Unfortunately, von Schelting's errors in interpreting Weber were taken by Parsons as adequate understandings; consequently, he misjudged the usefulness of Weber's methodology here. For a more detailed account, see Uta Gerhardt, *Idealtypus: Zur methodologischen Begründung der modernen Soziologie* (Frankfurt: Suhrkamp, 2001), esp. chapters X and XI.

[114] *Structure*, p. 31.

[115] Ibid., pp. 283, 395. See also below.

[116] Ibid., p. 395. The next two quotes are from the same page.

justification of Nazi methods of control of opinion." No doubt, he distinguished between coercive enforcement and a genuine moral basis of conformity of opinion. He invoked National Socialism to characterize the former when he insisted that Durkheim had explained the latter.

A more open reference was in the other footnote that referred to Nazism. Its previous mention was in an unpublished manuscript of his, written in 1935 (preserved in the Harvard University Archives), entitled "Pareto and the Development of Social Theory." There, through discussing Pareto, he attacked unscientific thought which he identified with Nazi quasi-science. He distinguished between two kinds of intellectual milieu beyond a genuinely science-prone environment, one producing pseudoscience whereas the other produced blatantly unscientific doctrine. His point hinged on Pareto's distinguishing between "foxes" and "lions" – Pareto's two main types of élites in society. As Parsons discovered, Pareto found that there were two types of "non-scientific systems of ideas but with a highly interesting difference."[117] One was an intellectual milieu based on skepticism (associated with Pareto's "foxes"), involving ideas that were, Parsons said, "*pseudo*-scientific": They assimilated themselves as closely as possible with science, "they involve such 'deities' as 'Reason,' 'Science,' 'Positivism,' so that it takes some discernment to distinguish them from the real thing." In contradistinction, other systems of ideas were based on faith (associated with the "lions"). These were "avowedly idealistic, anti-materialistic, involve 'higher' entities such as Intuition, Faith etc." The latter, Parsons stated, were conspicuously unscientific whereas the former pretended to be what they were not – science. Pareto, he assured, had been opposed to both when – contradicting "the main positivistic-utilitarian tradition"[118] – he formulated "the conception of rational empirical science and that of rational action as action guided by scientific knowledge."

In *Structure*, apart from the conspicuously few direct mentions of Nazi doctrine, Parsons opposed social Darwinism when, for one, he rejected Darwinism. He not only contradicted the principle of heredity and environment, but also criticized the wider context of positivist utilitarianism or biological anti-intellectualism in the tradition of Spencer as well as others.

In Chapter III of *Structure*, when he analyzed "Some Phases of the Historical Development of Individualistic Positivism in the Theory of Action," he explicitly addressed Darwinism. Malthus, he began, had been the real source of "positivistic anti-intellectualism... which steadily gained in force almost throughout the nineteenth century."[119] Its pinnacle, "radical positivistic theory... Malthus himself did not reach.... But, in part influenced by him, the tendency culminated in one of the great movements of nineteenth century thought, Darwinism, which when developed into a closed system and applied to human action in society constituted the most important radically anti-intellectualistic positivistic system ever promulgated."

---

[117] Parsons, "Pareto and the Development of Social Theory," p. 54. Cf. Parsons papers, HUG(FP) – 42.41, box 2; the next two quotes are from the same page.

[118] Ibid., p. 58; the previous and the next quotes are from the same page.

[119] Parsons, *Structure*, p. 111; the next quote is from the same page.

Darwinism, he explained, made three assumptions. They were, first, that a presumed population surplus "must be eliminated by... 'natural selection;'"[120] second, that this meant that a process of evolution took place, due to the alleged fact that "those which survive are not the 'average'"; and, third, that in this "the environment alone is the determining, direction-giving element" – not human agency. He added, with a view not so much on Darwin but on Darwinism as practiced by Spencer and his followers, "Precisely in so far as this 'biologizing' tendency, which in fact took primarily the Darwinian form, gained ascendancy there was an abandonment of the utilitarian position in favor of radical anti-intellectualistic positivism."[121]

At this point, interestingly, generalizing from Darwinism to social Darwinism, he also included behaviorism in his warning against deterministic "theory which finds the ultimate explanatory principles in the objective non-normative influence of the conditions of action, usually of heredity and environment";[122] adding, "The most important thing is that both ultimately reduce the interpretation of human conduct to terms of a theory of biological selection."[123]

Such misguided theory, to Parsons, meant "radical anti-intellectual positivism." What made him so immensely critical of anti-intellectual positivism? In Chapter I, where he addressed "The Problem," he referred to a concrete historical situation in his time which was raison d'être behind his own intellectual endeavor. Characterizing his own present, he spoke of "a revolution of such magnitude in the prevailing empirical interpretations of human society... hardly to be found occurring within the short space of a generation, unless one goes back to about the sixteenth century.[124]

The main thrust of the anti-intellectualism of the 1930s, he felt, was "socialistic, collectivistic, organic theories of all sorts," and "the role of reason and the status of scientific knowledge as an element of action have been attacked again and again. We have been overwhelmed by a flood of anti-intellectualistic theories of human nature and behavior."

Referring to an intellectual revolution in his time, Parsons invoked the possibility that the ideological flood which he aimed to stem was a corollary of historic events. He addressed these as "certain basic social changes," but added that his book would not analyze them because he intended *Structure*, as he said, merely as a rejection of "Spencerian thought." His reference to a revolution in his own time, resembling the Renaissance in the early sixteenth century, interestingly, was positive rather than negative. What did he refer to? What could have been behind his somewhat cryptic sentences in Chapter I, supplemented as they were by some remarks in Chapter III?

Around the year 1500, revolutionary changes in religion, science, and art inspired the Renaissance, engendering the Reformation, Humanism, and, in general,

---

[120] Ibid., p. 112. The next two quotes are from the same page.
[121] Ibid., pp. 112–113.
[122] Ibid., p. 114.
[123] Ibid., p. 116.
[124] Ibid., p. 5. The next four quotes are from the same page.

individualistic expression of intellectual and artistic creativity. What in Parsons's own lifetime could be comparable? A reference to John Maynard Keynes in the subchapter on Darwinism might somewhat elucidate Parsons's reasoning. He argued: "It is unquestionably true that the economists' conception of a competitive order went far to provide the model for the biological theory of selection."[125] Nevertheless, he doubted whether the factual world was in a constant "state of war" which, he added, had been given the name of "struggle for existence." Against such a view he held his own, in the guise of a quote from Keynes. "The Principle of Survival of the Fittest could be regarded as one vast generalization of the Ricardian economics," Keynes had written. Parsons used Keynes's sentence verbatim, rejecting not only biologism but also the mechanistic determinism in classical political economy (which, to be sure, had been surpassed not only by Karl Marx as critic of political economy, but also, among many others, Max Weber and Keynes).[126]

Keynes's treatise, *General Theory of Employment, Interest, and Money*, just published in 1936, had become a classic upon publication, also informing Parsons's understanding of welfare state policies. Keynes advised state intervention through fiscal measures counteracting economic crisis in times of depression, suggesting anticyclical incentives programs as guarantors of public welfare.[127] Parsons, a follower of Roosevelt's New Deal, no doubt recognized Keynes for his non-Spencerian theory of the modern economy and state. Parsons cited Keynes at a point in *Structure* where he argued against the principle of struggle for existence. To Keynes, he stressed, the struggle for existence – a long overcome principle – denoted nothing but a "Hobbesian state of nature as the phrase 'nature red in tooth and claw' indicates."[128] Keynes thus was made a witness to Parsons's argument, warning that Darwinism had abandoned classical utilitarianism "in favor of radical anti-intellectualistic positivism."[129]

His criticism of Spencerian Darwinism, which was worse than classical political economics conceptualizing competition, obviously, expounded that the struggle for existence was a sham. He said about the notion of apparent cut-throat competition in classical political economy, as contrasted with the ideology of social Darwinism, "There too the 'unfit', the high-cost producers, the inefficient were eliminated, or ought to be, though only from the market, not from life!"[130]

Rejecting classic Ricardian but also Spencerian as well as Sumnerian liberalism, Parsons found empirical positivism to be akin to the Hobbesian "War of All Against All." How could he assume that positivistic utilitarianism was connected with "radical anti-intellectualism," and how could he presume that "war of all against all" was intimately tied to a philosophy of rugged individualism?

---

[125] Ibid., p. 113.
[126] Ibid., p. 113 (footnote). He quoted from John Maynard Keynes, *The End of Laissez-faire* (London: L. & V. Woolf, 1926; New York: New Republic, 1926), p. 17.
[127] John Maynard Keynes, *General Theory of Employment, Interest, and Money* (London: Macmillan, 1936; New York: Harcourt, Brace & Co., 1936).
[128] Parsons, *Structure*, p. 113.
[129] Ibid., pp. 112–113.
[130] Ibid., p. 113.

The answer to this question lay in a work cited extensively in *Structure*, Elie Halévy's *The Growth of Philosophic Radicalism*.[131] In an intellectual biography of Jeremy Bentham spanning the time period between the 1770s and 1840s and linking Bentham's thought to that of his contemporaries David Ricardo and James Mill, among others, Halévy showed how Bentham in the course of his life developed a philosophy of unlimited individualism. The latter legitimated forces of free trade and industrial capitalism as they culminated in triumphant, ruthless so-called Manchester liberalism. "The doctrine of Bentham," Halévy summarized, was meant to be as revolutionary in nineteenth-century England as that of the French Revolution had been earlier in other parts of Europe.[132] "It is undeniably a morality of pleasure," Halévy judged about the radical positivism which he found in Bentham,

> but a morality of pleasure which, in order to establish itself, postulates rationalism and individualism, defined as we have said. Founded on these bases, it is incessantly appealing to two distinct principles, which are in a sense in competition within the system: the one in virtue of which the science of the legislator must intervene to identify interests which are naturally divergent; the other in virtue of which the social order is realized spontaneously, by the harmony of egoisms.

For Parsons, Halévy's treatise contained a warning against philosophical radicalism which developed in English positivist utilitarianism through Bentham and others. Halévy's book ended on the note that Spencer had eventually superseded Bentham. Spencer's *Social Statics*, according to Halévy, was the eventual ambivalent triumph of "Manchester philosophy."[133]

By criticizing positivist utilitarianism, among other things, as anti-intellectualism when he adopted Halévy's criticism directed against radical,

---

[131] Elie Halévy, *The Growth of Philosophic Radicalism* (London: Faber and Faber, 1934), originally *Le développement du radicalisme philosophique* (3 volumes, 1901–1904). The English translation carried an introduction by Balliol College's legendary warden, A. D. Lindsay. Lindsay was the revered mentor of American Rhodes scholars in the 1930s, among them historian Gordon Craig, economic historian Charles Kindleberger, government official and diplomat Philip Kaiser, and politician-economist Walt Rostow – all of whom were involved in the eventual restoration of Germany after World War II.

[132] Ibid., p. 508. The next two quotes are from the same page. What Halévy meant by rationalism he had explained earlier in his book. With regard to the group of Utilitarians to whom Bentham belonged, he had said, "They demanded that, if social science is to exist, it must abandon the deductive method for the statistical method, which was criticized by Smith and ignored by Ricardo, and must be constituted on the pattern not of abstract sciences but on the sciences of observation" (p. 496). Individualism of philosophical radicals such as Bentham was, in the eyes of Halévy, basically justifiable, however: "The very appearance and success of individualistic doctrines would alone be enough to prove, that, in western society, individualism is the true philosophy. Individualism is the common characteristic of Roman law and Christian morality.... The individual may be constrained by the violence to which he is submitted by another individual, or may submit to the influence of another individual by sympathetic imitation. In any case, the Philosophical Radicals were right in seeing in the individual the principle of explanation of the social sciences" (pp. 504–505).

[133] Ibid., p. 514. Spencer's "A New Theory of Population, Deduced From the General Law of Animal Fertility," Halévy noted, when it was first published in 1852 in the *Westminster Review*, appeared in this journal founded in 1824 "by Bentham and his friends" (Halévy, p. 483).

rationalistic individualism in *Structure* Parsons did two things at once. He expressed both his rejection of social Darwinism and his sympathy for Keynesian ideas propagating democratic welfare-state capitalism.

The Matter of Facts

Social Darwinism in the United States and racism in Germany, no doubt, was a line of thought incompatible with Parsons's theory of action based on voluntarism. *Structure*'s line of thought rejected reasoning in the Anglo-Saxon world ranging from Spencer to Sumner, mirrored in Germany by racism ranging from Ploetz to the Nazis. These ideas represented the "dead" thought whose presumptive God, Evolution, allegedly had betrayed Spencer and also other disciples. Against this doctrine, still widely influential in the 1930s, Parsons wrote *The Structure of Social Action*. Darwinism cast a long shadow not only over the past but also the present at the time, affecting the foreseeable future of both sociology and society in the 1930s.

My view is that the book contrasted democracy with fascism (totalitarianism), a view which renders plausible its enormous success not in its first but its second edition, from around 1950 onward.

A consistent theory of society, not merely a history of sociology, was what Parsons intended. In the preface, he announced that *Structure* was "a study in social *theory*, not *theories*,"[134] clarifying that he was interested in "a *single* body of systematic theoretical reasoning the development of which can be traced through a critical analysis of the writings of this group," namely the "group of [recent European] writers" whose salience was the "keynote" in the "primary aim of the study." As mentioned earlier, Parsons informed his reader that, when he began writing this book, not even he himself had known that the four authors could be seen contributing to "a single coherent theoretical system,"[135] when he admitted freely, "The basis on which the four writers were brought together for study was rather empirical."

The book's argument may be reconstructed from the perspective of the question: What, then, was the empirical basis? What facts were assembled through critical appreciation of the oeuvres of, mainly, Pareto, Durkheim, and Weber? What was the nature of empirical society, constructed not through empiricism, which Parsons clarified using the theories of these "European writers"?

Interestingly, his printed introduction mentioned mainly economic issues that constituted empirical reality as he perceived it. He saw the four theories analyze "the main features of the modern economic order, of 'capitalism', 'free enterprise', 'economic individualism.'" However, in the abandoned version of his preface written one month previously, in September 1937, he had referred to the social component of economic order more directly, writing, "The four men treated in this study ... were all vitally concerned with the modern socio-economic order."[136]

---

[134] *Structure*, p. xxi; the next four quotes are from the same page (emphasis original).
[135] Ibid., p. xxii; the next two quotes are from the same page.
[136] "Preface," September 1937, p. 2; Parsons papers, HUG(FP) – 42.41, box 2; the next quote is from the same page.

This meant, as he continued, "Many of (the unsatisfactory versions of economic theory) were not, as the institutionalists and Sombart maintained, due to the theoretical scheme being simply wrong, but to certain non-economic assumptions involved in reaching these empirical conclusions."

He then interpreted his own endeavor. Indicating that his book identified noneconomic phenomena which, no doubt, were societal, through re-interpreting empirical economic issues, he announced that he would not only point out what were the mistakes of most contemporaneous economic theories. Through the looking-glass of the theories of mainly Pareto, Durkheim, and Weber, he pronounced, he provided an understanding of society in its empirical logic. Since the objective of the four theories had been to show that the "empirical significance"[137] of the subject area in the various economic theories was of more than economic relevance, he would use the four theories to piece together the facticity of modern society through the eyes of some of its major analysts. Among the not-quite economic aspects of economic life which he had come to understand, he recounted, were "the various possible meanings of ir- and nonrationality,"[138] "the interpretation of religious ideas and ritual in relation to action,"[139] and "the role of religious ideas and ethics in the modern economic order."

Recapitulating his train of thought in the nineteen chapters that obviously had been written prior to his summing up his argument in the (abandoned) preface, he related that his empirical interest had been only his original motive.[140] When he realized that there were common elements in the four theories, he had diagnosed convergence, and: "With the understanding of this convergence the empirical circle was closed."[141] However, his endeavor, he admitted, had not ended there. Instead, there had been a change of emphasis converting what had started as an empirical

---

[137] Ibid., p. 3.

[138] Ibid., p. 4.

[139] Ibid., p. 5; the next quote is from the same page.

[140] There would have been twenty chapters as were in the original outline preserved in the Harvard University Archives, had he not eliminated original chapter XVIII, the first half of which was what later was called the "lost chapter" on Georg Simmel.

[141] "Preface," September 1937, p. 5. The entire text in the abandoned preface summarizing his argument was as follows: "The fruitful starting points for this analysis proved to be the means-end schema and the conception of rationality as formulated with peculiar clarity by Pareto. This had the effect of broadening the range of theoretical considerations to that of the relations of valid empirical knowledge to action, and of the various possible meanings of ir- and nonrationality when rationality was conceived in these terms. This mode of analysis proved, surprisingly, to fit Durkheim's methodological approach, contributing greatly to the understanding of the complexities of his thought. Thus, in turn it was possible to bring his treatment of the empirical problems of economic individualism, above all as developed in his *Division of Labor*, into direct relation with his theoretical approach. In the work of both Pareto and Durkheim it was evident that consideration of the setting of economic problems, of the 'non-logical' on the one hand, of the 'non-contractual element of contract' on the other, led them eventually far afield, into such problems as that of the interpretation of religious ideas and ritual in relation to action. Particularly Durkheim, in the last phase of his work, worked out an elaborate explicit system of analysis of these phenomena. Surprisingly it turned out that on the outline of this system he had converged almost exactly with Max Weber in such a way that their common categories were directly applicable to, and helped to make understandable, Weber's analysis of the role of religious ideas and ethics in the modern economic order. With the understanding of this convergence the empirical circle was closed," pp. 4–5.

study into a theory of modern society. "In the course of this process another range of problems began slowly to emerge into prominence," he reported:

> Though the author's own analysis, and that of the writers studied, had developed largely in direct relation to the problems of economic individualism, it began to appear that in the course of their work with these problems there had been emerging, independently of each other, the outline of a generalized theoretical system of far broader application than to these particular empirical problems alone. The convergence which began to be so striking in relation to the empirical problems was associated with a deeper convergence on the analytical level itself. Hence interest gradually shifted from the range of empirical problems for their own sake, to interest in the theoretical system.[142]

My topic, in Parsons's words, is: In what way could the voluntaristic conception of action account for issues such as "ir- and nonrationality," "ritual in relation to action," or "religious ideas and ethics" addressed as empirical problems?

Parsons, in his abandoned preface, revealed that the empirical had been his primary interest, and that, subsequently, the theoretical "synthesis" came as a secondary gain. While he was writing his study, he told his readers, his "interest gradually shifted from the range of empirical problems for their own sake, to interest in the theoretical system," and (as mentioned) he added, as if to caution the reader who might otherwise be inclined only to see the theoretical impetus, "It is, however, worth while noting that this was not the original emphasis."

I wish to follow this track, venturing that his original interest was in understanding the empirical society of his time. In the 1930s, the latter comprised a dual reality between the totalitarian *Führerstaat* in Nazi Germany and the democratic welfare state of the New Deal in the United States.[143]

My thesis is that against the background of contemporary societies where he searched for the explanation of empirical reality, he found an analytical theory. This sociological theory accounted for the facts of social structure, not only in his own time but also on a more general plane. When he emphasized the unsuspected yet striking correspondence between Weber's and Durkheim's thought, at the end of his elaborate reconstruction in *Structure* of the theories of these writers, demonstrating that they stood on the shoulders of the giants who were their predecessors (including philosophers such as Immanuel Kant), he made clear that what made their theories converge was nothing other than the facts. "There is no trace of mutual influence," he exclaimed about the relationship between Weber and Durkheim. "There is not a single reference in the works of either to those of the other. It may be suggested that such an agreement is most readily explained as a matter of correct interpretation of the same class of facts."[144]

My reconstruction suggests that empirical facts which constituted society presupposed, according to Parsons, a two-pronged structure of social action. The

---

[142] Ibid., p. 5; the next six quotes are from the same and previous page.

[143] In "On Building Social System Theory" (first published, 1970), he remarked in a footnote that personally he had supported the general politics of President Roosevelt at the time of *Structure*. See in *Social Systems and the Evolution of Action Theory* (New York: Free Press, 1977), p. 30.

[144] *Structure*, pp. 669–670.

extremes of such structure were, on the one hand, a type of anomic society, and, on the other, one of integrated society. The search for anomic structures, I venture, guided his analysis of three major phenomena that he found addressed by the four European theorists, namely, force and fraud, anomie, and ritual or charisma. These phenomena, I think, constituted his understanding of the traditional-type society, which he derived from the "European writers," an anomie-driven coercive system of society. As a counterpart and modern solution, he developed the opposite type of structure of social action. The integrated system, I think, was the image behind Parsons's emphasis on legality, security, and rationality. The two opposite types of social system were extreme poles on a continuum. They contrasted anomie with value integration when the mixed form would definitely exist in the actual historical world.

The Anomic Society

Anomic society, I maintain, in the order in which they emerged in the book, comprised the themes of force and fraud, anomie, and ritual and charisma.

The topic of *force and fraud* was first introduced where Parsons discussed the War of All Against All: "In the absence of any restraining control men will adopt to this immediate end (viz. to destroy or subdue each other, as mentioned through a quote from Hobbes) the most efficient available means. These means are found in the last analysis to be force and fraud."[145] In this vein, force and fraud characterized, for Hobbes, a state of society that was to be avoided, through submission of subjects in a realm to near-total authority of the sovereign.

In this scenario, force and fraud had political as well as economic sides. With regard to the political, Parsons clarified, "use of coercion would result in a conflict which in the absence of constraining forces would degenerate into a 'war of all against all,' the reign of force and fraud."[146] With regard to the economic, he continued, classic economic theories had meant to rule out the utter disorganization resulting from ubiquitous force and fraud. They postulated beneficial effects of the invisible hand of market forces, hoping to thus preempt disorder. This, Parsons explained, had been the mistake that Marshall (but also John Locke) unknowingly made: Utilities had been acknowledged governing individual choices (regulating individuals' wants or activities which, rightly, Marshall had recognized as crucial), but system forces were underestimated that were effective on disenfranchisement and repression of the powerless (force), as well as deception, deprivation, or exploitation of the poor (fraud), Parsons argued. Classically liberal societies (proclaiming, e.g., so-called Manchester liberalism), therefore, had been deficient with regard to nonmarket community ties. Marshall, Parsons felt, had suggested wrongly that force and fraud had been overcome, whereas Pareto had rightly realized that this was not so: "Pareto lays great stress on the role of force and fraud in social life – an opinion he shares with Macchiavelli and Hobbes. This again is in the strongest

---

[145] Ibid., p. 90.
[146] Ibid., p. 236.

contrast to Marshall's views."[147] Wrongly, Parsons held against Marshall, the latter "would relegate (these phenomena) to the early stages of social evolution."

Pareto's conception of the circulation of élites, he explained, could be read as better adapted to the reality of society, allowing for clarification of the role of force, fraud, and faith. He reconstructed Pareto's theorem with an eye on the modern world: A changeover to a régime of "lions," Pareto had thought, followed the reluctance of the "foxes" to wield the instruments of force. Their inability to use force ruthlessly and indiscriminately would cause their eventual downfall and defeat.[148] In the realm of the economy, likewise, "forceful coercion" plus conservatism would dominate the economy in the type case of what Pareto called the "rentier," replacing the more versatile but less traditionalistic "speculator" type.

Parsons, commenting on this in a footnote, made explicit mention of Nazism. He reminded his reader that there were similarities between "lions" and Nazis, as contrasted with "speculators" and Weimar Germans. He remarked, indicating his concrete analytical interest, "Pareto has a most interesting note (Traité, 2336) in which he remarks that anti-Semitism has as a "substratum" a reaction against the speculators, of whom the Jews serve as a symbol. Hence the propensity for rentier classes to take it up. The history of Nazi Germany admirably bears out Pareto's view (written more than twenty years ago) on this point."[149]

Pareto's third element, Parsons noted, was faith. Faith partly accommodated ideologies. Pareto had found that ideologies could mean two things. They either meant skepticism in the name of "reason," in which case, Parsons stressed, ideologies "assimilate themselves as closely as possible to science."[150] Or ideologies enforced faith, in the guise of "principles . . . which 'dictate' to the facts instead of vice versa, as in science."

The three features belonged to two patterns which Parsons sketched: "The period of predominance of the 'foxes' and speculators is also one of skepticism – that of the 'lions' and the rentiers one of faith." To be sure, force and fraud prevailed in both such patterns, although to a differing degree.

Interestingly, Parsons suggested that the two patterns of power-driven structure of social action applied to European rather than American history and society. He judged that humanitarianism such as embraced Pareto was "a kind of diluted Christianity."[151] The latter, he remarked, "has been a conspicuous attribute of the European elite since the eighteenth century and may be considered one important cause of the peculiar instability of the present situation." This surely meant that both of Pareto's alternatives – the coercive traditionalism of the "lions"/rentiers and the skeptic antitraditionalism of the "foxes"/speculators – were similar inasmuch as both "may be considered a symptom of lack of social integration."[152] For

---

[147] Ibid., p. 179. The next quote is from the same page.
[148] As Parsons explicated, Pareto suggested that, unless the "lions" killed or otherwise disposed of newly emerging "fox" leaders, the "foxes" – promoting humanism and skepticism – would come to water down and eventually topple the regime of brute force of the "lions."
[149] *Structure*, p. 283 (footnote).
[150] Ibid., p. 284; the next two quotes are from the same page.
[151] Ibid., p. 290; the next quote is from the same page.
[152] Ibid., p. 291.

Americans, he reflected, both were unacceptable because both represented cultural pessimism, which, he commented, "is an Old World pessimism which it is difficult for Americans to understand."[153]

Force and fraud featured again in Parsons's discussion of Durkheim. Adopting Durkheim's distinction between contractual elements in contracts and normative rules which represented noncontractual elements in contracts, constituting generalized morality, he found an antidote against force and fraud. Only impartial, procedurally grounded morality, he knew, could effectively counteract fraud and forestall force. On this note, he postulated a negative generalized rule, namely a normative orientation that banned force and fraud. He found it explicated in Durkheim's *Division of Labor*.[154]

Eventually, he discussed Weber. He returned to the topic of force and fraud as noneconomic means. These would easily dominate economic exchanges if "on the one hand – norms of efficiency, the norm of legitimacy, or moral obligation, on the other" were lacking or ineffective.[155] More precisely, ineffectiveness due to failure of moral obligation involved economic as well as political circumstances of disorder. Disorder, in this vein, suggested "employment of what may be called non-economic means," in particular "force, fraud and the exercise of authority (in Weber's sense)."[156] Parsons thought that some, if not all "authority (in Weber's sense)" belonged to a type of social structure which, if not checked by normative controls, could ultimately be conducive to force and fraud.

To summarize his views on force and fraud: For one, force and fraud were unintended consequences of the type of society envisaged in traditional economic theory. In the then contemporary world, the early decades of the twentieth century, force and fraud prevailed in European societies, as remnants of eighteenth-century authoritarian régimes. To Parsons, lack of integration of the social order there was obvious. When he mentioned antidotes against force and fraud, which by the same token had to be features of integrated social structure, he explicitly mentioned legal authority[157] and also recognizied rational (noncoercive) persuasion.[158]

The next of the three basic features was *anomie*. Anomie was not entirely separate from force and fraud, but they could be seen as two stages of a process of deterioration of community ties which signaled anomie. When force and fraud prevailed, other types of social relations weakened. In a scenario of increasing anomie, force would be dominant in a first stage of "breakdown of the persistence of aggregates."[159] Fraud, in turn, constituted the second stage. This dynamic process of deterioration of societal community, however, would not continue unchecked. Frequently, in history, the stage of fraud would not be fully reached; reintegration

---

[153] Ibid., p. 293. This remark might be an indirect critical comment on Sorokin's *Social and Cultural Dynamics*, a work whose first three volumes were published in the same year as *Structure*. See also below.

[154] *Structure*, pp. 311–312.

[155] Ibid., p. 651; the semicolon in the text has been changed into a comma in the quote.

[156] Ibid., p. 657.

[157] Ibid., p. 132.

[158] Ibid., p. 101; see also below.

[159] Ibid., p. 291.

would set in. Thus, an outbreak of utter disorder spreading anomie would be cut short. The sequential relationship between force and fraud, as an issue in anomie, was listed in the index of *Structure* under the heading of "anomie," but was not dealt with under this label in the text.[160]

The phenomenon of anomie came under four different perspectives. The first explicit mention of anomie was in the reconstruction of Durkheim's *Division of Labor*,[161] referring to the breakdown of social order. The next mention, interpreting Durkheim in *Suicide*, focused on a completely different aspect of anomie. The scenario was now: "The relation between means and ends, between effort and attainment is upset. The result is a sense of confusion, a loss of orientation. People no longer have the sense that they are 'getting anywhere.'"[162] This type or side of anomie involved suicide as one severe indicator of loss of orientation; lesser forms of similar "social and personal void in which orientation is disorganized" were frustration and insecurity.[163]

A third aspect of anomie was that calculability overshadowed all other considerations in action orientation. This undoubtedly signaled an absence of genuinely moral obligations in social interchange. In Durkheim's earliest conception, Parsons noted, the notion of the individual had been strictly utilitarian, and the basis of rationality for the individual had been calculability: "His attitude is one of calculation. Here the 'individual' is still thought of in utilitarian terms as pursuing his own private ends under a given set of conditions. The only difference is that the conditions include a set of socially sanctioned rules."[164]

But Durkheim, Parsons continued, had soon realized that when the social environment allowed for such calculability, the world was without moral restraints. "In so far as the true attitude of the criminal toward the rule is the morally neutral one of calculation of consequences," Parsons explained, Durkheim had realized that society might function somehow. Despite its lack of integrative order, a society where calculability was all-pervasive could be held together through coercive forces ensuring more or less drastic punitive control, due to the fact that "sanctions, efficiently applied, act as real deterrents."[165] Force could therefore be connected with anomie in a society whose "order" was based on punitive social control.

[160] Ibid., p. xliv.
[161] Ibid., p. 326.
[162] Ibid., p. 335.
[163] Ibid., p. 336. Both these concepts, frustration and insecurity, referred to the discussion in the 1930s of approaches explaining violence. Frustration had first been addressed by Norman Maier in the late 1920s, in research investigating a state of loss of capacity for purposive action. See, for a retrospective written one decade later which summed up Maier's work on frustration as the breeding ground of unending motivation for violence, Norman Maier, *Frustration: The Study of Behavior Without a Goal* (Ann Arbor: University of Michigan Press, 1949). Insecurity had been analyzed by political scientist Harold Lasswell, as a mental state of modern masses willing to prefer dictatorship over democracy – as they had done in then contemporaneous Germany, and also Russia, and elsewhere. See Harold Lasswell, *World Politics and Personal Insecurity* (New York: Macmillan, 1934). Parsons returned to Lasswell's thesis in "Some Sociological Aspects of the Fascist Movements" (1942), now reprinted in *Talcott Parsons on National Socialism*, pp. 203–218. See also below.
[164] *Structure*, p. 380.
[165] Ibid., p. 403.

In other words, a world was possible where anomie reigned; in it, authority of contracts was guaranteed mainly by brute force, exercised by those who dictated enforced contractual relations: "A state of purely contractual relations would not be order but *anomie*, that is, chaos."[166]

Undoubtedly, anomie verged on social disorganization, the War of All Against All: "In so far as the immediate ends of particular acts are removed from ultimate ends..., there is need for a regulatory system of rules, explicit or implicit, legal or customary, which keeps action, in the various ways detailed above, in conformity with that system. The breakdown of this control is *anomie* or the war of all against all."[167]

A fourth part of Parsons's argument identified anomie with a stage of change in the dynamics of history. Had it not been for his theory of adventurers' capitalism, wrote Parsons about Weber, the latter would have been guilty of overlooking the potential for change of system structures, which Durkheim had recognized in analyzing anomie: "The emergence of this phenomenon is due to a process of emancipation from ethical control, the setting free of interests and impulses from normative limitations, traditionally and rationally ethical."[168]

Parsons pointed out that in Weber's view, but also that of other theories, adventurers' capitalism meant "the centrifugal 'bombardment of interests and appetites,' their tendency to escape control" – that is, here Weber diagnosed an overwhelming absence of community ties, in a bygone world but also a contemporary scenario for rampant egoism. All main authors, even Weber, Parsons found, had seen clearly that reversal from integration to disintegration, from social order to anomie, was possible:

> It is essentially the process involved in Pareto's process of transition from dominance of the residues of persistence to those of combination, equally in Durkheim's transition from solidarity or integration to *anomie*. It is a process the possibility of which is inherent in the voluntaristic conception of action as such. Its complete absence from Weber's thought would have given grave reason to doubt the accuracy of the above analysis. But it is there. Only, like the explicit role of ritual, it is pushed out of the foreground of attention by the peculiarities of Weber's own empirical interest.[169]

Anomie, in this view, became a transient stage in the precarious albeit irresistible modernization of modern societies. As Parsons exemplified through Weber's notion of adventurers' capitalism, as Durkheim had rightly argued, there could be "transition from solidarity or integration to anomie."[170] In other words, a lasting change of social dynamics could occur, as a loss of modernization, even once a society had reached a certain stage of integration. Such change could plunge a social order into major crisis, producing ever more obvious anomie.

---

[166] Ibid., p. 346.
[167] Ibid., p. 407; emphasis original.
[168] Ibid., p. 685; the next quote is from the same page.
[169] Ibid., pp. 685–686.
[170] *Structure*, p. 686. As mentioned, he found the same process in "transition from dominance of the residues of persistence to those of combination" in Pareto, ibid., p. 685.

40   *Understanding* The Structure of Social Action

To summarize what Parsons said about anomie: The four aspects yielded a picture of a process of deterioration of social integration on the system level and loss of moral obligation in exchanges on the action level in social structures. In this process, the orientational force of values, and consequently norms, diminished. If such deterioration was not checked, if only through introduction of effective punitive social control, a dangerously low ebb of *conscience collective* might result. A society could emerge where force and fraud prevailed. The latter, it appeared to Parsons, represented a type of social "order" not only quantitatively but also qualitatively different from others that meant progress in social-historical development. Frequently a loss of level of civilization previously attained could result. Anomie marked a state of affairs in society where calculability defined the only regularity in social life. This latter situation resembled generalized criminality, of the kind that would prevail in the absence of noncontractual guarantees that protected contractual relationships. Mafia-like coercive relationships would then dictate the contents and conditions of contracts. Such a state of societal anomie equaled chaos or the War of All Against All. Such anomie involved a succession of stages, once anomie had engulfed a society: Force marked the initial such stage, whereas fraud came to prevail subsequently.

Anomie, in the context of this analysis, had two meanings. For one, anomie marked a theme in the discussion refuting utilitarian theories. Moreover, anomie represented the negative pole of the structure of social action, nadir to social integration.

Parsons's third topic was *ritual* and *charisma*. He pursued the topic under separate headings in which the respective issues surfaced in the works of the "recent European writers." He analyzed ritual in connection with the work of Pareto and Durkheim, and he addressed charisma through the work of Weber. The three theories, he found, converged in their focus despite their use of different concepts when analyzing ritual/charisma. He expressly stated that such convergence existed. For him, therein lay sufficient proof that here was a basic element of social life.

To be sure, his interest was in the facts when he found the agreement between Pareto, Durkheim, and Weber in their treatment of ritual/charisma. He marvelled "that such an agreement is most readily explained as a matter of correct interpretation of the same class of facts."[171] What, then, were the relevant facts as they, in his view, spurred the agreement between the three classic theories? What was the reality on which their different conceptualizations converged?

The groundwork was to understand *ritual*, he explained. Pareto had made reference to logically residual actions where the means–end relationship was symbolic. An example was the fisherman in classical Greece sacrificing food to Poseidon before going out to sea. As Parsons saw it, Pareto emphasized that for the fisherman the means–end relationship in his action was real.[172] From this followed, he argued, that even if the non-normative factors of, say, physiological processes impinging

---

[171] Ibid., pp. 669–670. See also above, my reference to the abandoned preface.
[172] Ibid., pp. 208 ff.

on (social) action were left aside, another class of nonrational factors could clearly be identified, namely ritual orientations. They were normative: Their means–end relationship, albeit nonobservable to an outside observer, was undoubtedly real for the actor. From this interpretation of Pareto's concepts, which paralleled Durkheim's much better known identification of ritual with religious forms in society, Parsons arrived at the following understanding of ritual at the end of his discussion of Pareto: "Ritual involves, as Durkheim defined it (and his definition will be accepted here) in addition to the role of symbolism, the criterion that it is action in relation to sacred things. It may hence be defined as a manipulation of symbols, in some respects regarded as sacred, which operations are held subjectively to be appropriate means to a specific end."[173]

What made ritual a type of social action, he remarked at the end of his discussion of Pareto, was that *effort* was involved.[174] With regard to effort as one major element of social action, he remarked elsewhere, its importance could hardly be overestimated. Effort, he clarified there, delineated the scope of human freedom of choice which, in turn, defined the realms of active and evaluative creativity in interpersonal life. He made this insight a tenet of his, Parsons's, voluntaristic action theory: "It is an element the analytical status of which in the theory of action is probably closely analogous to that of energy in physics."[175]

Durkheim, as Parsons reported, had discovered ritual relatively late in his career of understanding society. Eventually, in his last major opus published nearly twenty years after *The Division of Labor*, Durkheim had identified the sacred as it was incarnated in things and ideas. Parsons explained: "Anything *is* sacred so long as people believe it is; it is their belief which makes it sacred."[176] The sentiment produced by the sacred, and expressed, for example, in ritual, he understood, was respect, a voluntary affective orientation: "Mere physical force may arouse fear, but not respect. Society is a moral reality and it is the only empirical entity which . . . has moral authority over man. This is the path by which Durkheim arrives at his famous proposition – that God or any other sacred object is a symbolic representation of 'society.'"[177]

Consequently, religious ideas provided sense to the world through the "fulfillment of ritual as a type of social action," which in turn meant respect expressed for "sacred things."[178] Thus, the world became filled with symbolic relationships. Their reality was equally compelling to actors as were intrinsically rational means–end relationships: "(R)itual is the expression in action as distinct from thought, of men's active attitudes toward the nonempirical aspects of reality."[179]

---

[173] Ibid., p. 258.
[174] Ibid., pp. 298–299. In other words, ritual was not mechanistic behavior but contained agency, precisely because the actor aimed to attain his ends through deliberate use of ritual, showing effectiveness of effort.
[175] Ibid., p. 719.
[176] Ibid., p. 415.
[177] Ibid., p. 417.
[178] Ibid., p. 419.
[179] Ibid., p. 432.

It was noteworthy, Parsons stressed, that Durkheim had taken religion as a primary medium of social cohesion irrespective of whether or not deities or other "sacred things" were involved. What mattered was that "religious ritual effects a reassertion and fortification of the sentiments on which social solidarity depends."[180]

Charisma, he pointed out as he turned to Weber's sociology of religion, was a quality given to objects that made them extraordinary (he used Weber's original German term, *ausseralltäglich*). Objects endowed with charisma, he explained, had a striking similarity to the sacred in Durkheim's terms, commanding an attitude of respect. He argued thus: "The fruitful starting point is rather the observation that religious as distinct from secular actions involve qualities, forces, etc. which are exceptional, removed from the ordinary (*ausseraltäglich*), to which a special attitude is taken and a special virtue attributed. This exceptional quality Weber calls *charisma*. It is exemplified in such conceptions as mana."[181]

The quality of charismatic sacredness could be acquired by persons (e.g., prophets), he pointed out, but also ideas which thus became religious ideas. The latter frequently offered guidance for practical life inasmuch as they structured the way in which actors oriented themselves to certain ideals even of economic life: "From this basal idea Weber draws one of his fundamental theses, that the first effect of 'religious ideas' on action including economic action – an effect everywhere present – is to sanction the stereotyping of tradition."[182] In this vein, Parsons found Weber saying, as a first tenet, that charismatic forces were what made "any of the great spheres of conduct, economic or political activity, love or war... traditionalized."[183]

But charisma even held a revolutionary potential. Through its double nature as religious quality and type (even an ideal type) of political authority, charisma became a powerful antidote against the forces of social order. Weber, Parsons felt, had realized this by addressing charisma as "as such, '*spezifisch wirtschaftsfremd*',"[184] which meant a genuinely political quality of hermetic coerciveness in the aura of a charismatic leader: "Applied to a person the charismatic quality is exemplary (*vorbildlich*) – something to be imitated. At the same time recognition of it as an exceptional quality lending prestige and authority is a duty."

This pointed to the peculiarly coercive quality of the kind of respect owed to and demanded from his followers by a person with "charismatic quality": "The charismatic leader never treats those who resist him or ignore him, within the scope of his claims, as anything but delinquent in duty" – which, in turn, meant that draconic punishment could be inflicted upon those "delinquent in duty" insofar as a charismatic leader commanded respect as a sacred figure.

This analysis was carried further to show that charismatic authority, nevertheless, was legitimate when it dominated a political regime of hermetic coerciveness

---

[180] Ibid., p. 435.
[181] Ibid., p. 564 (emphases, and also misspelling of *ausseralltäglich*, are original).
[182] Ibid., p. 565.
[183] Ibid., p. 566.
[184] Ibid., p. 662; the next four quotes are from the same page.

or even criminal infringement on human rights. Legitimation, which explained why authority was possible, Parsons asserted, explicating Weber, was the basis of voluntary as well as nonvoluntary aspects of action in political institutions. However, comparing the two for their inclusiveness, he noted that legitimation was less comprehensive than charisma; indeed, charisma involved a wider concept: "Legitimacy is the narrower concept in that it is a quality imputed only to the norms of an order, not to persons, things or 'imaginary' entities, and its reference is to the regulation of action, predominantly in its intrinsic aspects. Legitimacy is thus the *institutional* application or embodiment of charisma."[185]

Charisma, therefore, was a phenomenon extending beyond but certainly implying legitimacy. Inasmuch as legitimacy was the core realm of political authority, an individual had to accept the legitimacy of a dominant régime – even in a totalitarian country and even when based on nothing but charisma. This, no doubt, might involve strain from conflicting loyalties: "The fact that an order is legitimate in the eyes of a large proportion of the community makes it *ipso facto* an element of the *Interessenlage* of any one individual, whether *he* himself holds it to be legitimate or not. Supposing he does not, his action, to be rational, must be none the less oriented to this order."[186]

To summarize what Parsons said about ritual and charisma: These were two closely related aspects of the symbolic orientation to ultimate ends in social action. Religious ideas, whether incarnated in ritual or charisma, could pervade the meaning of actions serving nonrational symbolic as well as more rational purposes. Ritual, Parsons noted, was discussed by Pareto, who pointed out that symbolic action involved effort to solve empirical as well as transcendental problems of life. Ritual was also discussed by Durkheim, for whom formalized action was thus addressed, carried out in the spirit of the sacred that pervaded society inasmuch as the latter was a collectivity also forming a community. Weber, who did not discuss ritual, focused on charisma. Weber, Parsons found, discussed similar phenomena as Pareto or Durkheim. But he analyzed them with respect to their specific economic or political qualities – pointing to the noneconomic and antidemocratic political sides of charisma.

The three topics of force and fraud, anomie, and ritual/charisma, I venture, belonged together. Parsons highlighted connections between them, and he contrasted them with an integrated social order. What were the connections? How would these patterns contradict social integration? Force and fraud, for one, were "symptoms of the state of the deeper lying forces which Pareto speaks of as 'determining the social equilibrium' which, in a somewhat different context may be said to determine the state of integration of a society."[187]

Between force and fraud, mainly force, on the one hand, and charisma or faith, on the other, was a connection. Parsons hinted at that connection when he discussed Pareto's "association between idealism and the use of force,"[188] stating, "A

---

[185] Ibid., p. 669.
[186] Ibid., p. 652.
[187] Ibid., p. 291.
[188] Ibid., p. 289; the next three quotes are from the same page.

leading characteristic of a faith, for Pareto, is its absoluteness.... Such a faith, it is to be remembered, has definite consequences for action. The man of strong faith in general tries to make others conform to the standards demanded by his faith by whatever means are available." Inasmuch as faith involved others who were forced to comply, faith suggested charisma and also involved ritual. Pareto's "man of strong faith" who "turns readily to force," legitimated by his charisma, might act as analyzed by Weber. He might use power to punish those "delinquent in duty"[189] who failed to obey his uncompromisingly authoritarian commands. What connected force and fraud with ritual/charisma was therefore religious in the sense of Durkheim's identification of the sacred, symbolizing collective beliefs in a society.

Anomie, Parsons suggested, could be seen as a disorder whose apparent remedy was ritual/charisma. Discussing Durkheim in the chapter on "Empiricially Verified Conclusions" (Chapter XVIII), Parsons suggested that Durkheim had introduced ritual as an antidote against anomie: "(R)itual to Durkheim was... of great functional importance in relation to social 'solidarity,' a mode of revivifying and strengthening the common value elements.... Ritual is one of the fundamental defense mechanisms of society against the tendency of *anomie*."[190] To recapitulate the relationship between force and charisma, on the one hand, and force and anomie as well as anomie and ritual, on the other: Force (and, to a lesser extent, fraud) invited charisma which, in turn, enforced faith; anomie resulted therefrom but could be neutralized, to a certain extent, through ritual stemming societal disintegration. Taken together, the three elements constituted "as a polar type the state Durkheim called *anomie*."[191]

Drawing together Pareto's, Durkheim's, and Weber's work, Parsons found, using Weber, that he could detect not three but two basic types of systems structure of social action. The one, he argued, on an action level, using Weber's terms, was a conglomerate of "(a) affectual, (b) *wertrational* or (c) religious"[192] subjective value orientations, as the alternative distinct from "'interest', certain expectations of external consequences," namely egoistically based motives. On a social-system level, he found that Weber, in effect, had proposed a conjunction of the four elements of "(a) traditional, (b) affectual, (c) *wertrational*, and (d) held to be legal by positive institution (*Satzung*)," into a type of pattern: "'The legitimacy of an order by virtue of the *sanctification* of tradition is everywhere the most universal and original case.' This linking of traditionalism with *sanctity* is a conspicuous feature of his (Weber's) treatment of the former (religious motives) throughout."[193]

Parsons suggested that Weber had, in actual fact, discovered a duality of types of social action or system(s) of structure of such action – of which the social order was the one obvious side. Parsons, in due course, rejected the idea of tripartite authority structure of social action/system(s), which Weberians defend until this

---

[189] Ibid., p. 662.
[190] Ibid., p. 713.
[191] Ibid., p. 291 (footnote).
[192] Ibid., p. 659; the next two quotes are from the same page.
[193] Ibid., p. 660. The quotation is from Weber, *Wirtschaft und Gesellschaft* (Tübingen: Mohr [Siebeck], 1922), p. 19.

day. Parsons pointed out that Durkheim had made a similar discovery. Both authors, he asserted, contrasted "a legitimate order... with a situation of the uncontrolled play of interests," stating triumphantly,

> Thus Weber has arrived at the same point Durkheim reached when he interpreted constraint as moral authority. Morever, Weber has approached the question from the same point of view, that of an individual thought of as acting in relation to a system of rules that constitute conditions of his action. There has emerged from the work of both men the same distinction of attitude elements toward the rules of such an order, the interested and the disinterested. In both cases a legitimate order is contrasted with a situation of the uncontrolled play of interests. Both have concentrated their special attention on the latter element. Such a parallel is not likely to be purely fortuitous.[194]

The one side of the continuum, signifying anomie or lack of social integration, featured private, even egoistic utilitarian interests; the other side, however, showed a society dominated by orientations of *societal community denoting disinterestedness*.[195]

What anomie was not, he stated, was a social order that could be "looked upon as an expression of values, hence to be lived up to because it is valued for itself or for the values it expresses." He added in a footnote a further part of the sentence that again revealed how much advocacy of pro-democracy, anti-Nazi politics was on his mind. He added to the statement that a legitimate order was valued for its intrinsic values, as a footnote, "Or combated for disinterested motives."[196]

The Integrated Society

The three topics of force and fraud, anomie, and ritual/charisma epitomized the one pole of the dualist structure of (systems of) social action. What, in contradistinction, characterized the opposite pole, namely, an integrated society or genuinely democratic or moral social order?

Parsons, in *Structure*, refrained from explicitly outlining the features of value integration in a modern industrial society. He sandwiched his image of the integrated society into his interpretations of the three (four) theories, focusing on how they analyzed disintegration when implicitly he thereby also discussed integration. My account merely sketches this viewpoint. I see three aspects of an integrated social order explicated in *Structure*, namely, *legality*, *security*, and *rationality*.

Parsons introduced *legality* where he interpreted Marshall. The latter, he remarked, took for granted in a functioning economy what were, in fact,

---

[194] Ibid., p. 661.
[195] Ibid., p. 659; the next two quotes are from the same page. Disinterestedness, in Parsons's early works, meant what his later conception of pattern variables named collectivity orientation. This one among five structural alternatives denoted, among other institutional spheres, medical practice. To Parsons, medical practice represented a particularly moral type of democratic system configuration. For an appreciation of the resultant importance of trust, see Bernard Barber, *The Logic and Limits of Trust* (New Brunswick, N.J.: Rutgers University Press, 1983).
[196] He thus invoked the possibility that a legitimate order could be combated for disinterested motives.

extra-economic (noncontractual with respect to contracts) forces representing society's moral norms. Marshall had assumed competition, satisfaction of wants, mobility, and divisibility of resources, Parsons wrote, but had also assumed that consumers in such competitive order were protected from force and fraud, "partly by competitive pressure, partly by a legal authority which sets up rules of the game and penalizes infractions of them."[197] Parsons knew, however, that such legal authority was not to be taken for granted. Only a functioning moral order could secure noncontractual norms regulating contractual relations.

When he discussed Weber, he also touched upon legality. Evidently, legality was what made Weber's type of rational authority one of rational-legal regulation for social relations. According to Weber, an independent judiciary committed to laws established by a constitutionally legitimated legislative body accountable to the public, he maintained, was indispensable for order as opposed to anomie. Only a normative system based on legality could "work" in a modern democracy.[198] He insisted that respect for legality had to prevail in public administration, thereby strengthening the legislative function of government.[199]

Parsons introduced the second aspect, *security*, indirectly. In a lengthy passage, explicating Hobbes's ideas as against Locke's conjectures on social order, he eventually arrived at his own thesis emphasizing security. He endorsed Hobbes's ideal that only the sovereign's near-total authority could contain force and fraud, which otherwise would prevail.[200] Locke and his many followers in the eighteenth and nineteenth centuries, he held as he supported Hobbes, had overlooked how unrealistic the assumption was that "passion" would not rule behavior:

> As against Hobbes, Locke consistently minimizes the problem of security.... Thus, for Locke, government instead of being the dam which precariously keeps the angry floods of force and fraud from inundating society and destroying it becomes merely a prudent measure of insurance against an eventuality which is not particularly threatening, but which wise men will nevertheless provide against. Indeed so much is this the case that security against aggression really becomes a subordinate motive of participation in civil society.[201]

---

[197] *Structure*, p. 132.

[198] Weber, to be sure, had discussed these issues in his *Politische Schriften*. He had also dealt with the topic in his memorandum on value neutrality, revised and published in 1917. There, he had rejected syndicalism on the grounds that it curtailed democratic freedom when he strongly opposed the actual use of the State's monopoly in political power (for Weber, the State was to deliberately refrain from such use). See Weber, "Der Sinn der 'Wertfreiheit' der soziologischen und ökonomischen Wissenschaften," in his *Gesammelte Aufsätze zur Wissenschaftslehre*, 3rd edition, Johannes Winckelmann, ed. (Tübingen: Mohr, 1968), pp. 489–540 (especially, with regard to State power, p. 540).

[199] This tenet which Parsons would not explicate in *Structure* accounted for two references in the bibliography, namely Carl J. Friedrich and Taylor Cole, *Responsible Bureaucracy* (Cambridge, Mass.: Harvard University Press, 1932), and Friedrich, *Constitutional Government and Politics* (New York: Harper and Brothers, 1937); see *Structure*, pp. xxxiii, xxxvii. The former of the two books dealt with the administrative structure of Switzerland; the latter compared U.S. constitutionalism with Nazi plebiscitarian "democracy."

[200] *Structure*, p. 87 ff.

[201] Ibid., p. 95.

This meant that Hobbes's theory was the more realistic, whereas "Locke's more or less wishful postulation of the natural identity of interests"[202] grossly underestimated the importance of security.[203] For Hobbes, though, realistic concern for security had overshadowed all considerations for individual freedom when proving a viable standpoint: "The mode of thinking which Hobbes employed, applying it as he did in an empiricist sense, led empirically to an intensive concentration on the problem of a minimum of security. So intense was this concentration that the sheer difficulty of attainment of this minimum far overshadowed any possibilities of positive advantage to be derived from social relationships beyond security itself."[204]

The third aspect of the integrated moral community, I suggest, was *rationality*. Parsons warned, with Pareto, that science could not form a reliable basis for rational behavior. Any kind of rationality based on science might deny that other options were tolerable, he warned. Therefore, science-based models of rationality might imperceptibly undermine individual freedom of choice. However, he presupposed, freedom of choice was indispensable for modern democratic society. From this angle, then, rationality derived from scientific discoveries could not be the answer to the problem of how rationality governed modern social action.

Neither could relativism granting equal justification to all sorts of systems of thought, presumably emanating from viewpoints typically related to different social stata or groups, provide an acceptable answer.[205] The answer lay in specifying that rationality was not a one-way affair. Rationality could not be induced, let alone enforced, by individuals possessing rational orientations, but had to be evoked or often invited through reciprocally noncoercive *persuasion*. Parsons distinguished "between two classes of means in the rational pursuit of ends, those involving force, fraud and other modes of coercion, and those involving rational persuasion of advantage to be gained by entering into relations of exchange."[206]

In Parsons's discussion of Pareto, he elaborated on this distinction. On the one side, quasi-rationality was based on imposition, and, on the other, rationality persuasion. He interpreted Pareto's "man of strong faith" to be, by definition, opposed to rationality as contained in persuasion: "Given the inherent limitations on securing conformity by rational persuasion, the man of strong faith turns readily

---

[202] Ibid., p. 97.

[203] Harold Lasswell's analysis of political connotations of security applied here. Lasswell first used the insecurity thesis to explain how countries such as Nazi Germany or Russia had turned totalitarian, in his "The Psychology of Hitlerism," *The Political Quarterly,* vol. 4, 1933, pp. 373–384. See also below, Chapter 2.

[204] *Structure*, p. 97.

[205] Throughout his life, Parsons never ceased to doubt Karl Mannheim's sociology of knowledge (*Wissenssoziologie*). Mannheim apparently wished to combat relativism by a seemingly ingenious stratagem, namely advocating, as did his mentor Alfred Weber, the coming of a "free-floating intelligentsia." Parsons mistrusted this particular solution. In *Structure*, he mentioned explicitly that he would not deal with the issue. He placed the problem of *Wissenssoziologie*, which he attributed to Max Scheler as much as Mannheim, outside the realm of "the scope of this study" (p. 672).

[206] Ibid., p. 101.

48   *Understanding* The Structure of Social Action

to force."[207] Elsewhere, he clarified, "(T)o persuade anyone to do something you must not only show him how to do it, but also get him to see why he should do it at all. Where values are involved which are not facts which everyone must admit to be true or false, but which are 'subjective,' there is no rational means of getting another to accept the end."[208]

In this guise, persuasion was the means of a democratic society. Precisely because at times persuasion might be in vain, in the event when individuals chose to resist it, rationality represented a mutual endeavor, a reciprocal achievement.

Legality, security, and rationality epitomized Parsons's image of an integrated social order. Moral values, that is, normative principles of common concern, were behind all three of them: "(T)he order is looked upon as an expression of values, hence to be lived up to because it is valued for itself or for the values it expresses."[209] In the idealized case, this meant institutionalization through voluntary commitment. In most societies, legitimate rational-legal authority (in Weber's sense) might serve the purpose of order to a certain extent, he conceded: "(P)urely voluntary agreement is the limiting case where the element of legitimacy is reduced to a minimum."[210]

Such advocacy for disinterestedness, no doubt, showed Parsons's concern for a democratic society. He shared it with his near-contemporary at the University of Chicago, philosopher cum social psychologist George Herbert Mead.[211] Both proposed a normative credo which made them, Mead and Parsons, forerunners of the modern idea of civil society.

What About Heredity and Environment?

As an afterthought to *Structure*'s two-pronged theory of the structure of social action, its reference to heredity and environment might be clarified. At the end of his book, Parsons distinguished between three types of social theory, only the first of which took notice of the issue. These were, first, a theory focusing on heredity and environment as presumptive sources of action, suggesting a deterministic conception denying individual agency; second, another focusing on strictly rational means-end relationships where the sources of action lay in either utilitarian motives or externally experienced constraints stemming from coercive power; and a third one focusing on the individual as a responsible purpose-oriented actor basically

[207] Ibid., p. 289.
[208] Ibid., p. 277.
[209] Ibid., p. 659.
[210] Ibid., p. 660–661.
[211] George Herbert Mead, in the part of *Mind, Self, and Society* that explains society, clarified what Parsons called disinterestedness which he, Mead, termed universalism: It was the physician, Mead understood, who as a professional sought satisfaction in his work when he found his self-realization in the welfare and well-being of another, his patient. Parsons, in his article "Society" written for the *Encyclopedia of the Social Sciences* (1934), had stressed the same point, discussing the importance of service orientation in society. See Mead, *Mind, Self, and Society: From the Standpoint of a Social Behaviorist*, edited by Charles Morris (Chicago: University of Chicago Press, 1934), p. 288; Parsons, "Society" (1934), reprinted in *Talcott Parsons Early Essays*, pp. 109–121.

responsive to others' orientations and judgment.[212] The latter, voluntaristic theory of action, took into account normative as well as conditional elements of action,[213] he clarified, whereas the former two were more or less confined to conditional elements.

At the beginning of his book, to be sure, Parsons had dismissed heredity and environment as entirely irrelevant, "nonsubjective categories in relation to the theory of action."[214] He had stated, "(T)he concepts of heredity and environment... play no substantive role in the central theoretical argument of the study."[215] Where he addressed Darwinism, he had attributed to heredity and environment a falsely "rationalistic" schema of presumptively "objective non-normative influence of the conditions of action."[216] At various further points where he interpreted the thoughts of Pareto and Durkheim, he had mentioned how they more or less completely dismissed heredity and environment.[217] And Weber, Parsons found, had been occupied with "matters of taste"[218] when, in this context, heredity and environment counted among "the sources of ignorance and 'determinate' error," which were empirically somewhat relevant but had no theoretical significance for the theory of social action.

In the summary at the end of *Structure*, Parsons distinguished between three meanings, all theoretically unimportant, that could be given to heredity and environment. One was that these issues accounted for "failure to attain the rational norm"[219] and might therefore explain error, and so on; another was that hedonism presumably derived from hereditary drives and could instigate an organism's basically irrational behavior; and third, on a more general plane, "hereditary elements" could more or less shape everyday life. All this was of little theoretical relevance. What mattered in the last instance, he summarized, was whether the principle of heredity and environment merely was used in a "positivistic theoretical system" as the counterpart of the norm of intrinsic rationality, or became a mainstay defining the "radical positivistic pole" of a utilitarian position. The latter stance was problematic as it made heredity and environment an "extrapositivistic, metaphysical prop" in a theory forcibly establishing "the postulate of the natural identity of interests" – the latter formula, I suspect, invoking coercive utopianism as prevailed in Nazi-prone doctrines.

The Realm of Sociology

In the very last subchapter of *Structure*, as Parsons stated his tenet regarding "The Place of Sociology," he tentatively formulated knowledge that today is taken for

---

[212] *Structure*, pp. 718–719.
[213] Ibid., p. 719.
[214] Ibid., p. 82.
[215] Ibid., p. 84.
[216] Ibid., p. 114.
[217] See, for a summary of these various references, ibid., pp. 464–465.
[218] Ibid., p. 718; the next quote is from the same page.
[219] Ibid., p. 701; the remaining quotes in this paragraph are from this page.

granted. He maintained that society formed a third sphere of social life, separable from while connected with that of the economy and politics. He referred to such a truly sociological realm of society as a matter of facts, although he stressed its tentative quality, invoking

> a common reference to the fact of integration of individuals with reference to a common value system, manifested in the legitimacy of institutional norms, in the common ultimate ends of action, in ritual and in various modes of expression. All these phenomena may be referred back to a single general emergent property of social action systems which may be called "common-value integration." ... If this property is designated the sociological, sociology may then be defined as "the science which attempts to develop an analytical theory of social action systems in so far as these systems can be understood in terms of the property of common-value integration."[220]

Today it might appear strange that Louis Wirth, in his book review in the *American Sociological Review*, would not acknowledge the reality of society. Whereas Wirth praised *Structure* for its scholarly depth, he refused to see that it had rightly aimed at a realm of sociology accounting for genuinely social facts that were beyond the analytical spheres of economics and political science. Instead, Wirth insisted that the social should not be separated from, when it had to be conceptualized as an aspect of, the worlds of the economy and politics. Parsons, refuting Wirth's criticism in his long letter written in the fall of 1939, admitted that his definition of a field of facts for sociology was tentative but nevertheless insisted that it had a reality of its own:

> The definition of the field of sociology which I ventured at the end was meant to be highly tentative. I do not propose a complete reform of the American academic world in its terms but wish only to provoke thought. I have followed through in terms of the status of economic theory that analytical systems such as economic theory or the corresponding types of sociology not only are not but cannot be adequate schemes for the analysis of classes of concrete phenomena for all purposes. On the contrary, there are sociological elements not only in the political world as we ordinarily understand it but in the economic world and vice versa, there are economic and political elements even in, let us say, a church. In view of the emphasis which I placed in this discussion on the distinction between the classification of theoretical systems and that of classes of concrete phenomena, I do not think that the objections you raise can be sustained.[221]

I believe that the reality he (had) traced through the theories of the three (four) theorists suggested that the structure of societies (including that of social action, conceptualized in a model "unit act," its elementary form) was two-pronged. On the one hand, force and fraud, anomie, and ritual/charisma were the characteristics of social disintegration which he saw prevail in variable degree in most empirical societies, most certainly in Europe where authoritarian and fascist régimes in the 1930s reigned in the majority of countries. On the other hand, an integrated social system could be envisaged which, if only as an "ideal type" of civil society, united

---

[220] Ibid., p. 768.
[221] Letter, Parsons to Wirth, dated Oct. 6, 1939, p. 7; Parsons papers, HUG(FP) – 42.8.2, box 2.

legality, security, and rationality into a community of voluntary common moral value-orientation.

It is my view that Parsons was convinced that the War of All Against All prevailed in Nazi Germany. In contradistinction, although not denying that it was fraught with certain, even serious problems, he held that the United States under the New Deal represented an emergent integrated moral order, a realistic alternative to Darwinism-prone authoritarianism.

Summary

The Structure of Social Action has so often been named a compendium recapitulating previous, classic theories that proof has been urgently needed that this never was its purpose nor knowledge interest.

The two prefaces written in September and October of 1937, albeit with different emphasis, stressed two things. One was that the aim was analysis of empirical society, or societies, for that matter, concentrating on the facts as ascertained by scientific study. The other point was that the voluntaristic theory of the structure of social action was "synthetic" – as opposed to analytical, in the Kantian sense, no doubt. The "synthetic" characterization referred to the search for patterns or structural types, in the event juxtaposing the antagonistic system types of anomie or War of All Against All, on the one side, and integration or social order, on the other.

My argument followed three leads. One was that politics were involved in the definitively value-neutral – in true Weberian fashion – understanding of the structure of social action. As Parsons pointed out to Wirth, responding to the latter's book review, to practice value-neutral sociology did not mean that the sociologist analyzing society need not have values which made him judge social reality accordingly. Such judgment would take notice of concrete power relationships from the perspective of values held by the sociologist as a citizen. As a person, he was (or should be) a morally integral member of his society, respecting human equality and dignity and similarly deeply entrenched values of Western civilization. As such, as he wrote Wirth, the sociologist needed to recognize that concrete power relationships were to be reconciled with values.

That this meant that politics were clearly to be distinguished from sociology implied two things. One was that Parsons, like Weber, rejected politicization of the discipline and wished to keep sociology free from advocacy for political aims or groups. The other was that coercive political régimes as they denied, above all, occidental values such as human dignity were part of the world of the present. As such, they had to be taken into account in the sociological conceptual perspective, if only as the obverse of democratic, modern possibilities. It was in this perspective that Parsons, using Schumpeter as his mouthpiece, had his book introduced as "'civics' in the highest sense."

As a first line of thought, my argument has tried to follow this lead through the text. That the terms which in the 1938 lecture(s) clearly were used to analyze National Socialism as contrasted with American democracy, were the same as those explained in *Structure*, became obvious in my reconstruction of the text. Under the general idea that here were the facts on which converged the various theories of the "European writers," the main concepts constituting the anomie type of society were distinguished from those constituting the integrated type of society.

My second lead was that his knowledge interest was directed against social Darwinism, in various variants. For one, I ventured, he opposed Spencer who, as the history of science evidences, was the forerunner who inspired Darwin's principles of survival of the fittest and struggle for existence. Furthermore, he turned against contemporary utilitarianism and positivism in American sociology in the 1930s, as these continued the unacceptable trend to mechanistic Evolutionism which had long been overcome by European theories such as those of Durkheim and Weber. By the same token, he vigorously rejected the pseudoscience of racism which had become the official doctrine of Nazi "science." On this note, he commented on heredity and environment, dismissing such alleged principles in biology (as frequently stated at the time) as utterly irrelevant for systematic sociology.

His third lead was that he introduced, if surreptitiously as an antidote against the arrogance of economics and political science, an ideal of social reality postulating emergence of a modernizing democratic society. It was on the basis of evolution that he hypothesized a dynamics of democratization in the modern world itself. He endorsed the New Deal as a seminal achievement because it attenuated impoverishment and contained the dangers of political turmoil that had engulfed Weimar Germany. It was on the background of his knowing that society was real – not merely a construct used by sociology – that he could see a two-pronged dynamics between democracy (as in the United States) and dictatorship (as in Nazism), a fluidity of structure and process between complementary extremes borne out in the contemporary scenario of the 1930s.

To understand *The Structure of Social Action* means to place the book into this triple context. Only when these three leads are followed in the reading of the text, I propose, would the reader do justice to the multidimensional knowledge interest and sophisticated argumentation which Parsons pursued in the book.

As such a multidimensional, sophisticated endeavor, however, the book has not been recognized. Indeed, considering its ambitious program of methodological cum theoretical analysis couched in the terms of empirical study, the book may have been something of a failure: Not only was its half-chapter on Simmel omitted – whose use of *a prioris* of sociation, conditions of both society and knowledge about it, would have enlightened Parsons greatly if only he had understood Simmel's truly groundbreaking construction (he could have used it to reconcile Whitehead's warning of the fallacy of misplaced concreteness and endorsement of perspectivism with Weber's idea of ideal type). It may even be said that Parsons himself underestimated the breathtaking salience of his argument. His crucial reference to phenomenology remained strangely vague despite its undeniable importance for the methodological grounding of his theoretical argument. He grounded the development of the orientation of empirical-historical social actors in a phenomenological structure but failed to explore in detail the conditions and corollaries of this postulate.

On this note, *The Structure of Social Action* was the work of a genius but suffered from weaknesses in its argument that called for further clarification. In due course, Parsons reverted to *Structure* all his life, adding elements to its argument or adding further "European writers" such as Bronislaw Malinowski or Sigmund Freud, or American thinkers such as George Herbert Mead or W. I. Thomas, to substantiate *Structure*'s groundbreaking line of thought. He returned to the two-pronged theory of society in all four phases of his intellectual biography, never again couching his postulate in such abstract terms as in *Structure*, where he used other theorists' work to ground his own thoughts. Subsequently, he continued his two-pronged analysis with clearer focus on the world around him, always intent on defense of democracy in each contemporary era.

Postscript: What about Cultural Pessimism?

In Parsons's own time, as he unequivocally contended through Brinton in the first paragraphs of *Structure*, Benthamite political philosophy was a thing of the past; even its sequel, Darwinism, particularly in the guise of Spencer's social Darwinism, to him appeared long "dead." However, pessimism, deploring dangers to Western civilization coupled with an appeal to political adventurism, was not obsolete, not even in his immediate environment at Harvard. Sorokin's *Social and Cultural Dynamics*, a four-volume book whose first three volumes were being written during the same time period as Parsons's *Structure* (between 1932–33 and 1937),[222] represented a major opus promulgating cultural pessimism when it purported to prove through empirical analysis that an eventual rise of an authoritarian charismatic régime was likely, even desirable.

Sorokin's forerunner, no doubt, had been Oswald Spengler's vastly successful *Der Untergang des Abendlandes* (1918), translated as *The Decline of the West* (1922).[223] It had set an example of cultural criticism, denouncing modern science and art when it served the purpose for German intellectuals of rejecting Weimar culture. Spengler, in a universal history of occidental culture, argued that the modern world was doomed. Unproductive relativism had swept away the "Faustian" potential, he lamented, producing instead, in the wake of modernity, the atrophy of the presumably indispensable forces of "soul-image" and "life-feeling."[224] As Spengler emphasized, Einstein's relativity theory and Heisenberg's nuclear physics, causing the collapse of the Newtonian world view, aggravated an already obvious collapse of "the great style of ideation... in architecture and the forms of art."[225] Such a breakdown of the pillars of the century-old world view that had originated in classical Greece, he stressed, made clearly visible that the "gently

---

[222] Pitirim Sorokin, *Social and Cultural Dynamics*, vols. I–III (New York: American Books, 1937); Vol. IV, 1941.

[223] Oswald Spengler, *Der Untergang des Abendlandes. Umrisse einer Morphologie der Weltgeschichte* (Berlin/Leipzig: Wilhelm Braunmüller, 1918); translated *The Decline of the West* (New York: Knopf, 1922).

[224] These were the titles of chapters IX and X.

[225] *The Decline of the West*, p. 420.

sloping route of decline" of Western civilization apparently was irresistible.[226] The prospect, no doubt, was universal disaster. It would be brought about by ubiquitous chaos in the wake of the breakdown of normative order, caused by the emergence of relativistic culture and science. Eventually there would emerge a lifeless, soulless world, governed by means of "de-sensualized"[227] systems management and based on intractable mathematics that would reign supreme. Its barren, mechanical grounding would be in functions mapping the world into a gridlike "vast system of morphological relationships."

Sorokin, when he announced his major opus in an article published in German in *Sociologicus* as early as the spring of 1933,[228] let it be known that he took Spengler seriously. He discussed the question whether fine art could be the field in which objective measurement could assess the inherent creativity of culture, as it apparently inspired what he termed the vigor of an era or style. The main thrust of his *Social and Cultural Dynamics*, however, related to the question whether the decline of the West meant the end of culture. Sorokin's elaborate, even quantitative analysis in the self-styled Philosophy of History covered the entire span of high cultures since circa 2500 B.C. With such analysis, Sorokin claimed, he aimed, for one, at "an investigation of the nature and change, the dynamics of integrated culture: its types, its processes, its trends, fluctuations, rhythms, tempos."[229] Second and more important, however, "as a child of this culture..., resigned to the possibility of its decline,"[230] he wanted to clarify that despite the profound "contemporary crisis... after a trying transitory period, there looms not an abyss of death, but a mountain peak of life" – an era of renewed ascendancy for Western culture. In other words, his topic was the prospect of Western civilization, and his aim was to prove that the current irresistible decline of cultural vigor would eventually be followed by an era of charismatic heroism, the ultimate pinnacle of the history of mankind.

His method was relatively simple. He identified three basic types of culture: Ideational, Idealistic, and Sensate. Their epistemological basis that supposedly made these types true, suggesting historico-intellectual adequacy, he established through mere citation of Edmund Husserl's Phenomenology.[231] His definitions of Ideational, Idealistic, and Sensate cultures were made plausible by distinguishing between specific mentalities which, in turn, were said to structure a vast array of phenomena in art, politics, social life, and so on, throughout history. Apart from characterizing entire epochs as outflow of one of the three types (or mixed forms), Sorokin asserted that fluctuation of types was frequent. In particular, he wished to demonstrate that even though a culture did not have to "die" once its ideational, sensate, etc., vigor deteriorated, such deterioration was obvious in

---

[226] Ibid., p. 425.
[227] Ibid., p. 427; the next quote is from the same page.
[228] Pitirim Sorokin, "Studien zur Soziologie der Kunst I," *Sociologicus*, vol. 9, 1933, pp. 45–65.
[229] Sorokin, *Social and Cultural Dynamics,* vol. I, p. x.
[230] Ibid., p. xiii; the next quote is from the same page.
[231] Ibid., p. 58.

early twentieth century America. At the same time, he argued that new life could impregnate a previously declining culture, which, he warned, necessarily required complete destruction prior to subsequent rebirth. He demonstrated this thesis, which was geared at his own lifetime and country of refuge, using as an example the crisis transforming the Middle Ages (Ideational) into the Modern Age which, in his view, had lasted until the nineteenth century (Sensate). His own time, the post–World War I period, he diagnosed, was one of epochal crisis, characterized by revolutions, wars, and obvious loss of civil liberties in connection with the widespread emergence of totalitarian régimes.

As a specimen of crisis of culture, he named Nazism. Together with similar other régimes, he stated, it was "compulsory and mechanical slavery: soulless, mirthless, compassionless, largely devoid of real altruism, real familism, real solidarity... very successful in destruction but of little value in the construction of the familistic relationship and a really collectivistic society."[232] His antagonism to Nazi anti-humanism, however, he warned, did not mean that he believed in social reform, let alone supported the politics of the New Deal under President Franklin D. Roosevelt. On the contrary, he considered Roosevelt's America different only in shade from the totalitarianisms in the Soviet Union or Nazi Germany. "The Communism, the State Socialism, the Corporate State, the Nazi Reich, the Rooseveltian policy, the policies of other dictatorial states all are a manifestation of the same trend toward a totalitarianism of various shades and forms and away from liberalism," he stated[233] – designating as liberalism *not* what in the 1930s probably was called Progressivism.[234] Instead, his notion of liberalism, whose decline he regretted, was modeled on Spencer's belief in self-regulating individualism, called by Sorokin "singularity" (as contrasted with "universalism").[235]

Although for him the crisis of his time meant more or less uncontrolled use of power by the strong over the weak, he did not regret its immediate effect, namely, the War of All Against All. "'Bellum omnium contra omnes,' each person, faction, group, and class trying to procure, by any means whatever, everything for which their sensate wishes clamor"[236] was in his view a necessary stage in the coming of the new age. He ended his voluminous book in a spirit of prophetic hope. The dynamics of crisis, which in his view extended from Babylon to the end of the Middle Ages, followed a model of a four-stage process characterized by the formula "crisis – catharsis – charisma – resurrection."[237] In his own lifetime, Sorokin therefore concluded, neither was totalitarianism the end of history; nor

---

[232] Vol. III, p. 338.
[233] Vol. II, p. 575.
[234] What in the 1930s was named Progressivism apparently came nearest to Parsons's own politics at the time. See above.
[235] Vol. II, pp. 261–304. It should also be noted that a society encompassing universalism thought to undo individualism was what Othmar Spann proposed in his *Gesellschaftslehre* (2d edition, 1923; 3rd edition, 1930). See above.
[236] Vol. III, p. 177.
[237] Vol. IV (1941), p. 778.

was liberal democracy the last stage of irreversible decline: "Ahead of us lies the thorny road of the dies irae of transition. But beyond it there loom the magnificent peaks of the new Ideational or Idealistic culture as great in its own way as Sensate culture was at the climax of its creative genius."[238]

Nothing is known about Parsons's opinion on the book. However, Sorokin's doctrinaire style and cultural pessimism aroused Brinton, Parsons's colleague and collaborator in the Harvard Pareto Circle of the early 1930s, in a review preserved as an offprint in Harvard College Library.

Brinton's reaction to Sorokin was scathing.[239] He addressed Sorokin's approach as "Socio-Astrology," heaping ridicule on what he skillfully revealed as dilettantism rather than science. "We don't really know much about the mentalities of the masses of mankind, but Mr. Sorokin finds it convenient to classify them," was how he introduced his listing of Sorokin's types, adding that there were mixed ones and "apparently Mr. Sorokin would even grant a mixture of the mixed."[240] But Brinton primarily wanted to expose Sorokin's cultural pessimism, comparing it unfavorably with that even of Spengler,[241] calling both authors together with others of similar world view "prophets of immediate doom."[242] "It is true that Mr. Sorokin does not prophesy our absolute annihilation but only another, and, since our children or grandchildren will enjoy the dawn, brief Dark Age,"[243] he chided. The charge was that Sorokin had only contempt for the common man on whom hinged, as it always had, according to Brinton, the dynamics of real life in society. Brinton's message was that sociology, if it was at all scientific, had to carefully observe the thin line between analytical concepts and empirical reality. To make sense of modern or any society, sociology had to take seriously experiential qualities of the lived-in social worlds of all citizens.

Although Brinton's criticism of Sorokin might have mirrored Parsons's own disdain for pseudoscience preaching empirical positivism in the guise of idealism, Brinton antagonized Parsons as he generalized from Sorokin and others to sociology as such. In a book review in 1939, entitled "What's The Matter With Sociology?" Brinton judged: "Sociologists are on the whole a modest lot, and their occasional outbreaks into prophecy are but natural compensations for their permanent inferiority complex."[244] Subsequently, when Parsons in a letter objected "particularly to (the article's) superior, and shall we say, contemptuous tone,"[245] Brinton admitted that he had meant to denigrate what most sociologists appeared to do, but had not wished to include Parsons and, moreover, had not yet read *Structure*

---

[238] Ibid., p. 779.
[239] Crane Brinton, "Socio-Astrology," *Southern Review*, vol. 3, 1937, pp. 243–266; reprinted Harvard University College, 1937.
[240] Ibid., p. 247.
[241] Ibid., p. 257.
[242] Ibid., p. 261.
[243] Ibid., p. 262.
[244] Brinton, "What's the Matter With Sociology?," *Saturday Review of Literature*, May 6, 1939, p. 3; reviewing Robert Lynd's *Knowledge for What?* (1939).
[245] Parsons, letter to Brinton, dated July 11, 1939, Parsons papers, HUG(FP) – 42.8.2, box 2.

(though Parsons had had it sent to him some time earlier). He added a somewhat cryptic sentence, presumably wishing to compliment Parsons on the quality of his work as he drew an implicit comparison between him and other sociologists and also insinuated a merely elementary stage of the development of sociology as a science: "I will say I think the number you would accept is really damned small – growing, I agree, and perhaps on the eve of getting where physiologists got after Harvey and chemists after Lavoisier."[246]

[246] Brinton, letter to Parsons, dated July 19, 1939, p. 2; Parsons papers, HUG(FP) – 42.8.2, box 2.

2
Parsons's Sociology of National Socialism, 1938–1945

Introduction

Secondary reconstruction of Parsons's oeuvre has it that the time period of the two classics, *Structure* published in 1937, and *The Social System* which first appeared in 1951, were an "early" and a "middle period," respectively. Two decades of theory endeavor, subsequent to *Structure*, supposedly led up to eventual development of a "late period" featuring a multidimensional systems analytical approach.[1] The "middle period," continuing from *Structure*, apparently incorporated above all *The Social System* as an epitome of systematic, abstract theory.

This categorization of Parsons's oeuvre lumps together as "middle period" two phases in American history that were remarkably different when both had an impact on his work. They were the era of World War II, until 1945, and that of the postwar period including the emergent Cold War in the years culminating in the outbreak of the Korean War.

In this chapter, I wish to argue that World War II was a backdrop to a special phase in Parsons's work. I suggest that he proposed a sociology of National Socialism, counterpart to his analysis of democracy featuring American democracy.

Parsons's sociology of National Socialism followed from his two-pronged theory of the structure of (systems of) social action. In *Structure*, he elaborated on two types of social system, indirectly contrasting then contemporary societies, the United States and Nazi Germany. This chapter renders further credence to the view that he had contemporary society in mind. My hypothesis: In the time period between the pogrom of November 1938 in Germany, and the defeat of National Socialism and end of World War II, his sociology was utterly concerned with existing reality in his contemporary world. He sought to understand the mechanisms behind social problems such as, for instance, police terror or mass aggressiveness – in due course taking seriously the then often-raised question of what to do with Germany in the aftermath of the Nazi régime.

---

[1] Jeffrey Alexander, *The Modern Reconstruction of Classical Thought: Talcott Parsons* (Berkeley: University of California Press, 1983), esp. pp. 46–72; Peter Hamilton, *Talcott Parsons* (London: Tavistock, 1983), pp. 85–114.

Introduction

This chapter focuses on Parsons's sociology of National Socialism which relied heavily on the distinction between anomie and integration, drawn in *Structure*. He incorporated obviously empirical facts into his theory of two-pronged structure of society, to a truly astonishing degree. Indeed, in a large number of articles, speeches, memoranda, etc., he explored the nature of Nazi society in detail worthy the attention of historians. He saw in it the type representing the obverse of American (Anglo-Saxon) democracy, and he proved this through abundant factual evidence.

My narrative of his analytical understanding of National Socialism distinguishes five episodes. Although I begin with his formative years in the 1920s, when he acquired his interest in the two main foci of his work – professionalism on the one side, and the relationship beween economy and religion on the other – my main focus is on the years between 1938 and 1945.

My thesis is that Parsons, alarmed by the danger to Western civilization which National Socialism incurred, engaged himself in thorough study of the nature of that regime; at the same time, he outed himself as a political activist propagating his openly anti-Nazi convictions. He pursued the defense of democracy, for the first time openly, on the first occasion after the infamous Nazi pogrom against Jews on November 9, 1938. Throughout the years of 1938–1945, I wish to argue, his activism and his analysis of Nazi-type social structure went hand in hand.

In 1969, in his fourth collection of essays, *Politics and Social Structure*, he reprinted four of his articles analyzing Germany in the context of National Socialism. He recollected how at the time he had divided his time and energy between the two purposes of activist stance and analytical endeavor:

> For all observers of social and political processes in the Western world of the time, the Nazi movement presented not only intellectual, but also profoundly moral, problems.... It is obvious that there are at least two ways of reacting to such disturbing phenomena: to try to "do" something about them, and to try to understand them. As an academic man, in a situation heading toward the danger and eventual outbreak of a new world war, I became relatively active as an anti-Nazi, but as a sociologist, particularly in view of the limited opportunities for action, I came under very strong "internal" pressure to try to contribute both to my own and to others' understanding of what had gone on.[2]

In "On Building Social System Theory: A Personal History," interestingly, he mentioned little of his World War II zeal. Rather, he focused on his theoretical interests after *The Structure of Social Action*, discussing "The Professions and the Two Aspects of the Rationality Problem." He hinted at wider concerns involved when he placed the problem of medical practice in the center of understanding modern society. He recalled,

> It was empirically nearly obvious that the "learned professions" had come to occupy a salient position in modern society, whereas in the ideological statement

---

[2] Parsons, "Part II. Historical Interpretations. Author's Introduction," *Politics and Social Structure* (New York: Free Press, 1969), pp. 60–61.

of the alternatives, capitalism versus socialism, they did not figure at all. Indeed, what is now habitually called the "private, nonprofit" sector of organization and activity which is occupationally organized, as distinct, for example, from kinship, did not figure ideologically. In retrospect it can be said that both ideological positions stated versions of the "rational pursuit of self-interest" – the capitalist version, grounded in utilitarian thought, the interest of the individual in the satisfaction of his wants, the socialist version, the interest of the collectivity (on lines deriving from Hobbes and Austin) in maximization of satisfaction of the public interest.[3]

The two recollections, both in the year 1969, referred to the time period after *Structure*. Parsons remembered different aspects of his intellectual biography. These should be joined together, showing how he remembered what happened on both occasions of recollection in 1969. My interest is as much in the documentation of how Parsons as American citizen was actively involved in opposing the Nazi menace as delineation of the progress of his sociological thought.

Some previous literature on Parsons has dealt with the topic of his analyzing National Socialism already in the 1980s. The first such essay, Rainer Baum and Frank Lechner's reconstruction of Parsons's understanding of National Socialism, unfortunately, failed to distinguish between the theses Parsons took from contemporaries such as Harold Lasswell or Margaret Mead, and those he added to or developed far beyond others' conjectures when he wrote his various analyses.[4] Another such endeavor, William Buxton's account of Parsons's lifetime oeuvre in the terms of an allegedly dominant political activism befitting an advocate of the U.S. capitalist nation-state, charged Parsons with lifelong "commitment to the redemptive principles of liberal Calvinism."[5] Neither of the two standpoints, I submit, did justice to his concerns in the time period between 1938 and 1945. Both standpoints surely fell short of recognizing that as a citizen he engaged in pro-democracy activism, while as a sociologist he occupied himself with analytical theory during this period in his life. That the latter was very much a theory of the historico-political society of the day is the focus of my concern in this chapter.

I understand Parsons, in the time period of 1938–1945, moving back and forth between theoretical concern and political engagement. He rightly saw the United States under the threat of Nazi imperialism, but he also considered Germany where he had lived for a year and come to know Germans (some of whom he could help escape Nazism) as well as their society, in the 1920s.

I argue that his sociology of National Socialism was part of his larger endeavor. He had a theoretical interest in the sociology of democracy, and, at the same time, a personal commitment to American society as well as, dating back to his

---

[3] Parsons, "On Building Social System Theory: A Personal History" (originally written, 1969), in *Social Systems and the Evolution of Action Theory* (1977), p. 33.

[4] Rainer Baum and Frank J. Lechner, "National Socialism: Toward an Action-Theoretical Interpretation," *Sociological Inquiry*, vol. 51, 1981, pp. 281–305.

[5] William Buxton, *Talcott Parsons and the Capitalist Nation State* (Toronto: University of Toronto Press, 1985), esp. pp. 97–116, cit. front page (unpaginated).

student days, Germany, to his sojourn there. From this vantage point, he wanted the emergent theory of social systems to be able to help understand contemporary events, further to the analytical framework proposed in *Structure*, his first major work. His interest in empirical society as a source and arena of proof for the theory of the structure of social action still prevailed. In the time period between 1938 and 1945, he devoted his analytical genius to the historical crisis incurred by National Socialism, in order to contribute to the understanding of the structure of social action in even more concrete terms than he had been able to do in the 1930s.

Between 1938 and 1945, Parsons published nine articles and wrote three manuscripts unpublished in his lifetime on the subject of National Socialism. He also wrote a large number of radio broadcasts, lectures, speeches, and memoranda for various occasions and associations, all of which are preserved in the Harvard Archives. These materials are being used in this chapter, attempting to put into chronological order his work from those years. As a rough guide to his intellectual biography in those years, five phases are distinguished. Their main organizing focus was World War II, dividing his intellectual biography into a pre-war period, three stages parallel to U.S. war history, namely a pro-intervention stance prior to Pearl Harbor, an interest in issues of propaganda and power in the year 1942, a year of crisis in the Far Eastern and European theaters of operation, and a time when postwar democratization of the Axis countries, especially Germany, was pivotal prior to VE-Day. Last but not least, under the title of "Beyond Victory," I wish to highlight Parsons's contribution to re-education policy planning for Germany, as consultant to the Foreign Economic Administration Enemy Branch between March and October 1945.

The Pre-War Period

On November 23, 1938, Parsons published his first article openly dealing with National Socialism, entitled "Nazis Destroy Learning, Challenge Religion."[6] It appeared in the *Radcliffe News*, the student newspaper of Radcliffe College, the women's college linked with Harvard University. Two weeks earlier, on November 9, the Nazis had seized the opportunity of the assassination of a German diplomat by a young Polish Jew to escalate persecution of Jews in Germany and Austria to hitherto unrivalled cruelty.[7]

In his short article Parsons argued that in the United States, National Socialism was frequently mistaken for a variant of an authoritarian régime. Americans, he observed, expected Nazism soon to be mitigated by the normal political process. Instead, he warned, it represented a revolutionary antidemocratic movement

---

[6] Parsons, "Nazis Destroy Learning, Challenge Religion," reprinted in *Talcott Parsons on National Socialism*, pp. 81–83.
[7] On the importance of the persecution of November 9, see Gerald Schwab, *The Day the Holocaust Began: The Odyssey of Hershel Grynspan* (New York: Praeger, 1990); *Night of Pogroms: "Kristallnacht" November 9–10, 1938* (Washington, D.C.: U.S. Holocaust Memorial Council, 1988); also Raul Hilberg, *The Destruction of the European Jews* (Chicago: Quadrangle, 1961), esp. pp. 22–30.

bent upon the destruction of the modern world, one taken for granted by most contemporary Americans. National Socialism, he charged, was "the most formidable threat to many of the institutional fundamentals of western civilization as a whole which has been seen for many centuries."[8] To substantiate this claim, he focused on two particularly pernicious endeavors of National Socialism, namely replacement of liberal learning by partisan science and destruction of religious universalism that had prevailed since the Reformation in the early sixteenth century.

In the field of science, that is, liberal learning as practiced and taught at universities, he saw that "National Socialism is deeply hostile, in particular to the spirit of science and the great academic tradition and more generally to the whole great cultural and institutional tradition of which these are an integral part,"[9] and the Nazis were "destroying the great academic institutions in which Germany was so eminent.... In philosophy, history and the social fields the destruction is virtually complete."[10]

Regarding the Nazi challenge to religion, Parsons condemned the policy whereby Jews were excluded by birth from eligibility to the ministry of the Protestant church.[11] This meant that, under the Nazis, the principle of universality of salvation that had inspired Christian faith since St. Paul's epistles was being abandoned: "To my knowledge no European authority, religious or secular, ever before has in principle excluded a group from eligibility to religious goods on grounds of birth alone, however bitterly they may have persecuted Jews so long as they persisted in what was in Christian terms their heresy."[12] Parsons concluded that National Socialism was "a deadly enemy for us [;] we must oppose it with all our strength,"[13] which, for him, was also a "hidden agenda" describing his own intellectual development.

How did his stance in favor of liberal learning and universalistic religion emerge, which became the linchpin of his first explicit accusation waged against the Nazi danger to Western civilization? How did he acquire the world view in which these two foci were epitomes for democratic structure when their denial spelled unprecedented danger to the essence of civilization itself?

From his undergraduate days at Amherst College in the early 1920s to his tenure as an associate professor of Harvard's Department of Sociology at the end of the 1930s, the two themes were, for Parsons, not only foci of sociology but also his understanding of the historical process in contemporary societies. Each theme suggested another equally important topic for him. Liberal learning suggested the idea of science and the professions, and universalistic religion embraced the idea of modern capitalist economic structure.

---

[8] "Nazis Destroy Learning etc.," p. 81.
[9] Ibid., p. 83
[10] Ibid., p. 82
[11] See Alan Davies, "Racism and German Protestant Theology: A Prelude to the Holocaust," *Annals of the American Academy of Political and Social Science*, vol. 450, 1980, pp. 20–34.
[12] "Nazis Destroy Learning," p. 82.
[13] Ibid., p. 83.

Liberal Learning, Science, and the Professions

Parsons's concern for liberal learning stemmed from a commitment originating in his college education, 1920–1924. During Alexander Meiklejohn's presidency, 1912–1924, Amherst became noteworthy for its reform conception of the substance and objective of college education. Main tenets in the liberal college which Meiklejohn instituted were freedom of inquiry and excellence of knowledge, pursued in the service of the nation as a whole. The liberal college, Meiklejohn maintained in his educational philosophy, aimed to transcend the classical philosophical program of *Bildung*.[14] Though *Bildung* liberated the person from undue dependency on the necessities of everyday life, Meiklejohn knew, *Bildung* as predominantly academic pursuit also tended to estrange the student from his contemporary society. The idea was to educate citizens to use their knowledge responsibly in order to promote the well-being of each individual person as well as the entire community. The student was encouraged to think beyond the narrow confines of specialized disciplines and grasp the dynamics of his or her contemporary world. The freshman, Meiklejohn stated, was "to face the problems of his people, to begin to think about those problems for himself, to learn what other men have learned and thought before him, in a word, to get himself ready to take his place among those who are responsible for the guidance of our common life by ideas and principles and purposes."[15]

Students were to be committed to reform. They were to work for the good of their society through their use of knowledge and common sense during "The Next Hundred Years" – which latter title Meiklejohn named his Centennial Exercise Speech at Amherst in June 1921.[16] Such education made philosophy a vehicle of practical learnedness rather than erudition alone. "To know philosophy in any effective sense," Meiklejohn wrote, "one must do more than read: One must find a problem which seems to him real and must then let his reading and thinking develop from that."[17]

The program met with students' noteworthy enthusiasm. A contemporary account of the invigorating atmosphere created by Meiklejohn's reform carried the title *Prophets Unawares*.[18] This book depicted the missionary spirit evoked in the average student, stating about the type of student which Parsons evidently became

---

[14] Wilhelm von Humboldt's classic idea, to a certain extent, had spurred the reform of American universities in the early twentieth century, at least inasmuch as in the wake of Abraham Flexner's mission to Germany and eventual influential report evaluating the quality of colleges and other institutions of higher learning throughout the United States, American higher education had been modeled after the idea of *Bildung*. As Parsons understood in his later life, however, one crucial element in the American university made it differ from, and superior to, the traditional German university. Whereas the latter cultivated a spirit of "each for himself" among professors, the American system involved the faculty establishing community-like relationships between professors. See also below, Chapter 4.

[15] Alexander Meiklejohn, *The Liberal College* (Boston: Marshall Jones, 1920), p. 48.

[16] Meiklejohn, "The Next Hundred Years," in *Freedom and the College* (New York/London: Century, 1923), pp. 101–144.

[17] Meiklejohn, *Philosophy* (Chicago: American Library Association, 1926), pp. 47–48.

[18] Lucien Price, *Prophets Unawares: The Romance of an Idea* (New York: Century, 1924).

in his college years: "After four years of the Amherst method, his education has begun. It was to continue the rest of his life, and, in many if not most cases, I think it will." [19]

Parsons, an ardent disciple of Meiklejohn's ideals, took sides in the conflict with the college's trustees that led to Meiklejohn's resignation. A spokesman of the students, defending Meiklejohn's program in a co-authored article in *The New Student* in October 1923, his first publication ever, he emphasized about himself and those with whom he felt in agreement that "those educational ideas have become so supremely worthwhile as to be the issue on which we will stake a great deal."[20] The importance of liberal learning for a democratic type of society was thus imprinted upon him during his college years.

After leaving Amherst and following subsequent study abroad, he joined the Department of Economics at Harvard University. His first research project, in which he participated around 1930, was in medical economics. He was part of a program yielding thirty-five research reports commissioned by the Committee on the Cost of Medical Care whose chairperson and main sponsor was Ray Lyman Wilbur, Secretary of the Interior in the second Hoover administration (Wilbur Committee) in the preparatory years for the New Deal.[21] His identification was with professionalism, inviting reforms such as health insurance (known at that time as "sickness" insurance).

Professions were at the center of a 1937 book review that focused on education and the professions, indirectly taking account of the fact that Nazis interfered with both.[22] Parsons's review of University of Chicago President Hutchin's book emphasized the importance of universities as institutions of unfettered scientific inquiry, cherishing the cultural heritage whose origin was classic civilization, European culture. "In their common concern with learning in this sense, both professionally specialized learning and common liberal learning," he wrote, "lies perhaps the most important single unifying principle of the professions. And therein lies the

---

[19] Ibid., p. 47.

[20] Talcott Parsons and Addison T. Cutler, "A Word from Amherst Students," *The New Student* (October 20, 1923), p. 7 (quoted from *Talcott Parsons Early Essays*, p. 292). On the story of Meiklejohn's presidency of Amherst and his forced resignation, see Camic's introductory essay in *Early Essays*, pp. xii–xiii.

[21] In an autobiographical account, written in the early 1960s, he recalled that when the Committee's Report came out in 1932, the American Medical Association denounced national health insurance as proposed by the Wilbur Committee – the accusation being that "medical soviets" were being planned. This, Parsons recalled, had been not only a starting point of his career as a medical sociologist, but also the starting point of his sociology of the professions. See Parsons, "Some Theoretical Considerations Bearing on the Field of Medical Sociology," in *Social Structure and Personality* (London: Routledge and Kegan Paul, 1964), esp. pp. 325–326; see also *Medical Care For the American People, Final Report of the Committee on the Cost of Medical Care* (Chicago: University of Chicago Press, 1932). Wilbur, a physician, served as president of Stanford University between 1916 and 1943. He chaired the Committee on the Cost of Medical Care in the years 1928–1932. Parsons participated in one of the research projects commissioned by the Wilbur Committee most likely upon recommendation by Walton Hamilton, one of his college professors.

[22] Parsons "Remarks on Education and the Professions," *International Journal of Ethics*, vol. 47, 1937, pp. 365–369; see also "The Professions and Social Structure," *Social Forces*, vol. 17, 1939, pp. 457–467.

basis of their relation to the universities. For Universities are, in the great European tradition, par excellence the trustees of learning – the agencies responsible for its perpetuation, transmission, and advancement."[23]

Destruction of liberal learning by the Nazis was the theme of a book by Parsons's younger colleague and collaborator, Edward Y. Hartshorne. *The German Universities and National Socialism*[24] documented the introduction of the so-called *Führerprinzip* replacing collegial academic self-government. Hartshorne reported on the loss of one-third and even over one-half of the professors and younger staff in most disciplines, with the heaviest losses concentrated in the social sciences due to emigration subsequent to harassment or dismissal, witnessing the threat to the liberal spirit of science at German universities.

"The National Socialist Revolution aims at *totalitarianism* in a double sense," wrote Hartshorne, explaining, "In the first place all political power is monopolized by one group of agents, and in the second place this group aims to extend its sphere of influence over the whole field of activity within the social group it governs."[25] At German universities prior to Nazi ascendancy to power, Hartshorne showed, this had meant slander and intimidation of liberal and leftist professors by organized National Socialist students.[26] After January 1933, it often had meant loss of livelihood (even of life tenure as a civil servant) when Jews but also Social Democrats and those unwilling to pay homage to the Nazis were excluded.[27]

Hartshorne's book documented how the "Hitler greeting" became compulsory in class, quickly making life intolerable for those who had hoped to stay aloof from Nazi practices. He reported that theories elaborated by Jews were being extinguished from the canon of permissible academic work in Germany. He described how the German university's traditional semiautonomous administration and independence of its academic teachers had all but collapsed under relentless state control on behalf of the Nazi doctrine and *Führer* type hierarchical organization.

Hartshorne, together with Robert Bierstedt, Kingsley Davis, George Devereux, Robert Merton, and others participated in a discussion group in the winter and spring of 1937 which, under Parsons's spirited guidance, occupied itself with types of influence and the problems of authority and propaganda, focusing on

---

[23] "Remarks on Education and the Professions," p. 366.

[24] Edward Y. Hartshorne, Jr., *The German Universities and National Socialism* (London: Allen and Unwin, 1937). He used data from the Academic Assistance Council (Society for the Protection of Science and Learning) in London as well as German statistics from various sources, mainly the Friedrich-Wilhelm-Universität, Berlin, plus most illuminating anecdotal and life history material. He traveled in Germany in 1935–1936 to gather first-hand evidence on the plight of German universities.

[25] Ibid., p. 13.

[26] For student terror, see Michael Stephen Steinberg, *Sabers and Brown Shirts: The Students' Path to National Socialism, 1918–1935* (Chicago/London: Chicago University Press, 1973). For the role of professors in the destruction of liberal learning, see Leon Poliakov and Joseph Wulf, *Das Dritte Reich und seine Denker* (Berlin: Arani, 1957). Regarding the "revolutionary changes" establishing totalitarian society, see David Schoenbaum, *Hitler's Social Revolution* (Garden City, N.Y.: Doubleday, 1966).

[27] Correspondence from Parsons's previous co-students at Heidelberg alerted him to personal disaster that was being inflicted on many enforced refugees from Germany.

Nazi Germany as one of the examples used to analyze, as one among a range of topics, the importance of the knowledge of the expert in modern society.[28]

The group, who met at Adams House between January 12 and May 18, 1937, and whose sessions were summarized in a report authored (edited) by Davis, elaborated between them a scheme for the analysis of influence in relation to authority and propaganda. Regarding types of relationship where an actor A had an impact on an actor B, the group identified, for one, one type of influence that in turn consisted of three subtypes: Rational enlightenment, Economic exchange, or Coercion. In contradistinction, authority, another type of influence, was comprised of subtypes Expert, Office, Charisma, and Power. Interestingly, when the group under Parsons's leadership outlined the connotations of Rational enlightenment, the prerequisite was that the respective knowledge needed to be checked on all accounts in order to warrant a relationship of influence, "A explains, B learns, and action is a consequence of what is learned."[29] Regarding "The Expert," one sociologically highly relevant feature was disinterestedness grounded in the ethical requirement of service which focused on the actor's counterpart, who was the target and beneficiary of the expert's competence, "Since it is implied that A will act in B's interest in that sphere where B is incompetent, there must be solidarity (i.e., common identity of ends) at least to the extent that A will not take advantage of B's weakness. This explains the ethical requirement of professional disinterestedness."[30] Summing up, after three meetings, what had been achieved so far, Devereux described the classification of modes of influencing behavior thus (as protocolled by Davis): "This classification ... distinguished influence by *enlightenment* and *free exchange*, from influence involving *authority*. Under the latter heading were included the influence of the *expert*, that of the *officer*, and that of the *charismatic leader*. All of these modes of influence were in turn distinguished from *coercion*.[31]

In the last two sessions, the topic of propaganda was raised: "It was in the first place suggested by Hartshorne that propaganda is a mode of influencing other people to a specific end. And this was done, added Parsons, through their attitudes or ends rather than through their situations.... Propaganda is more than merely informative; it aims to convince by playing on the sentiments."[32] Such influence certainly was far removed from science and fit easily into the picture of German contemporary reality:

> Hartshorne brought to light some interesting facts about ritualistic speaking choruses used for political purposes in present-day Germany. He used this as an illustration of the idea that once propaganda has been thoroughly inculcated, then the imparting of the same ideas, or repetition of the same phrases tends to become a bore, and to give way [to] ritual. Ritual it was agreed, tends to go with a feeling

[28] "Parsons' Sociological Group, Reports on Meetings." Parsons papers, HUG(FP) – 42.45.4, box 1.
[29] Ibid., p. 3.
[30] Ibid., p. 5.
[31] Ibid., p. 9.
[32] Ibid., p. 20.

of security and stability. Propaganda tends to go with a stage of social change where an attitude is being inculcated.[33]

These issues most certainly were on Parsons's mind when in November 1938 he made himself known as a committed anti-Nazi as he identified the two major dangers emanating from Germany in his short article in *Radcliffe News*.

The topic of academic freedom, for him, was the linchpin of the democratic mission of (social) science. It was the theme of an unfinished manuscript of 1939, which was left untitled but carried the penciled working title of "Academic Freedom," where he elaborated on the academic profession's democratic anchorage.[34]

His organizing question was why the "academic person cannot 'do as he pleases' " while enjoying authority, to which he gave two answers. One stressed that the professions' liberal and learned traditions originated in the history of Western civilization and safeguarded the values of rationality and human dignity. This history was the root cause for the peculiar limitations to personal indulgence and the ban on unchecked manipulativeness, which were institutionalized in such normative orientations as disinterestedness or functional specificity. The professional's authority, though limited insofar as it covered only a particular field of competence, was unlimited on the condition that the knowledge it relied on followed no other than scientifically established standards. Consequently, academic knowledge meant responsibility hinged on genuine freedom of thought. Freedom of "a liberal profession," he stated, could only be granted to someone who resisted prejudice or doctrine; it could not be extended to him "who approaches a subject with a fixity of attitude or preconceived ideas, or with a dominance of emotion or sentiment which precludes any important range for this rational process."[35]

The other answer rejected the alternative of German science in the 1930s, which dictated to scientists what their findings were. Academic freedom in Germany had been replaced by party-induced anti-intellectualism, which at the time meant that the natural sciences were given considerable leeway, particularly "certain branches of science which have yielded important practical results in fields like that of military technology,"[36] whereas the social sciences were being ostrasized. However, scientists' technical or laboratory successes were only a pretext used by Nazi authorities to give the "Nazi revolution" or the "new Germany" moral authority, trumpeted in public statements by scientists ostentatiously supporting the Nazi régime. This undeniably destroyed any historical raison d'être of professional authority. Liberal learning underlying freedom of inquiry could not be compromised by becoming a hostage to totalitarian militaristic government. To epitomize what he criticized, he used the example of medicine. He compared the situation of the university in Germany with a group of doctors who were ordered by an all-powerful lay agency to diagnose certain cases as cancer or else lose their jobs. "Hence," he stated, "for problems genuinely within the technical range of an academic field,

---

[33] Ibid., p. 22.
[34] "Academic Freedom (1939)," see *Talcott Parsons on National Socialism*, pp. 85–99.
[35] Ibid., p. 89.
[36] Ibid., p. 95.

any attempt to lay down on nonacademic grounds what the findings of academic work or the opinions of academic people must be, is intolerable."[37]

Universalistic Religion and the Modern Economy

The second focus of Parsons's warning of 1938 against National Socialism was religion. In the American academic tradition until the end of the 1920s, religion from a social-science point of view had been closely connected with the ethical side of economics.

In the Age of Reform between the 1890s and the 1930s,[38] religious values such as justice, equality, and peaceful community had spurred American economics (23 out of 181 members of the American Economic Association's first published membership list had been clergymen). Richard T. Ely,[39] analyzing the evolution of economic production from early pastoral times to the modern industrial era, criticized modern monopolistic capitalism on moral grounds. "Is there a real equality of opportunity?" he asked, and the answer was, "Vast differences in wealth stand in the way of such equality."[40] The solution was social reform safeguarding democracy while overcoming economic inequality.[41]

The union of social ethics and economics inspired the so-called Social Gospel,[42] a movement whereby scholarly analysis acknowledging equality before God seriously envisaged how equality of opportunity could be promoted. The movement aimed to overcome economic individualism but also rejected monopoly and trust capitalism; it proposed to abandon exploitation of labor, create a social order based

---

[37] Ibid., p. 96.
[38] Richard Hofstadter, *The Age of Reform: From Bryan to F.D.R.* (New York: Vintage, 1956); see also James T. Kloppenburg, *Uncertain Victory: Social Progressivism in European and American Thought, 1870–1920* (New York: Oxford University Press, 1986).
[39] Harvard's Widener Library keeps thirty-six editions of twenty-two books by Ely, among them *Recent American Socialism* (Baltimore: N. Murray Publications, Johns Hopkins University, 1885); *Social Aspects of Christianity* (New York: Thomas Y. Crowell, 1889); *Monopolies and Trusts* (New York: Macmillan, 1900); *Property and Contracts in Their Relation to Distribution of Wealth*, 2 volumes (New York: Macmillan, 1914); *World War and Leadership in a Democracy* (New York: Macmillan, 1918).
[40] Ely, *Studies in the Evolution of Industrial Society* (New York: Macmillan, 1903; 11th printing 1918), p. 81; regarding the importance of Ely for economics and sociology before 1920, see Edward S. Mason, "The Harvard Department of Economics from the Beginning to World War II," *Quarterly Journal of Economics*, vol. 97, 1982, esp. pp. 391–393.
[41] Part II of Ely's *Evolution of Industrial Society* discussed various solutions to the problem of social reform in industrial society, advocating how to improve on equal opportunity when guaranteeing individual liberty. German professors, Ely held in the concluding part of his book, were an example of how to combine science orientation in their teaching with advocating reform and participating in public life outside the classroom (p. 487). The reference was, most likely, to German economists Adolf Wagner und Gustav (von) Schmoller at Friedrich Wilhelm University Berlin who in the 1890s had advocated welfare politics such as had been introduced by the Bismarck government, as an antidote against both the socialism of the German Social Democratic Party and poverty and squalor in the lives of the masses.
[42] Parsons's father, Edward Parsons, belonged to the Social Gospel movement; he published *The Social Message of Jesus* (New York: National Board of YWCA, 1912).

on the idea of service and voluntary commitment, and use science in the interest of truth and progress. As quoted by Camic, evolution and reform, as Edward Parsons's phrase went, were to help achieve "perfect humanity."[43]

Parsons's professors at Amherst, especially Clarence Ayres and Walton Hamilton, represented the tradition of economics advocating social reform. Ayres taught philosophy when Parsons had him as a teacher,[44] but became an economist after leaving Amherst on the occasion of Meiklejohn's resignation. His *The Nature of the Relationship between Ethics and Economics*, published in 1918, dealt separately with ethical and economic theory but suggested drawing together the "two sciences": "(T)he problems both of ethics and of economics must center in the structure of society and the changes it is undergoing.... The ethical problem is the general problem in contrast with which it is possible to speak of others as 'special.' ... (T)he problem of economics is to contribute its study of industrial society to the solution of the problem of living."[45]

Hamilton's work was in economics which, for him, as for the majority of economists at American universities in the 1920s, was to serve the betterment of living standards by way of democratic channels. Hamilton's *Control of Wages* (1923) urged that workers organize themselves in cooperatives when fighting for decent wages.[46] His textbook *Current Economic Problems* (third edition, 1925) followed the "primary desideratum" that the student "learn to think intelligently in terms of a complex industrial situation" rather than merely become familiar with a "vast collection of 'principles' that formally explain its working."[47] The readings

[43] Camic, characterizing the elder Parsons's outlook, used verbatim quotations from two articles written prior to the book of 1912: "Alarm over the moral consequences of the 'industrial system,' with its selfishness, economic individualism, exploitation of labor, and tendency toward social 'disorder'; receptivity to improvements that might emerge from 'scientific investigation, higher criticism, rationalism, philosophical speculation' and even 'Christianized socialism'; and hope that partisans of the divergent ethical viewpoints would unite around a 'common store of truth and principle' to work with the church, 'the inspirer of all life,' for progress toward a 'perfect humanity.'" Introduction to *Early Essays*, p. x; see also Howard Brick, "The Reformist Dimension of Talcott Parsons' Early Social Theory" (University of Oregon, Eugene, 1991, mimeo), pp. 6–7.

[44] It was for his classes that Parsons prepared the essays entitled "A Behavioristic Conception of the Nature of Morals" (March 27, 1923) and "The Theory of Human Behavior in Its Individual and Social Aspects" (undated; Parsons papers, HUG(FP) – 42.8.2, box 2). His short reminiscence "Clarence Ayres's Economics and Sociology," written in the 1970s, mentioned that Ayres's institutional economics inspired him, Parsons, to eventually become a professional sociologist but failed to recall the moralistic message of Ayres's economics of the time. In William Breit and William Patton Culbertson, Jr., eds., *Science and Ceremony: The Institutional Economics of C. E. Ayres* (Austin/ London: University of Texas Press, 1976), pp. 175–180.

[45] Clarence Ayres, *The Nature of the Relationship between Ethics and Economics* (Chicago: University of Chicago Press, 1918), pp. 54, 55–56, 57.

[46] Walton Hamilton and Stacy May, *The Control of Wages* (New York: George H. Doran, 1923). The title page introduced Hamilton as "Professor of Economics, Amherst College, Instructor, Amherst Classes for Workers," and May as an instructor of the Amherst Classes for Workers. The book's dedication read: "The psalmist has said that a book on wages is like grass which in the morning flourisheth and groweth up and in the evening is cut down and withereth. But he must have been looking through his glass darkly that day, for he did not really see how frail are the pages whereon it is written of what hire the laborer is worthy" (p. v).

[47] Walton Hamilton, ed., *Current Economic Problems: A Series of Readings in the Control of Industrial Development*, 3rd ed. (Chicago: University of Chicago Press, 1925), p. 17 (1st ed. 1915,

in the textbook were to "represent emotionally as well as intellectually (for feelings count as strongly as logic in the practical affairs of our everyday world) the conflicting views and arguments which contemporary society is bringing to bear upon its problems."[48]

Religion and economics were also reconciled by another academic teacher during Parsons's years of study. Before he took up his lifelong position at the London School of Economics, Richard Tawney taught at Amherst in the summer of 1920 and again once or twice in the remaining years of the Meiklejohn presidency. His *Religion and the Rise of Capitalism*, published in the year following Parsons's sojourn at the London School of Economics, ventured the hypothesis that capitalism had historically developed under the guise of Christian values but had become a cynically unjust system. Tawney criticized Max Weber for overlooking that the truly religious and the capitalist economic orders were incompatible.[49]

Parsons studied with Tawney at the London School of Economics in 1924–1925. From there he went on to Heidelberg University, where he became familiar with the work of Max Weber, analyzing the relation between religion and economics. Weber's *Collected Essays on the Sociology of Religion* (of which *The Protestant Ethic and the Spirit of Capitalism* was part of the first volume) became an eye-opener for Parsons, who made Weberianism his own lifelong tenet. Weber drew together religion and economics under the analytical perspective of how and why rationality had developed in Western civilization. Parsons eagerly absorbed the new standpoint and made it his own. His doctoral dissertation explored the topic,[50] and he translated *The Protestant Ethic* into English (published 1930, with a preface by Tawney).

The relationship between religion and economy as one of the "spirit" which spurred social action became pivotal for Parsons. In his criticism of H. M. Robertson's critique of Weber, he held forth authoritatively what Weber's actual thesis on Protestantism and capitalism had been. "As he put it," he wrote in defense of Weber, "ascetic Protestantism placed peculiarly powerful 'psychological sanctions' on certain types of conduct and the source of these sanctions lies in the

---

rev. ed. 1919). It is not unlikely that the second edition was among the books studied by Parsons as an undergraduate.

[48] Ibid., p. 15.

[49] Richard H. Tawney, *Religion and the Rise of Capitalism* (New York: Harcourt, Brace & Co., 1926); the book has been translated into seven other languages.

[50] Parsons, "Capitalism in Recent German Literature: Sombart and Weber," *Journal of Political Economy*, vol. 36, 1928, pp. 641–654 and vol. 37, 1929, pp. 31–51 (reprinted in *Early Essays*, pp. 3–37) appears to have been a somewhat rewritten version of the dissertation. When the two chapters of Parsons's original German manuscript had been "lost" by Edgar Salin's (his doctoral dissertation supervisor's) assistant, Parsons wrote, as a third chapter, an English version, which was accepted as the required work by Heidelberg University's *Philosophische Fakultät*. On his year in Heidelberg, see his "On Building Social System Theory: A Personal History," *Daedalus*, vol. 99, 1970, pp. 828–830, and also Camic, "Introduction," in *Early Essays*, pp. xix–xxii, and Alexander, *Modern Reconstruction*, p. 23. Documentary evidence of Parsons's unusual experience of eventually being promoted *Dr. phil.* is preserved in Heidelberg University Archives, call number UAH H IV, 751/21.

way in which Protestant dogma, above all the doctrine of predestination, canalized the individual's attitudes and conduct in a certain peculiar direction – that of systematic, rational mastery over the external environment, and lent these attitudes a very special ethical intensity."[51]

His "The Role of Ultimate Values in Sociological Theory"[52] further explored the use of the sociology of Weber, in action theory for the 1930s. He re-analyzed Weber's original solution to the problem of ultimate values in light of the newly emergent salience of ritualism, an alternative to rationality. The dilemma was, as had been stated by Weber, between *Gesinnungsethik* and *Verantwortungsethik*.

The question of ethics, applied to the problems of economics, became the apex of *The Structure of Social Action*, mainly written in 1934–1935.[53] Through four theories developed between 1880 and 1920, the book analyzed how the structure of action in social systems was either deemed utilitarian, which invoked anomie contained in coercion, or understood as normative, which suggested societal integration. The advertisement McGraw Hill, the publisher, ran stated: "This volume...contributes not only to a branch of scientific sociology but also to 'civics' in the highest sense."[54]

The book's culminating part focused on how Weber's sociology of religion explained worldwide differences of economic history, introducing "the mutual relations of prophecy, rationalization, and traditionalization."[55] He analyzed the legitimacy of social order as based either on due process or routinization of power, legitimacy that could even derive from charisma providing action-inducing " 'meaning' of the world."[56] Charisma, he clarified in the footsteps of Weber, "is the quality which attaches to men and things by virtue of their relations with the 'supernatural,' "[57] and, "The charismatic leader never treats those who resist him or ignore him, within the scope of his claims, as anything but delinquent in duty."[58] In this vein, he found aspects of religious structure, particularly the imperatives of the sacred, in the apparently profane order of charismatic rule, detecting traditionalized immobilism in conditions which outwardly might appear as innovative change: "(F)or Weber the two main characteristics of traditional authority (are) a traditional body of norms held sacred and unalterable and...an area of arbitrary personal authority of the ruler, legitimized by his generally charismatic personal

---

[51] Parsons, "H. M. Robertson on Max Weber and His School," *Journal of Political Economy*, vol. 35, 1935, pp. 688–696, quoted from *Early Essays*, p. 59; Hector Menteith Robertson, *Aspects of the Rise of Economic Individualism: A Criticism of Max Weber and His School* (Cambridge: The University Press, 1933).

[52] "The Role of Ultimate Values in Sociological Theory," *International Journal of Ethics*, vol. 45, 1935, pp. 282–316.

[53] Parsons, *The Structure of Social Action: A Study in Social Theory with Special Reference to a Group of Recent European Writers* (New York: McGraw Hill, 1937); 3rd edition, 1968. See also above, Chapter 1.

[54] For the advertisement, see Parsons papers, HUG(FP) – 42.8.2, box 2. See also above.

[55] *Structure*, p. 685.

[56] Ibid., p. 667.

[57] Ibid., p. 668.

[58] Ibid., p. 662.

quality. By this process, from being the specifically revolutionary force charisma becomes, on the contrary, the specific sanction of immobile traditionalism."[59]

The book, among other things, challenged the formula of "Economic Man." The latter was to be supplemented by a theory of the two-pronged structure of social action, mirroring tendencies in the empirical world of the day. In less indirect fashion than Parsons, Peter Drucker's *The End of Economic Man*, published in spring 1939,[60] analyzed the collapse of democracy and the rise of totalitarianism in several European countries, notably Italy and Germany, consequent upon conspicuous failure of economic rationality there. After the masses had sacrificed the security of their traditional society during the Industrial Revolution, Drucker argued, their hopes for equality and freedom nevertheless had been smashed subsequently. The demonic forces of war and unemployment, in World War I and the Great Depression, would not remedy their plight. National Socialism appeared a solution to the Germans. It represented a noneconomic society, Drucker emphasized, organized like an army and based on a "war economy," an antidote against capitalism and socialism alike. However, even the demise of Economic Man had not produced sufficient political integration; the persecution of Jews had become a prop for the German masses to perpetually create the antitype whose destruction signified ersatz success sustaining the régime of National Socialism, Drucker wrote.

A review of the book published on May 6, 1939, by Harvard economist Eli Ginzberg was kept by Parsons and has been preserved in the Harvard Archives. Ginzberg pointed out that the purpose of a "war economy" was eventual war. He conceded that unemployment had been overcome by the Nazis, and opportunities for prestige and power had been opened up for the underprivileged, although at considerable cost to the country and its citizens, and even more at the expense of Germany's European allies tricked into unequal deals by the Nazis. The war economy had been costly in the preceding years of peace, Ginzberg wrote, but "even worse cost must still be met. In a world of strident nationalism, external victories will eventually be checked."[61]

Before Pearl Harbor

On September 1, 1939, war broke out in Europe. On September 7, A. J. R. Fraser Taylor, a lawyer from Hove, England, wrote to Parsons asking him to explain American neutrality in "the War which has just broken out between the European democracies and Germany."[62] In particular, Taylor enquired why the United States appeared to favor isolationism, and he offered three alternatives for an explanation: Would an American entry into the war invite a Japanese or Russian attack on its

---

[59] Ibid., p. 664.
[60] Peter F. Drucker, *The End of Economic Man: A Study of the New Totalitarianism* (New York: John Day, 1939).
[61] Eli Ginzberg, "The Dynamics of Nazism" (review of Drucker's book), *Saturday Review of Literature*, May 6, 1939, p. 5; the review is among the Parsons papers, HUG(FP) – 42.8.2, box 2.
[62] Letter, A. J. R. Fraser Taylor to Parsons, September 7, 1939; Parsons papers, HUG(FP) – 42.8.2, box 3.

"ill-defended Pacific coasts," or had "the Nazi party somehow got the ear of Congress," or was "the deadweight of ignorant Middle West isolationalists" responsible for the inaction? On September 28, Parsons replied that the first and second suggestions seemed unimportant. But the third, he admitted, was valid.

He felt that internal affairs played a major part in keeping the United States out of the war despite President Roosevelt's attitude. He cited Harold Lasswell's insecurity hypothesis to account for isolationism:

> There is a vast mass of the kind of personal insecurity which is inevitable in such a great country where there has been an extremely rapid growth and social change and a prolonged period of economic distress. This type of thing is relatively easily mobilized by highly emotional movements and leaders and as in other cases "patriotism" has been one of the things around which it can be most easily mobilized. For a variety of reasons, patriotism is readily identified with isolationism and even the type of sentiment which in other situations might be readily mobilized in favor of an aggressive war.[63]

Lasswell had first raised the insecurity hypothesis in 1933 to account for "The Psychology of Hitlerism,"[64] and extended his idea one year later into a comprehensive political psychology in his *World Politics and Personal Insecurity*.[65] Insecurity, in Lasswell's terms, meant loss of identification with traditional authorities or values in the wake of the industrial revolution or due to drastic political changes. Bereft of personal security, the individual lost his sense of belonging, which, in turn, made modern masses prone to turn to any symbol that held a promise of restoring personal security and thus alleviate all-pervasive anxiety. If mass anxiety was insufficiently relieved by existing political or economic institutions, he warned, the masses might turn against minority groups whom they made into scapegoat objects for their intractable hatred. In the United States, orators with strong antidemocratic bias such as Huey Long had a large following, in the Soviet Union Communist dictatorship proved an obvious antidote against mass insecurity, and in Nazi Germany, he found, ethnocentric hatred reconciled the deprived lower-class unemployed with the upper-class antidemocratic circles:

> Smarting under the humiliation of defeat, burdened by the discriminatory aftermath of Versailles, racked by the slow tortures of economic adversity, ruled in the name of political patterns devoid of sanctifying tradition, the German mentality has been ripening for an upsurge of the masses.... Hitlerism is a concession to cultural fundamentalism in a far deeper sense than that it defends property from communist expropriation.... Hitler was able to say, in effect, "You are not to blame for the disaster to your personality involved in the loss of the war. You were betrayed by alien enemies in our midst.... Germany must awaken to the necessity of destroying the alien at home in order to prepare to dispose of the enemy abroad."... In general, the symbols of Hitlerism have assuaged the emotional

---

[63] Letter, Parsons to Fraser Taylor, September 28, 1939; Parsons papers, HUG(FP) – 42.8.2, box 3.
[64] Harold Lasswell, "The Psychology of Hitlerism," *The Political Quarterly*, vol. 4, 1933, pp. 373–384.
[65] Lasswell, *World Politics and Personal Insecurity* (New York: McGraw Hill, 1934).

conflicts of the lower bourgeoisie, while the acts of Hitlerism have lowered the labor costs of the upper bourgeoisie.[66]

Using Lasswell's insecurity hypothesis, Parsons explained to Taylor that isolationism was an alternative to war for those who were too demoralized through recent social changes (including rapid industrialization and population growth but also the Great Depression), and this group, he knew, represented a majority of Americans, for the time being.

He immediately worked personally toward changing this. On the same day as his letter to Taylor, September 28, 1939, he wrote to Senators David I. Walsh and John Cabot Lodge, Jr., of Massachusetts.[67] He justified his approaching the senators through his opinion that those who disagreed with the Senate majority's vote which laid an embargo on military aid to Britain and France "should be heard from lest their cause go by the board simply because they are inarticulate." Three aims, he stated, naturally were in the interest of the United States: (1) eventual victory for the Western powers, (2) minimizing social and economic damage and cost to the United States, and (3) staying out of the war. But, he added, the latter should not mean peace at any price, similar to Chamberlain's appeasement policy. He warned that the embargo provisions of the Neutrality Act would jeopardize the prestige of Congress: "In accepting those restrictions, we are going to pay a heavy national price for whatever protection of our neutrality they may yield." The gain might even be zero, he added, when the Germans would tend not to credit the United States for its restraint; it might first sacrifice its allies from World War I – Britain and France – and then be confronted with Nazi power alone.[68]

Parsons campaigned for intervention on behalf of Britain in a speech on Harvard Yard at a rally organized by the Militant Aid to Britain Committee on April 26, 1940. He invoked the contemporary crisis which could be interpreted either way between two alternatives that were before the citizens of the United States:

> One is that our society is experiencing a deep-seated change which is the inevitable product of the operation of historical laws, and of its own history. War and revolution, violence and the challenge to our moral standards, are only symptoms, surface phenomena. The basic processes will, whatever we do, take their inevitable course. The best we can hope to do is to mitigate some of the more unpleasant disorders, but this can best be done in our own bailiwick, at home. This kind of fatalistic acceptance of inevitability is heard in many quarters, right and left from the "wave of the future" to some of our Marxist friends. From this point of view the outcome of the present war is a matter of quite secondary importance,

---

[66] Lasswell, "The Psychology of Hitlerism," pp. 373, 378, 380, 384.
[67] Letters (identical wording), to Senators Walsh and Lodge, September 28, 1939; Parsons papers, HUG(FP) – 42.8.2, box 3.
[68] Lodge, in his answer, took a position that contradicted that of Parsons. "To my mind," Lodge wrote, "we can take sides or we can stay at peace. We cannot do both." He added, speaking on a personal note, "I do not feel that as an American official I have a right to have any goal other than that of preserving peace for America." Letter, Lodge to Parsons, October 3, 1939; Parsons papers, HUG (FP) – 42.8.2, box 3. It might be remembered that U.S. ambassador to Britain at the time, Joseph P. Kennedy, took the same position as Lodge did in his letter to Parsons.

it will make only a superficial difference anyway. The other view is that we may be at one of the great turning points in the history of civilization.[69]

U.S. Democracy Versus Nazi Germany

In August 1940, the Council for Democracy was founded in New York. Its first chairman was Parsons's colleague and close collaborator, Carl J. Friedrich, professor of government at Harvard. The council's aim was to help the American public to understand the need to fight fascism, through elucidating those features of democracy that distinguished America from Germany. A large number of social scientists and public figures joined the council, especially its highly active Committee for National Morale. Among them were Gordon W. Allport, Gregory Bateson, Walter Cannon, Hadley Cantril, Eliot D. Chapple, Elmer Davis, Leonard Doob, Friedrich, George Gallup, Geoffrey Gorer, Ernst Kris, David Levy, Kurt Lewin, Margaret Mead, Gardner Murphy, Henry A. Murray, Ralph Barton Perry, Edmund Taylor, Goodwin Watson, and Robert Yerkes.

Parsons's first major analytical text in which he openly compared U.S. society with Nazi social structure was a memorandum prepared for the Council for Democracy, with the working title, "The Development of Groups and Organizations Amenable to Use Against American Institutions and Foreign Policy and Possible Measures of Prevention."[70] The memorandum was written, as he wrote to Murray on April 21, 1941, "at the end of last summer at Friedrich's request and turned over to him when it was finished." But it was never published in his lifetime, and Parsons complained to Murray, "I am not aware that the Council for Democracy has made any use of it or has any immediately in mind."[71]

The memorandum had two parts, one delineating the "General Sociological Background," the other "The Practical Problem." The introductory part clarified that weak points of American social structure could be exploited by German antidemocratic propaganda. These included class conflict as well as ethnic differences and social disorganization, whose dangerous sides meant that they could lead to emotional insecurity and psychological pathologies. The latter, to be sure, could make groups or individuals susceptible to Nazi tactics. Modern society's occupational-economic structure, Parsons acknowledged, had failed to provide every citizen with satisfactory earnings and a sense of worth and security. Modernization in the economic and religious realms had devalued social traditions,

---

[69] The text of the speech is among the Parsons papers, HUG(FP) – 15.2, box 3. The rally, as may be learned from a newspaper clipping from *The Crimson*, was picketed by the Harvard Student Union, which had invited the objectors to the British Aid meeting from all Harvard student houses, the Teacher's Union, the Law and Architecture Schools, Wellesley, Simmons, and Radcliffe Colleges, Tufts University, M.I.T., the CIO and the AFL, all Cambridge high schools, the Womens' Neighborhood League of Cambridge, the YWCA, and the Pacifist League. Newspaper clipping from *The Crimson*; Parsons papers, HUG (FP) – 42.8.2, box 3.

[70] The memorandum remained unpublished during Parsons's lifetime, being preserved in Parsons papers, HUG(FP) – 42.41, box 2; with permission of the Harvard University Archives the memorandum was eventually published in *Talcott Parsons on National Socialism*, pp. 101–130.

[71] Letter, Parsons to Henry A. Murray, April 21, 1941; Parsons papers, HUG(FP) – 15.2, box 3.

whereas rational action was frequently being overemphasized. A backlash reaction on a mass basis was "fundamentalism," which urgently was to be avoided: "The appeal of the Nazi movement, though not primarily religious, has a good many resemblances to that of fundamentalism."[72]

These weaknesses of liberalism in U.S. society suggested that a movement such as National Socialism "does not come out of the blue, without, in the content of its developing tradition, continuity with that of the society out of which it has grown."[73] From this vantage point, Parsons outlined five characteristics of National Socialism, "five principal elements around which its principal goals and symbols have come to be organized."[74] He described them in considerable detail as (1) nationalism bound up with racism (race being defined as German or "Aryan" blood), (2) socialism decreeing equality of Germans inasmuch as they were folk-comrades in the proclaimed folk-community, (3) anti-intellectualism in the guise of "fundamentalist" anti-rationalism, (4) militarism, and (5) particularism realized in the *Führerprinzip*, a special type of hierarchical organization. It abolished the notion of office and, consequent upon the absence of division of power in the Nazi realm, favored a monolithic pyramide-like authority structure, "culminating in the supreme leader. The latter has unlimited powers with no legal definition, and each sub-leader has undefined authority, limited however, by his subordination to his superiors."[75]

Democracy in American liberalism, in contradistinction, could be described in terms of four tendencies, namely,

> at least our present relative freedom of opportunity for occupational achievement and status; the dominance of universalistic criteria in this field, with favorable conditions for the development of science and technology; institutional guarantees of individual freedom and liberties; a political system in which authority is subject to law and respect for the rights of the governed, is limited to the powers of constitutionally defined office.[76]

From the vantage point of the four tendencies of American democracy, he outlined a scenario of six "elements of our social tradition which, from the point of view both of intrinsic desirability and effective appeal it seems should be most heavily stressed in any appeal to the sentiments around which national solidarity should and can be integrated."[77] In other words, the following six elements were important enough to be made into thematic areas for the educational work of the Council for Democracy, as it made Americans aware of the strengths and achievements of their democracy. The six elements were: (1) constitutionalism, or rule of law as distinct from rule of men, (2) civil liberties, (3) equality of opportunity, (4) commitment to the community of citizens, engaged in disinterested activity to realize values on behalf of every individual member of the society,

[72] Parsons, "The Development of Groups," p. 111.
[73] Ibid., p. 113.
[74] Ibid., p. 114.
[75] Ibid., p. 119.
[76] Ibid., p. 106.
[77] Ibid., p. 120.

(5) rational-critical spirit which particularly concerned the importance of science and technology as impulses for social life, and (6) activism.

The memorandum juxtaposed the two types of social order. However, Parsons warned that they were not entirely distinct from each other. For one, the first three elements characteristic of National Socialism, namely, nationalism, socialism, and anti-intellectualism, if in attenuated form, could also be found in U.S. society. (Only militarism and the utter particularism of *Führer* authoritarianism were special for Germany under the Nazis.)

Furthermore, four danger zones existed resulting from structural strains such as class or ethnic inequality. These danger zones, which invited subterfuge from German propaganda apt to undermine the American creed in democracy, were fundamentalism, particularism, personification of political groups and issues, and discrimination against minorities. " 'Fundamentalism,' not only in religion, but in any field,"[78] Parsons warned, could alienate Americans from rational thinking. Particularism, valuing one's own group more highly than others, he stressed, made Americans insensitive to some values of democracy (particularly, equality). Personification of "interests" and "groups," he charged, was dangerous when a person was judged in terms of group membership, particularly when "careless and indiscriminate use of epithets like 'Fascist' or 'Communist' "[79] prevented genuine appreciation of an individual's personal merits. Discrimination against minorities, he concluded, was based on prejudice against "such groups as the Irish, French-Canadians, and Italians," but also Jews and Blacks.[80] Such discrimination, in turn, produced feelings of resentment on the part of the targeted minorities, feelings that could be used by German hate-mongers to induce antidemocratic movements in the United States. He therefore warned against "any sense of inferiority (that) is readily exploited to fan resentments against real or alleged discrimination."

The memorandum relied on contemporary social-science knowledge focusing on democracy as contrasted with totalitarianism, in two fields. One pertained to the nature of political power, as analyzed in Friedrich's comprehensive *Constitutional Government and Politics*.[81] Friedrich argued that modern systems of government meant division of power between the legislative, executive, and judicial branches, based on pluralism of manifestation of interest and intent, in the context of European history. Politics in the modern age, he warned, could mean that interest groups pressurized the government, producing a skewed balance within the body politic. Nazi rule was a deterioration of "direct popular action," destroying constitutionalism completely.

National Socialists, Friedrich maintained, used the plebiscite to "serve the purpose of demonstrating a united front in support of the aggressive foreign policy

---

[78] Ibid., p. 124.
[79] Ibid., p. 125.
[80] Ibid., p. 126. The next quote is from the same page.
[81] Carl J. Friedrich, *Constitutional Government and Politics. Nature and Development* (New York: Harper and Brothers, 1937; rev. ed. entitled *Constitutional Government and Democracy*, Boston: Little, Brown, 1941).

of the government."[82] "All political power is subject to abuse, no matter what the legal form of its exercise," Friedrich contended, "But concentrated power is very much more easily abused than divided power."[83] He ridiculed the Nazi claim that their rule was democratic as they commanded an overwhelming majority of nearly 100 percent in "elections" that had been nothing but pro-Hitler plebiscites. Such manipulation, Friedrich chided, could not "provide 'real democracy,' as the German propaganda minister [Goebbels] would try to make us believe."[84] He called Goebbels's claim "a Utopian dream or a sorry sham."

The second line of discussion in Parsons's memorandum touched upon *morale*. The theme was widely acknowledged in the late 1930s and first half of the 1940s. For example, in *War In Our Time*, a collection of essays by some members of the Graduate Faculty of the New School for Social Research, emigré sociologist Hans Speier addressed the issue of "Morale and Propaganda."[85] In modern mass society, he argued, symbol warfare was unavoidable, that is, mass media would wield manipulative means of propagandistic persuasion. Propaganda in war, he wrote, had three uses. It affected morale, it manipulated symbolic meanings of facts, and it directed loyalties. Regarding the morale aspect, he linked it to "the psychology of fear and anxiety,"[86] and he clarified: "Morale can be strong in the face of danger, particularly when it rests on the notion that one is prepared to meet it; undefined danger, which causes anxiety, destroys morale."[87]

Morale in the guise of demoralization was recognized, for instance, by psychiatrist Harry Sullivan. He analyzed, among other then-recent events, that millions of French had fled the Germans, blocking the roads and hindering the mobility of the French army in June 1940.[88] Another approach was "An Analysis of the Conception of Morale," by Scottish psychologist P. E. Vernon. He investigated war attitudes in a democratic society, testing personality "qualities presumed to be

---

[82] Friedrich, *Constitutional Government* (1937), p. 494.
[83] Ibid., p. 499.
[84] Ibid., p. 500; the next quote is from the same page.
[85] Hans Speier, "Morale and Propaganda," in *War In Our Time*, Hans Speier and Erich Kähler, eds. (New York: Norton, 1939), pp. 299–326. The New School for Social Research, founded in 1919, from 1933 onward became a major destination and haven for exiled social scientists from Germany and countries such as Belgium, Czechoslovakia, France, Holland, Italy, and Poland. In 1933, the University in Exile was established, renamed the Graduate Faculty of Political and Social Science of the New School for Social Research when it started academic teaching on October 1, 1933. Among its first representatives were German emigré sociologists Hans Speier and Emil Lederer, psychologist Max Wertheimer, political scientists Karl Brandt and Eduard Heimann, economists Gerhard Colm and Arthur Feiler, and educationalist Frieda Wunderlich. A recent list of names of scientists and artists who were helped by the New School for Social Research between 1933 and 1945 includes over 180 names. See Claus-Dieter Krohn, *Wissenschaft im Exil. Deutsche Sozial- und Wirtschaftswissenschaftler in den USA und die New School for Social Research* (Frankfurt: Campus, 1987), esp. pp. 227–232.
[86] See, for reference, John Dollard, "Hostility and Fear in Social Life," *Social Forces*, vol. 17, 1938, pp. 15–26; Theodor Reik, "Aggression from Anxiety," *International Journal of Psychoanalysis*, vol. 20, 1939, pp. 7–16.
[87] Speier, "Morale and Propaganda," p. 312.
[88] Harry Stack Sullivan, "Psychiatric Aspects of Morale," *American Journal of Sociology*, vol. 47, 1941, pp. 271–301.

connected with morale." He found, as he summarized in an abstract, that factors "of stability, optimism and trustfulness, cheerfulness, adaptability to hardships, and enthusiasm" pervaded democracy-prone personality qualities. In these, he found "a group factor representing a rational, liberal and altrocentric outlook."[89]

Kimball Young, in his masterly essay concluding the Committee for National Morale's annotated bibliography on German psychological warfare, invoked the "total" citizen. The American, though low in belligerence or determination for aggression, Young explained, was unequivocally strong when it came to defending himself (or herself) against attack. The Nazi follower was strongest when firmly organized in a hierarchical structure, but Americans, if the need arose, could fend for themselves one by one, each individual a fortress of strength and determination.[90]

The two themes, constitutionalism and morale as characteristic of democracy, entered into Parsons's comparison between U.S. and Nazi society in his memorandum for the Council for Democracy.

In the fall of 1941, he undertook to completely rewrite his memorandum. It was now entitled "Sociological Reflections on the United States in Relation to the European War."[91] It aimed to address "concern over the defense of the United States" under four headings: "What are we defending? What are we defending it against? In what respects are we vulnerable? and The outlook and questions of policy."[92]

Of the four proposed sections, only the first has been written. What was being defended in what at the time of writing apparently still was "the European war," was democracy in the Anglo-Saxon world. This entailed four general principles of democratic social organization: activity (activism), rationality (rational-legal, or means-end action orientation), ethical universalism, and functional specificity. These characterized three systems of liberal organization of society, namely the occupational sphere or "economy" (quotation marks Parsons's), the government as based on constitutionalism of which democracy was one predominant form, and a sphere of regulation of interpersonal relationships through contractual rules established in procedural laws. The latter included institutionalization of civil liberties. The four principles characterizing the three main systems (or systemlike aspects of modern society as described by Weber) were specific for Western liberalism.

---

[89] P. E. Vernon, "An Analysis of the Conception of Morale," *Character and Personality*, vol. 9, 1940, cit. p. 294. Also noteworthy were L. M. Hurvich, T. W. Huntington, and G. W. Allport, *Beginnings of a Bibliography on Psychological Factors in Morale* (Harvard University, Cambridge, Mass., 1940, mimeo); Stanley Washburn, "What Makes Morale?," *Public Opinion Quarterly*, vol. 5, 1941, pp. 519–531; Clyde R. Miller, "Some Comments on Propaganda Analysis and the Science of Democracy," *Public Opinion Quarterly*, vol. 5, 1941, pp. 657–665; and a sequel to the Allport bibliography, Irving L. Child, "Morale: A Bibliographical Review," *Psychological Bulletin*, vol. 38, 1941, pp. 393–420.

[90] Kimball Young, "What Is To Be Learned From This Survey," pp. 84–88, in Ladislas Farago, L. F. Gittler, Gordon W. Allport, John G. Beebe-Center, Edwin G. Boring, Floyd L. Ruch, Stanley S. Stevens, and Kimball Young, *German Psychological Warfare. Survey and Bibliography* (New York: Committee for National Morale, 1941).

[91] First published in *Talcott Parsons on National Socialism*, pp. 189–202.

[92] Ibid., p. 189.

The democracy thus envisaged extended beyond the realm of politics: "[The four pattern elements] define a broader type of social structure (than what is in the popular opinion called democracy)... (A)ll four of them can be shown to be seriously threatened in the present world situation."[93]

The structural features of National Socialism in terms of the renewed analysis were only hinted at in the completed first part of the manuscript. From what Parsons explained there in passing, four elements mattered. They were "fatalism," ritualism, ethical particularism, and functional diffuseness. "Fatalism," he found, constituted the opposite of activism and had been "widely noted in connection with the oriental civilizations."[94] Ritualism, as already mentioned in *The Structure of Social Action* as analyzed by Durkheim,[95] suggested that "mysterious, supernatural forces and entities hold sway."[96] Ritualism also invited a certain type of nonempirical action justification, to which he (explaining its obverse, reciprocity-prone rationality) objected when he insisted "that projections be treated as capable of proof that they are true or false, that projected actions be weighed in the light of this efficiency as means to an end and the like."[97] Ethical particularism, no doubt, dominated the race doctrine distinguishing between Aryan and non-Aryan blood, which was even a determinant in Nazi Germany of the right to live. Finally, functional diffuseness meant that, eventually, the "Western tradition of science and learning and the social organization which centers about its transmission and development" would be destroyed.[98] Technical competence, he reported, had already been replaced by ideological reliability in the university in Nazi Germany. Authority in the totalitarian society had become total as it was no longer defined by competence or related to task-specific skills. In regression to patrimonial traditionalism, "the clear distinction" was becoming blurred "between the sphere of office with its powers and that of the private capacity of the incumbent in which, whatever his personal prestige or influence, he does not exercise the specific legally defined powers of his office, hence rational-legal authority in the sense of this discussion."[99]

Threat to Democracy

Parsons joined the American Defense Harvard Group as it was founded in the summer of 1940. Its purpose was to place the skills of democracy against the totalitarian threat. In its statement of purpose and activities dated July 1940, eight

---

[93] Ibid., p. 194.
[94] Ibid., p. 191. He obviously referred to the thesis that National Socialism resembled "oriental despotism," established in Karl August Wittfogel, "Die Theorie der orientalischen Gesellschaft," *Zeitschrift für Sozialforschung*, vol. 7, 1938, pp. 90–122.
[95] See Parsons, *The Structure of Social Action*, esp. pp. 673–677.
[96] "Sociological Reflections on the United States...," p. 192.
[97] Ibid. See also, for an earlier treatment of the topic of ritualism as a type of relationship in social action between means and ultimate ends, his "The Place of Ultimate Values in Sociological Theory," published in 1935.
[98] "Sociological Reflections...," p. 199.
[99] Ibid., p. 200.

specific purposes were listed,[100] among them support of measures for military and industrial mobilization in the United States on behalf of countries engaged in war with totalitarian powers; relief for foreign refugees and children from England; help "in developing real and visible national unity without regard to race, creed, or party"; advocating universal national service "without distinction of class or color, thus making it clear that the nation stands united and strong in its determination to preserve American liberties"; and, last but not least, "maintenance of a fearless and united national morale determined to resist every totalitarian encroachment on America, whether by armed force, economic action, or internal movements to appease rather than resist totalitarian powers."

He became vice-chairman of the Group's Committee on Morale and National Unity (renamed from National Service) in the fall of 1940, and chairman of the renamed Committee on National Morale in February 1941.[101] In this function, he drafted a resolution which was meant to be voted on by members, depicting National Socialism as the antitype of democracy. The draft text began,

> German National Socialism is not only in principle incompatible with modern liberal society – it has now become an immediate and acute threat to its very existence. It is unfortunately not composed of retiring persons who obligingly mind their own business, but is in essence a militantly expansive movement, tending inherently to strive for power, conquest and domination. Moreover, it expands by the means against which a liberal society is most reluctant to defend itself, and attacks at points where we are least likely to comprehend the danger. It has not only succeeded in organizing a great nation, with a thoroughness not equalled since the time of Sparta, for the exercise of military power, not only for defense but even more for conquest. It has, in addition, woven this military power into a larger strategy including a remarkably subtle use of propaganda as a technique for undermining resistance, and a degree of development of conspiracy and fraud, as technique of policy which is unprecedented.[102]

Between February and April 1941, Parsons and Hartshorne as chairman and vice-chairman, respectively, organized a discussion group on German social structure. It strove to pull together what social-science knowledge had evolved in Nazi Germany so that competent conclusions could be drawn also regarding American policy and postwar planning.[103]

---

[100] "Letter to the Faculties and Staffs of American Colleges and Universities, from members of the American Defense Harvard Group," Cambridge, Massachusetts, July 1940; Parsons papers, HUG(FP) – 15.2, box 3.

[101] Other members of the committee were Allport, Paul H. Buck, Bernard de Voto, William Y. Elliott, Hartshorne, James A. McLaughlin, Arthur M. Schlesinger, and Arthur M. Schlesinger, Jr.; among those who also participated in the committee's work were George Devereux, Sheldon Glueck, Elton Mayo, Murray, Robert Ulich, Caspar W. Weinberger, and William F. White.

[102] Typewritten text in three parts (no title, no author), beginning with "German National Socialism"; Parsons papers, HUG(FP) – 15.2, box 3.

[103] Parsons prepared a session on regional, economic, political, and cultural aspects of German society prior to 1914; Hartshorne prepared one on how World War I had affected German attitudes and Weltanschauung; emigré historian Herbert Rosinski talked about the German army as the backbone of militarism tied up with the monarchy under the Second Empire, but also a reservoir of anti-Nazi feelings among officers of Junker descent serving the Nazis in World War II; and Dr. Wyatt,

Transcripts of stenographic notes taken at the sessions show that he had an ambitious goal for these discussions among Harvard scholars, "(I)f we could get at it, what kind of alterations in the German situation might be within the realm of some reasonable possibilities which, even apart from its conforming with whatever ideal patterns we had in mind, might at least make it a quiescent region of non-conformity rather than an actively spreading one."[104]

The question he addressed in his talk on German pre–World War I society, in due course, was what elements there had contributed to Nazism, and whether these could be altered in the longer run. He characterized the society of the Second Empire through Junkerism, elitism, religion as represented in the jealously dominant Protestant churches in Prussia (briefly touching upon anti-Semitism as well as discussing Jewish influence), industrialization, and urbanization. These latter had incurred rapid social change after 1870, he emphasized. The bureaucracy was the rational-legal type but caught up in legalism and formalism, and, last but not least, regional divergence was important although it had been conspicuously dominated by Prussian hegemony in the political system, which discouraged citizen participation. Moreover, Parsons mentioned the fact that the Reich government had not been responsible to the *Reichstag*, imperial Germany's parliament. Summing up what had been tensions in Germany facilitating susceptibility to subsequent totalitarianism, he pointed at anomie in two respects. On the one hand, tremendously rapid industrialization and urbanization had uprooted large segments of the population and led to widespread loss of the sense of a secure future (for instance, Berlin had grown from two hundred thousand to over four million inhabitants in some fifty years). On the other hand, there had been in Germany "organization of anomie in the Social Democratic party.... They were Marxists, which meant they were atheistic and anti-religious. This was

---

a collaborator of Murray, addressed the issue of German authoritarian family structure. Wyatt's material was from the volume edited by Max Horkheimer, Erich Fromm, and others of the exiled Frankfurt Institute of Social Research, entitled *Studien über Autorität und Familie (Studies on Authority and Family*, published in Paris, 1936). Two other discussion groups were to follow, one on Japan and one on the United States, aiming at devising strategies relevant for American morale on a comparative basis. See "Report of the Committee on National Morale, submitted by the Chairman" (1941); Parsons papers, HUG(FP) – 15.2, box 3, and letter, Parsons to Bernard de Voto, October 1, 1941; Parsons papers, HUG(FP) – 15.2, box 3. On Rosinski's and Wyatt's background and material: Rosinski had taught history at Kiel University in Germany before he fled to England and later the United States. His groundbreaking work, *The German Army*, was published in 1939 by the Hogarth Press in London and in 1940 by Harcourt, Brace & Co. in New York. The English edition was reprinted in 1940, and the American one in 1944 by Infantry Journal Press, Washington. The book first appeared in German under a pseudonym: Miles, *Deutschlands Kriegsbereitschaft und Kriegsabsichten im Spiegel der deutschen Fachliteratur* (Zurich: Europa Verlag, 1939). Wyatt's material, in particular, was Fromm's seminal essay on the social psychology of authoritarianism, published as one of three introductions to *Studien über Autorität und Familie* (Paris: Félix Alcan, 1936). Fromm's theorem was that German authoritarian family structure favored the personality tendency to submit to, out of feelings of both helplessness and grandeur, a movement such as National Socialism.

[104] "Discussion Group on German Social Structure, February 14, 1941 (Dr. Parsons)," p. 1; Parsons papers, HUG(FP) – 15.2, box 10.

what greatly facilitated the Nazi definition of the situation – of radicals as anti-religious."[105]

In addition to using sociology as a backdrop to understanding the then present-day as well as past German social structure, Parsons worked to explain then current world politics to an audience outside Harvard. From August 29, 1940, to June 5, 1941, he regularly commented on the news of the day over a local radio station, WRUL. Once or twice a month, he discussed events that had occurred as well as policies and measures taken or considered by President Roosevelt or the Senate, interpreting them in light of the worldwide war situation. He did not hesitate to stress how tremendous the threat was to democracy. When the Axis powers formed the Triple Alliance with Japan on September 27, 1940, he warned that "the new pact will probably prove to be a historic event" since it meant "an explicit and direct challenge" to the very existence of American democracy.[106]

Regarding Religion

At about that time, Parsons completed a draft version of his article on anti-Semitism. However, it took nearly two years until the article was actually published, in a version that, to Parsons's dismay, he had not authorized. The article appeared in an anthology devoted to the problem of anti-Semitism entitled *Jews in a Gentile World*.[107] Isacque Graeber, the book's main editor, had approached Parsons in late 1939,[108] and Parsons had written a manuscript over fifty pages long by the spring of 1940 but had to defend his argument against Graeber; in September 1940, he sent it for comment to emigré political scientist Eric Voegelin.[109]

In December, Graeber requested a one-page "general statement of theory," which Parsons supplied.[110] According to this abstract, the argument was as follows: Anti-Semitism was a phenomenon of interdependency between two separate but related social systems. Jewish cultural individuality had religious roots,

---

[105] Ibid., p. 8.
[106] "News report, September 30" (1940); Parsons papers, HUG(FP) – 15.2, box 3.
[107] Isacque Graeber and Steuart Henderson Britt, eds., *Jews in a Gentile World: The Problem of Anti-Semitism* (New York: Macmillan, 1942). Contributors were, among others, Harvard political scientist Friedrich with a statement "Anti-Semitism: Challenge to Christian Culture," Harvard anthropologist Carleton Stevens Coon writing about "Have the Jews a Racial Identity?," Kansas University and Menninger Clinic psychologist Junius Hagg Brown discussing "The Origin of the Anti-Semitic Attitude," as well as sociologist Jessie Bernard on "Biculturality: A Study in Social Schizophrenia," sociologist Everett Stonequist addressing "The Marginal Character of the Jews," and German emigré sociologist Carl Mayer from the New School for Social Research dealing with "Religious and Political Aspects of Anti-Judaism."
[108] Letter, Parsons to Graeber, December 8, 1939; Parsons papers, HUG(FP) – 42.8.2, box 3.
[109] Letter, Parsons to Voegelin, September 11, 1940; Parsons papers, HUG(FP) – 42.8.2, box 3. Voegelin, for whose entry into the United States Parsons had provided an affidavit, taught at the University of Alabama Birmingham, at the time.
[110] Accompanying letter, Parsons to Graeber, dated December 14, 1940, warning Graeber, "Anything in the way of the formulation of the main argument of my paper beyond what is already there would be seen to be out of place." Parsons papers, HUG(FP) – 15.2, box 17.

historically entrenched: "It is a religious type quite different from any branch of Christianity."[111] Assimiliation of Jews into societies in Europe and America was more successful in spheres where universalistic standards prevailed, mainly in the occupational realm where equality of opportunity was least curtailed by *gemeinschaft* social traditions. Jews frequently suffered from incomplete institutionalization of universalism in their surrounding society; anti-Semitism prevailed where strains were widespread, particularly strains that "place the individual in a position of conflict and insecurity." Jews in modern society suffered considerably from the "unsettling effects of rapid emancipation," and "the result is widespread emotional instability, involving aggressive sentiments which are readily mobilized." Such susceptibility to aggressiveness, evidently, made Jews unnecessarily conspicuous and provoked aggressive reactions against them: "In respect to the great masses of the non-Jewish population the Jew serves as a peculiarly vulnerable symbol on which to project their aggression."

Graeber made unauthorized changes in Parsons's text. He defended his editorial alterations, pleading, "I beg you not to castigate me for having cut your chapter. In fact, I had instructions to rewrite yours as well as several others. Please believe me that I did this – yours especially – with pains in my vitals."[112] Parsons responded by writing eleven inserts that were to be entered into the text. Of these, however, Graeber only used two in the published text.[113]

What was the conflict about? The issue was whether condemnation of anti-Semitism as amoral should stand at the end of the article, as Graeber found and wrote into the manuscript, replacing Parsons's insisting on the primacy of scientific study. "I definitely intended this to be a scientific analysis rather than an attempt to press any particular policy,"[114] he insisted to Graeber. Instead of ending on the note that "anti-Semitism can be dealt with effectively only by fully apprehending all the problems involved in it. In other words, it is by means of serious study, by means of an objective analysis, and not through emotional thinking that a successful tackling of the problem may be attempted,"[115] the article's last sentences now read, "[A] rational policy toward anti-Semitism cannot consist in suppressing and punishing its expressions, but only in some analogous way in an attempt to control its deeper causes. Mere indignant repression of an evil is the treatment of symptoms, not of the disease."[116]

---

[111] One-page outline attached to letter to Graeber, December 14, 1940. All quotes in the remaining paragraph are from this same page.

[112] Letter, Graeber to Parsons, August 16, 1941; Parsons papers, HUG(FP) – 42.41, box 2.

[113] The original version of the paper, as much as it could be reconstructed on the basis of material preserved in the Harvard Archives, has only been published in *Talcott Parsons on National Socialism*.

[114] Letter, Parsons to Graeber, March 1, 1940; Parsons papers, 42.8.2, box 3.

[115] This is the restored version of Parsons's text as published in *Talcott Parsons on National Socialism*, pp. 150–151. See also, for the context, Gerhardt, "Die soziologische Erklärung des nationalsozialistischen Antisemitismus in den USA während des Zweiten Weltkrieges," *Jahrbuch für Antisemitismusforschung*, vol.1, 1991, pp. 253–273.

[116] Parsons, "The Sociology of Anti-Semitism," in Graeber/Britt, eds., *Jews in a Gentile World*, p. 122. Parsons, to be sure, refrained from having the article reprinted in any of his five collections of essays;

In his correspondence with Voegelin on the occasion of inviting comment on his analysis of anti-Semitism, Parsons ventured a hypotheses on the atavistic religious side of Nazism. Voegelin, writing to Parsons on September 11, had characterized German attitudes toward Jews by three elements, namely helplessness which resembled anomie, competition between two "chosen peoples" which plunged the Germans into a curious state of "monadologism," and anti-Christianity. Parsons, replying on September 27, reported that in order to understand the problems raised by Voegelin, he, Parsons, had reread Weber's "Ancient Judaism" three or four times.

Answering Voegelin's first point, namely that vis-à-vis Jews Germans felt helpless due to the fact that Germans lacked a cultural ideal guiding their behavior such as was the gentleman for England or the gentilhomme for France, he reached a tentative conclusion.[117] "From a Lutheran point of view," he wrote to Voegelin,

> the world was accepted as frankly and inevitably evil. Men were expected to sin and were released from the psychological tension by repentance. It seems to me this could easily work in the direction of greatly diminishing the force of the obligation of Christian charity, more generally of universalistic ethics. The Calvinist active positive obligation to build up a kingdom of God on earth, on the other hand, gives a very much stronger sanction for the literal enforcement of Christian principles. It seems to me that in this connection people of a Lutheran background allow their aggressive impulses which are in contradiction to Christian ethics a much freer rein than has been possible so far in societies with a Calvinist background. As long as American society has strong sentiments which follow the Calvinist patterns, I feel we are considerably better protected against mass outbursts of this kind of utterly un-Christian aggression than Germany has been.[118]

On Voegelin's second point, competition between "chosen peoples," he wrote as he contrasted German feelings of being a chosen people with Jewish Messianism, holding both against Calvinism:

> One of the essential differences is that in the Anglo-Saxon world this has not been combined with the peculiar Jewish humility, with the acceptance and expectation of persecution and dependency as a punishment for their previous delinquency, combined with the Messianic hope of eventual domination. I suspect, therefore, that not so much for reasons of this sort as for historical reasons the German conception of the chosen people is closer to the Jewish than ours is. This also ties up, I think, with what I previously called the German inferiority feeling which I should think had been considerably conditioned by the combination of

in fact, it is the only one so treated of his essays on fascism and related problems from the 1942–1947 period. The issue seems to have troubled him nevertheless. In 1979, he wrote a postscript to the article, which addressed the problem of Germany's change since 1945 and also noted that the horrendous scope of Nazi atrocities had become known only after his article had been published. The latter manuscript kept in the Harvard Archives carries the handwritten note by Victor Lidz, "to be edited and prepared for publication by S. Z. Klauszner after T. P.'s death." It was published in *Contemporary Jewry*, vol. 5, 1980, pp. 31–38.

[117] Letter, Parsons to Voegelin, September 27, 1940, pp. 2–3; Parsons papers, HUG(FP) – 42.8.2, box 3.

[118] Ibid., p. 3; the idea has been discussed also in Gordon A. Craig, *The Germans* (New York: Meridian, 1991), pp. 15–34.

consciousness of a great past in the early medieval empire and a century-long condition of political helplessness during the period of domination of Europe by the Western states, particularly France.[119]

He concluded by suggesting, "Perhaps one source of anti-Semitism connected with this is the kind of spiteful *resentment* which combines these ethical religious attitudes with sheer envy who can live on that order of hopes."[120]

Regarding Voegelin's third point, Parsons cited Weber's sociology of religion. He stressed that Christianity was further advanced in rationalism than Judaism, an advantage which National Socialists in their quest for nihilism had annulled when they destroyed the one with the other: "It seems to me that from this point of view National Socialism can be considered, as you say, an outburst of new religious force which centers around a re-orientation of precisely these fundamentalist sentiments.... This in turn, of course, is very closely connected with the nihilism in the Nazi elite of which Rauschnig [sic] makes so much."[121]

The Weberian View

Parsons had promised an article about the Weberian view on contemporary politics to *The Review of Politics* in 1938, in the wake of his dealing with Weber in his *The Structure of Social Action*. In particular, he had promised to write on Weber's types of authority with regard to modern totalitarianism.[122] So far nothing had come of this.

In the *Boston Evening Transcript* on September 28, 1940, in the style of a newspaper reporter who accounted for facts in a characteristic journalistic manner, he now wrote a Weberian style analysis attempting to clarify where National Socialism was going. As if reporting on a speech, analyzing the known facts, he outlined how Germany was on its way to plunging the world into a new "dark ages" if it would win the war.[123] The type of society toward which Nazi Germany was heading, he avowed, had little to do with modern rational-legal rule. The term feudalism could characterize such a type of society as it was about to (re)emerge in Germany – except that the basis for the feudal-like fief-vassal relationship would not be land but racist *weltanschauung*:

> From this longer run point of view, then, perhaps we stand at one of the really critical junctures of history. Perhaps the outcome of the present struggle with revolutionary National Socialism will determine whether Western society as a whole is to continue the path of development which has brought it its most distinctive

---

[119] Letter, Parsons to Voegelin, September 27, 1940, pp. 3–4.
[120] Ibid., p. 4; the next quote is from the same page.
[121] Ibid., p. 5. The reference was to Hermann Rauschning, *The Revolution of Nihilism: Warning to the West* (New York: Alliance, 1940; originally in German, Zürich: Europa-Verlag, 1938, 2d edition).
[122] Letter, Waldemar Gurian to Parsons, December 11, 1939, and letter, Parsons to Gurian, December 21, 1939; Parsons papers, HUG(FP) – 15.2, box 17.
[123] "New Dark Ages Seen If Nazis Should Win," in *Talcott Parsons on National Socialism*, pp. 153–157.

achievements, or to fall backward into what must be regarded in relation to all the fundamental values of our history, as a more primitive state.[124]

Now he decided to detail the argument that German fascism meant regressive social change based on the routinization of charisma as outlined by Weber.[125] The article was written in the summer or early fall of 1941 and published in two parts in the *Review* in its January and April 1942 issues.[126]

Its first part carefully reconstructed Weber's conceptual distinction between rational-legal, traditional, and charismatic types of authority. The second part applied the typology, clarifying in four points in what way Hitlerian Germany was different from the United States as a democratic society of the rational-legal type. The article used Weberian thought to show in what respect Nazi Germany's charismatic type authority structure meant grave danger for the preservation of occidental culture itself.

Parsons's first point was that the Nazi Party was no party at all, but a revolutionary movement destroying the pluralist party system. "Democracy and the Party System" stressed that the Nazi leader demanded obedience when Germans who refused were persecuted as delinquent. Comparing democratic and Nazi practices, he clarified, "There is no one objectively *right* cause which it is a duty of the electorate as a whole to support. But in a charismatic pattern this is precisely the case – for those who fall within the range of his claims, it is delinquency in duty not to heed the call of the leader."[127]

His second point outlined how the charismatic rule underwent a process of routinization leading to a personal rule of local fiefs. Such development, he clarified, would especially be possible for a time period subsequent to Nazi victory, if it were to happen, and Hitler's death.

As regarded the characteristic features of National Socialism, in Weberian terms of charismatic régime, he stressed replacement of achievement through ascriptive action orientation there. Germans entirely restructured their society on the basis of the ascriptive quality of race denoting the German *Volk*,

> Thus for instance, "race" membership in the "mystical body" of the German people, in all cases supercedes any considerations of individual quality or competence. This constitutes a fundamental break with the ethical significance of universalistic standards, in a variety of fields of application, such as rational knowledge, the personal rights and liberties of a human individual as such, technical competence and the like. In place of these, in its racial and party particularism, and in its emphasis on unlimited loyalty to the *Führer*, it puts patterns that are much more appropriate to a traditionalistic organization of authority than a rational-legal one.[128]

---

[124] Ibid., p. 157.
[125] In a letter dated October 21, 1941, Gurian acknowledged that *The Review of Politics* had accepted Parsons's article for publication, suggesting minor revisions; Parsons papers, HUG(FP) – 42.45.4, box 1.
[126] Entitled "Max Weber and the Contemporary Political Crisis," *The Review of Politics*, vol. 4, 1942, pp. 61–76, and pp. 155–172; reprinted in *Talcott Parsons on National Socialism*, pp. 159–187.
[127] Ibid., p. 173.
[128] Ibid., p. 174.

In this vein, he pointed out as particularly striking in his recapitulation of Weber's three types of authority, that charismatic authority was *wirtschaftsfremd*, to use Weber's own term. The charismatic régime characteristically was uninterested in promulgation of a normal economic life:

> During the charismatic phase it is possible for both the means of administration and the remuneration of the administrative staff to be provided, out of resources which are placed at the disposal of the movement or of the leader personally, and which he in turn dispenses to his followers according to *ad hoc* exigencies, or which they acquire independently in the course of their activities. But such a system is, in the long run, impossible both from the point of view of internal relations within the administrative staff, and of its relations with the general population.... On the other hand, especially where provision originates in contributions and compulsory levies, these can very readily become "appropriated" by the members of the administrative staff who are closest to their sources, and, along with the authority over the sources which is involved, as their "private" property, that is as perquisites of their status within the group.[129]

These two elements gave rise to a third, the destruction of rule of law, the abolition of *Rechtsstaat*. The reversal of the division of power that destroyed an independent judiciary, leading to partisan legislation and jurisdiction, involved large groups of Nazi officials being placed above the law – thus rendering impossible even the persecution of the bulk of crimes committed. Murdering designated anti-Nazis who were even entire "races," such as Jews or Slavs, remained unchallenged, as the Gestapo, S.S., and Party functionaries were protected from prosecution even in cases of crimes against humanity.

> Thus, for instance, the inviolability of the regular system of courts from interference is fundamental to a system of the "rule of law." In Nazi territory the secret police is above the courts and need give them no accounting for its actions. Beyond that, every person with authority in the party hierarchy is in an important sense above the law. Any of the regular state system of law enforcement agencies which tried to touch him, unless he were delivered to them by his party superiors, would do so at their peril.[130]

Summing up his view on "Probable Consequences of the Permanent Consolidation of National Socialist Power," he referrred to regression from rational-legal type authority to totalitarian patrimonialism, through charismatic rule and its unavoidable routinization, in Germany:

> When considerations of the ideological content of National Socialism are combined with those of the dynamics of routinization of the charismatic movement the evidence seems to be overwhelming. The consequence of its political predominance for a considerable period would with a very high degree of probability be the transformation of the area concerned into a system of institutional patterns of a strongly traditionalistic character. Other elements of the social system which in the Western world have been relatively independent of the political organization

---

[129] Ibid., p. 166.
[130] Ibid., pp. 176–177.

as such, such as the dominant forms of private property and economic enterprise, market relationships, education and cultural activities, could hardly avoid being drawn into the same basic course of change. That the most distinctive cultural features of our civilization could not long survive such a change, would scarcely seem to need to be pointed out.[131]

Parsons's third point concerned "The Outcome of War and the Development of Institutions." Weber's reference to preservation of Western civilization on the occasion of classic Greece winning the battles of Marathon and Salamis against the Persians in the fifth century B.C. was applicable, to comprehend the danger facing humankind. "It is altogether possible that we now stand at another equally critical point of decision for the course of history as a whole," Parsons warned, cautioning, "There are those who feel that the rationalized liberal culture of the Western world has played itself out, that it has no further creative potentialities."[132] He went on to doubt, however, that there really could be a serious scholar advocating "domination over the principal Western cultural area by such a movement as National Socialism?"[133] (To be sure, his colleague Sorokin's last volume of his opus on cultural and social dynamics that had just appeared in 1941 announced a new millennium through redemption by a charismatic leader.)

His fourth point concerned the two types of ethical commitment, contrasting "fundamentalism" with liberal modernism, *Gesinnungsethik* with *Verantwortungsethik*. Only the latter, far more difficult to adopt than the former, was adequate in the struggle for democracy pervading the "contemporary political crisis" of 1941–1942:

> There can be no doubt that, to Weber, not only was *Gesinnungsethik* "irrational" in the sense that he held all orientation to ultimate values to lie beyond the competence of rational analysis, but also that it was a force which inhibited what possibilities of rational orientation to problems of conduct exist.... [M]ovements which, today, mobilize the forces which threaten the basic modern Western institutional system, are such as appeal to the *Gesinnungsethik* type of orientation... This is true of National Socialism... Conversely, there can be little doubt that any ability to assume the burdens of responsible action in Weber's particular sense constitutes one of the most important conditions for the successful preservation of a rational-legal system of authority and... the potentialities of human development which our Western "great society" holds.[134]

The Year 1942

The year 1942 was the first year of full participation of the United States in the hostilities. With the Japanese attack on Pearl Harbor, the United States entered into World War II; thus ended isolationism. At dawn on December 7, 1941, Japan

---

[131] Ibid., p. 179.
[132] Ibid., pp. 180–181.
[133] Ibid., p. 181.
[134] Ibid., pp. 183–184.

bombarded the assembled American fleet, an attack that preempted deployment of U.S. naval forces to stop Japan's imperialist conquest of Korea, China, Malaysia, and Indochina. With Pearl Harbor, a turning point in American history, at once chance and destiny,[135] ended a period of *Night Over Europe*, and *Design for Power* by the totalitarian Triple Alliance.[136] Advocates of intervention, such as historian Edward Earle, no longer stood *Against This Torrent*.[137] Now the pledge for a better world was that *America Is Worth Fighting For*.[138] Hitler declared war on the United States on December 11, 1941. From then on, the United States dealt with the Nazis and their Axis allies in the only way that would be effective: superior military force.

Parsons's work subsequent to Pearl Harbor accounted for the fact that the United States now participated actively in the war, in three noteworthy ways. For one, he turned to understanding German warfare and occupation policy against defeated nations; also, he anticipated Germany's defeat and discussed policy vis-à-vis Germany subsequent to U.S. victory; third, he gave more thought to the type of democracy that existed in the United States in light of America's (future) mission to re-educate Germany (and Japan).

The "Occupied Countries Study"

In the first half of December 1941, on the occasion of a luncheon at the Harvard Faculty Club with emigré Dutch sociologist Bartholomew Landheer, Parsons planned research which focused on societies attacked in war or under hostile occupation. He named the project "Occupied Countries Study."

Landheer had been rescued from Europe as a beneficiary of a Rockefeller Foundation fellowship and was working for the Netherlands Information Bureau in New York. The study with Landheer, originally entitled "Social Aspects of Invasion,"[139] aimed at "a series of studies of the sociological consequences of conquest and occupation in the German-occupied countries of Europe."[140] These were to be Holland, France, Czechoslovakia, and Poland. The Dutch case was to be researched by Landheer. France was to be tackled by Georges Gurvitch, who was director of the *Centre d'Études Sociologiques* at the *École Libre des Hautes Etudes*, the newly detached French wing of the New School for Social Research in New York. Czechoslovakia was to be dealt with by Conrad Arensberg from Brooklyn College, who was to work closely with a Dr. Safranek from the Czech exile government's information institute. Poland was to be studied by Theodore Abel from

---

[135] Oscar Handlin, *Chance or Destiny: Turning Points in American History* (Boston: Little, Brown, 1954), chapter 8, "Pearl Harbor," pp. 167–190.
[136] Frederick L. Schumann, *Night Over Europe: The Diplomacy of Nemesis* (New York: Knopf, 1941); *Design for Power: The Struggle for the World* (New York: Knopf, 1942).
[137] Edward Mead Earle, *Against This Torrent* (Princeton, N.J.: Princeton University Press, 1941).
[138] Ralph Ingersoll, *America Is Worth Fighting For* (Indianapolis/New York: Bobbs-Merrill, 1941).
[139] Letter, Landheer to Parsons, December 13, 1941; Parsons papers, HUG(FP) – 15.2, box 15.
[140] Letter, Parsons to Hartshorne, January 5, 1942; Parsons papers, HUG(FP) – 15.2, box 16.

Columbia University, who was originally Polish and had been in the United States since the early 1920s.

Abel, to be sure, was not eager to take part. In the middle of February, Parsons heard through Robert Merton that Abel felt sociology was utterly unable to deal with what went on in Poland. "His point, if it may so be dignified," wrote Merton to Parsons,

> is that the utter chaos in such countries as Poland, Holland and Greece which followed upon the occupation makes it a purely sterile, "unrealistic" question to consider the changes in the social structure. "There is no social structure there today; anything goes. Also, to say that most of the population look back to the days prior to the occupation as preferable is such an understatement as to be entirely absurd." The upshot of it is that I do not expect any close cooperation on his part; he wants to get out and "do things," devise methods of saving some of those in enemy hands, etc.[141]

Nor was Parsons successful in finding funding for the study. In early January 1942, he approached Hartshorne, who had joined the Psychology Division of the Office of the Coordinator of Information (COI) in Washington, D.C., to interest his agency in the research. "Surely," Parsons reasoned, "I should think an organization which is responsible for propaganda policy to European countries could hardly fail to be interested in this type of study."[142] Hartshorne, however, was unable to convince COI to officially endorse the study, although he was allowed cooperation in the project.[143]

Nor could Parsons enlist support from the Rockefeller Foundation,[144] nor even his own university. He asked Harvard president James Conant, hinting at the possibility that COI and the Rockefeller Foundation might sponsor or finance the research, that the university formally endorse the project:[145] "Since we did not feel qualified to attempt direct practical action," he wrote of himself and Hartshorne as chairpersons of the Harvard Defense National Morale Committee who now wished to launch the study together, "our aim was to do an academic job in bringing to bear our own sociological knowledge of and approach to the social situation of those countries in order to clarify some of the principal factors which must underlie any intelligent practical policy." From this vantage point, he described the aim of the study, regarding German-occupied countries as "the most adequate broad understanding of the 'state of the social system' in the relevant respects." The uses, he continued, could be "such practical fields as propaganda policy, the rather general orientation of foreign policy, and perhaps most important of all the problems of post-war settlement."

---

[141] Letter, Merton to Parsons, February 17, 1942; Parsons papers, HUG(FP) – 15.2, box 15.
[142] Letter to Hartshorne, January 5, 1942.
[143] Letter, Hartshorne to Parsons, January 23, 1942; Parsons papers, HUG(FP) – 15.2, box 15.
[144] Letter, Parsons to Joseph Willetts, May 28, 1942; letter, Parsons to Roger Evans, June 11, 1942; letter, Parsons to Willetts, November 18, 1942; Parsons papers, HUG(FP) – 15.2, box 15.
[145] Draft of a letter from Parsons to Conant, undated (probably early March 1942); Parsons papers, HUG(FP) –15.2, box 15.

Anticipating What to Do With Germany

In a book published in 1941, *Two-Way Passage*,[146] Louis Adamic had suggested that German emigrés and those who had immigrated in previous centuries fleeing European antiliberal régimes could repay their new home country by now emulating America when reestablishing Europe. Parsons, who disagreed with Adamic, expressed his view in a letter. "Positing a United Nations victory and the failure of Russia to become the dominant influence in Central Europe," he wrote Adamic in March 1942,

> it is of course inevitable that we should come to have a very important influence in the disposition of that part of the world. It seems to me, however, that there is a considerably greater chance of success if formal authority and responsibility is in the hands of domestic elements in the countries in question. Of course when there has been such a violent revolution as the Nazi one this becomes a matter of very great difficulty, and perhaps it is a question which difficulties are the greatest.[147]

He suggested to Adamic that Americans of European descent should be used primarily in functions such as relief work, whereas the Germans themselves were to take responsibility for their country's restitution and (re)democratization. He gave two reasons. One was Germans' propensity to feel humiliated and accuse others of injustice to them. "Even under the best conditions there is bound to be a tremendous volume of humiliation, disillusionment, and hardship," and this

> in turn means that those who bear formal responsibility are the objects of all kinds of antagonisms and hostility, reasonable and unreasonable. The Weimar Republic was, among other things, surely severely handicapped by giving the impression that it was a regime imposed by and patterned after those of the victors. If those who bear responsibility are actually citizens of a victor nation that difficulty would seem to me almost inevitably accentuated and the tie of ancestry would not be sufficient to overcome it.[148]

Another reason pertained to Germans' biased image of Americans.

> In Germany, from my experience, the attitudes are very deeply ambivalent. On the one hand, most Germans feel a tremendous superiority to us which is expressed in what, long before Hitler, was the extremely common talk about American materialism, greed, acquisitiveness, etc. The general tenor, at least in circles which I met, was thinking of America as a land of crass materialism and Germany of the higher spiritual values. There was much talk about Europe being corrupted by the influx of American jazz, advertising, and other vulgar things. Along with this and the German national humiliation of the period between wars, there was also very strong resentment of what was felt to be our patronizing attitude and our smug self-satisfaction in our, to them, fabulous wealth and good fortune. Naturally the propaganda about the Fourteen Points and such things was also in the picture. There is at the same time a very genuine respect and admiration particularly for American technical achievement, but I doubt very much if this goes far enough

---

[146] Louis Adamic, *Two-Way Passage* (New York: Harper and Brothers, 1941).
[147] Letter, Parsons to Adamic, March 24, 1942, p. 3; Parsons papers, HUG(FP) – 15.2, box 16.
[148] Ibid., p. 4.

to form a very solid basis for overcoming the sources of suspicion, mistrust and sense of superiority.[149]

The nature of German society, therefore, was one not only corrupted by Nazism such that the latter's defeat would automatically bring back acceptable institutional structures. But Germany's society needed thorough overhaul as it harbored serious premodern inadequacies.

"Democracy and Social Structure in Pre-Nazi Germany,"[150] an article presumably originally devised as a chapter for a book on Germany to be co-authored with Hartshorne,[151] elaborated on elements of German traditionalism which had made Weimar Republic democracy unstable:

> From a sociological point of view, the "democratic," or better "liberal-democratic," type of society which has reached its highest degree of large-scale realization in such countries as England and the United States, has developed from a complex combination of structural elements. Some of these elements have been common to the modern Western world as a whole, while others have played a part particularly in these two countries. By contrast Germany presents a rather bewildering array both of similarities and of differences.[152]

Whereas Germany during the period of its Second Empire and the Weimar Republic definitely had been a country with a highly developed industrial and bureaucratic system, it had also retained, unlike, for example, the United States, a

---

[149] Ibid., p. 3.
[150] "Democracy and Social Structure in Pre-Nazi Germany," *Journal of Legal and Political Sociology*, vol. 1, 1942, pp. 96–114; reprinted in *Talcott Parsons on National Socialism*, pp. 225–242. The article was commissioned by George Gurvitch for the *Journal of Legal and Political Sociology*, a journal started at the newly founded Centre d'Études Sociologiques of the New School for Social Research. On the occasion when Parsons asked him to participate in the "Occupied Countries Study," Gurvitch obtained Parsons's promise to write on Germany. Interestingly, when he accepted the task, Parsons cautioned Gurvitch on what he could or would not see done to himself by an editor:

> I should naturally have no objection whatever to editorial changes with respect to length and literary style, or to checking of specific questions of fact, or to considering suggestions as to problems which ought to be considered which I have neglected to pay attention to. I have, however, had some unfortunate experiences in editorial revision of my manuscripts without due submission to myself for approval and involving what seemed to me very serious changes in my own position and analysis. I could not undertake to write an article unless I am assured that what will appear will be my own work in all the essential respects and that after I have put a great deal of work into it I should not be subjected to any pressure to have it seriously altered with respect either to technical sociological analysis or to political attitude.

Letter, Parsons to Gurvitch, February 20, 1942; Parsons papers, HUG(FP) – 15.2, box 15.
[151] Parsons and Hartshorne, in the summer of 1941, had planned a book together, to be entitled *German Social Structure and National Psychology*. In a letter addressed to psychoanalyst Robert Waelder, Parsons had outlined the book whose second chapter was to deal with pre-Nazi Germany. See letter, Parsons to Waelder, December 17, 1941; Parsons papers, HUG(FP) – 15.2, box 10. (The book project came to none due to the fact that Hartshorne had to refrain from publishing scholarly work as long as he remained in government services, as he served with COI, and OSS subsequently. See also below, Chapter 3.)
[152] "Democracy and Social Structure," in *Talcott Parsons on National Socialism*, p. 225.

landed aristocracy with strong tendencies toward the feudal background of traditional European society. This had been particularly noticeable in Prussia, whose *Junker* families set the tone for dominant militarism in the entire society: "[T]he armed forces under the old German constitution were not under the control of the civil administration but were responsible directly to the Kaiser.... [T]he officer's corps, in continuity with the whole Junker class, carried on a highly distinctive 'style of life' which was in sharp contrast with everything 'bourgeois,' involving a strong contempt of industry and trade, ... even of liberal and humane culture."[153]

The contradiction between an impressive level of industrialization, on the one hand, and strong forces of feudal-like traditionalism, on the other, was reconciled in a tendency of German culture toward interpersonal relationships couched in the terms of formal rank and titles. In this vein, he reported, "the honorific title of *Rat* is differentiated into an indefinite number of subclasses according to the particular occupation of the incumbent *Kommerzienrat, Justizrat, Sanitaetsrat, Rechnungsrat*, etc."[154] Women in this type of culture were no attenuating influence but rather cultivated a life concentrated on the home, on husband and children, even refraining from participation in community life unless formally identified with their husband's rank and authority.

Proceeding to how this type of society had responded to the pressures for social change in the early twentieth century, particularly following World War I, Parsons stated that the speed of urbanization, industrialization, and so on had procured "a good deal of free-floating aggression, a tendency to unstable emotionalism and susceptibility to emotionalized propaganda appeals and mobilization of affect around various kinds of symbols."[155] What Weber had called the process of rationalization had yielded in Germany secularization of religious values, emancipation from traditional patterns of morality, and "the general tendency of rational criticism to undermine traditional and conservative systems of symbols."[156] Such "emancipated" value patterns, however, were not without problems. Though creating a spirit of modernity, they also eventuated a conspicuous split in the interpretive world view, where both "these polar attitude patterns tend to bear the marks of psychological insecurity, to be 'overdetermined.' This is true on both sides: on the emancipated side in the form of a tendency to a compulsive 'debunking' and denial of any elements of legitimacy to all traditional patterns, on the traditional side of a 'fundamentalist' obstruction to all progress, a traditionalist literalism with strongly emotional attitudes."[157]

At the leftist end of the political spectrum, the outcome was radicalization. During the Weimar years, the labor movement had overly relied on a somewhat compulsive rationalism embracing a futuristic kind of utopianism. At the opposite end of the political spectrum, utopianism had also prevailed, though with retrospective regressive intent. The political right had preached escapism from the reality of

[153] Ibid., p. 227.
[154] Ibid., p. 231.
[155] Ibid., p. 236.
[156] Ibid., pp. 236–237.
[157] Ibid., p. 237.

a society torn in the cataclysms of inflation and political instability. Radical traditionalists had romanticized Germany's mission, anticipating an unrealistic return to the age of the lost Empire. In this scenario, moderate conservatives had been caught haplessly in between the two opposite camps, eventually losing ground to the rising flood of demagogues.

"The element of formalism in the patterning of the basic institutional system of Germany ... seems to indicate a stronger general tendency to romanticism than exists in the Anglo-Saxon countries,"[158] he concluded, specifying again what aspects of social structure set Germany apart from other Western countries, even before Nazism: "The existence of such romantic elements is inherent in the nature of modern society. That, however, their manifestation should become structured in such a pattern and placed in the service of such a movement is understandable only in terms of specific features of the social structure of pre-Nazi Germany which differentiated it from that of other Western countries."[159]

Another text, also written in 1942, couched Parsons's argument concerning Germany's lapse into fascism and future treatment in the terms of a more general theory. His presidential address delivered at the annual meeting of the Eastern Sociological Association on April 25, 1942, on the topic of "Some Sociological Aspects of the Fascist Movements,"[160] involved three points: For one, social theory had at last understood how to approach the issue of threat to civilization:

> Whatever was sound in [the] older attempts, as of a Comte, a Spencer or a Marx, tended to be so intimately bound up with scientifically dubious elements of grandiose speculative construction and methodological assumption and dogma that the whole genus of analysis has tended to become discredited as a result of the general reaction against speculative theories.... Perhaps in the last few years more strongly than at any other time have there been signs that warrant the hope of an ability in the social sciences to apply generalized theoretical analysis to such problems in a thoroughly empirical, tentative spirit which will make possible a cumulative development of understanding.... The very breadth of the problem of diagnosis of the state of a great civilization creates a strong demand for such a method.[161]

Anomie, he knew, procured "susceptibility to the appeal of movements of the general sociological type of fascism,"[162] anomie as lodged in economic and life-world destabilization (urbanization, migration, etc.) during the Industrial Revolution. Exposed to these forces, the individual, on whom a "burden of decision" was thrust to control his own life situation in a world of uncertain fate, tended to "be attracted to movements which can offer them 'membership in a group with a

---

[158] Ibid., p. 239. He finished his article just before the deadline of August 1, and Gurvitch congratulated him on the "very impressive and interesting article," calling it "a brilliant example of sociological analysis in the field." Letter, Gurvitch to Parsons, August 1, 1942; Parsons papers, HUG(FP) – 15.2, box 17.

[159] "Democracy and Social Structure," p. 241.

[160] Originally published in *Social Forces*, Vol. 21, 1942, pp. 138–147; reprinted in *Talcott Parsons on National Socialism*, pp. 203–218.

[161] Ibid., p. 203.

[162] Ibid., p. 207; the next quote is from the same page.

vigorous *esprit de corps* with submission to some strong authority and rigid system of belief, the individual thus finding a measure of escape from painful perplexities or from a situation of *anomie*.' "[163]

He then focused on the larger "process of rationalization" as in the Industrial Revolution. Weber had analyzed rationalization authoritatively, and Spencer and Tönnies had made contractualism a standard for social relations in the newly established industrial world, sustaining individual liberties but also "concentration of the various rights which taken together we call ownership into a single bundle rather than their dispersion."[164] The process as a whole, as a corollary, promoted science and technology and also evoked professional private practice and large-scale organizations based on the principle of functional role specificity. These developments, although undoubtedly positive, had an unanticipated consequence: "The present concern is not whether the patterns of rationality in these different areas are in some sense superior to those they have tended to supplant, but rather the relation of their relatively rapid process of development to the functioning of the social system."[165]

The crux was that "the patterns of rationality" could result in widespread anomie. "It should be clear that their development is in itself perhaps the most important single source of anomie." Social changes engendered through modernization left the masses without clear-cut guidance regarding their own prospects of security in life, and circumstances which had prevailed, for one, in Germany and Italy drove them into the arms of movements offering them an authoritatively reassuring view of the world. One of these movements was Marxism, which concentrated on labor as the mainstay of self-realization and well-being. It harbored utilitarianism and therefore could not offer a viable solution.[166] Another such movement was fascism, equally protesting capitalism's alleged inability to secure justice or equality. He explained, "The 'profit motive' has become the object of deep reproach,"[167] "Inequality, unemployment, and new forms of unjust privilege have been brought into the limelight," and, "This reaction against the 'ideology' of the rationalization of society is one principal aspect at least of the ideology of fascism." [168]

Third, the paper analyzed the event that a fascist movement took over the government. In the situation of takeover of power, the movement presented itself as mass based, due to the fact that insecurity made large parts of the population prone to seek stability in the antidemocratic organization. But as soon as the fascists had a large following, they aligned themselves with big business. They therefore became committed to fulfill industry's vested interests in high production, profit,

---

[163] Ibid.; the quotation was from Theodore W. Sprague, Jehovah's Witnesses: A Study in Group Integration. Ph.D. dissertation, Harvard University, 1942.

[164] "Some Sociological Aspects," p. 208.

[165] Ibid., p. 209; the next quote is from the same page.

[166] "With the shift . . . from 'economic individualism' in the direction of socialism, especially Marxism, certain changes of emphasis on different factors have occurred but a fundamental constancy of cognitive pattern, the 'utilitarian,' has remained." Ibid., p. 210.

[167] Ibid., p. 211; the next quote is from the same page.

[168] Ibid., p. 212.

and absence of strikes. Parsons recalled Drucker's thesis of "the fascist tendency immediately to mobilize the economy in preparation for war."[169]

What, then, could sociology do? What were the possibilities for sociology, keen to help eradicate fascism? He determined: "Sociological... analysis... perhaps... will serve in a humble way to illustrate a direction in which it seems possible to utilize the conceptual tools of sociology in orienting ourselves, at least intellectually, to some of the larger aspects of the tragic social world we live in."[170]

What the possibilities were, with regard to Germany's future in the wake of its defeat, he explored in a radio broadcast on May 21, 1942. He raised the question whether in a future scenario of Germany's redemocratization, the German people should, on principle, be identified with National Socialism, or what difference if any there was between Nazism and Germans. The Nazi movement, he knew, revealed "how grandiose were its plans of conquest, how ruthless its exploitation of every possible means of increasing its power, not only by armed force, but by economic pressure, propaganda, diplomatic trickery and subterfuge and the organization of fifth columns."[171] But should or could the German people be excused from being part of the problem?

Parsons substantiated: "Are the German people of such a character that, given an opportunity they will always and inevitably break out in domineering aggression, or are they merely the innocent victims of a small band of political adventurers?"[172] Both standpoints, he knew, were wrong. Neither was it wise that "the German people must, as a condition of stability, be forever deprived of access to political power and responsibility"; nor could it be true that "all that is necessary is to remove the wicked men and all will be well." Nazi rule had exacerbated trends characteristic of German society since the nineteenth century and before (Prussian militarism, elitism, excessive bureaucracy, and formalism). Furthermore, disorganization and anomie in the wake of World War I, inflation, and eventually depression after 1929 had facilitated the Nazi ascendancy to power at the end of the Weimar Republic. German sentimentalism had added an undue element of romanticism to Nazi prophecies of a cure for all societal ills. In this way, "deep-lying features of German national character and society"[173] had contributed to the country's falling victim to the Nazis.

Five "broad suggestions of policy toward Germany," which he enumerated, resulted, namely, (1) Having ousted the Nazis, the United Nations should aim at Germany's economic and political stability; more than anything else this would preempt tendencies toward a new radicalism fed on German feelings of injustice. (2) Any "un-German" impression of the military government was to be avoided.

---

[169] Ibid., p. 217.
[170] Ibid., p. 218.
[171] "National Socialism and the German People," handwritten manuscript marked "Radio Broadcast, WRUL, May 21 1942"; Parsons papers, HUG(FP) – 15.2, box 10; reprinted in *Talcott Parsons on National Socialism*, cit. p. 219; see also, discussing a similar issue, Albert P. Martin, "The Plain People of Germany," *Yale Review*, vol. 29, 1940, pp. 461–483.
[172] "National Socialism and the German People," p. 219; the next two quotes are from the same page.
[173] Ibid., p. 222.

(3) A firm moral stance was to be taken, based on Christian values. Military government should condemn crimes both as perpetrated by the Nazis and as tolerated by the general population. Thus shame and guilt would be reinforced and eventual restitution could take its course. (4) Prussian militarism as well as the Junker class would have to be thoroughly uprooted. (5) Finally, Germans' romanticizing their nation should become utterly impossible.[174]

At the end of his broadcast on WRUL, he added an audacious suggestion, "The most radical solution would be for the German people as such to cease to be ... a unit [of struggle for power] but be incorporated into a larger one such as a central European Federation."[175]

To be sure, this was no starting point of a debate on Germany's future. In the previous November, Harvard historian Sidney Fay, in the first issue of *Current History*, a journal he had helped found, had already pleaded that "Germany Should Not Be Dismembered."[176] He had warned, "To impose on a defeated Germany a dismemberment of the country would embitter a great many of the best patriotic Germans who are opposed to Hitler and his mad militarism,"[177] suggesting instead, "A federal Germany, composed of a score of fairly equal states, with large powers residing in the federal government, somewhat like what was intended by the Weimar constitution, would not be turning the clock back too far. It would satisfy the majority of Germans who are liberal, democratic, and peaceful, if they are not goaded by a sense of injustice."[178]

"Propaganda and Social Control" – An Early Pattern Variable Scheme

That a national propaganda agency should coordinate American morale, boosting efforts at civilian defense, had become a policy of the Roosevelt administration in 1940.[179] In the summer of 1941, the Office of Facts and Figures had been created, and in September, the COI had been established against German psychological warfare onslaught in the (then, still) European war. Both agencies met with lukewarm or outright skeptical reactions from the public. The problem was, as

---

[174] See ibid., pp. 223–224.
[175] Ibid., p. 224.
[176] Sidney Fay, "Germany Should Not Be Dismembered," *Current History*, vol. 1, November 1941, pp. 12–15.
[177] Ibid., p. 12.
[178] Ibid., p. 15. The reference was to Edwar Ansell Mowrer, *Germany Puts the Clock Back* (New York: Macmillan, 1933), a book widely read which, in late 1933, gave a vivid picture of the infringements on civil rights and destruction of democratic institutions under the Nazis. Upon reading Parsons's article "Democracy and Social Structure in Pre-Nazi Germany," Fay commented, "I find myself in substantive agreement with it." Letter, Fay to Parsons, November 26, 1942; Parsons papers, HUG(FP) – 15.2, box 17.
[179] See Richard W. Steele, "Preparing the Public for War: Efforts to Establish a National Propaganda Agency, 1940–1941," *American Historical Review*, vol. 75, 1970, pp. 1640–1653, and also Allan M. Winkler, *The Politics of Propaganda: The Office of War Information 1942–1945* (New Haven, Conn./ London: Yale University Press, 1978), esp. pp. 1–7.

observers remarked, that American propaganda during World War I had retrospectively come to be judged as an overwhelmingly negative endeavor.[180] Perceiving the urgency of convincing the public to know the nation's mission and join efforts of preparation for intervention, Congress in the summer of 1941 agreed to establish an information agency which was to also handle propaganda.

In June 1942, partly replacing COI, the Office of War Information (OWI) was established[181] whose function was to divulge information on the war as well as on countries with whom the United States was at war. Its aim was not persuasion at any price. Its guiding principle was "a strategy of truth."[182] This noteworthy strategy, informing the public by addressing them as adults capable of thinking for themselves, was unprecedented. In "Issues of Informational Strategy," a contribution to a special issue of *Public Opinion Quarterly* published early in 1943 analyzing the principles and policies of OWI, political scientist Friedrich emphasized that government announcements required truth as the ideal standard. It was the "strategy of truth," which suggested what were justifications for measures involving the public, approximating full disclosure of facts if at all feasible in the circumstances of war. Friedrich held that a population not lied to by its government was by far more willing and able to voluntarily make sacrifices and work toward the common goal of defeating the enemy. If there was an informational strategy that would harm the enemy when it helped the home front, Friedrich wrote, it was "the widely heralded 'strategy of truth,' or 'propaganda of the truth.' It was claimed by men in very high authority that this was the weapon of democracy in the propaganda struggle and was an answer to the question of how to counter the incessant barrage of totalitarian phrases, slogans and word-symbols. Truth, it was said, will fight our battles for us in the great struggle for the mind of mankind."[183]

Analyzing "War Propaganda for Democracy," John Perry of OWI related both propaganda and democracy to postwar peace envisaged. He cited Eleanor Roosevelt, a public figure on whom to hinge the spirit of truth and effort:

> Mrs. Roosevelt put it this way in a recent column, "I hope that in every factory today, and in every Army camp, young people are discussing the kind of world they intend to build when this war is over." And that awareness would be expressed in war production, in fighting strength and in defense of the home front.... Can this be done by propaganda? Not in a fascist state, where propaganda flows only from the government to the people, is backed by force and recognizes no right of reply or dissent. But the purpose of propaganda in a democracy is not to "mold" public opinion or to win popular support for the predetermined programs of a select group of bureaucrats. And so long as people have free access to information and ideas

---

[180] See, as a study cited in this connection, Harold Lasswell, *Propaganda Technique in the World War* (New York: P. Smith, 1938).

[181] Executive Order 9182, "Consolidating Certain War Information Functions into an Office of War Information," June 13, 1942; *Federal Register* (June 16, 1942): 4468–4469.

[182] The phrase was first used by then Librarian of Congress and Director of the Office of Facts and Figures, Archibald MacLeish, at an inaugural dinner at Freedom House on March 19, 1942 (Winkler, *Politics*, p. 13). It became widely used in public speeches and newspaper commentary. MacLeish became a director of OWI.

[183] Friedrich, "Issues of Informational Strategy," *Public Opinion Quarterly*, vol. 7, 1943, pp. 78–79.

from all sources, and the right to discuss among themselves and arrive at their own conclusions, such propaganda would not be more than partially and temporarily successful. But government propaganda has been and can be used to provoke and stimulate group discussion. Information, facts and figures, ideas can be expressed in words and charts or pictures and transmitted through the channels which will ultimately bring them into the conversations of farmers, laborers, housewives and young people.... There is one weapon which the Axis can never use against us, a weapon that has left a record of power and victory in the history of nations. It is the enormous striking power, willingness to sacrifice and lasting determination of free people, who are joined together by the bonds of mutual interests rather than by the rule of tyrants.[184]

Parsons devoted an essay to the problem, written in the summer of 1942. "Propaganda and Social Control" analyzed two problems in conjunction. One was variation of types of propaganda, in defense of democracy and anticipating redemocratization of fascist societies in the postwar world. The other was that a conceptual scheme was needed, to distinguish normative action in a democracy from coercive conformity in an authoritarian society.

The leading question was why Germany and Japan had become aggressive powers while the United States had not. One answer was that the Axis countries had fallen victim to aggressive mass movements whose leaders had seized their governments and managed to destroy all resistance, whereas the United States had remained a democracy. The question raised by this answer was how the population of the Axis countries had come to define their situation in a way that their problems had looked as if they could be solved by electing criminal adventurers into office of what soon became all-powerful governments. The answer was that propaganda had made them distrust their own sense of right and wrong. A certain type of propaganda had spurred them to adopt an antidemocratic, antihumanist ideology, which they felt obliged to believe lest they be accused of lacking commitment to their embattled nations. This invited the question why such a stratagem would not work in the United States. One answer was that its level of "free-floating aggression" was lower owing to a lesser degree of national humiliation such as Germany had experienced after World War I, and of economic chaos following thereafter. However, since some "free-floating aggression" prevailed even in the United States, due to a certain level of ever-present insecurity and disorganization, the question was why its effect was less drastic. The answer invoked American tendencies to strengthen rather than weaken others' motivation. What would sometimes appear as sheer optimism or naiveté in the American mentality and way of life turned out to have a protective effect on democracy. This tendency could be deliberately used, Parsons suggested, to bolster the war effort through "propaganda of reinforcement." Such strategy of truthful information was apt to strengthen awareness of positive and beneficial tendencies in the polity and society. Such propaganda could dwell on human rights and dignity, recognize rationality and intellectualism without debunking others'

---

[184] Cit., John Perry, "War Propaganda for Democracy," *Public Opinion Quarterly*, vol. 6, 1942, p. 443; in similar vein, see William Garber, "Propaganda Analysis – To What Ends?," *American Journal of Sociology*, vol. 48, 1942, pp. 240–245.

emotions and personal feelings, or explain and underscore constitutional division of power and citizens' resultant obligation of everyone to take responsibility.

As one contribution to social theory, the article made two distinctions, which related to types of propaganda, and types of social control. Propaganda comprised two anomic types (revolutionary, debunking), on the one hand, and one befitting integrated society (reinforcement). Likewise, social control had a coercive form characteristic of anomie, and a voluntaristic one belonging to the integrated type society.

Propaganda, in general, was an "attempt, whether or not it is clear to the person what is being done, to change his 'attitudes' or to influence his definition of the situation."[185] Propaganda was "one important mechanism for controlling action – not of course necessarily in the interest of checking deviant tendencies, quite possibly of promoting them – through appeal to the 'subjective,' non-situational aspects of action."

Two of the three types of propaganda belonged to anomie or authoritarianism. "One type," he wrote, "is the 'revolutionary' in that it is oriented to the 'conversion' of people to a pattern of values and definition of the situation which is specifically in conflict with fundamental aspects of the existing basic institutional structure and its attendant values and definitions."[186] And, "A second fundamental type of propaganda is 'disruptive.' Its goal is not winning people over to an alternative set of values and definitions of the situation, but undermining their attachment to the existing institutional system as such."

The third type was "that of 'reinforcement,' of strengthening attachment to the basic institutional patterns and cultural traditions of the society and deliberately and systematically counteracting the very important existing deviant tendencies."[187]

All three types, inasmuch as they were related to policy, aimed at a certain definition of the situation in the society at large. Against this background, propaganda shaded into social control. Among the two types of social control, one was coercive and one voluntary.

Social control, in general, involved "two kinds of channels through which 'pressure' to control behavior may be exerted – whether 'deliberately' by any controlling agency or unconsciously is indifferent for present purposes."[188]

Coercive control, the fascist version, was based on an unrealistic definition of the situation, frequently spelling totalitarianism. For instance, Germany, a social system with a truly irrational official ideology and policy, practiced coercive control where paranoia-like prejudice served as fake justification for persecution. "The Jew" was the supposedly all-pervasive source of Germany's fate, and killing millions of Jews appeared within the Nazi system a logical conclusion. Forms of deviance such as psychosis and criminality appeared acceptable to the Party élite and the S.S., but also hundreds of thousands of party members and even

---

[185] Parsons, "Propaganda and Social Control," in *Talcott Parsons on National Socialism*, p. 249; the next quote is from the same page.
[186] Ibid., p. 267; the next quote is from the same page.
[187] Ibid., p. 268.
[188] Ibid., p. 249.

ordinary citizens, when they participated in or consented to deportations or killings. Crime and attitudinal pathology fused, leading to "attitudes and definitions of the situation" far removed from the logic of voluntaristic control.[189]

Deviant social systems, establishing social control through coercion, interestingly, even in the presence of obvious "elements of strain and disorganization,"[190] would not easily disintegrate. On the contrary, they were held together by mechanisms of authoritarianism and utopianism which stabilized "the fascist alternative"[191] to modern Western industrial and cultural tradition. In contrast, voluntary social control, typical in a democratic setting, meant reciprocity as it was based in the ego, in terms of Freud's theory of personality: "On the one hand, the appeal may be to what psychoanalysts call the 'reality principle,' and the mechanism will then operate through the actual or potential alteration of the situation in which people act."[192]

Such society was based on the reciprocity principle pervading social life. That is, "institutionally established behavior and reaction patterns undoubtedly have, among others, this latent function, that they provide the right stimuli to other persons to prevent them from embarking on too widely deviant trends of behavior."[193] In such society, normality prevailed or was reestablished by institutions such as medicine.

Parsons invoked medical practice to envisage reciprocal relationships with others and institutional patterns that functioned to facilitate actions of mutual service in the interest of a collectivity or community.[194] Indeed, medical practice in liberal society, epitomizing voluntaristic social control, was a paradigmatically important channel to overcome deviance, he explained. Partly insulating patients from their environment, which rendered them harmless, and partly through treating their deviance such that they became able to again fulfill their social roles, medical practice helped to reestablish patients' health.

Behind this explanation of how the medical profession helped to reintegrate a person into his social world stood an idea of how a deviant nation could be transformed into a democratic social order. Interestingly, Parsons explained this prospect preempting the scheme of pattern variables. He distinguished three dimensions of normative orientation of behavior characteristic of the physician as

---

[189] Ibid., p. 260.
[190] Ibid., p. 261.
[191] Ibid., p. 274.
[192] Ibid., p. 249.
[193] Ibid., p. 251.
[194] As mentioned above, Chicago philosopher-sociologist George Herbert Mead, in his classic *Mind, Self, and Society*, had illustrated what a truly democratic society meant using the example of a physician's taking the role of the other. A physician, Mead clarified, practiced a democratic attitude when he cared for his patient in a disinterested manner, as a professional doing his work. Mead held that "equality in a functional sense is possible, and I do not see any reason why it should not carry with it as deep a sense of realization of the other in one's self as the religious attitude. A physician who through his superior skill can save the life of an individual can realize himself in regard to the person he has benefited. I see no reason why this functional attitude should not express itself in the realization of one's self in the other." George Herbert Mead, *Mind, Self, and Society: From The Standpoint of Social Behaviorist*, p. 288.

an agent of voluntaristic social control. They were universalism, functional specificity, and affective neutrality. These three, he suggested, defining certain roles of high prestige in modern democratic societies, generally valued as desirable, could explain what was different in the action orientation typical in a democratic as distinct from authoritarian setting.

He even used the model of medical practice to elucidate how social science had a mission of service to modern society. Medical sciences as well as other fields of learning, particularly the humanities, were lodged within the universities, and "the universities, in short, are the primary formal carriers of the great Western rational-liberal cultural tradition."[195] Academic freedom in the university furnished the social scientist (and the tenured professor in his professional role) with responsibility to society in a crisis. Through relentless efforts at securing objective knowledge, the sociologist was to contribute to constant self-defense of democratic society. Against the onslaught of fascist propaganda and the temptations toward structures of coercive control, the sociologist serving his society would responsibly use the knowledge gained under the protection of his tenure in the university.

It was in this sense that Parsons referred to medical practice when he explained how Germany and Japan had become aggressive nations whereas the United States had not. He thus suggested a model idea of how Western society could become a "socialization agent" for the rehabilitation of Germany or Japan:

> It is the principal thesis of this paper that the structure of Western society in its relation to the functions of social control provides an extraordinary opening for the deliberate propaganda of reinforcement as an agency of control. Just as deliberate psychotherapy in the medical relationship is in a sense simply an extension of functional elements inherent in the structure of the rôle of the physician, so, on the social level, the propaganda of reinforcement would be simply an extension of many of the automatic but latent functions of existing institutional patterns.[196]

"Propaganda and Social Control" was published in November 1942. It marked the end of Parsons's scholarly analysis of National Socialism for the next two years. Only in 1944 did he again write on the topic, then concretely anticipating Germany's (re)democratization.

The reason for his abandoning the sociological work but not, of course, his political effort opposing Nazism, for the time being, might have been a book published in the latter part of 1942. Franz Neumann's *Behemoth*[197] made many a contemporary study obsolete, and Parsons readily adopted its findings although

---

[195] "Propaganda and Social Control," p. 262.
[196] Ibid., p. 269.
[197] Franz Neumann, *Behemoth: The Structure and Practice of National Socialism* (New York: Oxford University Press, 1942). Two years later, after Neumann had accumulated new evidence and found a revised conceptual framework for his approach, he added over a hundred pages of appendix and called the second edition, *Behemoth: The Structure and Practice of National Socialism 1933–1944*. The extended revision of the work became possible after Neumann, in the summer of 1942, joined the Central European Section of the Office of Strategic Services. See Barry Katz, *Foreign Intelligence: Research and Analysis in the Office of Strategic Services 1942–1945* (Cambridge, Mass.: Harvard University Press, 1989).

not its analytical framework. Neumann's work took its title from Thomas Hobbes's second book, presumably written in the 1660s, unknown until 1889. Hobbes's well-known *Leviathan*, first published in 1651 subsequent to replacement of monarchy in England by government of the Long Parliament under Oliver Cromwell, had focused on the semblance of legitimacy accorded the sovereign in an apparent authoritarian régime. Hobbes's *Behemoth*, focusing on the last two years of the decade when utter lawlessness had prevailed after the death of Oliver Cromwell, likened "government" that was nonexistent to a prehistoric monster.

Neumann used the analogy between the chaotic years of the late 1650s and the present in the 1930s/1940s to focus on the demise of any state authority in Nazi Germany. In its place, four all-powerful blocs of vested interests had evolved, he maintained. These power blocs were locked in a struggle to dominate each other, when they nevertheless converged in repressing the population in hitherto unprecedented totality. The power blocs were the higher echelons of the (Prussian and Reich) ministerial bureaucracy linked with the élitist Junker class, the Nazi Party hierarchy, the Armed Forces, and monopolitic Big Industry. Their chaotic and all-pervasive rule was made amenable to the masses through an ideology of the "Grossdeutsches Reich (Living Space and Germanic Monroe Doctrine)," Neumann argued. He saw this rule built on a theory of racial imperialism, which he equated with "German Imperialism" based on a totalitarian race concept. Hitler as charismatic leader in this "leadership state," Neumann elucidated, derived his charisma from the idea of "Blood Purification and Anti-Jewish Legislation."[198] The society in Germany, therefore, was built on the dialectics of murder and yearning for salvation. Germany's four power blocs were locked in deadly struggle for total supremacy.

Parsons, who eagerly adopted Neumann's diagnosis, using it in 1944/1945 in his next article on Germany, was convinced, at the end of 1942 and early in 1943, that it was premature to expect fascism to collapse. Indeed, Neumann's analysis could help explain why that utterly lawless social entity (the term lawlessness was coined for Germany under the Nazis by Friedrich in 1943) would persevere despite its undeniable, forcibly compensated disorder.

When a research assistant of Allport's, Mrs. A. Goldstein from Boston University's department of psychology, conducted an informal opinion poll in the spring of 1943, Parsons was asked the following two questions: (1) Would recent military defeats (El Alamein in North Africa, Stalingrad in Russia) destroy the German population's allegiance to the Nazis, and (2) Was Hitler's or the Nazi Party's popularity waning, which might soon hasten Germany's defeat. He answered in the negative, giving a view of coercive structures in the war situation.

Did allegiance to the Nazis shrink due to military setbacks? He admitted that industrial workers and the churches would be most likely to have or act out antifascist feelings, thus weakening "morale in Germany."[199] But "on structural grounds,"

---

[198] The three quotations are from headlines of chapters or subchapters, respectively.
[199] Letter, Parsons to Mrs. A. Goldstein, March 29, 1943; Parsons papers, HUG(FP) – 15.2, box 9; the next six quotes are from the same location.

he felt, the middle-class, youth, and women who had been "most susceptible to a fanatical Nazi appeal, because of their peculiarly pronounced insecurity" would not submit to a realistic judgment of the situation, however hard their lives became. They had acquired "a vested interest in the Nazi regime" as had, for different reasons, the army. The latter would hold on to the régime, he emphasized, if only because the German army tradition did not allow for insubordination, and a revolt meant that "the honor of the German cause as such and especially of the officer is at stake."

Answering Goldstein's second question, Parsons conceded the Nazi Party's loss of grip on the population. He added, however, "that the principal sentiments upholding morale now are nationalistic in the broadest sense and those associated with the solidarity of that nation in that it is extremely difficult to see any way of saving the situation except continuing to fight." By this he referred to crimes providing a paradoxical rationale for Germans' reluctance to overthrow the Nazis. He wrote:

> An unconscious element underlying the fruitfulness of this appeal to national solidarity in terms of the fear of the consequences of defeat is the accumulation of guilt feelings relative to the events of the whole last decade. There seems to be a great deal of evidence of this both in relation to the Nazis' internal misdeeds and still more to the treatment of the occupied countries since the war. In the present situation, however, there are very strong obstacles to the direct expression of this, and it takes the form of anxiety which probably exaggerates the consequences of defeat and the probable vindictiveness of the victors.

Toward VE-Day
Concerning Re-education

On December 29, 1942, Vice President Henry A. Wallace addressed the nation in a radio speech, entitled "Postwar Policy at Home and Abroad." President Roosevelt had included the issue of postwar reconstruction in his radio address on the occasion of the seventh anniversary of the Philippines Commonwealth Government on November 15, and Wallace now devoted an entire broadcast to it. He said about the Germans: "The German people must learn to un-learn all that they have been taught, not only by Hitler, but his predecessors in the last hundred years, by so many of their philosophers and teachers, the disciples of blood and iron.... We must de-educate and re-educate people for Democracy.... The only hope for Europe remains a change of mentality on the part of the German. He must be taught to give up the century-old conception that his is a master race."[200]

The catchword, then, was re-education. Some educationalists were engaged in discussing the practical problems involved. One suggestion was to place the educational endeavor concerning postwar Germany in an international frame, to preclude repercussions on Americans' own democratic attitudes. In an article in the *New York Times*, Walter M. Kotschnig suggested a permanent International

---

[200] Radio address, Wallace on "Postwar Policy at Home and Abroad," printed in *New York Herald Tribune* (December 29, 1942).

Office of Education attached to the emergent United Nations Organization. He warned, however, from a missionary spirit, "We shall be most effective in the work of educational reconstruction if we rid ourselves of all messianic complexes. We shall do our best work if we learn to work with other countries rather than to impose our ideas upon them."[201]

O. Hobart Mowrer at Harvard raised twenty "Questions to be Asked and Answered," which, to him, concerned the problem of how education could be effective regarding Germany's transformation. Among the questions that Mowrer discussed with American Defense before he incorporated them into an article published in the *Journal of Abnormal and Social Psychology*, were the following, which he raised in a draft paper, among others:

> (2) To what extent must the ideal of "freedom" be correlated with responsibility and restraint?... (4) Can formal education effectively compete with unfavorable economic and political conditions?... (6) To what extent should the citizens of all nations be made aware of the use of displacement (the scapegoat mechanism) as a means of diverting attention from direct to less direct causes of frustration and failure? (7) Is it true that "personal security" is a product of the way in which an individual is socialized, as well as of such environmental factors as are subsumed under the Four Freedoms?... (9) Do literacy and other indices of educational achievement correlate with political wisdom and self-governing capacity? (10) Can it be said that Democracy is to questions of value what science is to questions of fact, or must questions of value be settled on authoritarian or metaphysical grounds?... (12) How can the conception of administration as "service" rather than as "control" be extended not only in the political sphere but also in the schools?... (15) How can the vivifying psychological and social effects of fascism and war (full employment, reduced in-group competition, etc.) be achieved in a Democratic peace-time economy? (16) Do the "fittest" survive only through competition or is cooperation perhaps an even more potent means of ensuring security, productivity, and a meaningful life?... (18) How can educators work most effectively with psychiatrists, social workers, journalists, lawyers, and other professional groups for purposes of reconstruction? (19) Should students be indoctrinated in Democratic ideals or is Democratic indoctrination a contradiction in terms? (20) In what new ways may educational techniques and objectives be adapted to special opportunities created by the war?[202]

---

[201] *New York Times* (December 13, 1942); see also I. L. Kandel and W. M. Kotschnig, "The Messianic Complex," *School and Society* (February 6, 1943).

[202] O. H. Mowrer, "Educational Considerations in Making and Keeping the Peace," draft paper for discussion in American Defense Morale Group meeting. The draft paper, possibly written in January 1943, is among the Parsons papers, HUG(FP) – 42.45.4, box 1. The references which Mowrer made to contemporary analysis, when he listed knowledge that could be used to answer the twenty questions, were (a) Erich Fromm, *Escape from Freedom* (New York: Rinehart, Winston and Holt, 1941); Harold Lasswell, *World Politics and Personal Insecurity*; (b) William Temple, *Christianity and the Social Order* (New York: Penguin Books, 1942); (c) Alfred D. Simpson et al., *Schools of the People: Report of the Barrington Survey* (Cambridge, Mass.: Harvard Graduate School of Education, 1943); (d) Gustav Bychowsky, "Psychological Reconstruction in Post-war Europe," *New Europe* (August 1942); and (e) Clarence Leuba, "Psychological Aspects of International Reconstruction," *Journal of Applied Psychology* (August 1942). Mowrer's paper was published in a revised version in *Journal of Abnormal and Social Psychology*, vol. 38, 1943, pp. 174–182.

Mowrer's catalogue of questions concerned themes which, since 1941, involved three disciplines in the discussion of postwar prospects: psychology, psychiatry, and political science.

In 1943, psychologist Kurt Lewin, an emigré, wrote articles on "Cultural Reconstruction"[203] for Germany, and "The Special Case of Germany."[204] As he had done since 1939,[205] he maintained that Germans had never learned how to elect leaders nor work together to accomplish a task in a group. Germans, in their cultural heritage, only knew group structures that were either authoritarian or laissez-faire, and literally had to learn what was a democratic structure.[206] An American contribution to German redemocratization, wrote Lewin, could be, in addition to political change, cultural change in postwar Germany through collaboration between Germans and non-Germans (e.g., Americans) in what he labeled self-reeducation. Lewin hoped that experiencing democratic group life might spur a "process of self-reeducation."[207]

The psychiatric theme, a national issue for attention in 1943, was the German cultural trend of paranoia. Richard A. Brickner, neuropsychiatrist at Columbia University, took as a point of departure the psychiatric viewpoint that typical German cultural reaction patterns were remarkably similar to paranoid psychosis.[208] Brickner,[209] collaborating with cultural anthropologist Margaret Mead (who advised him on the relationship between cultural values, family structures, and general personality tendencies), focused on four characteristics of German politics and culture to elaborate his diagnosis. He ventured that the German world view resembled, on a group level, the perception of a paranoid adroit to defend delusions against any apparent foe, if need be through murder. The characteristics were (1) megalomania, that is, a heightened sense of a mission to heal the world from ills; (2) absolute demand for German leadership; (3) persecution complex; and (4) retrospective distortion of facts (mystification), as in the widespread conviction that World War I had not been lost but ended by a "stab in the back" when Social Democrats had established "un-German" democracy.

---

[203] Kurt Lewin, "Cultural Reconstruction," *Journal of Abnormal and Social Psychology*, vol. 38, 1943, pp. 166–173.

[204] Kurt Lewin, "The Special Case of Germany," *Public Opinion Quarterly*, vol. 7, 1943, pp. 555–566.

[205] See, for instance, Kurt Lewin, Ronald Lippitt, and Ralph K. White, "Patterns of Aggressive Behavior in Experimentally Created 'Social Climates,' " *Journal of Social Psychology*, vol. 10, 1939, pp. 271–299.

[206] He cited Alex Bavelas, "Morale and the Training of Leaders," in *Civilian Morale*, Goodwin Watson, ed. (Boston: Houghton Mifflin, 1942), pp. 143–165, but could equally have referred to Alex Bavelas and Kurt Lewin, "Training for Democratic Leadership," *Journal of Abnormal and Social Psychology*, vol. 37, 1942, pp. 115–119. Lewin, an emigré who had held a professorship at the University of Berlin, was bicultural and could therefore discern the crucial dearth in German group attitudes and images.

[207] Lewin, "Special Case," p. 566.

[208] Richard A. Brickner, "The German Cultural Paranoid Trend," *American Journal of Orthopsychiatry*, vol. 12, 1942, pp. 611–632.

[209] Brickner, *Is Germany Incurable?* (Philadelphia: Lippincott, 1943).

What could be done? Psychiatry, Brickner explained, could corroborate the findings of cultural anthropology that national character had little to do with genetic endowment, but depended on cultural settings instead. He knew that re-education had become the most successful therapy for paranoid psychotics since the 1930s. The answer to the title question of *Is Germany Incurable?* was that re-education was a promising road for postwar Germany's conversion to democracy. Re-education could overcome Germany's paranoid culture trend. Under protection of the Allies, the democratic or "clear" elements of the "Germany group" could be made a starting point for eventual democratization of postwar Germany.[210]

Political science took a different viewpoint. In "The German People and the Postwar World,"[211] election statistics until the very end of democratic rule proved that a majority of Germans had never voted for the Nazis or, in fact, a nationalistic party. This suggested that once freed from Nazi rule, Germans would revert to democratic, non-nationalist parties by majority vote. Friedrich, in *The New Belief in the Common Man*,[212] argued that democracy had a strong appeal of its own, the most humane form of government yet invented. The task of the future was to introduce democracy through military government. "Conceived as it is in terms of the law of war, it will be in a position to re-establish the rule of law in lands which have been deprived of that first condition of self-rule. In thus re-establishing the government of laws, and not of men, American military government will make a substantial contribution toward the re-establishment of self-rule among the enslaved peoples of the world."[213]

Friedrich, as director of the School of Overseas Administration at Harvard in 1943–1945, collaborated with Parsons in the effort to help prepare Germany's democratic reconstruction. In the preparatory phase for the program to train future military government officers, Parsons drafted a memorandum for the first meeting of the steering committee (the minutes of which are preserved in the Harvard Archives), on February 11, 1943, "Memorandum on a Possible Sociological Contribution to the Proposed Training Program for Military Administration."[214] He outlined what sociology could achieve for preparing future military government officers, referring to his "Occupied Countries Study," for which he still sought funding. He also cited evidence from research on the social structures of various European countries as well as the United States which he had accumulated through his teaching sociology at Harvard for more than a decade. The memorandum

---

[210] For details on the spectacular success of Brickner's book, see Gerhardt, "Re-Education als Demokratisierung der Gesellschaft Deutschlands durch das amerikanische Besatzungsregime," *Leviathan*, vol. 27, 1999, pp. 355–385, esp. pp. 364–368.

[211] Sydney L. W. Mellen, "The German People and the Postwar World. A Study Based on Election Statistics, 1871–1933," *American Political Science Review*, vol. 37, 1943, pp. 601–625; the article was among the reading materials assigned to the Area Specialized Training Program of the School of Overseas Administration at Harvard, for classes which Parsons taught in 1943–1944.

[212] Friedrich, *The New Belief in the Common Man* (Boston: Little, Brown and Co., 1942).

[213] Friedrich, "Military Government as a Step Towards Self-Rule," *Public Opinion Quarterly*, vol. 7, 1943, p. 541.

[214] Parsons's memorandum is being preserved in the Harvard University Archives, under the call number of UA V 663.8, box 2.

insisted on grounding military government preparation in proper social science research: "The most fruitful research program would consist in studies of the social structure of a series of different countries in terms of a common conceptual scheme in such a way as to promote systematic comparative analysis."

Parsons became a staff member of the School of Overseas Administration during its planning period and taught there from its beginning. After two months, he became chairman of the Planning Committee of the Foreign Area and Language Program, Central European Program, where his responsibility was for instruction as well as personnel.

His lecture topics: institutional structure of Europe (seven lectures); German universities; the status of liberal professions in Germany; the Protestant church, the Catholic church; the press in Nazi Germany; public meetings in Germany; anti-Semitism (three lectures); etiquette in personal relations; etiquette in business and official relations; family observances; social and psychological aspects of authority; the special role of authority [in human relations]; why the Nazis won (two lectures); the German people and its character; and family, tradition, and customs in Italy (with anthropologist Clyde Kluckhohn), among others.[215]

A research proposal which he prepared with Kluckhohn on German and Italian family systems was drafted with military government in occupied countries in mind.[216] The project wished to answer the questions, among others: "(1) What are the respective roles of husband and wife, both within the family and in relation to outsiders, with respect to authority, initiative, and the mutual attitudes expected? In particular, what is the range of independence and responsibility accorded to women and what are its limits? . . . (7) What sentiments of family loyalty might most easily be disturbed by foreigners who did not understand the local situation?"[217]

One part of the proposal was entitled "Practical Utilities," whose draft version contained the following paragraph (stating the proviso, "Such knowledge is undoubtedly of the greatest practical utility to both the military and the civilian administrator"):

> For instance if food is to be distributed or rationed it is essential to know what groups ordinarily pool their resources and what individuals are accustomed to take responsibility in such matters. Public relations releases need to take account of the particular sentiments associated with the family. Punishments will have very different repercussions on others than the particular offender according to the nexus of kinship relations in which he is placed. Any program affecting children or young people will need to take account of traditional conceptions of parental jurisdiction. Where in this country it might be all right to work through the school without direct reference to parents in another it might be essential to secure parental cooperation directly. In general knowledge of

---

[215] For details, see the material in the Harvard University Archives, HUE 67.143.75.5.

[216] The proposal was unsuccessful. A letter from the chairman of the Harvard University Committee on Research in the Social Sciences, John D. Black, dated September 28, 1943, acknowledged that Parsons had withdrawn the application but also that no member of the committee had approved the project.

[217] "Research Project for the Study of the German and Italian Family Systems," research proposal submitted by Parsons and Kluckhohn. Parsons papers, HUG(FP) – 15.2, box 9, pp. 2–3.

the customary location of authority and influence is essential to administrative efficiency. Any strains of consistency for a nation as a whole which can be established would naturally simplify the administrator's task but would in addition also have an important bearing on broader questions of policy toward that nation. For instance in predicting reactions to various kinds of propaganda appeal.[218]

In July 1943, Italy – which was to seek a truce with the Allies – was occupied by the Nazis, thus opening up another front when the Allies entered via Sicily. Hartshorne, who was now a member of the Psychological Warfare Division, joining a team that interrogated German prisoners of war, first in Algier and subsequently in the Italian campaign, commented in his letters to Parsons on the amazing apathy and docility of captive Germans.[219]

Parsons, in a letter to a former teaching assistant who was working in an army prisoner-of-war camp involved in the program for teaching Germans democratic attitudes and organization, assured that "a good deal of pretty tough-minded and realistic thinking is called for." He detailed what he meant:

> [It] seems to me exceedingly unlikely that the society of Europe in our lifetime will be at all pleasant to look at from almost any point of view. I personally feel that order and security will have to be the primary keynotes, and we simply cannot undertake to implement any very large humanitarian ideal. When you add up the terrific disorganization there is bound to be with the fact that every important move in Europe will have to reckon with the sensitivities of the Russians, I don't think we ought to build up the idea that we are going to introduce an Utopia over there.[220]

"Germany After the War"

On March 29, 1944, a Joint Committee on Post-war Planning, on behalf of the American Psychiatric Association, the American Orthopsychiatric Association, the American Branch of the International League against Epilepsy, the National Committee for Mental Hygiene, the American Association of Mental Deficiencies, the American Neurological Association, the American Psychoanalytic Association, and the American Society for Research in Psychosomatic Problems, invited Parsons to a "Conference on Germany After the War." It was "to approach the German situation as a cultural rather than purely political and economic problem, employing what insight the psychologically oriented disciplines – anthropology, psychiatry and psychology and some branches of sociology – can supply." [221]

---

[218] "Research Project" draft version, typed, p. 3 (the paragraph was erased from the proposal submitted to the Harvard Committee on Research in the Social Sciences). For concerns related to those discussed in the paragraph, see Katherine Thomas, *Women in Nazi Germany* (London: Victor Gollancz, 1943).

[219] See his correspondence, among the Parsons papers, HUG(FP) – 15.2, box 11.

[220] Letter, Parsons to Charles O. Porter, February 15, 1944; Parsons papers, HUG(FP) – 15.2, box 15.

[221] Letter, Lawrence K. Frank to Parsons, March 29, 1944; Parsons papers, HUG(FP) – 15.2, box 10.

The conference was organized by Brickner, the psychiatrist.[222] He proposed in the preparatory statement[223] to discuss three issues, inviting pre-conference written statements from participants, consultants, and others:

 I. What has German culture made of the German people?
 II. How may the German people be expected to react to defeat?
 III. What methods and procedures could be utilized for securing the re-education and re-culturalization of the German people? Can the American people... especially after their anger has cooled, carry out a corrective program for Germany?

The corrective program, as it was tentatively named, was to involve German disarmament and punishment for German war guilt, but also German participation in international communication and transportation, scientific advance, as well as economic measures such as deindustrialization but also German access to their own raw materials. Last but not least, the attitudes of American personnel in the military government toward German crimes and betterment as well as relief operations such as the United Nations Rehabilitation and Relief Agency (UNRRA) were to be discussed.

At the first meeting, a controversy developed between psychoanalysts Kubie and French. Their positions clashed in regard to whether destructive elements in German attitudes had completely replaced constructive ones, as Kubie insisted, or whether resocialization of the Germans could be achieved, as Mead (whose position French took) supposed. The latter was supported in a written statement by Alexander, who reasoned that Germany's authoritarianism needed to be changed urgently.[224]

---

[222] Among the invited participants of the conference were psychiatrists Lauretta Bender, Carl Binger, Adolf Meyer, and Douglas A. Thom, neurologist Tracy J. Putnam, clinical physician Alvan L. Barach, psychoanalysts Franz Alexander, Thomas French, and Lawrence S. Kubie, psychologists Richard Crutchfield and Gardner Murphy, philosopher Harry S. Overstreet, anthropologist Margaret Mead, and sociologists Theodore Abel and Parsons. Among invited consultants and guests were Gustav Bychowsky, Hans Ernst Fried, Heinz Hartmann, I. L. Kandel, Walter Kotschnig, Ernst Kris, Rhoda Metraux, Koppel Pinson, Sigrid Schultz, Sigrid Undset, and Robert Waelder. Special assistance was acknowledged in the conference report from, among others, Erik Erikson, Erich Fromm, Kurt Lewin, and Laura Thompson. Ruth Benedict took part in the first part of the conference and contributed a comment toward its concluding memorandum. The original plan was to have two two-day meetings on April 29–30, and June 3–4, 1944. However, as the discussions became heated, further meetings in between were scheduled on May 6, and 13–15, changed to 20–21. Parsons took part only in the first and last of these but received the material regarding the May meetings.

[223] "Conference on Germany After the War. April 29th and 30th, and June 3rd and 4th, 1944. New York City," statement signed by Lawrence K. Frank (National Committee for Mental Hygiene), Edward Humphreys (American Association for Mental Deficiency), George Stevenson (American Orthopsychiatric Association), Douglas A. Thom (American Psychiatric Association), and Edwin Weiss (American Society for Psychosomatic Research); Parsons papers, HUG(FP) – 15.2, box 10.

[224] Franz Alexander, M.D. "Conference on Germany After the War. Suggestions Concerning the Joint Statement Prepared at Conference April 29th–30th" (working paper, mimeo); Parsons papers, HUG(FP) – 15.2, box 10. Alexander had emigrated from Germany in 1930.

Parsons, in his memorandum entitled "The Problem of Intervention in German Society," which was written after the April meeting, compared the positions taken by Kubie and French when he adopted Alexander's main point. "It seems to me," he observed,

> that Dr. Kubie thinks of the problem too exclusively in psychiatric terms. He perhaps, tends to forget that the successful psychiatric treatment of a child, like any patient, is not conditioned by the specific procedures of the psychiatrist alone. The great bulk of the patient's time is spent in a series of social situations over which the psychiatrist has only partial control at best. The society in which most psychiatrists operate is, within limits, relatively normal and the influences his original social relationships exercise on the patient in large part cooperate with the psychiatrist, rather than thwarting him. Indeed, the primary goal of his therapy is to promote adequate adaptation to the expectations of others in the patient's social situation.[225]

The idea of dualist German national character structure was what Mead proposed. Her memorandum entitled "Regularities in German National Character,"[226] written in the summer of 1944, described Germans' strong status orientation and superordination-subordination, their tendency to aggressive action, and impersonal attitudes toward other individuals as main targets for consideration for change. She suggested the German national character composed of two partly contradictory tendencies. They were, on the one side, a Type A typical pattern that originated in the relationship of the child to his mother, producing features that made Germans "emotional, idealistic, active, romantic" – a pattern which "may be constructive or destructive and antisocial."[227] On the other side, a Type B typical pattern originated in the father as punishing figure in the authoritarian family, the resultant typical attitudes of which gave Germans an "orderly, hardworking, hierarchy-preoccupied, methodical, submissive, gregarious, materialistic" zest. Mead felt that the two components were to a certain extent irreconcilable. Nazism, she ventured, had welded the two types into one dualist structure: "Nazism made possible more type A behavior after adolescence than any previous regime. Type A behavior is inclined to anarchy, destruction; type B . . . to obsessiveness, accumulation, sado-masochism. Types A and B are only mutually exclusive at any given moment; in

---

[225] "Memorandum – The Problem of Intervention in German Society," p. 1; Parsons papers, HUG(FP) – 15.2, box 10.
[226] Parsons thought that Mead was the sole author of the memorandum. See his letter to Perry, July 21, 1944, HUG(FP) – 15.2, box 15. Mead, however, kept a draft among her papers preserved in the Library of Congress which carried the names of five authors, namely Ruth Benedict, Geoffrey Gorer, Mead, Rhoda Metraux, and Alfred Metraux. See Library of Congress, Margaret Mead Papers, box 31, "Institute of Intercultural Studies," Folder: "Conference on Germany . . . Reports." Benedict wrote a "Comment on 'Statement on Regularities in German National Character'" where she referred to the "joint anthropological memo on German character structure." See Parsons papers, HUG(FP) – 15.2, box 10.
[227] "Regularities in German National Character," in "Germany After the War. Round Table – 1945," *American Journal of Orthopsychiatry*, Vol. 11, 1945, p. 392; the next quote is from the same page. Brickner's "Report on the Conference on Germany After the War," originally "Confidential," was published under that inconspicuous title in 1945.

the course of a life history varying amounts of each type will be manifested in different situations."[228]

In a letter to Parsons dated May 12, Mead acknowledged that her and Parsons's positions taken at the conference were remarkably similar. She rephrased the French-Kubie controversy, in three questions: (1) Could a society be cured by the imposition of outside force? (2) Was there enough interchange between the individual and society that an influence exerted upon social institutions was equally effective as a planned change of methods of individuals' socialization? (3) Was German character structure a fixed given, derived from centuries of unchanged cultural practices, such that the duality of national character would appear and reappear no matter how much its disappearance would be on the agenda of controlled social change? She doubted, as she said in her letter which answered Parsons's ideas, whether it was enough to "expedite industrialization, the emancipation of women, etc., and rely on this basically sound 'basic character' to express itself."[229] Parsons replied to Mead on May 19, referring to her own theory of dualist mentality:

> Whether the practical action is dangerous or not depends on how far the situation favors the expression of one or another of the possibilities. I feel for instance, that much could be accomplished if the German nation could cease to be a unit in a competitive struggle for power however that may be achieved. I think for instance there is reason to believe that Sweden with a similar Lutheran background would and probably in the time of Gustavus Adolphus and Charles XII did show similar aggressive tendencies. But once out of the running in the competition of the great powers the tendency was for the orderly, industrious, conscientious component to be dominant and to create situations where the dominance-submission pattern gradually faded away. I should think much the same could be said about the German-Americans who have been conspicuously "good citizens" in the American environment. Thus, I should think the general nature of the problem was pretty clear.[230]

On September 21, Parsons sent his thoroughly revised memorandum to Brickner, apologizing for its length and explaining that it contained a general theoretical introduction and application to the German case.[231] On September 28, he sent it to Mead who made a number of suggestions for change of minor points in a letter dated October 28. Brickner responded in November, when he informed Parsons that his text had been dismembered. The theoretical part was now Appendix V among ten appendixes of Brickner's final report prepared for the Marshall Provost General's Office. These appendixes carried no names of authors, and Parsons's text partly was Appendix V (which contained only his "Analytical Introduction") and partly a number of inserts interspersed with other text, which dealt with Political and Economic Rehabilitation of Germany. Brickner wrote to Parsons about cutting his memorandum, "There were some parts of it which were covered in other places, and there were a few spots in which it didn't seem that we could speak as representing

---

[228] Mead, "Regularities in German National Character," p. 393.
[229] Letter, Mead to Parsons, May 12, 1944; Parsons papers, HUG(FP) – 15.2, box 10.
[230] Letter, Parsons to Mead, May 19, 1944, p. 1; Parsons papers, HUG(FP) – 15.2, box 10.
[231] Letter, Parsons to Brickner, September 21, 1944; Parsons papers, HUG(FP) – 15.2, box 10.

the feeling of the conference as a whole – such things as the idea of encouraging re-industrialization of Germany."[232]

In his reply, Parsons emphasized why he had taken the position he had: "In the terms in which I analyzed the situation, most alternatives about which people are thinking would tend to have a 'regressive' effect to consolidate and confirm the patterns which have [been] the source of the trouble rather than to lead away from them."[233]

"The Problem of Controlled Institutional Change"[234] consisted of two parts: Its "Analytical Introduction" located the sociological focus in the "definition of the situation" in a society. The collective dimension of meaning structure in a society was a locale for peaceful change from a charismatic-type to a rational legal-type social system, depending on understanding cultural forces in the social system.

The theory of society, sketched in the "Analytical Introduction," identified points of leverage for institutional change in postwar Germany through military government. Institutions, he began, were the "backbone" of the social system. Their realization in social action had two inputs – the motivational forces and the situation. These converged in the definition of the situation. If change aimed at remodeling a certain definition of the situation, it had to be based on knowledge of what were the elements of rigidity or flexibility in an institutional structure. "Vested interests" lodged with existing institutions could otherwise be the seedbed for blocking change. As a strategy, the potential for flexibility could be strengthened, producing new or different definitions of the situation in due course.[235] Channels of change needed to be explored carefully, lest the population react negatively to the policy. Such backlash, naturally, would render reformist policy ineffective, which, in the case of Germany, would prolong the threat to the world.

He distinguished between a democratic and a fascist type society. Democratic societies, though sufficiently integrated, nevertheless harbored conflict and tension, even prejudice, elitism, and fundamentalism; universalism and achievement orientation, indeed, were continuously challenged by tendencies to particularism and ascription. On the other side, fascist societies contained elements of universalism and achievement valuation. On that note, Parsons maintained that many of Germany's "most important culture patterns and structural elements shade imperceptibly into those on the democratic side."[236] The Nazis had eradicated some democratic orientations incompletely, no doubt. To be sure, this had happened

---

[232] Letter, Brickner to Parsons, November 13, 1944; Parsons papers, HUG(FP) – 15.2, box 10.
[233] Letter, Parsons to Brickner, November 17, 1944; Parsons papers, HUG(FP) – 15.2, box 10. For further clarification of the thought, see below.
[234] Parsons's memorandum, which Brickner shortened in his conference report, was published in full length in *Psychiatry*, vol. 8, 1945, pp. 79–101; reprinted in *Talcott Parsons on National Socialism*, pp. 291–324.
[235] As an example of a definition of a hermetic, inflexible situation effective for the actor (widely beyond Western reasonableness), he referred to Japan's Kamikaze fliers. In the event, in the last phase of the war, some three hundred Allied warships were sunk by Kamikazes, killing some fifteen thousand troops.
[236] "The Problem of Controlled Institutional Change," p. 298.

under pressure, which could mean that some of the changes imposed by the Nazis could soon be reversed by military government policy.

Where was such policy to start? Addressing "The Case of Germany," he invoked Mead's distinction between the A and B components of German character structure:

> In the traditional pre-Nazi Germany society it is overwhelmingly the *B* component which has become institutionalized. The *A* component arises from two principal interdependent sources: certain features of the socialization process in the German family, and the tensions arising from life in that type of institutional order. It is expressed in romantic, unrealistic emotionalism and yearnings.... The peculiarity of the Nazi movement is that it has harnessed this romantic dynamism to an aggressive, expansionist, nationalistic political goal – and an internal revolution – and has utilized and subordinated all the motives behind the *B* component as well.... The first task of a program of institutional change is to disrupt this synthesis and create a situation in which the romantic element will again find an apolitical form of expression.[237]

The dualistic character structure, together with German "formalism" (which Parsons had analyzed in his essay on pre-Nazi German social structure), and remainders of feudal or quasi-feudal mentality (which he had analyzed in "Some Sociological Aspects of Fascist Movements") were to be overcome, specifying three objectives:

> To eliminate the specific Nazi synthesis of the two major components of German character, or to divert it from its recent distinctive channels of expression if this is possible. To eliminate, or at least seriously reduce, the structural role of the hierarchical, authoritarian and formalistic elements in the "conservative" German institutional structure – in particular its focus on the army and the military class should be broken. To displace the conservative pattern and to reduce the tension by systematically fostering those elements of the pattern of modern Germany, especially of industrialism, which are closest to their counterparts in the democratic countries.[238]

Three types of social control – regressive, permissive, and direct – were to achieve these objectives.[239]

Regressive control concerned the four power blocs as outlined by Neumann. The Nazi Party was to be ousted completely. The Junker class was to be dispersed or repressed, most likely through Soviet occupation policy. The military class was to be broken up and the army undone in the wake of its decisive defeat. The civil service and bureaucracy were to be stripped of militarism, elitism, and formalism.

---

[237] Ibid., p. 300.
[238] Ibid., p. 302.
[239] Reprinted versions of the article in Parsons's various editions of *Essays in Sociological Theory* and also in *Politics and Social Structure* changed the term from *regressive* to *representational* control. In my view, the use of the term "regressive" related to reverting regression into patrimonialism of Nazism as a type of authority as explained in "Max Weber and the Contemporary Political Crisis." The version reprinted in *Talcott Parsons on National Socialism* used the original version of 1944/1945.

Big industry, to be sure, had only relatively recently come under the Nazi spell.[240] This, Parsons implied, made industry whose "intrinsic characteristics" of universalism and achievement were to be fully restored, if not decisively enhanced, a chosen locale for strategic social change. That such change simultaneously would strip German industry of its "integration with a militaristic state and conservative class structure"[241] could spell hope for the future.

Permissive control meant to facilitate acceptable changes. Parsons scrutinized four institutions as potential venues. Direct interference with the family would, he felt, belie the values of privacy and freedom. Influencing education would arouse boomerang reactions from a population loath to be instructed what to think. Government, in turn, would all too easily become distorted into an Allied import to be contrasted unfavorably with undemocratic indigenous German traditions. The only sphere for successful institutional control was, he found, the economic-occupational system. It was the least unproblematic on all three criteria of effectiveness of change, salience, feasibility, and inconspicuousness.

A change in the economic-occupational system from ascription to achievement, he ventured, would have beneficial repercussions on the other institutional systems as well. That is, the family would benefit from the father's self-determination in the workplace; the school would benefit since teachers would have influence over their own work and could apply their own judgment in their teaching; and government would equally benefit in many evident ways. At any rate, the economic-occupational sphere was an institutional realm where universalism-achievement type values prevailed in a seemingly natural fashion; such values were then imperceptibly strengthened and did not need to be introduced from the cold. In this way, economic liberty and security could establish a focus of democratic orientation beyond the political sphere, effective cultural reorientation. The pattern of the Weimar Republic would disappear, which, with its solely political focus of democracy, had proved vulnerable to nondemocratic mass movements.

He emphasized two advantages of the proposed change: It would reduce the conservatism of the urban middle class and the rural population, and it would reduce formalism. When status would be made a consequence of achievement rather than occupational promotion hinged on submission to superiors, as had been the pre-Nazi as well as Nazi pattern, the Germans' mentality would noticeably change in the direction of democratic attitudes.[242]

Considering American policy plans in the fall of 1944 to deindustrialize Germany, Parsons's conclusions may have sounded outrageous not only to Brickner:

> The essential thing is that there should be a policy of fostering a highly productive, full-employment, expanding economy for Germany. The inherent tendencies

---

[240] See, for details, L. Hamburger, *How Nazi Germany Has Controlled Business* (Washington, D.C.: The Brookings Institution, 1943).

[241] "The Problem of Controlled Institutional Change," p. 306.

[242] Ibid., p. 313.

of the modern, industrial economy are such that if this is achieved its influence on institutional change will be automatically in the right direction. Conversely, tendencies to particularism, the breakdown of functional specialization, overemphasis on group solidarity are overwhelmingly defensive reactions to the insecurity attendant on a contracting field of opportunity. It is not modern industrialism as such, but its pathology and the incompleteness of its development which fosters these phenomena.[243]

Direct control, as the third type of social control, dealt with outlawing anti-Semitism and other ideological doctrines. To be sure, the role of " 'ideas' in shaping social structures and culture patterns"[244] was more than precarious. The question was, How much and what kind of propaganda of reinforcement was called for? Obvious praise of American business successes, at any rate, would only arouse German prejudice against American materialism. Because what Mead had called the type A and type B components of the German national character were to be split up, and the former discouraged and the latter redirected, no new creed was to be established that could attract fundamentalist hopes, not even in economic prosperity. He suggested:

> Western civilization as a whole has been a moral community historically – although never anywhere nearly perfectly integrated.... Despite differentiated versions, distortions, and contradictory values there, these values are by no means dead in Germany.... A cautious propaganda appeal to these sentiments may be considered – by word and deed. In doing so, ... the appeal should as far as possible be *dissociated* from anything to do with the status of the German nation as a unit. It should be made to the rights and duties of persons or citizens and groups as such, not as Germans, and to impersonal patterns such as truth or freedom. The obviousness of the inclusion of Germans under the universality of such values should be the main context.[245]

The institutional changes, Parsons cautioned, might be slow nonetheless. They were to have their effects only over years or decades. "Cautious" appeals might occasionally be made using propaganda of the right kind. Positive reinforcement might be given by recourse taken to "the values of Christianity and certain... related secular values – such as those of science and free inquiry, the dignity and freedom of the person, even equality of opportunity." These appeals were to picture Germans as members of humankind, which included everybody. He expected that Germans who had denied their victims participation in these values under Nazism would set free their presumptively latent, all-pervasive guilt feelings. That the latter existed he did not doubt, and their release would bring Germans closer to the spirit of the Western societies.

Transformation from charismatic dictatorship to rational-legal type democracy, therefore, was feasible through careful application of sociological knowledge, he envisaged. His suggestion was not to mastermind change through "imposition" of

---

[243] Ibid., p. 314.
[244] Ibid., p. 315.
[245] Ibid., p. 321; the next quote is from the same page.

democracy by policy authorities. But in light of the dichotomy of social action structures ranging from anomie to integration, he advised to goad Germans' own definition of their situation in their society away from anomie and coercion and toward integration and voluntary commitments.

Upon its publication, the article in *Psychiatry* drew criticism and praise. Friedrich – with whom Parsons prepared an unsuccessful research proposal concerning "Patterns and Dynamics of the German Social Structure," in November 1944[246] – found the argument misplaced. It bothered him that Parsons used the idea of national character, of which he, Friedrich, strongly disapproved.[247] Parsons replied that it had provided a useful hinge to introduce his policy recommendations regarding reindustrialization, as a better strategy than what was widely understood as a promising road to German re-education.[248]

Wilbert Moore, who co-edited an anthology for which, in the spring of 1945, Parsons wrote his first genuinely theoretical paper since 1938, praised him for thoroughness and depth: "It has more meat per square inch than anything I've seen lately," he complimented him. "It makes most of the discussions of 'what to do with Germany' seem superficial if not irrelevant."[249]

Prejudice

In May 1944, the American Jewish Committee organized a conference on anti-Semitism,[250] bringing together, among others, emigré scholars Theodor Adorno, Edward Bibring, Max Horkheimer, Paul Lazarsfeld, Kurt Lewin, and Frederick Pollock, with American social scientists Gordon Allport, John Dollard, Clyde Kluckhohn, Albert McClung Lee, Rensis Likert, and Lloyd Warner. The objective was to work out a pragmatic approach on how to deal with anti-Semitism in America.

Another occasion for discussing anti-Semitism was the 1944 meeting of the *Conference of Science, Philosophy and Religion in Their Relation with the Democratic Way of Life*. The Conference chose the general title "Unity and Difference in the Modern World." Parsons chose for his paper the session "Group Tension as a Social Problem," where he proposed to speak on the topic, "Racial and Religious Differences as Factors in Group Tensions"[251] (other speakers on the same panel were Lawrence K. Frank and Harry Overstreet).

---

[246] See Barry Katz, *Foreign Intelligence* (1989), p. 204.
[247] Letter, Friedrich to Parsons, April 16, 1945; Parsons papers, HUG(FP) – 15.2, box 9.
[248] Letter, Parsons to Friedrich, May 7, 1945; Parsons papers, HUG(FP) – 15.2, box 9.
[249] Letter, Moore to Parsons, May 1, 1945; Parsons papers, 15.2, box 13. The formulation hinted at Louis Nizer, *What To Do With Germany* (Chicago: Ziffe-Davis, 1944; 2d edition, 1945), a bestseller at the time.
[250] "Conference on Research on Anti-Semitism, May 20 and 21, 1944, New York City"; Parsons papers, HUG(FP) – 15.2, box 4.
[251] The essay was published in the conference proceedings which carried the title *Approaches to National Unity*, edited by Lyman Bryson, Louis Finckelstein, and Robert McIver (New York: Harper and Brothers, 1945), pp. 183–199. It is reprinted in *Talcott Parsons on National Socialism*, pp. 275–290.

He began with an inconspicuous remark:

> Not so long ago the prevailing temper of the Western world was one of what we now feel to be naively utopian optimism. Economic and technological progress, a rapidly rising standard of living for everyone, were thought of as combined with increasing tolerance and internal and external harmony, so that altogether the millennium was near at hand. From this utopian dream our generation has been rudely awakened by the spectacle of a whole world at war, by the rise of movements which challenge the very foundations of our social and moral order.[252]

Not only had "the magnificent technological genius of the time [been] devoted to destructive ends" but "even under the unifying pressure of war, . . . Anti-Semitic disturbances, race riots, labor troubles [were] all too prominent a feature of the news."

Prejudice, resulting from "free-floating" aggression in the wake of mass insecurity, was the reverse side of the fact that racial or ethnic groups were an important source of solidarity in the modern society. Nevertheless, here lay "subtle and formidable barriers to mutual communication and, hence, to adjustment" in the sense of universalism that characterized democracies.[253]

Group solidarity was frequently connected with religious traditions shared by culturally and more often than not ethnically homogenous groups. This was even true for the " 'advanced' religions, . . . Christianity and Mohammedanism." "The universalistic ideal has never yet been realized for more than a fraction of humanity and the movements themselves have always split up into sectarian subgroups which have erected new barriers among themselves."[254]

From this vantage point, he addressed the sources and mechanisms of group tension that led to violent prejudice and murder. The main mechanism expressing conflict in the manner between "the possessors of the one true religion"[255] as against "proselytizing 'pagans' and 'heretics' " was that not only were disenfranchised groups excluded from economic privileges or jurisdictional justice, but "[T]hese intrinsic conflicts are enormously aggravated by distortions in the definition of the situation and the accompanying emotional reactions. There may be a realistic basis of conflict between Jew and Gentile, but the picture of the Jew painted by the rabid anti-Semitic is one of a malevolence out of all proportion to the occasion. This is an example which illustrates a mechanism of extremely widespread operation, that of 'scapegoating.' "

The basis of scapegoating were "exaggerations" of elements present in a situation, but the mode of thinking operative in such definition of the situation was entirely divorced from rationality. It amounted, in psychoanalytical terms, to crude rationalizations of negative feelings. Such ratiocinations making for fake justifications of a violent behavior took the form of "extreme simplification and stereotyping, of 'tabloid thinking.' "[256] Parsons concluded,

---

[252] "Racial and Religious Differences," p. 275; the next two quotes are from the same page.
[253] Ibid., p. 279.
[254] Ibid., p. 280.
[255] Ibid., p. 282; the next two quotes are from the same page.
[256] Ibid., p. 283.

Thus, we have a situation where a number of factors are in a state of interdependence. There are (1) actually existent cultural and other differences between groups, creating barriers to communication and understanding. There are (2) elements of realistic conflict of value and interest. There are (3) internal tensions and insecurity in group life and structure, which create a need for the scapegoat reaction. There is (4) the relative adequacy or inadequacy of the other mechanisms of control or neutralization of the aggressive impulses generated by insecurity. There is (5) the symbolic appropriateness of an out-group as a scapegoat relative to particular tensions in the in-group. Finally, there are (6) the patterns of rationalization which justify scapegoating and make it subjectively acceptable to people.[257]

Racial tensions as had been analyzed in Gunnar Myrdal's then-recent *An American Dilemma*,[258] he addressed subsequently as "The Practical Problem of Control." He acknowledged that Myrdal's suggestion to wage a systematic educational campaign against the severe group antagonism in the American South might be important and do a lot of good. But the dangers were, first, that negative attitudes against racial equality could thus be activated rather than attenuated, which made success so much harder for policy measures; second, a campaign recommending racial equality might inadvertently become simply an outlet for aggression on the part of those who thereby denounced alleged conservatives or indifferents whom they charged for prejudice in a manner conspicuously prejudicial.

At the end of his essay, he warned against a vicious circle of group tension. When no policy measures were taken to weaken disintegration in a system, a spiral of increase of prejudice could result from the very policy intending an increase of tolerance. As regarded the forces which could strengthen equality and weaken prejudice, he hinted at the possibility that tendencies toward integration were frequently present even in a society that gave the impression of being ruled by group tension and deviance. Such tendencies, in due course, needed strengthening. Contrary to the tendencies toward anomie looming large in the social fabric, a tendency toward integration, he assured, inhered "social systems... [just like] other organic systems. 'Integration' or 'social health' is an inherent tendency of most societies, even though it is not as such a tangible 'factor' susceptible of direct control."[259]

Beyond Victory

Early in August 1944, after the Bretton Woods conference set up the International Monetary Fund and World Bank to facilitate postwar reconstruction in Europe and worldwide, in the interest of avoiding the collapse of the economy of the United Kingdom at the end of the war, Secretary of the Treasury Henry Morgenthau, Jr.[260]

---

[257] Ibid., pp. 283–284.
[258] See Gunnar Myrdal, *An American Dilemma*, 2 volumes (New York: Harper and Brothers, 1944)
[259] "Racial and Religious Differences," p. 288.
[260] For the following, see E. H. Penrose, *Economic Planning for the Peace* (Princeton, N. J.: Princeton University Press, 1953).

suggested a transfer of export markets from Germany to Great Britain. The only safe way to achieve demilitarization of Germany and thus preclude future belligerence of this extremely aggressive nation, he felt, was to deindustrialize Germany thoroughly. As a nation economically sustained by agricultural production, Germany would be harmless to its neighbors. In particular, the Rhine-Ruhr area, as the major heavy-industry region of Central Europe, was to be either internationalized under United Nations jurisdiction, or eradicated as an industrial region and converted into pastureland.[261] At their Quebec meeting on September 15, 1944, Roosevelt and Churchill agreed tentatively that Germany be made pastoral.[262]

Parsons reacted to the prospect of the Morgenthau policy by thoroughly revising his memorandum in September when it was due for Brickner's final report. He reworked his original statement, with the aim to prove that Morgenthau's objectives could be reached with completely different policies.

To practice what he preached, he took his only position ever in Washington, D.C. Between March and October 1945, he held a part-time advisory function in the *Foreign Economic Administration Agency*, Enemy Branch (FEA),[263] whose task was to draft disarmament and deindustrialization measures for Germany.[264]

Before he began this work, he summed up what he could contribute in a letter to Arthur R. Burns, deputy director of the Enemy Branch of FEA, dated March 6, 1945.[265] Enclosing the Brickner memorandum which at the time was due to appear in *Psychiatry*, he then summarized his personal contribution to the FEA's postwar planning task, in his letter to Burns:

> I think the topics on which I could make a contribution would be of two principal kinds. First, there would be the level of industrial change, which is the main subject matter of this paper. This would include the internal balance of different major groups in the social structure and the somewhat subtler but, I think, equally important level of patterns of relationship. What I mean should be evident, I think, from the paper. The second set of problems is that of ideological reactions. As I said in the last section of the paper, I think it is very difficult to accomplish much

---

[261] Morgenthau elaborated his position in *Germany Is Our Problem* (New York: Harper and Brothers, 1945). Goebbels's propaganda press from the fall of 1944 onward seized upon the opportunity to malign Morgenthau, exploiting the fact that he was Jewish.

[262] The complete text of the agreement may be found in Henry A. Stimson and McGeorge Bundy, *On Active Service in War and Peace* (New York: Harper and Brothers, 1947), pp. 576–577. The negative reaction of the American press to the agreement of September 1944 forced Roosevelt to withdraw from its position. To a certain extent, its spirit was preserved in the Joint Chiefs of Staff Directive 1067, which laid down the military government policy toward Germany in February 1945. It may be mentioned that Morgenthau's policy suggestions had more notoriety than actual political impact and were never carried out by the military government for Germany.

[263] President Roosevelt had entrusted the FEA with planning the economic policy for Germany some two weeks after the Quebec Conference in September 1944.

[264] For context discussion, see Uta Gerhardt, "Talcott Parsons and the Transformation of German Society After World War II," *European Sociological Review*, vol. 14, 1996, pp. 291–325.

[265] Letter, Parsons to Burns, March 6, 1945; Parsons papers, HUG(FP) – 15.2, box 9. The next two quotations are also from this letter. Burns (1895–1981), professor of economics at Columbia University, was also a long-time personal friend whom Parsons had first met during his sojourn at the London School of Economics in the 1920s.

directly on this level but we do know enough to see certain specific dangers and it should be possible to avoid policies which would directly arouse unfavorable reactions. This ought to be a very important policy and I should think something quite significant could be said about it.

From this general perspective, he proposed to Burns that he could "think it would be possible for me to take specific proposals for economic policy which have been worked out in your office and work out some sort of opinion as to the probable social repercussions they might entail. As you suggested, I think I could do much more significant work in connection with relatively long-run problems than with the more immediate phases."

Throughout the summer and into the early fall, he formalized his ideas in memoranda directed either to Burns, Philip M. Kaiser, Chief of the Planning Staff, or Henry Fowler, director to the FEA's Enemy Branch. As it happened, he travelled to Washington at least once a month during the remaining part of the academic year, and several times during the months of July and August when he had all-day meetings with the staff of the FEA Enemy Branch on Saturdays. These meetings, well remembered as they are by Kaiser, were discussion forums in which Parsons presented his ideas to the experts, writing up what had been discussed subsequently in his memoranda, which he placed at their disposal.[266]

Possibly antedating these memoranda was an undated and untitled four-page manuscript, opposing the view that "late monopoly capitalism" was the root cause of German fascism and ought to be controlled in Germany.[267] Admitting that militarism and "violent aggressiveness of National Socialism" were what had to be abolished forever, he reasoned: "Deep seated as this militaristic pattern has become, there is no reason to believe that it is rooted in the biological characteristics of Germans, or is in the long run unmanageable," suggesting: "The policy of military and economic disarmament, properly conceived and implemented, should not only serve immediately to render Germany incapable of making war, but also to contribute toward a re-orientation of the German people which is compatible with the interests and values of the United Nations."

This, he envisaged, would mean "to start redirecting German energies into peaceful channels." Since "it is essential to insist on a maximum of German responsibility" in the transformation, which "should in no sense be a matter of our taking care of them and doing the job for them," he found that a policy of controlled economic recovery would serve the purpose of redirecting Germany

---

[266] Personal communication. Philip M. Kaiser, whom I had the privilege of meeting in November 1995 in Washington, D.C., now lives in retirement after having served in government and diplomatic service.

[267] Memorandum, starting with the sentence, "A persistent tendency toward militarism and continual orientation of national policy towards war, has been characteristic of Germany for a long period." Parsons papers, HUG(FP) – 15.2, box 9. All quotations in the next four paragraphs are from this memorandum. The addressee most likely shared the view propounded by Max Horkheimer but also Franz Neumann, in the context of the so-called Frankfurt School, that fascism was the highest form of development of monopoly capitalism, and the latter had to be abolished if the former was to be overcome. See, for this view, Neumann, *Behemoth*, pp. 221–361, esp. pp. 225–292.

better than any other strategy. "I feel very strongly," he explained, "that Germany should not be prevented from industrial and commercial development, but should be encouraged in those lines which are compatible with the policy of economic disarmament." This, he elucidated, would also virtually "weaken the older conservative elements, notably the landed aristocracy and the older-type of higher Civil Service." Moreover, it would put "personal achievement" into a more prominent place in the German value hierarchy, he felt, "in non-military lines of course, and much less on hereditary position, than before. The integration with the economy of Europe, which guides attention away from possible military uses of industry and away from national self-sufficiency, seems to be the best direction of development."

One memorandum to Fowler, written some two weeks before the beginning of the Potsdam Conference, detailed two minor points, which he said "were brought up... in a conversation with an expert in another agency."[268] They were, first, that Germans' sense of security under the military government régime might be enhanced if an agency was established "to facilitate rapid reunion of... scattered families.... The psychological significance of this problem is certainly far beyond its economic significance." The second was "that there is serious danger as the employment situation in Germany shifts that larger numbers of women who have been accustomed to employment and a good deal of responsibility will be unable to secure it." In order to preempt subsequent relapse of the German family into notorious authoritarianism, he recommended that something be done about women's employment: "Anything that can contribute to the independence and self-respect of women is an important step in the direction of reorienting the German people."

Another memorandum, dated August 7, 1945 and addressed to Kaiser, dealt with the subject of "Separation of Western Territories from Germany."[269] Since the subject went beyond "'purely economic' matters," he wished to deal with its "social and political aspects, and to treat them in direct conjunction with the fundamental political settlement in Europe." He warned of dire consequences in case of annexation of the Rhine-Ruhr area by France, as had been discussed until only days before at Potsdam. The "international political order created by the victorious nations" would be compromised from the start if "the European system as one of national units competing for positions of power" would be accentuated. Moreover, "the stability of the solution... would maximize our own responsibilities in continental Europe in the least desirable way," if only because German nationalism would be incited to recover an irredenta: "It would make virtually impossible any progress toward a social situation which could hope to influence the

---

[268] "Memorandum to Henry A. Fowler, from Talcott Parsons," July 2, 1945; Parsons papers, HUG(FP) – 15.2, box 9. The expert might well have been Mead who, in July 1945, invited Parsons to become a regular member of the National Research Council's Committee on Food Habits, which she chaired. All quotes in this paragraph are from this memorandum.

[269] "Memorandum to Philip Kaiser, from Talcott Parsons. Subject: Separation of Western Territories from Germany." Parsons papers, HUG(FP) – 15.2, box 9. All quotes in this and the next four paragraphs are from this memorandum.

German people in the direction of integration with Western democratic patterns." In other words, far from being weakened, German aggressiveness would be given a rather just cause, and the patterns of paranoid ethnocentrism would inadvertently be preserved or restored through Allied policies.

The second part of the memorandum started with the statement, "The proposal to place this area under government of the United Nations organization seems to me to be quite a different matter and to deserve very careful consideration." Internationalization of the Rhine-Ruhr, he suggested, "might well provide an opportunity for contributing to quite fundamental changes in the whole European politico-economic system, which could be of profound importance." Politically, "this could serve as a prominent symbol of the superceding of the old political constitution of Europe as a system of competing power units" – which, he marvelled, might teach the Germans a lesson inasmuch as "a practical demonstration that the pattern of national self-interest can be transcended right on their own door step could conceivably have a greater effect than any amount of propaganda on our part."

Parsons saw two economic advantages. First, "it would not be necessary to carry out such drastic industrial disarmament within the territory as if it were left within German jurisdiction." This would amount to "an experimental test of the degree to which the German economy in that region was autarchic in that much more specifically economic criteria could be applied in guiding industrial redevelopment and reorientation." Second, Germany's neighbors would be less fearful in their economic relations with Germany. The reason was that "international administration might provide a basis of mutual confidence which would greatly facilitate freedom of trade and therefore a desirable type of economic development."

In terms of social structure, he saw two advantageous repercussions. The Rhine-Ruhr area, to be sure, despite its having belonged to Prussia from the early nineteenth century onward, never had been a predominant domain for *junkerism*. Its independent development would mean "the loosening up of their [the Junker and Prussian civil service groups'] previous monopoly position, not only in business as such but socially, so as to leave opening for the advent of new blood.... Particular attention should be paid by the International Administration to higher education, as a channel for the emergence of a new elite. This area would include several universities, notably Bonn, Cologne and Frankfurt, possibly Heidelberg. They are the natural channel for new blood to come into positions of leadership."

Lastly, the trade-union movement could be reestablished on a desirably large scale. In all, an internationalization of the Rhine-Ruhr area could plant the seeds for European unification: "It could be hoped that eventually it would work into a general restructuring of the European political system as a result of which national states as units would come to have a drastically altered significance. Indeed, it is precisely as an experiment in restructuring European society in this direction that the proposal has its greatest appeal to me."

The next memorandum was written ten days later, on August 17, 1945. It was again directed to Kaiser, and undertook to give "General Comment on THE FEA

DISARMAMENT PLAN, draft of Aug. 6."[270] The disarmament plan on which he commented obviously was a document containing the "TIDC recommendations," or "TIDC policy in reorienting the German economy,"[271] part of the Economic Planning directives which were agreed upon at Potsdam. He noted as a point of departure that the report expressed "our firm determination that the kind of disturbance of the peace which has emanated from Germany shall not be allowed to happen again." It was unrealistic to assume that Germany's transformation would result from the destruction of economic resources for war alone, he stated. The type of peace economy that would work as a bulwark against Germany's future warmongering was market capitalism. He phrased the recommendation thus:

> The right kind of repressive action can have positive functional value in facilitating the process of reorientation while conversely the right kind of "leniency" can have a positive repressive effect. This statement may sound paradoxical, yet in a sense it is the key to the whole problem.

What did "leniency" entail? For one, "institutional disarmament" meant conversion of the entire economy from war production in cartelized industries to consumer production in small-scale capitalist businesses. In the process of re-establishing a consumer-oriented economy, he explained, "the 'lenient' aspect can contribute to the actual disarmament of Germany in so far as it effectively reorients the people and their sentiments and interests away from military values and the dream of German supremacy by military force." In this vein, "by imposing 'stronger' controls, we are actually risking weakening the effectiveness of the total control system, because at the same time we are strengthening the resistance to control more than that of the controls." He summarized the gist of his argument thus:

> For purposes of analyzing the concrete implications of a series of assumptions, I should suggest that the possible repressive measures which are under consideration be rated along two scales, first their descending order of strategic significance in effectively crippling Germany's capacity to make war, second the seriousness to the functioning of the kind of peacetime economy we think of as acceptable for Germany. Other considerations such as interdependence will of course have to be taken into account. But having worked out such a classification it should be possible to distinguish a small number of relatively distinct levels of completeness of disarmament and attempt to analyze the resulting situation as a whole for each.

Instead of imposing controls upon Germans, therefore, "[I]t would be very much healthier for us to be thinking of what positively we were trying to bring about, and of the others as obstacles to that." In this vein, he believed, a peaceful prosperous German economy would eventually even help overcome the compartmentalization of economies and separation of countries in Europe, in the wake of a wise disarmament policy: "I am convinced that most of what could be shown to be necessary to effective continuing disarmament would fit naturally into this conception of, once

---

[270] "Memorandum to Philip M. Kaiser, from Talcott Parsons. Subject: General Comments on THE FEA DISARMAMENT PLAN, draft of Aug. 6." Parsons papers, HUG(FP) – 15.2, box 9. All quotes in this and the next two paragraphs are from this memorandum.

[271] The acronym presumably stands for some Industrial Disarmament for Germany Committee.

having performed the surgical operation to eliminate grossly autarchic elements of Germany's industrial structure, promoting the development of a healthy European economy."

Accompanying the memorandum was a draft paper, outlining "Psychological and Social Aspects" of the FEA Disarmament Program. This draft paper invoked that the Junker class (and higher civil service), the military, and big industry would disappear or lose their power position (in addition to the Nazi party which had been dissolved already). The paper urged conversion of the German economy to small-scale capitalism, plus a revival of professionalism, as the best way to change institutional spheres in German society in the direction of a "liberal democratic type of society." He recommended not restricting the German economy too severely, while destroying its war potential through decartelization, reparations, and so on. Such policy, he felt, would eventually benefit equally "the recovery of the rest of Europe."[272]

Two further memoranda written in September and October 1945 elaborated further on these points. After the FEA had been dissolved on October 15, 1945, and some of its staff transferred to the Germany and Austria Division in the State Department, the latter's director, economic historian Charles Kindleberger, recommended Parsons's last memorandum (dated October 11, 1945) to his staff as a source for planning German postwar policy.[273]

Some twenty-five years later, in his "Building Social System Theory: A Personal History," his intellectual biography up to the end of the 1960s, Parsons wryly recollected. "During the latter part of the war period I served as a consultant to the Enemy Branch of the Foreign Economic Administration, dealing with the postwar treatment of Germany. I wrote several memoranda in opposition to the so-called Morgenthau Plan."[274]

Summary

Parsons's wartime work failed to receive due attention in secondary literature until the 1990s. It was during the years between 1938 and 1945 that he solidified his sociological analysis through expressly targeting Nazi Germany, contrasting

---

[272] The text of the entire paragraph ran: "The ultimate test of the disarmament program will be its effects on the attitudes of Germans and upon the social structure of Germany. If the attitudes that have underlain the last two wars and the German social structure upon which German desire and capacity for aggression have rested survive or are consolidated security can be obtained only by long continued repressive control. But a program can be designed and executed that will help to eradicate German militarism and to reintegrate Germany under a stable European society." "VI. The Social and Psychological Aspects of the F.E.A. Disarmament Program," Parsons papers, HUG(FP) – 15.2, box 9.

[273] See "Office Memorandum United States Government, State Department, Germany and Austria Division," from Kindleberger to all main staff of GA, December 15, 1945, National Archives, Record Group 59, General Records State Department, Decimal Files, 1945–9 Control (Germany), box 3672.

[274] Parsons, "On Building Social System Theory: A Personal History," in *Social Systems and the Evolution of Action Theory*, p. 39.

it as he did with U.S. society. He engaged in anti-Nazi activism, as a citizen and academic. He participated in, for one, voluntary associations such as the Council for Democracy and American Defense, but he also volunteered to counsel a government agency on postwar politics vis-à-vis Germany, in 1945. In general, he condemned National Socialism as a coercive, charismatic system but he also concerned himself with German redemocratization at the end of World War II.

My argument divided his concern into five phases. The earliest phase, cultivating the spirit of citizenship inculcated into Amherst students during the Meiklejohn era, had two foci. One was higher learning, involving professionalism that denoted social organization beyond economic patterns of either capitalism or socialism. The other focus was religion that involved the economy (in Weber's theory, a major accomplishment). The two issues were his main points in his first article openly accusing National Socialism of destroying Western civilization, in late November 1938.

In the time period until Pearl Harbor, he ardently advocated intervention. He systematized his analysis juxtaposing the two type systems, Nazi Germany as charismatic-traditional, and the United States as rational-legal authority societies. This culminated in his "Max Weber and the Contemporary Political Crisis."

In the year 1942, he turned to the problem, What to do with Germany? Since the war against Germany (and Japan) was underway at last, he could now concern himself with what the future should entail. He published five essays on the topic in 1942 (one in two parts), when his interest gradually shifted to the prospects for re-education.

In the next two years, among many other activities, Parsons participated in the Harvard School of Overseas Administration training future military government officers. In this function, he applied his systems approach to Germany, suitably adapted to the historical situation which it had to fit. In his memorandum, originally written for "Germany After the War," he suggested controlled institutional change to overcome particularism and ascription, and fully re-establish universalism and achievement. His suggestion was, based on sociological expertise, to modernize the economic structure there.

In the time period until October 1945, as consultant to the FEA, he advised policy planners to follow a sociologically grounded idea. Social change for Germany, he contended, meant modernization of German society.

More than in any other period in his life, in the years 1938–1945, he concerned himself with the society that was the experienced lifeworld of millions. He was an activist in defense of democracy, but he also used sociological theory to placate the utter danger to civilization that National Socialism entailed.

During these years, his focus of work was not only American democracy (which nevertheless remained one pivotal theme), but also its obverse, German Nazism. That he knew Germany from his sojourn at Heidelberg may have been helpful in spurring his concern. His analysis of two-pronged structure of (systems of) social action carried over into his endeavor of explaining contemporary societies in that age of world war. His *The Structure of Social Action* had elaborated on the conceptual scheme, but he now gave it life when he applied it successfully to the goings-on in the "Contemporary Political Crisis" of World War II.

Parsons went out of his way, often quite literally, to convince others that his sociological deliberations made sense, in many quarters. Probably more than at any other time in his life, he combined defense of democracy with analysis targeting the enemies of democratization.

1. Edward Smith Parsons (1863–1943) came from a family a prominent member of whom had been Edward Pamelee Smith, U.S. Commissioner of Indian Affairs in the administration of Ulysses Grant in the Civil War era. He had a Divinity degree, and in the early twentieth century was a member of the Social Gospel, an intellectual movement aiming to reconcile living conditions in contemporary capitalism with the ethics of Christ's Sermon of the Mount. He was a scholar of English and published on Milton. In 1919, he was elected president of Marietta College (Ohio). An unconfirmed story has it that in the spring of the following year, he and his young son Talcott traveled to Germany where they visited with Max Weber in Munich.

2. Mary Augusta Ingersoll Parsons (1863–1944). Her father was a great-grandson of the theologian Jonathan Edwards (1703–1753). Her mother was born Katherine Talcott; she and also the Ingersoll family came from western Massachusetts. Mary Parsons grew up in Cleveland and married Edward Parsons in 1889. She is said to have supported progressive causes in her time, even having been a suffragist. She had five children of whom her son Talcott was the youngest. The first four were Esther (1890–1965), Charles Edwards (1892–1940), Elizabeth Ingersoll (1894–1957), and Edward Smith, Jr. (1898–1960).

3. Talcott and Helen Parsons's three children were born in 1930, 1933, and 1936, respectively. Two of their children became scholars in their own right. Their daughter Anne, the oldest, grew up to be a social scientist; she held a doctorate from the Sorbonne and did research in Italy as well as Boston. She died in June 1964. Their son Charles was to teach philosophy, first at Columbia and later Harvard University. As of 2001, he has been Edgar Pierce Professor of Philosophy at Harvard. In Emerson Hall, his office happens to be on the same floor as the one occupied by his father until 1965.

4. Parsons came from a large family. The picture taken at Christmas 1928, shows his two brothers and sisters, parents, and niece and nephew, together with the young couple then recently married. Front (from left): Esther Parsons (oldest sister), Edward S. Parsons (father) with Joan Parsons (daughter of Edward S. Parsons, Jr.), Mary A. I. Parsons (mother) with Samuel Parsons (son of Edward S. Parsons, Jr.), and Margaret Allen Parsons (wife of Edward S. Parsons, Jr.). Rear (from left): Helen Walker Parsons (married to Talcott Parsons since 1927), Talcott Parsons, Charles Edwards Parsons (much-admired older brother), Elisabeth I. Parsons (sister), and Edward S. Parsons, Jr. Helen W. Parsons had been an American graduate co-student at the London School of Economics when she and Talcott met. They were married subsequent to his return to the United States after his sojourn at Heidelberg University (ending July 1926).

5. In 1949, on the occasion of the twenty-fifth anniversary of his graduation, Parsons received an honorary degree from his alma mater, Amherst College. In the photograph, he is at the right, in the rear row. The other professors who received honorary degrees with Parsons in 1949 were (back row, left to right): Frederic Marsena Butts (AC 1909), Henry Butler Allen (AC 1909), Frederick Waldbridge Hoeing (AC 1929), Joseph Ramsdell Kingman, Jr. (AC 1924), (front row, left to right) Willard Long Thorp (AC 1920), Sir Oliver Shewell Franks, Ralph Albert Van Meter, and Henry Plimpton Kendall (AC 1899). In the center position, front row, is Charles W. Cole, president of University of Massachusetts. In the postwar years around 1950, Parsons was approaching the summit of his unprecedented fame as thinker in American social theory.

6. In the 1960s, Talcott Parsons was indefatigable, traveling to an amazingly large number of symposia, conference meetings, and personal lectures in the United States and abroad, to familiarize his audience with his newly revised version of systems (symbolic interaction media) theory. He also held the office of member of Committee A of the American Association of University Professors (AAUP) in 1956–1961, and Committee C thereafter, was Secretary of the American Sociological Association in 1961–1963, and was elected to serve as president of the American Academy of Arts and Sciences from 1967 to 1971.

7. Harvard was Talcott Parsons's bailiwick throughout most of his academic life, from 1927 until his retirement in 1973 and beyond. In 1946, he and others founded the Department of Social Relations, which was a sequel to joint efforts of Harvard faculty preparing military government officers at the School of Overseas Administration in 1943–1944, uniting Sociology, Social Anthropology, Social Psychology, and Clinical Psychology. In the early 1960s, he helped negotiate the building of William James Hall, at last a common locale and home for the various disciplines in the department. In the photograph, William James Hall is the large building in front; Emerson Hall (situated in Harvard Yard) is a rectangular structure with pillars, to the left of Widener Library.

8. In 1964, Parsons took part in the Fifteenth German Sociology Congress in Heidelberg celebrating the one hundredth anniversary of the birth of Max Weber. On the occasion, Parsons gave the main paper focusing on Weber's idea of objectivity in social science. Together with the former president of the German Sociological Association, Otto Stammer, he had arranged for a program guaranteeing that Weber's critics of the "Frankfurt School" would not go unchallenged. In the photograph, Parsons is on the left. The others are, from left to right: (behind Parsons) Leopold von Wiese, *nestor* of German sociology who had been reactivated as academic teacher after World War II; Raymond Aron, *doyen* of French sociology; Ernst Topitsch, who taught philosophy of science at Heidelberg University in the 1960s; and Otto Stammer. Parsons and Stammer had met during the Sixth World Congress of Sociology in Washington, D.C., in September 1962, to discuss the arrangements for the Heidelberg conference.

9. In his later life, Parsons would not let up on his zest for knowing the newest literature and taking a vivid interest in the politics of the day. His family remembers him as occupied with a book or newspaper (preferably, the *New York Times*) most of the time when he was with them. On this occasion of an apparent preparation of a picnic, he seems to have minded to something cooking on a camp stove, obviously interrupting only briefly his reading a newspaper.

10. The family's summer home in New Hampshire was refuge and relaxation at the same time, serving Helen and Talcott Parsons long after his retirement from Harvard (and hers where she had been the heart and soul of the Russian Research Center for more than twenty years). He invited guests to Acworth, to discuss matters sociological, from the 1930s onward. For instance, in August 1941, Eric Voegelin, whom Parsons had rescued in the late fall of 1938 from persecution in Europe by securing him a temporary position in less than two days (which involved an affidavit), came to the summer house where they discussed Parsons's manuscript on anti-Semitism.

3
The Harvard Social-Science War Effort and *The Social System*

Introduction

The volume celebrating the three-hundred-fiftieth anniversary of Harvard University, *Harvard Century: The Making of a University to a Nation*, focused extensively on the contribution of Harvard natural scientists' research to the development and eventual deployment of the atom bomb during World War II. But no mention was made of the contribution of the Harvard social scientists in winning World War II.[1]

Other books, while not specifically dealing with Harvard, have given credit to wartime activities of social-science academics. *The Politics of Propaganda: The Office of War Information, 1942–1945* occasionally mentioned contributions by Harvard psychologists or historians, although the broader involvement of Harvard personnel in this wartime agency was not discussed.[2] Likewise, *Cloak and Gown: Scholars in the Secret War, 1939–1961* analyzed, though not extensively, the contributions of some Harvard as well as Yale professors to government agencies such as the Coordinator of Information Office (COI), the Office of Strategic Services (OSS), and the Office of War Information (OWI).[3] Also, *Foreign Intelligence: Research and Analysis in the Office of Strategic Services 1942–1945* has remembered the work of a number of scholars under the directorship of Harvard historian William Langer, though Harvard scholars whose work was discussed in some detail were only the Marxist economists Paul Baran and Paul E. Sweezy.[4]

By and large, evidence concerning Harvard's social scientists' war effort is scarce. Their various projects have not been documented comprehensively in any

---

[1] Richard N. Smith, *The Harvard Century: The Making of a University to a Nation* (New York: Simon and Schuster, 1986).
[2] Allan Winkler, *The Politics of Propaganda: The Office of War Information, 1942–1945* (New Haven/London: Yale University Press, 1978).
[3] Robin W. Winks, *Cloak and Gown: Scholars in the Secret War, 1939–1961* (New York: William Morrow, 1987).
[4] Barry M. Katz, *Foreign Intelligence: Research and Analysis in the Office of Strategic Services 1942–1945* (Cambridge, Mass.: Harvard University Press, 1989). Among the social scientists who were the explicit theme of the book were Felix Gilbert, Hajo Holborn, Charles Kindleberger, and Herbert Marcuse, among others, but only the two Marxist economists from Harvard.

one monograph. In the time period between the end of World War II and the outbreak of the Korean War, some general documentation was attempted, highlighting the accomplishments of social science in connection with what at the time conveniently was called the war effort. In some of these contemporaneous reports, Harvard social scientists were mentioned, but these analyses usually cast a wider net than Harvard and also sociology, often focusing on political science as particularly important.[5] In other analytical accounts, sociologists played a rôle as protagonists, such as in Daniel Lerner's monograph on psychological warfare against Nazi Germany. This book reported on the war work done by, among others, sociologists Hartshorne, Edward Shils (from the University of Chicago), and Morris Janowitz (educated at New York University Washington Square College).[6] As a type of war effort, Lerner focused on their work under a political-science (not sociology) perspective, which was Lerner's metier, and not in any way related to Harvard.

The contribution of Harvard's social sciences to the war effort in World War II has not received adequate attention yet. I submit that it is one widely unrecognized background to Parsons's *The Social System*. My aim in this chapter is to substantiate this background to Parsons's second major opus. I shall not only refer to various scenarios and outcomes of the war work at Harvard, but also account for Parsons's efforts prior and particularly subsequent to victory in World War II. His interest, as I shall document, was to secure a standing for sociology. He deemed it a discipline equal in importance to, for example, nuclear physics in regard to its value as a "basic national resource."[7]

Some Scenarios in the War Effort of the Social Sciences at Harvard

Since conclusive secondary literature does not yet exist, the necessary evidence comes from books and articles on various related topics as well as memoirs and unpublished materials. Four areas stand out in which Harvard social scientists, including Parsons, contributed to the war effort. Some such tasks were fulfilled in

---

[5] See, for instance, Leonard W. Doob, "The Utilization of Social Scientists in the Overseas Branch of the Office of War Information," *American Political Science Review*, vol. 41, 1947, pp. 649–667, Carl J. Friedrich, "Political Science in the United States in Wartime," *American Political Science Review*, vol. 41, 1947, pp. 978–990, or Paul M. A. Linebarger, *Psychological Warfare* (Washington: Infantry Journal Press, 1948).

[6] Daniel Lerner's *Psychological Warfare Against Nazi Germany, D-Day to VE-Day* (New York: Georg W. Stewart, 1949), a uniquely well-informed study, analyzing the scholarly approach to persuasion of the enemy taken by the *Psychological Warfare Division* (PWD), among whose staff were also Richard Grossman, who later was Home Secretary of the British government under Prime Minister Harold Wilson, or Klaus Mann, son of the Nobel Prize winner, writer Thomas Mann. For further information on Morris Janowitz, see Dennis Smith, *The Chicago School: A Liberal Critique of Capitalism* (New York: St. Martins Press, 1988), esp. pp. 184–188.

[7] See the title of Parsons's memorandum for the Social Science Research Council written between 1946 and 1948, "Social Science – A Basic National Resource." See below.

the nation's capital, Washington D.C., others further afield in the Far Eastern and European Theaters of Operation. And some wartime work was carried out within Harvard's own precincts.

Government Agencies

In September 1941, the COI was founded as an agency to prepare material on enemy countries that was collected in the Library of Congress and analyze it, among other uses, for the Armed Forces. Among the first to be hired by COI was Hartshorne, Parsons's collaborator in, among other contexts, the Harvard Defense Group National Morale Committee. At the time, the two were preparing to write a book together entitled *German Social Structure and National Psychology*.[8]

Another Harvard scholar who joined COI in 1941 was historian William Langer. In June 1942, Langer was appointed Director of the Research and Analysis Branch (R&A Branch) of the newly established OSS, one of the two successor agencies of COI.[9] "R&A," as it was frequently called, soon became a hotbed of academic work – producing high-quality memoranda analyzing the geography, history, economy, law, military organization, propaganda techniques, and various aspects of the cultural and social structures of the enemy countries.[10] Other Harvard social scientists working for R&A, to name but a few, were historians[11] Arthur Schlesinger, Jr., and Crane Brinton,[12] and economists Walt W. Rostow and George Mason, the latter leaving OSS in 1944 to become Assistant Secretary of State.[13]

Whereas OSS dealt with information concerning enemy countries, the OWI was meant to concentrate on the United States. One of OWI's tasks was to prepare handbooks on enemy countries for the use of the U.S. public, government, and military; another was to devise, within the confines of the "strategy of truth,"

---

[8] The publisher was to be Reynal & Hitchcock, New York/Philadelphia. See also above.

[9] Some details are in William Langer, *In and Out of the Ivory Tower: An Autobiography* (New York: Neale Watson, 1977).

[10] For appreciation of the wealth of material accumulated through meticulous research in R&A, see Petra Marquardt-Bigman, *Amerikanische Geheimdienstanalysen über Deutschland 1942–1949* (Munich: Oldenbourg, 1995).

[11] For a full list of historians involved in OSS, see Winks, *Cloak and Gown*, pp. 495–497.

[12] Brinton, historian of the French Revolution, had written on English political thought in the nineteenth century including social evolutionism. Parsons had referred to him in the opening paragraph of *The Structure of Social Action* (1937) when dismissing Herbert Spencer's utilitarianism as dead for modern social theory in the 1930s. Both had been members of the legendary "Harvard Pareto Circle" in the early 1930s, which had been a venue for anti-Darwinist discussion; cf. Barbara Heyl, "The 'Harvard Pareto Circle,'" *Journal of the History of Behavioral Sciences*, vol. 4, 1968, pp. 316–334. See also Chapter 1.

[13] Smith, *Harvard Century*, p. 170. Of the latter two, Rostow became an influential adviser to Presidents Kennedy and Johnson in the 1960s, and Mason was Undersecretary of State at a time when the Acting Secretary of State was Joseph C. Grew, a career diplomat and Harvard graduate, who was also a committed supporter of social science as a resource for government policy.

approaches securing public support for government measures in wartime;[14] and still another was to interrogate prisoners of war on Nazi Germany, in locales near the battlefields, or to prepare and train personnel for this work abroad in a training center located on Long Island. Hartshorne, Parsons's collaborator, did the latter work in the winter of 1943 before he was sent to Algiers and Rome on related missions.

Between March and October 1945, Parsons offered his services as an adviser to the government agency Foreign Economic Administration Enemy Branch (FEA), who employed him on a part-time basis. His memoranda recommended a policy of demilitarization and decartelization but not deindustrialization for Germany, cautioning against renewed German nationalism as it might inadvertently result from U.S. occupation policy.[15]

The Conference on Germany After the War in which Parsons took part received financial support from the War Department's Provost Marshall General's Office.[16]

Voluntary Associations

In the summer of 1940, the Council for Democracy began as a voluntary association for scholars and public figures intent on fighting fascism by strengthening American democracy. Harvard political scientist Friedrich, founding member of the Council for Democracy, invited Parsons to join the Committee of Correspondence, pointing out that issues of democracy as obverse of fascism were to be "worked out by the process of discussion in the light of all available facts." He continued, "As consultants, I am seeking men and women in the various social sciences who on short notice would be prepared to supply information on specific points bearing on one or another of the policies involved in our work as they fell

---

[14] In 1943, *Public Opinion Quarterly* devoted an entire issue to policies and programs of OWI that aimed at the U.S. population. Accounts there included Jerome Bruner, "OWI and the American Public," A. H. Feller, "OWI on the Home Front," Carl J. Friedrich, "Principles of Informational Strategies," and Robert J. Landry, "The Impact of OWI on Broadcasting," among others. See *Public Opinion Quarterly,* vol. 7 (1943, spring issue), pp. 3–185. See also Chapter 2.

[15] For various previous accounts on this work of Parsons, see my essays, "Talcott Parsons als Deutschlandexperte während des Zweiten Weltkrieges,"*Kölner Zeitschrift für Soziologie und Sozialpsychologie*, vol. 43, 1991, pp. 211–234; "Die Geburt Europas aus dem Geist der Soziologie," *Ruperto Carola, Wissenschaftsmagazin der Universität Heidelberg.* 2/1996, pp. 24–30; "Talcott Parsons and the Transformation of German Society at the End of World War II," *European Sociological Review*, vol. 12, 1996, pp. 303–323; and "Talcott Parsons und die amerikanische Besatzungspolitik," *Schweizerische Zeitschrift für Soziologie*, vol. 24, 1998, pp. 121–151. See above, Chapter 2, and below.

[16] The eventual outcome of the Conference was Richard Brickner, *Report on a Conference on Germany After the War* (no date, no location) (November 1944; New York). The report was made available to selected government agencies in December 1944. It was published in 1945, under the inconspicuous title, "Germany After the War – Round Table 1945," *American Journal of Orthopsychiatry*, vol. 11, 1945, pp. 381–441. See also above, Chapter 2. Focusing mostly on the Brickner conference: Gerhardt, "A Hidden Agenda for Recovery: The Psychiatric Conceptualization of Re-education for Germany in the United States during World War II," *German History*, vol. 14, 1996, pp. 297–324.

within their field."[17] In December 1941, the Council for Democracy was awarded *Variety* Magazine Plaque for Patriotic Leadership for successfully explicating America's democracy to the nation's citizens.[18]

An extension of the Council for Democracy was the Committee for National Morale, which, as its first major task, prepared a comprehensive annotated bibliography on German Psychological Warfare compiled in 1941 and published as a book in 1942.[19]

Another voluntary organization involving Harvard staff[20] was American Defense. Its Harvard Group was established in June 1940, and with philosopher Ralph Barton Perry as chair, the Group was active until after VE-Day. According to the "Blue Print for Organization of an American Defense Group," the central purpose of American Defense was "to defend America against actual or potential enemies abroad, and against disruptive factions at home.... There must be at one and the same time a sense of emergency, an enduring fidelity to the country and a faith in the social and human values for which it stands."[21] Parsons as chair, with Hartshorne as vice-chair, organized a discussion group of the subcommittee on morale, on German social structure from pre–World War I Germany to Nazism, followed by groups on Japanese society and American ideology.[22]

Another voluntary association which was founded in 1940 and lasted until the 1960s was the Conference of Science, Philosophy and Religion in Their Relation to the Democratic Way of Life. Its organizers, Lyman Bryson, Louis Finckelstein, and Robert MacIver (who were editors of the volumes of conference proceedings during the war and immediate postwar period) were connected with Columbia University and Teachers' College, New York. The Conference in its first years and throughout the 1940s attracted a large number of social scientists, in addition to public figures such as Dwight D. Eisenhower or nuclear physicist J. Robert Oppenheimer. Contributions to the symposia were papers organized around conference themes such as "Freedom," "World Peace," "Unity and Diversity," "Power and Conflict," or "Progress Toward Integration, 1939–1949," to name but a few which were tackled in the 1940s. Members of the Conference who nominally convoked the symposium together were, in 1949, Franz Alexander, Karl W. Deutsch, Waldemar Gurian, Clyde Kluckhohn, Harold D. Lasswell, Margaret Mead, Alexander Meiklejohn, Henry A. Murray, Parsons, Ralph Barton Perry, Arthur Upham Pope, George N. Shuster, Samuel A. Stouffer, Louis Wirth, and Quincy Wright,

---

[17] Letter, Friedrich to Parsons, October 8, 1940, Parsons papers, HUG(FP) – 42.8.2, box 3.

[18] Cedric Larson, "The Council for Democracy," *Public Opinion Quarterly*, vol. 6, 1942, pp. 284–290, esp. p. 288.

[19] Ladislas Farago et al., *German Psychological Warfare. Survey and Bibliography* (New York: Putnam and Sons, 1942; previously, New York: Committee for National Morale, 1941). See also above, Chapter 2.

[20] Another voluntary association whose aim was fulfilled in a relatively short time period was the Harvard Military Aid to Britain Campaign. It lasted until the end of 1940, when the Senate passed the Lend-Lease Bill.

[21] The "Blue Print for Organization of an American Defense Group" for Harvard is filed among the Parsons papers, HUG (FP) – 42.8.4, box 3; the quotation is from p. 3.

[22] Letter, Parsons to Perry, May 24, 1943, Parsons papers, HUG (FP) – 15.2, box 3.

among a list of nearly two hundred.[23] During the 1940s, Parsons prepared for the Conference his papers on "Religious and Racial Tensions" (1944), "Origins and Patterns of Aggressiveness" (1946), as well as a twenty-nine-page manuscript entitled "The Institutionalization of Social Science and the Problems of the Conference," destined for the 1947 conference whose working title was "How Can Scholarship Contribute to the Relief of International Tensions?"[24]

Research

Sociologists frequently investigated issues related to, including the war against, Nazism. For instance, in 1938, Columbia University sociologist Theodore Abel had published a study based on biographical accounts of members of the Nazi Party, entitled *Why Hitler Came Into Power*.[25] In 1940, emigré sociologist Hans Gerth, who had taught at Harvard in 1938–1939, analyzed the composition and leadership of the Nazi Party in order to explain how they came to power.[26]

At Harvard, in a project lasting until April 1, 1940, Allport, together with historian Sidney B. Fay and Hartshorne, invited emigré Germans throughout the world to submit autobiographical reports covering the topic, "My Life Before and After January 30, 1933." Two hundred thirty-four reports were sent in, often comprising hundreds of pages (such as, for instance, that of philosopher Karl Löwith who from his temporary country of refuge, Japan, described his relationship with Heidegger, his experiences of being shunned by colleagues even before the Nazi takeover, and his eventual flight from Germany[27]). Allport, together with Jerome Bruner and another collaborator, published a preliminary interpretation of the material using an analytical perspective of personality under social catastrophe.[28]

Research projects were being conducted all around Parsons. Parsons's former student, Robert Merton, previous chairman of the Sociology Department of Tulane University and in the early 1940s changing to Columbia University, was commissioned to conduct a study of war bond advertising by a companion agency of

---

[23] "Program. Tenth Conference on Science, Philosophy, and Religion in their Relation to the Democratic Way of Life convoked by Mortimer J. Adler (first of a list of nearly two hundred names) at The Men's Faculty Club of Columbia University..., New York..., on... September 6, 7, 8 and 9, 1949"; Parsons papers, HUG(FP) – 42.8.4, box 8.

[24] The manuscript, which appears to have been a draft version of a paper not presented on the occasion of the 1947 conference, carries the handwritten specification, "Conference on Science, Religion, and Philosophy"; Parsons papers, HUG(FP) – 42.8.4, box 8.

[25] Theodore Abel, *Why Hitler Came Into Power* (Englewood Cliffs, N.J.: Prentice Hall, 1938).

[26] Hans Gerth, "The Nazi Party: Its Leadership and Composition," *American Journal of Sociology*, vol. 45, 1940, pp. 517–541.

[27] Löwith's extended essay has been published posthumously as a separate autobiographical account, Karl Löwith, *Mein Leben in Deutschland vor und nach 1933* (Stuttgart: Metzler, 1986).

[28] Gordon W. Allport, Jerome Bruner, and Erich Jandorf, "Personality Under Social Catastrophe," *Character and Personality*, vol. 10, 1941, pp. 1–22; Hartshorne compiled a book from the interview material on the pogrom of November 1938, in which he contrasted the moving and alarming autobiographical reports of Nazi victims with Nazi press coverage and also press reports in the United States and England, under the working title of *Nazi Madness*. The book, unfortunately, never found a publisher.

COI, the Office of Facts and Figures (OFF).[29] Throughout the period of active combat, the OSS R&A Branch studied German social structure and politics in some two thousand reports, eventually preparing material for the prosecution of Nazi leaders by the Nuremberg International Tribunal trial starting in November 1945, collecting and analyzing, among other topics, materials documenting the criminal responsibility of Nazi leaders, or Nazi plans to dominate Europe including planning genocide in concentration camps in Poland and farther West in the German *Reich*.[30]

Another example of research from that time was the work done by Margaret Mead and Gregory Bateson. One striking representation was Bateson's analysis of a German film about a boy who converted from communism to the Hitler Youth, picturing the ideology of sacrifice as denial of personal independence and even identity – such research being the study of fascism, to use a phrase later coined by Mead, targeting Germany as "culture at a distance."[31]

Another research endeavor became known as the United States Strategic Bombing Survey. This large-scale study, whose reports eventually filled thousands of pages, was directed by psychologist Rensis Likert, one of the most experienced research coordinators in wartime work (following his stint at the OFF he had chaired the Division of Program Surveys investigating issues of morale via opinion polls, before directing the Strategic Bombing Survey). In December 1944, Hartshorne worked as an adviser to Likert on the construction of questionnaires for use in defeated Germany. The latter were destined to study not only the effect of bombing on German morale but also the mentality of Germans immediately after cessation of hostilities; data were collected through interviews with Germans between March and July 1945.[32] Similar research was conducted on Japan.[33]

Parsons, to be sure, did not participate in these various endeavors. He did, however, make several attempts to obtain a research grant for comparative work. In early 1942, under the co-directorship of Dutch emigré Bartholomew Landheer, together

---

[29] The outcome of this research was published after the war, namely, Robert K. Merton, *Mass Persuasion* (New York: Harper and Brothers, 1946) (with assistance of Marjorie Fiske and Alberta Curtis).

[30] See, among others, R&A Report No. 3110, "Leadership Principle and Criminal Responsibility" (22 pp.), July 18, 1945; No. 3114, "Nazi Plans for Dominating Germany and Europe" (95 pp.), August 7, 1945; No. 3113.1, "Principal Nazi Organizations Involved in the Commission of War Crimes, Criminal Responsibilities in Connection with the Purge of 1934" (18 pp.), June 15, 1945; No. 3113.3, "Legislative Agencies Involved in War Crimes" (30 pp.), August 28, 1945; No. 3114.2, "Nazi Plans for Dominating Germany and Europe. Domestic Crimes" (68 pp.), August 13, 1945; and no. 3114.3, "Nazi Plans for Dominating Germany and Europe. The Criminal Conspiracy Against the Jews" (15 pp.), August 15, 1945.

[31] See Margaret Mead and Rhoda Metraux, eds., *The Study of Culture at a Distance* (Chicago: University of Chicago Press, 1953).

[32] The two main publications resulting from the study were, United States Strategic Bombing Survey, *The Effects of Strategic Bombing on German Morale*. Vol. I (Washington, D.C.: Government Printing Office, July 1947), Vol. II (Washington, D.C.: Government Printing Office, December 1946). Some of the attitudinal data were analyzed separately in Helen Peak, "Observations on the Characteristics and Distribution of German Nazis," *Psychological Monographs*, vol. 59 (1945), no. 6 (entire issue).

[33] It may suffice to mention here that Parsons deemed this latter research highly successful in regard to the war effort in the Far East (see below).

with colleagues such as Abel, Conrad Arensberg, Georges Gurvitch, Hartshorne, and Merton, who were each to investigate the situation in a particular nation, he devised a study of the social structure of countries under occupation by Nazi Germany.[34] In the summer of 1943, as an offshoot from teaching in the Army Specialized Training program,[35] he drafted a research project, together with anthropologist Kluckhohn, on German and Italian Family Systems; these were to be studied through emigré families in the Boston area.[36] One small study, however, was carried out in late 1944 under the auspices of the Cambridge Community Council. The study investigated race relations (ethnic groups) with Radcliffe College and Wellesley College students as interviewers under the direction of Parsons and Elizabeth Schlesinger, who was a faculty member at Wellesley School of Community Affairs.[37]

Civil Affairs Training Schools

In May 1942, the first School of Military Government was founded at the University of Virginia, inaugurated by the newly established Civil Affairs Division (CAD) of the War Department, which was directed by General John Hilldring.[38] The three-month-long courses of the Civil Affairs Training Program (CATP) were open to younger military men who had at least a high school background, and the nine-month Army Specialized Training Program (ASTP) was reserved for applicants who had had a professional or university education, were fluent in at least one foreign language, and were on average between thirty and fifty-five years old.[39]

Harvard started out in June 1943 with both CAT and AST programs, the latter comprising some 900 hours of teaching on an advanced graduate level. Of these, more than half were occupied with training in various languages, either Far

---

[34] See above, Chapter 2; details are in two letters, namely, Parsons to Roger F. Evans at the Rockefeller Foundation, dated June 11, 1942; and Parsons to Joseph H. Willits at the same institution, dated November 18, 1942; both letters, it appears, followed up personal visits during which Parsons explained the study; none appears to have been as much as answered. Parsons papers, HUG(FP) – 15.2, box 15.

[35] See next section.

[36] The completed "Application for Grant Form from the Harvard University Committee on Research in the Social Sciences," a five-page draft elaboration on the project, "Research Project for the Study of German and Italian Family Systems," and a five-page draft statement of its objective are filed among the Parsons papers, HUG(FP) – 15.2, box 9.

[37] See "Memorandum to the American Defense Steering Committee," by Elizabeth Schlesinger, dated September 21, 1944, filed in Parsons papers, HUG(FP) – 15.2, box 3.

[38] In 1943, programs for training future military government personnel were opened at nine other universities, namely Boston, Chicago, Harvard, Michigan, Northwestern, and Stanford in the summer, and Western Reserve, Wisconsin, and Yale in the fall.

[39] For details, see Earl F. Ziemke, *The United States Army in the Occupation of Germany 1944–1946* (Washington, D.C.: Museum of Military History, 1975). Applicants for both types of courses had to undergo highly selective interviewing by the universities. This meant that the approximately 2,000 military men who completed the CATP education in the last quarter of 1943 had been selected from among 25,000 applicants, and the 960 civilians of that period had been chosen from among some 50,000 applicants.

Eastern or European, and the remainder comprised instruction on matters such as geography, history, economy, law, political-administrative structures, and cultural traditions or mentalities of the countries in the respective areas.[40]

Parsons, who was an Associate Professor until 1944, was initially in charge of the teaching on the Central European area, especially Germany, for both ASTP and CATP, and he later organized the entire ASTP curriculum. According to an exact account of his schedule that he prepared for the use of the Dean of Social Science, he devoted five-sixths of his total working time to this task during the second half of 1943.[41] He was responsible for the agenda and minutes of the Planning Committee as well as planning the curriculum, recruiting staff, inviting outside speakers where experts were needed for various topics, in addition to preparing courses, lecturing, and testing students.[42]

Parsons's Themes Connected with Harvard's War Effort

In the period between 1939 and 1945, among Parsons's fifteen articles were seven that dealt with war-related topics. For instance, "Max Weber and the Contemporary Political Crisis" (published in two parts in January and April 1942), and "Racial and Religious Differences as Factors in Group Tensions" (originally a paper presented at the 1944 meetings of the Conference of Science, Philosophy, and Religion in Their Relation to the Democratic Way of Life) were clearly related to the war situation. He also wrote, apart from three unpublished manuscripts, at least fourteen radio speeches, and a host of ad-hoc memoranda, reports, minutes, or resolutions for various groups or agencies.

To recollect his sociology that entered into his war-related work, his memorandum for the Council for Democracy, an ad-hoc draft for a resolution of American Defense, his lecture notes for ASTP and CATP, his article on German re-education, and his memoranda for the FEA are briefly summarized, together with an essay on the topic of aggressiveness in Western society, originally a paper presented at the 1946 meetings of the Conference of Science, Philosophy, and Religion in Their Relation to the Democratic Way of Life. One important topic was that the atom bomb, reaching beyond the victory in the Second World War, raised the specter of

---

[40] In his annual report covering the period until February 1944, Friedrich, the director of the Harvard School of Overseas Administration, characterized the general purpose of the school as it had been voted on a year before by the Corporation of Harvard in the following way: "Its purpose was to develop intensive programs of regional research and study, with especial attention to the training needs of Americans who might go overseas in connection with the war and postwar tasks America is facing all over the world." "Annual Report, 1943. School of Overseas Administration." By the Director. Unpublished, 1944 (Filed in the Harvard University Archives under the call number HUE 67.143.75B), p. 1.

[41] Parsons, who had originally been assigned half-time to the Committees on Military Government and International Administration, explained in a letter to Dean Buck how much more of his time he was in fact using for the Civil Affairs program. Letter, Parsons to Dean Buck, December 8, 1943, Parsons papers, HUG(FP) – 15.2, box 9.

[42] At Harvard, CATP and ASTP courses on Japan continued until 1945 whereas those on Europe ended in April, 1944.

a Third World War – against which he invoked thoughts that had constituted the baseline of the Harvard social-science war effort.

The Memorandum for the Council for Democracy

The main tenet of this memorandum was that tensions between races, ethnic groups, social classes, or other elements of social structure produced social disorganization that, in turn, could result in anomie grounded in – on the level of action orientation – personal insecurity. Personal insecurity, according to Lasswell's thesis, encouraged allegiance to nondemocratic forces offering a semblance of security to the masses of modern citizens whose identification with nation, economic system, and so on, had been lost. In this diagnosis lay an explanation of how democratic countries could lapse into totalitarianism.

Two opposite types of social order could be seen. National Socialism, for one, showed the five dominant elements of "nationalism including race, socialism, anti-intellectualism, militarism and what may be called particularism as evidenced in the famous principle of leadership,"[43] a menace to Western civilization.

U.S. society, in contrast, was characterized by the six elements of (1) "Rule of law" as opposed to "rule of men" as had been analyzed by his colleague, Friedrich, under the label of "constitutionalism"; (2) civil liberties – which were, he cautioned, not to be extended indiscriminately to those who aimed to undermine democratic structures; (3) equality of opportunity – which, he stressed, deserved to be strengthened as well as grounded in other parameters of success than solely monetary achievement; (4) fairness standards of achievement, which were to emphasize voluntary service for the community; (5) a rational-critical spirit promulgating science, technology, and professional responsibility but eschewing negativism; and, last but not least, (6) activism, which meant the opposite of quietism or fatalism in the face of an imminent problem situation.

The Ad-Hoc Theory for the American Defense Committee on National Morale

Parsons believed that to understand the roots of fascism meant to be better able to fight it. He had a clear image that National Socialism created a society based on violence and fraud. He expressed his views in a text urging American support for Britain and also American intervention in the war. At the time when "Germany... has now gained control over the whole continent of Europe west of Russia,"[44] he drafted a resolution for American Defense in which he made a forceful plea for

---

[43] Parsons, "Memorandum: The Development of the Groups and Organizations Amenable to Use Against American Institutions and Foreign Policy and Possible Measures of Prevention" (unpublished, 1940), published in *Talcott Parsons on National Socialism*, pp. 101–130, cit. p. 114.

[44] Untitled text in three parts, starting with "German National Socialism," p. 1; Parsons papers, HUG(FP) – 42.8.2, box 3.

the fight against Nazism:

> We Americans face a fundamental choice. We can actively combat this scourge, or we can, passively and complacently sit back attempting merely to hold on to what we have.... We members of the _____ group accept this choice unequivocally. We understand it to mean that all the resources of the nation, moral and material, must be mobilized as rapidly as possible for a decisive struggle against National Socialism and its allies.... It means preparation for, and the probable expectation of, involvement in the war ourselves.... It means... active participation, each according to his ability, training and opportunity, in an intensive drive to realize them.[45]

Sociology of Germany for Future Military Government Officers

On June 14, 1943, at the opening meeting of CATP and ASTP, Friedrich, Dean Edward Fox, and also Parsons addressed the first group of "students."[46] "It is really a great opportunity to do something that really has not been done before," Parsons announced at the program. What was the novelty, then?

> [W]hat we are going to try to do is to give you a certain kind of training in social science. We want to take the subject as it is and attempt to mobilize its resources as best we can for this particular job. Now, this particular job as we conceive it is the understanding of a complex society and the understanding of it in its way which will be practically useful for people who are actually in working contact with people of that society. It will be increasingly evident, as our program unfolds, that it is an exceedingly complex society.[47]

In his teaching, over the next nine months, Parsons practiced what he had preached in his opening speech. He covered the topics of German population, family and kinship structures, institutional structures such as civil law, the structure of authority, local government, the education system and the liberal professions, the organization of religion – Lutheran and Catholic churches and their relation to the state, and military organization; furthermore, he dealt with the effects of regional differentiation within Germany.[48] In addition, such as in the section devoted to "Culture and Ideology" of the ASTP classes between November 12 and December 23, 1943, he addressed the topics of modern European thought,

---

[45] Ibid., p. 2.
[46] They were, in fact, men of often considerable standing in civilian life. As mentioned, participants in the two programs, particularly ASTP, were professionals (lawyers, doctors), university professors or others from higher education, top-level employees from industry, commerce, or municipal government, in short, often highly trained civilians aged on average between 30 and 55 years. See Ziemke, *The United States Army in the Occupation of Germany*, pp. 14–17.
[47] "School of Overseas Administration Harvard University Foreign Area and Language Program Advanced Phase, Opening Meeting – June 14, 1943," p. 9; Harvard University Archives, UA V 663.8, box 2.
[48] Material on the curriculum detailing the schedule of lectures, including those of Parsons, are preserved and filed in the Harvard University Archives, UA V 663.8, box 1.

the "socialist" (i.e., anticapitalist) element of Nazism ("Nazism II"), radical revolutionism, youth culture, and anti-Semitism in Nazism ("Nazism III"), the social implications of Christianity in European cultural patterns, "vested interests" and conservatism, the structural environment of German culture, the religious background of German culture, Nazism and the German national tradition, and differences between German and Anglo-Saxon democracy.[49]

His CATP lecture notes of July 25, 1943 on anti-Semitism may illustrate his approach.[50] He began by examining two reasons why Jews were selected as scapegoats in Gentile societies. These were, first, that the Jews at the same time were both an in-group and an out-group, inasmuch as they were members of society less remote than foreigners but set aside from Gentiles by the socioreligious character of their – more or less orthodox – community; and, second, that they were a "natural" symbol for any "fundamentalist" group opposing modernization in modern society, representing for "fundamentalists" a conspicuous epitome of all that was modern. No matter whether modern life was resented and rejected as economic capitalism, religious emancipation, or intellectualism – Jews always served as the symbol for resentful antimodernism. In his notes in which he jotted down only salient points in the shape of keywords or short sentences, Parsons clarified that the Jews were a "par-excellence symbol of emancipation," which meant that "fundamentalist" groups opposing emancipation could fight modernity by hating Jews. These, therefore, could be made to stand for capitalism, socialism (communism), intellectualism, and/or metropolitanism, he noted. Anti-Semitism could be equally anti-Christian or irreligious, since by nature it sprang from anomie and nihilism, and it represented more than one kind of immorality. Exponents of this catch-all prejudice, he said in his lecture, took issue with the presumed international character of Jews, and they presumed that economic life everywhere was controlled by supposedly all-powerful world Jewry; even in the United States, he made a point of saying, Jews were charged with controlling economic life.[51]

He then addressed two further main points concerning anti-Semitism, under the keywords of "Victims" and "Response to Victims." Under the former heading, he noted, "Distinguishable (visibility); Little possibility for retaliation; Accessibility; Previous blame; Personification," and under the latter, his main points were "Repression; Compliance + appeasement; Resistance – assimilation, contra-scapegoating, heightening of in-group feeling, temporary security."[52]

The remedy against such prejudice appeared in his lecture notes as "importance of reward, even praise in preventing prejudice." Such type of propaganda would

---

[49] See "School of Overseas Administration, Central European Program. Outline," dated September 29, 1943; Harvard University Archives, UA V 663.8, box 1.

[50] "CA Anti-Semitism, July 25," lecture notes, handwritten; Harvard University Archives, UA V 663.8, box 2.

[51] At this point, his lecture notes contained the somewhat cryptic sentence: "Case of the Chinese Emperor." While he did not explain the meaning of this, I suspect that he meant that the Chinese emperor was never seen eye to eye by practically all his subjects, and therefore they were free to fantasize what he looked like, just as anti-Semites might fantasize what a Jew looked like and what he or she "does" or "is."

[52] Lecture notes, "CA Anti-Semitism, July 25," p. 3.

reinforce the absence or disavowal of discrimination or ethnocentrism as a type of antiprejudice policy on the part of military government[53] (he was to revise this suggestion again in 1944/1945 when he elaborated on the three types of institutional control for Germany).

Re-Education for Germany as "Controlled Institutional Change"

Between September and early November 1944, Parsons revised his memorandum for the final report of the Conference on Germany After the War, convened by Columbia University psychiatrist Richard Brickner and sponsored by the War Department earlier that year.

The revised memorandum, which was published early in 1945, entailed three propositions. They were (1) that social change to overcome Nazism might be boycotted by "vested interest" groups unless re-education policy was so inconspicuous that it failed to be noticed by those who were the target of the policy; (2) that Margaret Mead's hypothesis was sound, to the effect that German national character had a dual structure vacillating between idealism and materialism; and (3) that Germans would readily collaborate with military government if the latter's policies were both firm and nondirective,[54] enabling Germans themselves to bring about their own re-education into a democratic nation.

Such institutional change was to apply three different kinds of policies of social control. They were *regressive control* which counteracted, in the terms of Weberian types of authority, regression to even more pronounced traditionalism than had developed already within the charismatic system of National Socialism.

Second, and sociologically most interesting, was *permissive* control. (Future) Allied Military Government policy, setting up specific institutional innovations, could undo the Nazi mentality surreptitiously through conversion to market capitalism of the economic-occupational system. Universalism and achievement-mindedness would be reinforced in Germans; their value orientations would tend in the direction of democracy, through change located initially in the economic-occupational world. Regarding prevention of World War III, a much-discussed topic at the time, he added that German reconstruction was no mistake because the clue to world peace lay in international control, not de-industrialization of Germany: "It is to a better system of international control, not to de-industrialization of Germany, that one must look for a solution of this problem."[55]

---

[53] In "Propaganda and Social Control," he made the distinction between communism's "revolutionary" propaganda, fascism's "destructive" or "debunking" propaganda, and democracy's "reinforcement" propaganda. These were related to two types of social control, namely repressive control in deviant (dictatorial) régimes, and permissive control in integrated (democratic) régimes. See his "Propaganda and Social Control," *Psychiatry*, vol. 5, 1942, reprinted in *Talcott Parsons on National Socialism*, pp. 243–274. See also above.

[54] This had also been the thesis of Emil Ludwig, a writer and German emigré who had testified in 1943 before the House of Representatives Committee on Postwar Policy to this effect; see Emil Ludwig, *The Moral Conquest of Germany* (Garden City, N.Y.: Doubleday, 1945).

[55] Parsons, "The Problem of Controlled Institutional Change," p. 314.

The third type of social control he called *direct*, one to approach racism and other features of Nazi ideology through unrelenting repression, destroy all appeal of "socialism" to the Germans, and convert their formalism into a sense of individuality – if only at the expense of a return to the Germans' notoriously legalistic stubbornness.

The Memoranda for the Foreign Economic Administration

In his memoranda worked out for the Foreign Economic Administration (Enemy Branch), Parsons specified what he meant by "applied social science."[56] In the memorandum discussing a policy of "Separation of Western Territories from Germany" he held the view that to teach the Germans a lesson of how democracy was more effective than any authoritarian structure meant utmost trust in the principle of economic self-determination in a market economy:

> Internally the most important thing would be the creation of a focal center for the development of a liberal-democratic society among the German population. So long as the moral-psychological situation is good, a favorable situation for relative economic prosperity and an expanding field of economic opportunity should work in that direction. It seems more likely that this would work out under International than under German administration because there would be less need for repressive controls over the economy.[57]

With regard to the FEA Disarmament Plan for Germany, he argued that institutional disarmament was to be the centerpiece of the redemocratization of Germany in at least three different respects. First, as far as the institutional sphere of the military was concerned, complete eradication of German militarism had to include not only the organization of the armed forces but also the prestige of militaristic values and traditions. Second, the economy was to be dissociated from the state. This meant that not only would cartels and monopolies be abolished, but quasi-governmental powers of so-called industrial groups[58] would also have to be scrapped; this left the economy as a competitive, de-politicized realm of society where market forces could prevail freely. Third, the use of international relations as a cloak for espionage or fraud was to be abandoned completely. In this way, international relations were to be freed from constraints and could become an arena for cooperation and exchange; in this vein, exploitation of the weak by the strong and powerful, as had been practiced in Europe by Nazi imperialism in a disastrous way, could be controlled or possibly prevented in the future, he ventured.

Such institutional change in the name of disarmament, to be sure, needed a rationale of positive goals. It was not enough to destroy undesirable Nazi structures;

---

[56] "The Problem of Controlled Institutional Change" carried the subtitle, "An Essay in Applied Social Science."

[57] Memorandum, Parsons to Philip M. Kaiser, dated August 7, 1945. Subject: "Separation of Western Territories from Germany," p. 4; Parsons papers, HUG(FP) – 15.2, box 9.

[58] These had been Nazi-induced amalgams of whole branches of the economy into state-dependent centralized complexes, operating beyond competition or market control under primarily political (i.e., party-directed) policies.

it was also necessary to conceive of democratic structures suitable for German society to replace them. "[T]he emphasis of the discussion should not be only on elimination and suppression of institutions."[59] "Their mere suppression would not solve the problem, since if German society is to survive at all it must be organized in some form, and whether we like it or not Allied policy will influence the development of this form." From this he concluded, "It is extremely important to analyze what probable alternatives may be expected to emerge in place of the structures which are destroyed and what can be done to guide developments in the direction of those alternatives which are most acceptable from our point of view."

Regarding Origin and Prospect of Aggressiveness in Western-Type Societies

In September 1946, the seventh symposium of the Conference of Science, Philosophy, and Religion in Their Relation to the Democratic Way of Life posed the topic of "power and aggression in western culture and methods for the transformation and integration of that culture itself;"[60] Parsons chose to reanalyze aggressiveness in light of the impact of the atom bomb. Lasswell's insecurity hypothesis, he felt, had lost none of its salience.

He started out by stating that "a few elementary facts about the psychology of aggression"[61] suggested that aggressiveness, as a cultural and not merely individual tendency, needed sociological attention. Three subsystems of modern society generated aggressiveness that could be converted into willingness to support antidemocratic movements or sustain the politics of an aggressive nation. They were, first, the kinship system which in modern Western urban and industrial society was no longer a harbor for personal privilege and security; this, in turn, created anxieties that could be exploited by political movements preaching aggressiveness. Second, the occupational system with its uncertain and less than equitable chances of advancement in hierarchies of income and influence could be a source of dissatisfaction, all the more since "there is in fact much injustice, much of which is very deeply rooted in the nature of the society, and because many [individuals] are disposed to be paranoid and see more injustice than actually exists."[62] He concluded, "Thus the kinship and the occupational systems constitute from the present point of view a mutually reinforcing system of forces acting on the individual to

---

[59] Memorandum, Parsons to Philip M. Kaiser, dated September 14, 1945. Subject: "Revision of Chapter 10 of the FEA Disarmament Plan Called Institutional Disarmament," p. 2; the following two quotes are from the same page. Parsons papers, HUG (FP) – 15.2, box 9.

[60] "Announcing the publication of *Conflicts of Power in Modern Culture*, autumn 1947, Seventh symposium of the Conference on Science, Philosophy and Religion in Their Relation to the Democratic Way of Life, distributed by Harper & Brothers, New York"; Parsons papers, HUG(FP) – 42.8.4, box 8.

[61] Parsons, "Certain Primary Sources and Patterns of Aggression in the Social Structure of the Western World," first published in *Psychiatry*, vol. 10, 1947, pp. 167–181; reprinted in *Talcott Parsons on National Socialism*, pp. 325–347, cit. p. 326.

[62] Ibid., p. 338; the next quote is from the same page.

generate large quantities of aggressive impulse, to repress the greater part of it, and to channel it in the direction of finding agencies which can be symbolically held responsible for failure and for deception and injustice to the individual and to those with whom he is identified."

The third subsystem held the worst danger. "Group hostilities," when they were exploited by a government that was not controlled by a democratic body politic, could easily become the driving force in aggressive imperialism. "The values about which the fundamentalist pattern of reaction tends to cluster are those . . . in the constitution and symbolization of informal group solidarities."[63] That such displaced aggression, targeting the "foreigner," was immensely dangerous, on principle, was due to the fact that, in the postwar era of the existence of the atom bomb, "national states now command such destructive weapons that war between them is approaching suicidal significance."[64]

The War Effort Realized by Three of Parsons's Harvard Colleagues

The war effort was not confined to Parsons alone, as has been noted. Many Harvard professors, either intermittently or continuously throughout the period between 1940 and 1945, contributed to the various programs and projects in some of which Parsons also participated. Also, for Parsons as for his colleagues, the themes that had dominated their war effort were not dropped abruptly on the occasion of victory but blended into some of their postwar work. To exemplify such concern and thereby further substantiate Parsons's claim that social science had a stake as a basic national resource, I shall sketch the context of three of them: Gordon W. Allport, Carl J. Friedrich, and Clyde K. M. Kluckhohn.

Allport

Allport, Professor of Psychology, in the 1920s had done some postgraduate work with Kurt Lewin at the University of Berlin. His main field of study, like that of his colleague Murray, was the origin and functioning of the human personality in the process of social life.[65] In 1940, he created a research interest at Harvard's Department of Psychology on the topic of morale[66] and with two collaborators

---

[63] Ibid., p. 341.
[64] Ibid., p. 342.
[65] See, as one major work, Allport, *Personality: A Psychological Interpretation* (New York: Henry Holt, 1937).
[66] This work initiated a series of *Worksheets on Morale* that were at the same time instructive and educative, meant for use everywhere in the nation. Topics included, among others, "The Analysis and Execution of Propaganda Campaigns," "Outline of a Course for Community Instructions in the Foundation of Morale," "Strategy and Tactics of Anti-Nazi Propaganda." See, for the list of topics up to 1942/1943, Allport and Helene R. Veltfort, "Social Psychology and the Civilian War Effort," *Journal of Social Psychology*, S.P.S.S.I. Bulletin, vol. 18, 1943, pp. 165–233, esp. pp. 225–226.

compiled a comprehensive bibliography.[67] When, with Lewin as its first president, the *Society for the Psychological Study of Social Issues* (S.P.S.S.I.) was founded in 1940, Allport became an active member. Its second Yearbook, to which he contributed, was the volume entitled *Civilian Morale*, containing scholarly articles on almost any aspect of morale, including industrial relations, race relations, or national character.[68] He became Counsellor of Harvard's American Defense Group in 1943 when he joined the staff of the School of Overseas Administration, both institutions where Parsons was his colleague.

A second topic: In 1942/1943, as editor of the *Journal of Abnormal and Social Psychology*, Allport invited eminent scholars from the United States and emigré Germans to write on issues of Nazism, war, and psychology. Under his aegis, Bruno Bettelheim and Curt Bondy published the first analytically elaborated eyewitness reports on life in a concentration camp.[69]

In 1945, the S.P.S.S.I. Yearbook tackled problems of world peace as they had been discussed at the Society's 1944 conference.[70] Allport contributed to the section entitled "World Order Within Our Grasp," recommending that the United Nations become an active peace organization immediately after the end of the war and urging swift decisions in international politics in order to incur psychological changes in favor of future peace: "Immediately after the war Europe will be in a very plastic state, but in time it will again harden in its old mold. Spheres of influence will be re-created and new nationalism and vested interests formed. Psychologically and politically the world will be ready for a peace organization at the close of hostilities. It can best be forged at the anvil left hot by war."[71]

Another topic was first discussed in a pamphlet from *Worksheets on Morale* and later developed into a scholarly theme,[72] namely the problem of rumor ("ABC's of Wartime Rumors," several revisions). Rumor was a device of propaganda feeding on anxiety and aggression as social-psychological forces. In this connection, Allport organized the *Massachusetts Committee on Public Safety*. Starting in 1942, this organization prompted the active involvement of at least forty newspapers across the nation, contributing to analyzing and counteracting rumors through

---

[67] L. M. Hurvich, T. W. Huntington, and G. W. Allport, "Beginnings of a Bibliography on Psychological Factors in Morale" (Cambridge, Mass.: Harvard University, unpublished, mimeo, 1940). He also published on the topic of morale in psychological journals. Most noteworthy was his and Helene Veltfort's documentation of over three hundred analytical papers concerning the "civilian war effort." See also above, Chapter 2.

[68] This Yearbook was published as Goodwin Watson, ed., *Civilian Morale* (Boston: Houghton Mifflin, 1942).

[69] Bruno Bettelheim, "Individual and Mass Behavior in Extreme Situations," *Journal of Abnormal and Social Psychology*, vol. 38, 1943, pp. 417–452; Curt Bondy, "Problems of Internment Camps," *Journal of Abnormal and Social Psychology*, vol. 38, 1943, pp. 453–475.

[70] This Yearbook was published as Gardner Murphy, ed., *Human Nature and Enduring Peace* (Boston: Houghton Mifflin, 1945).

[71] Allport and Sheldon J. Korchin, "World Order Within Our Grasp (Discussion)," in Gardner Murphy, ed., *Human Nature and Enduring Peace*, pp. 227–230, cit. p. 228.

[72] The systematic account written after the war was Allport and L. Postman, *The Psychology of Rumor* (New York: Henry Holt, 1947).

regular columns entitled *Rumor Clinics*.[73] This work aimed to neutralize propaganda in the short-wave radio broadcasts of *Auslandspropaganda* in the United States masterminded by the Goebbels Ministry in Berlin.

Starting out from a much-revised *Worksheet on Morale*, Allport's "ABC's of Scapegoating" (first published circa 1940) was distributed by the Harvard American Defense Group, in 1944, in 100,000 copies as a leaflet to educators throughout the nation.[74] Based on this wartime work, Allport's classic, *The Nature of Prejudice* (1954), acknowledged in its preface not only his indebtedness to the "continuing seminar on Group Conflict and Prejudice" that had arisen from his wartime interests, but also his intellectual debt and academic closeness, among others, to his colleague Parsons.[75]

Friedrich

Friedrich, a German national who first met Parsons in the 1920s when they were both students at Amherst College, had been writing about Germany ever since the Nazis had come to power in 1933.[76] His *Constitutional Government and Politics* (1937) distinguished between two modern forms of democracy, constitutional and plebiscitarian, vigorously rejecting *Volksgemeinschaft*.[77]

In November 1939, Friedrich opposed the Neutrality Act in a "letter to the editor" preserved among his papers in the Harvard University Archives:

> It seems to me that the vigorous support of the British and French in the hope that they will not be defeated by Hitler but on the contrary will be able to bring this unhappy war to as speedy a conclusion as possible is our one and only chance of staying out of it ourselves. The longer the war lasts the more likely we are to get in. Therefore anything that we do to prolong it, and undoubtedly the maintenance of the present Neutrality Act has that effect, the surer we are to get in.[78]

In 1940, Friedrich became a founding member and active campaigner of the Council for Democracy, serving on various subcommittees of the Council's Committee on National Morale and joining the Harvard Defense Group, the radio committee of which he chaired between 1941 and 1944. American values of strong-mindedness and truthfulness while fighting Nazi Germany were his concern, in 1942, in his *The New Belief in the Common Man* where he explained how an ability

---

[73] For further details, see Allport and Veltfort, "Social Psychology and the Civilian War Effort," p. 181.

[74] See Allport, "ABC's of Scapegoating," revised edition. Freedom pamphlet series (Chicago: Roosevelt College, and Anti-Defamation League of B'nai B'rith, 1948).

[75] Allport, *The Nature of Prejudice* (Reading, Mass.: Addison Wesley, 1954), p. xx.

[76] See, for instance, his undated manuscripts written in the early 1930s, entitled "National Socialism" (Harvard University Archives, HUG(FP) – Carl J. Friedrich – 17.60, box 18), and "Hitler, Prophet of Germany" (Harvard University Archives, HUG(FP) – Carl J. Friedrich – 17.60, box 24).

[77] Friedrich, *Constitutional Government and Politics. Nature and Development* (New York: Harper and Brothers, 1937), revised edition *Constitutional Government and Democracy* (Boston: Little, Brown, 1941).

[78] Letter, Friedrich to E. Skillin, Jr., editor of *Commonweal*, dated October 17, 1939; Friedrich papers, HUG(FP) – Carl J. Friedrich – 17.10, box 2.

to face hard facts cultivated the virtues of common sense that were at the heart of America's successful democracy.[79]

As Director of the Harvard School of Overseas Administration between 1943 and 1945, he followed the principle that the social sciences could best contribute to the war effort by preparing future military government personnel through excellent instruction. In an article published in 1943, he clarified that the only chance for democracy in postwar Italy, Germany, and Japan would be to replace "rule of men" by "rule of law" under the authority of the unparalleled powers bestowed upon military government.[80]

After the end of hostilities, he became political adviser to (Deputy) Military Governor of Germany (U.S. Zone), General Lucius D. Clay, in 1946 and again in 1948. He made valuable contributions when he helped plan a constitutional régime for the Federal Republic of Germany. He later remembered that he had advised the *Parlamentarischer Rat* in 1948 to lay down in the *Grundgesetz der Bundesrepublik Deutschland* the principle that change of governments was conditional upon the legislative chamber's, the *Bundestag*'s, qualified vote of mistrust, accompanied by a proposal for a candidate for Chancellor named beforehand – in this way, an acting head of government could not be ousted lightly, as had been one of the pitfalls of the Weimar system. Friedrich's experiences as adviser to Clay yielded his most instructive treatise on military government, which he conceived of as the last phase of World War II.[81]

Kluckhohn

Kluckhohn was an anthropologist whose fieldwork had been mainly with American Indians in the Southwest, particularly the Navaho. Together with anthropologists Mead and Bateson, he joined the Conference on Science, Philosophy, and Religion in Their Relation to the Democratic Way of Life at the time of its Second Symposium in 1941, devoted to the nature and future of democracy. Kluckhohn contributed by commenting on a paper by Mead advocating comparative study of culture. Mead proposed to ground changes from authoritarianism to democracy in the social-science knowledge accumulated by cultural anthropology and related disciplines, suggesting that no blueprints be issued but, rather, goals be pointed out on the basis of scientific knowledge. Such goals, Mead knew, would give direction to innovative efforts without either unduly restricting individual freedom of action or inadvertently converting citizens into dupes of doubtful social progress. Mead stressed how cultural anthropology could help to ensure a better world and improve on modern society.[82]

---

[79] Friedrich, *The New Belief in the Common Man* (Boston: Little, Brown & Co., 1942).
[80] Friedrich, "Military Government as a Step Toward Self-Rule," *Public Opinion Quarterly*, vol. 7, 1943, pp. 527–541; cit. p. 541.
[81] Friedrich and Associates, *American Experiences in Military Government in World War II* (New York: Rinehart & Co., 1948). He analyzed the time period from the summer of 1943 to the summer of 1946.
[82] Mead, "The Comparative Study of Culture and the Purposive Cultivation of Democratic Values," in Conference on Science, Philosophy, and Religion in Their Relation to the Democratic Way of Life, *Second Symposium* (New York: Harper and Brothers, 1942), pp. 55–69.

Kluckhohn supported her idea but qualified that a nation's culture was far from homogenous, and should not be so treated. He cautioned that the task of culture change with regard to democratization might be more difficult than Mead might expect. He warned, "We cannot 'implement plans for altering our present culture' until we know that culture in the same detailed and coherent way which we know certain of the best described non-literate cultures."[83]

In 1943, when the Conference symposium dealt with problems of future world peace, he contributed a paper entitled "Anthropological Research and World Peace,"[84] and in July 1944, when the Conference symposium's theme was "Unity and Diversity," he wrote an essay on how Navaho culture could help to envisage the tensions or potentialities of culture clash inherent in the future work of military government in the defeated nations.[85]

In 1944, he also published his *Navaho Witchcraft*. This book, which might on first sight appear far removed from the war effort, nevertheless had a lesson to teach (as Parsons found). Kluckhohn detailed the structural dynamics of the social context and type of motivationally relevant definition of the situation which, in Navaho society, led to suspicion of witchcraft, and frequently to subsequent persecution or even murder. Parsons, reviewing the book in 1946, praised the explanation of how anxiety and aggression could be channeled in a social system. Witchcraft, he reported Kluckhohn showing, could be seen as an indirect institutional mechanism facilitating the abreaction of group tensions.[86]

Between 1943 and 1945, Parsons and Kluckhohn both taught at the School of Overseas Administration, in the Far East Section but also in the Central European Program. (They designed a research project together in 1943.) In 1942, Kluckhohn became co-director of the OWI's Foreign Morale Analysis Division, whose target area was the Pacific Theater of Operations. Together with psychiatrist Alexander Leighton, he directed a series of research projects investigating Japanese morale as well as national character and mentality, explaining to the American military about the background of knowledge of the Japanese language,

---

[83] Kluckhohn, "Comment on chapter 'The Comparative Study of Culture' by Margaret Mead," in *Conference on Science, Philosophy, and Religion in Their Relation to the Democratic Way of Life, Second Symposium*, pp. 72–76; cit. p. 72.

[84] Kluckhohn, "Anthropological Research and World Peace," in Lyman Bryson, Louis Finckelstein, Robert MacIver, eds., *Approaches to World Peace* (New York: Harper and Brothers, 1944), pp. 143–159.

[85] Kluckhohn, "Group Tensions: Analysis of a Case History," in Lyman Bryson, Louis Finckelstein, and Robert MacIver, eds., *Approaches to National Unity* (New York: Harper and Brothers, 1945), pp. 222–231; reprinted in Kluckhohn, *Culture and Behavior* (New York: Free Press, 1962), pp. 301–322.

[86] At the end of his review, Parsons went beyond Kluckhohn, "It cannot but strike the reader who is a student of our own society that there is a close analogy between Navaho witchcraft and our own 'scapegoating.' But there is also a notable difference. Among the Navaho it is always an individual to whom witchcraft is ascribed. In our society, on the other hand, very often it is a social group, the Negro, the Jew, the 'Red.' What is the basis of the difference?" Parsons, "Navaho Witchcraft. By Clyde Kluckhohn. Cambridge: Peabody Museum of American Archaeology and Ethnology, Harvard University, 1944," Book review, *American Journal of Sociology*, vol. 51, 1946, pp. 566–569, cit. p. 569.

history, and culture, as well as the specifics of Japanese authoritarianism and war attitudes.[87]

In the spring of 1945, as Parsons was to mention in several papers, Kluckhohn came to the conclusion, on the basis of ethnographically collected material, that Japan's morale was seriously crumbling – a finding he obviously passed on to the War Department, among other parts of government, but with little immediate echo.[88] Parsons held Kluckhohn's research in exceedingly high regard.

Following on from such war work, Kluckhohn became the director of Harvard's Russian Research Center when it was founded in 1948. There, Kluckhohn and Parsons worked together, Parsons as a member of the Executive Council, as they also did in the newly founded Department of Social Relations, until Kluckhohn's untimely death in 1960.

Parsons's Reaction to the Deployment of the Atom Bomb

Approximately one week before VJ-Day, excluding Russian entry into the war against Japan, the atom bomb was dropped on two Japanese cities, Hiroshima and Nagasaki. Harvard's natural scientists, in Smith's *Harvard Century*, were later to be praised profusely for their achievement which had made the weapon possible and helped to end World War II. However, Harvard's social scientists, who also contributed to the effort that helped win the war, were not mentioned.

What was the nation's or academe's immediate reaction, one may ask, to the deployment of the bomb? More precisely, what was Parsons's view on the war effort, considering that the atom bomb was believed to be the utmost victory of the natural sciences, allowing for unparalleled destructive effectiveness of a weapon? To be sure, as much as can be reconstructed from archival material, Harvard's social scientists, among them Parsons, were not very enthusiastic about the atom bomb when they did recognize the enormous accomplishment thus made.[89]

On July 19, 1945, anticipating the deployment of the bomb by less than a month, National Scientific Advisor and chairman of the Office of Scientific Research and Development (OSRD) Vannevar Bush's report on wartime work was published in Washington, entitled *Science, the Endless Frontier*.[90] Bush's report, which relied exclusively on the scientific endeavors of the natural sciences such as nuclear physics, recommended a National Science Foundation (NSF) as a base for continuing the enormously valuable wartime work into the postwar period. On July 23, a bill to create this central scientific research agency of the federal government

---

[87] An outcome of this work was Alexander Leighton, *The Governing of Men* (New York: Octagon Books, 1945).

[88] This fact was mentioned by Parsons several times in his postwar writings. For one such reference, see especially Parsons, "Social Science – A Basic National Resource, 1948," p. 55; see next two sections below.

[89] Although initiatives similar to those of Parsons were taken by several of his Harvard colleagues (and some of this material has been preserved in the Harvard Archives), I shall concentrate here on Parsons, with little reference to his colleagues who acted similarly.

[90] Vannevar Bush, *Science, the Endless Frontier* (Washington, D.C.: Government Printing Office, 1945).

was introduced in Congress by Senator Kilgore of West Virginia and two other Democrats.

Dated July 22, a letter to the editor of the *New York Times* signed by Parsons appeared on July 25, entitled "Social Sciences Important. Provisions Sought for Them in Program of National Research." After briefly recapitulating the background to Bush's recommendation, he went on to say,

> It can readily be granted that the social sciences have not yet reached the level of maturity as disciplines which the medical and natural sciences have. They are, however, developing rapidly and have already made very significant contributions to the war effort as well as in other practical fields of application. When the history of the role of science in this war comes to be written the general public will be surprised to learn how important the contributions of social science have been, even though there has been no mobilization of its personnel for war research in any way comparable to that of the other groups in the Office of Scientific Research and Development.[91]

Parsons also wrote to Vannevar Bush, protesting "the exclusion of support of research in the social sciences from the scope of the Foundation," detailing "Indeed, for the long run I think that adequate support for research in social science can be argued to be at least as important for the future of our civilization as is that in natural science and medicine.... Hence, I feel that the omission of the social sciences from your proposed National Science Foundation would create very serious potential injury to the national interest."[92] Bush, in his reply dated August 7, cited a letter by President Roosevelt to whom he, Bush, had reported when first planning the national research agency.[93] Harvard President Conant, whom Parsons had also alerted in the matter, had replied to him a week earlier using the same excuse, "[I]t is quite clear from President Roosevelt's letter that he did not have the Social Sciences in mind."[94]

On the day following Bush's letter, Parsons wrote a draft for another letter to the editor of the *New York Times*. He used the event of the atom bomb having been deployed over Hiroshima (which had happened on August 6 and was reported on in the press the next day) to strengthen his argument on behalf of the social sciences:

> The startling news of the atomic bomb was significant on a scale beyond any familiar measure. Its prime significance is that it intensifies the immediate problem of the organization of the world for peace and progress.... The *New York Times* asked the logical question, "But can mankind grow up quickly enough to win the race between civilization and disaster?" It is when the whole story of the atomic bomb is set in context with certain other recent events and announcements that the

---

[91] Newspaper clipping, Parsons papers, HUG(FP) – 42.8.4, box 19.
[92] Letter, Parsons to Vannevar Bush, July 26, 1945; Parsons papers, HUG(FP) – 42.8.4, box 19.
[93] Letter, Bush to Parsons, August 7, 1945; Parsons papers, HUG(FP) – 42.8.4, box 19.
[94] Letter, James B. Conant to Parsons, July 31, 1945; Parsons papers – 42.8.4, box 19. Conant, rather condescendingly, added, "I was also very much interested in your statement about the important contributions to the war which have been made by the Social Scientists. I think it would be very valuable to present these cases to an intelligent lay audience and I hope this may be done at the earliest moment. I certainly would be interested in such a book."

urgency of this question becomes most apparent. The bomb was developed by the application of organization and management to a great group project involving many of the finest scientific brains.... The announcement by President Truman contained a very clear statement... "But the greatest marvel... of the enterprise... (is)... the achievement of scientific brains in putting together infinitely complex pieces of knowledge held by many men in different fields of science into a workable plan...." The immediate product of this scientific work is an agency of destruction out of scale with all past weapons, and therefore *ipso facto* a weapon in the hands of the rulers of the great industrial nations, which changes forever the balance of power among nations and the balance of power between rulers and ruled.... This leaves us with a glaring paradox. On the one hand the atomic bomb has already cost two billion dollars.... We have found that the exact sciences and their applied technology are indispensable to winning a war, and we have harnessed them to war with extraordinary success.... President Roosevelt called upon Dr. Vannevar Bush to... make recommendations concerning future encouragment of science by Government. On the other hand we find the social sciences omitted from the O.S.R.D. report, and not even mentioned among the necessary means to assure the world against the danger of atomic bombs.[95]

The message was clear: Only social sciences, which had been of strategic if largely unheralded importance in the war, could address the problems of international politics which were raised by the fact that henceforth the atom bomb would be a factor to be reckoned with regarding the fate and fame of the nation. He pleaded,

[T]he idea that human brains must solve the human problems of world peace is not an unfamiliar one. President Roosevelt stated in the address which he prepared for the Jefferson Day dinner, "Today we are faced with the preeminent fact that, if civilization is to survive, we must cultivate the science of human relationships...." Mr. Vinson, then head of OWMR, in his Memorial Day address at Arlington stated, "There is something wrong with us, with the systems of mankind that have caused war...." If these statements do not imply a definite method of approaching the problems which they state, they are only loose generalities. If they do imply a method, this method must be social science.... As an appropriate first measure the President should order a study of the position of the social sciences parallel to the study prepared by Dr. Bush of O.S.R.D. on the natural sciences.... It should most vigorously explore the needs which social science must fill in a world equipped for suicide, and the means to put social science brains in harness.

To substantiate his claim that social science was of crucial importance in the emerging world crisis subsequent to American command of the atom bomb, he followed two separate courses of action. For one, he alerted his colleagues in sociology to the necessity to actively campaign for inclusion of the social sciences into the NSF. For this purpose, he published an article detailing what science legislation meant regarding the role of social science in the endangered postwar political scenario of the United States.[96]

---

[95] Letter (draft), "To the Editor of *The New York Times*," dated August 8, 1945; Parsons papers, HUG(FP) – 42.8.4, box 19; the next quote is from the same source.
[96] Parsons, "The Science Legislation and the Role of the Social Sciences," *American Sociological Review*, vol. 11, 1946, pp. 653–666.

In addition, Parsons became a member of the Association of Atomic Scientists as well as the American Association for the Advancement of Science, presenting a paper at the latter's Symposium on Science Legislation in December 1946, which was published in the *Bulletin of Atomic Scientists* in January 1947. He then had the essay republished in *Political Science Quarterly*, to assure it wider circulation among social scientists whose role surely was at stake.[97] His concern was incorporation of the social sciences into the NSF, equal with the natural sciences, on the grounds of the importance of science as such for progress in the modern democratic world. He made four points which substantiated his concern in the context of a sociological theory of the social system, namely, (1) "Most scientists, as well as other intelligent citizens, would agree that the great problems of our time are not those of the control of nature but of the stability and adequacy of the social order;"[98] (2) "Our civilization as a whole is deeply committed to the great adventure of rational understanding of man and society, as well as the physical and biological world. Science as a body of technical knowledge and procedures is the most highly developed expression of this fundamental system of attitudes and values in our civilization;"[99] (3) "In fact, all science is a fundamental unity. It simply is not possible to draw sharp clear-cut lines between the natural and the social sciences.... Each side needs the contributions of the others, and many of the most important problems fall across the line;"[100] and (4) "To a very substantial and rapidly increasing degree, the actual functioning of our social order is dependent on a social technology which is in fact applied social science.... Technically trained personnel are playing a larger and larger part, for instance, in the administrative process, in the adjustment of industrial relations, in the field of communications, in the control functions of the economy as through the central banking system, in the operation of foreign trade, and various such fields."[101]

Against this backdrop, he emphasized that basic science was as important as applied science. And then, to epitomize the importance of social science often undervalued even by social scientists themselves, as one example among several which he cited, he referred to the research of the OWI's Foreign Morale Analysis Branch on decrease of morale in Japan in the early months of 1945, prior to Japan's eventual unconditional surrender – which implicitly rendered improbable the official story that deployment of the atom bomb had ended World War II:

> The study of Japanese military morale, conducted by Dr. Alexander Leighton, Dr. Clyde Kluckhohn and their colleagues ... formed a basis, in the latter period of the war in the Pacific, for a psychological warfare policy, which had begun before the end to have important practical results, and which certainly could not have been arrived at on the basis of common sense. They also unquestionably

---

[97] "Science Legislation and the Social Sciences," *Political Science Quarterly*, vol. 62, 1947, pp. 241–249.
[98] Ibid., p. 241.
[99] Ibid., p. 242.
[100] Ibid., pp. 242–243.
[101] Ibid., pp. 243–244.

had a good deal to do with the policies toward working out the surrender of Japanese forces without incurring the serious last-ditch resistance so many feared.[102]

To document what were the accomplishments which sociology in particular had attained during wartime, Parsons co-authored with Bernard Barber an article, "Sociology, 1941–1946," published early in 1948 in the *American Journal of Sociology*.[103] This article cited a host of wartime studies, including Hauser's "Wartime Developments in Census Statistics" (1945), Taeuber's "Some Recent Developments in Sociological Work in the Department of Agriculture" (1945), and Williams's "Some Observations on Sociological Research in Government During World War II" (1946), documenting analytical progress dating from the war period.[104] The article mentioned as locales for the development of scientific sociology between 1941 and 1946 a number of war-related government agencies, namely, OSS, OWI's Foreign Morale Analysis Division, and the "Army Civil Affairs Training Schools and the Army Specialized Training Division's Foreign Area and Language Programs,"[105] together with other agencies. The article, on close inspection, provided detailed documentation of wartime achievement of sociology, and indeed social science in general.

The last paragraph complained of a situation of apparent discrimination, however. Despite unquestionable contributions to winning the war in the time period between 1941 and 1946, sociology was in a sad state of professional development, Parsons and Barber observed. Nonetheless, they conveyed a spirit of optimism:

> When to these purely scientific problems are added the social responsibilities which all trained intelligence – but, above all, social science – must feel in a time like this, it is clear that to be a sociologist after World War II is to be in a situation of appalling difficulties. As a professional group we are committed to a venture which is in many ways without precedent and which, indeed, the pessimists freely predict to be impossible. It is a challenge worthy of the finest traditions of the American spirit of enterprise.[106]

The Fate of Parsons's Memorandum Analyzing the War Effort of the Social Sciences

At the end of November 1946, the Social Science Research Council officially asked Parsons to write a comprehensive "statement or report" on the topic of how the social sciences could contribute to the understanding and explanation of the

---

[102] Ibid., p. 247.
[103] Parsons and Barber, "Sociology, 1941–1946," *American Journal of Sociology*, vol. 53, 1948, pp. 245–257.
[104] See Philip M. Hauser, "Wartime Development of Census Statistics," *American Sociological Review*, vol. 10, 1945, pp. 160–169; Conrad Taeuber, "Some Recent Developments in Sociological Work in the Department of Agriculture," *American Sociological Review*, vol. 10, 1945, pp. 169–175; and Robin M. Williams, "Some Observations on Sociological Research in Government During World War II," *American Sociological Review*, vol. 11, 1946, pp. 573–577.
[105] Parsons and Barber, p. 249.
[106] Ibid., p. 257.

modern world. The background was the controversy over whether or not the social sciences should be incorporated into the National Science Foundation [NSF], the enabling legislation for which was in the process of being debated by Congress. However, the SSRC did not directly intend to commission a political statement but aimed at more fundamental expertise. In this vein, the committee minutes included a memorandum by Robert Yerkes, setting the guidelines for the memorandum from Parsons. The minutes named the following first and most important objective of the memorandum that Parsons was to write: "To inform and enlighten scientists and laymen about the status and developmental possibilities of principal areas of social science, with primary intent to educate and to convince them that like other natural phenomena those of human life and institutions which are the materials of the social sciences can and should be studied scientifically and that with great profit to mankind." [107]

It must have been obvious to Parsons that this invited a review of exactly the kind of social-science research and instruction that had been provided in the framework of the war effort at Harvard and elsewhere.[108] Material preserved in the Harvard Archives proves beyond doubt that he set out to diligently collect information and relevant data from a large number of experts who now either were employed by government agencies such as the National Resource Planning Board, the Bureau of Labor Statistics, the President's Research Board, the Public Health Service, and others,[109] or were colleagues at his own or other universities. To this he added knowledge gained through projects or programs in which he had participated himself, such as the Civil Affairs Area Instruction, or with which he had collaborated, such as the FEA. He contacted colleagues at Harvard such as Kluckhohn, with whom he was now involved in the creation of the Russian Research Center, or

---

[107] "Memorandum Concerning Social Science Research," prepared by Robert M. Yerkes, for the Social Science Research Council, dated November 26, 1946, p. 1; Parsons papers, HUG(FP) – 15.2, box 20.

[108] Regrettably, Parsons's concerns were misinterpreted by Samuel Z. Klausner, "The Bid to Nationalize Social Science," an interpretation of the Parsons memorandum of 1948 published in Klausner and Victor M. Lidz, eds., *The Nationalization of the Social Sciences* (Philadelphia: University of Pennsylvania Press, 1986), pp. 3–40. Klausner speculated that Parsons had been concerned with opening social science to control on the part of the SSRC, a national agency serving the interests of the government in Washington which, in turn, was said to represent the capitalist nation state.

[109] A list compiled for the preparatory work, entitled "Research Accomplishments or Research Programs," had four headings and listed under "I. Government" eleven agencies, beginning with the "Bureau of Agricultural Economics, a. Division of Farm Population and Rural Welfare" and ending with "United Nations Education, Scientific and Cultural Organizations" (with handwritten addendums such as "Food + Agriculture," "Federal Trade Commission," "TVA," etc.); under "II. War Experience" four agencies specified into nine programs and branches ranging from "1. Office of Strategic Services a. Research and Analysis Branch" to "4. Office of Price Administration"; under "III. Private Organizations" fifteen names (supplemented by three handwritten additions) ranging from "1. National Bureau of Economic Research" to "14. University of Chicago: Public Administration Clearing House. 15. Harvard University: Laboratory of Social Relations"; and under "IV. Foundations" eight names, namely "1. Rockefeller, 2. Carnegie, 3. Macy, 4. Millbank [sic]," supplemented in handwriting by "20th Century, Russell Sage, Commonwealth, Kellogg," with the latter concretized by a person, Harold Taylor. See Parsons papers, HUG(FP) – 15.2, box 23.

Samuel Stouffer, who had joined the newly created Department of Social Relations in 1946 after he had directed a major research program under the sponsorship of the War Department. The results of Stouffer's program were to be published in 1949, becoming known under the title of *The American Soldier in the Second World War*.[110] He also cast a wide net of requests for information to be obtained from a long list of agencies and experts.[111]

Parsons's memorandum, *Social Science: A Basic National Resource*, became available in July 1948.[112] It was a major piece of work detailing not only the function of science for the dynamics of modern society but also the merits of social science in terms of winning the war that had just ended. Social science, he claimed, had been enormously beneficial for victory because it facilitated otherwise difficult changes. Moreover, it helped that these changes were made in a way least disruptive and most effective. The contribution of social science had been to defuse dangers in comparatively normal life in the society despite its involvement in an ongoing war. This to him seemed the most laudable effect of social science as a basic national resource, benefiting everyone. He suggested, therefore, that in the postwar period social science had a self-evident task. Social science could de-escalate political threat before the latter had to be answered by force; social science could help conceive social reform to counteract social disorganization before fundamentalist movements could exploit structural conflict in a society.

His message was that social science had proven its merit and therefore should undoubtedly be made part of the scientific outlay to be enabled through the emergent NSF. Social science, a basic national resource, should on the basis of its proven merits definitely and deservedly become a field for research funding under the NSF, rather than only being considered for it.[113]

---

[110] See Samuel Stouffer, Edward A. Suchman, L. C. De Vinney, S. A. Star, Robin M. Williams, Jr., *The American Soldier*, 2 volumes (Princeton, N.J.: Princeton University Press, 1949). The third volume was, *Experiments on Mass Communication*, (Carl I. Hovland, Arthur A. Lumsdaine, and Fred D. Sheffield), Princeton, N.J., 1949.

[111] To Margaret Mead he wrote in July, 1947: "I think you know that I am working on a report for the Social Science Research Council on the relations of social science research to the public interest. In this connection I have been looking particularly for striking examples of the way in which research methods going well beyond common sense would produce results of practical importance." Letter, Parsons to Mead, July 10, 1947; Parsons papers, HUG(FP) – 42.8.4, box 14.

[112] Social Science Research Council, "Preliminary Draft: Social Science – A Basic National Resource," July 1948; Parsons papers, HUG(FP) – 15.2, box 20, quoted henceforth as Parsons, "Social Science – A Basic National Resource, 1948." The memorandum was published posthumously under the title of "Social Science – A Basic National Resource. A Report Prepared for the Social Science Research Council, July 1948. Preliminary Draft. Filed in Harvard University Archives," in Samuel Klausner and Victor Lidz, eds., *The Nationalization of the Social Sciences*, pp. 41–112; for comment, see also Bernard Barber, "Theory and Fact in the Work of Talcott Parsons," in Klausner and Lidz, eds., *The Nationalization of the Social Sciences*, pp. 123–130.

[113] Klausner and Lidz, who apparently were not fully aware of the contemporaneous context in which the memorandum was written, changed the wording of large parts of the manuscript, rewriting entire sentences or parts thereof as well as inserting headings to the chapters which Parsons had not used. Due to the subtle and sometimes not so subtle difference in meaning conveyed in the rephrasings of Klausner and Lidz, I shall here use the original memorandum.

How did he proceed when he made this point? In chapter II of the memorandum, he clarified how the modern world view was based on scientific knowledge, and in chapter III he showed that progress was often not recognized for what it was in the scientific world of the day (e.g., Pasteur in nineteenth-century France, or Freud in early twentieth-century Vienna). In chapter IV, he described different types of social research, with the aim of eventually, in chapter VI, venturing that since scientific progress would often not be noticed immediately, in any case education for research should be performed on the highest level possible, irrespective of publicity.

The main section of the memorandum, no doubt, was chapter V.[114] Parsons started by saying that the war effort had been a particularly rich field of research that had helped solve practical problems when the work often was of outstanding scientific quality. In this, he wrote, "a relatively new resource" had been "the knowledge and skill of social scientists... in that mobilization."[115] He hastened to say that since such research had mostly built on work completed prior to the war, the quality left nothing to be desired. Six fields of wartime research, he detailed, to him exemplified meticulous investigation, based on rigorous study designs and producing important results when its purpose had been related to wartime problems.

The first area which he listed was *war bond sales research*. He described it using as a model Merton's study on mass persuasion which had been conducted under the auspices of the Office of Facts and Figures, lodged with the Division of Program Survey in the Bureau of Agricultural Economics in 1940–1942. The war bond sales research was, for him, a topic where he could also emphasize that exemplary contributions could be made to social-science methodology when the aim of the project was clearly practical as it served the war effort. Methodologically, he stressed, the war bond sales research had yielded the insight that sometimes data filled in by interviewers paying home visits could be more reliable than mailed questionnaire data. Substantively, the research had yielded results proving how sometimes scientific studies could unexpectedly effect positive changes in policy.[116]

A second area was *psychological ability testing*. He used psychological ability testing to argue, first, that top scientific quality (e.g., findings reconcilable with Henry A. Murray's personality theory) could be accomplished despite the fact that the tests were application-geared such as, for example, the widely used Army

---

[114] Its heading, inserted by Klausner and Lidz in their version amended in 1986, is "Some Practical Achievements: the War Record." The original, however, only carried the Roman numeral V.

[115] Parsons, "Social Science – A Basic National Resource, 1948," p. 40. The wording of this passage in the Klausner and Lidz version, to give an example of their editing of Parsons's text, is: "World War II brought the most intensive mobilization of national resources in American history. It was only natural that a relatively new resource such as the knowledge and skill of the social scientist should be included in the mobilization." See in Klausner and Lidz, *The Nationalization of the Social Sciences*, p. 79.

[116] Parsons, "Social Science – A Basic National Resource, 1948," pp. 41–43. Merton's study was published as *Mass Persuasion* (New York: Columbia University Press, 1946; with Marjorie Fiske and Alberta Curtis).

General Application Test; second, that psychological ability tests could elucidate how validation procedures could help to clarify the valid uses to which a particular test could be put and what were invalid uses (e.g., during the war, he reported, certain tests had been found to satisfactorily measure ability for training but proved useless to assess ability for combat); third, psychological ability tests were frequently screened for bias, and this screening had shown bias lodged not only in the researcher applying the test but also in the setting where the test was taken by the applicants, among similar findings showing how complex the issue of validity was; fourth, improvement of a test instrument was possible as had been documented various times, on which he elaborated; and fifth, one positive outcome of the ability testing program had been that unnecessary casualties in the war appeared to have been avoided, namely, men thus selected frequently had been better suited for their tasks than men not assigned to their wartime responsibilities by scientifically grounded standardized attitude scales – which, in turn, had meant that those thus tested positive were less likely to endanger or abandon others in a situation of battle.[117]

The third example he offered was *mental health assessment*.[118] Programs of mental health assessment, he admitted, were mainly instrumental for army psychiatry. But they had also helped to test how suitable a person was for an assignment. If responsibility for others or secrecy were involved in a war situation, he affirmed, mental health was highly significant when lives were at stake when soldiers had to hold up under stress of combat. He mentioned another aspect which to him was obvious when he contended, "The perspective of the importance of group relations in the mental health problem... brings the scientific basis of psychiatry squarely into the domain of the social sciences... This is one of the fields of research where the sociological level articulates most directly with the subtle dynamic analysis of the motivations and mechanisms of behavior."[119] In this vein, he felt, psychiatry was a social science that would enrich "contributions to our basic knowledge of human behavior."[120]

A fourth topic which for Parsons held a hitherto seriously underestimated proof that social science had been of tremendous value in the war context was the Foreign Morale Analysis Division of OWI's research on the Japanese soldiers' will to fight and the Japanese population's readiness for unlimited endurance.[121] He used the research of the Foreign Morale Analysis Division to document how a conceptual scheme derived from social-science knowledge could be used to interpret written or oral material on a vastly different culture. Research on Japan, he recounted, had established from evidence as early as May 1945, that Japanese morale was at the point of collapse. He concluded, on an astonishingly apparent note of discontent, that the United States had ended World War II through deployment of two atom

---

[117] Parsons, "Social Science – A Basic National Resource, 1948," pp. 43–47.
[118] Ibid., pp. 47–52.
[119] Ibid., p. 52; the next quote is from the same page.
[120] David Levy, in his *New Fields of Psychiatry* (New York: W. W. Norton, 1947), took the same perspective on psychiatry, tracing the development of, among other fields, political psychiatry from a beginning as early as the 1920s.
[121] Parsons, "Social Science – A Basic National Resource, 1948," pp. 53–55.

bombs when they could have acted on the basis of reliable knowledge gained through professional social-science expertise. He wrote, referring to the Morale Analysis Division findings, "The work of this group furnishes another impressive example of one of the most important practical functions of social-science research. The 'experts' in the sense of practical men with experience in Japanese affairs were divided on such questions as the invulnerability of Japanese morale or the advisability of attacking the Emperor. On this practical level there was no reliable set of criteria to decide between the alternatives."[122] American politicians who instructed the military, he insinuated, should have listened to the social scientists. He concluded, "A society which refused to utilize such a resource would not seem to be acting very sensibly."[123]

In the fifth place, social scientists contributed ways to measure *combat organization and determinants of morale*.[124] He used the topic of combat organization and morale to show, first, how opinion polls could be used effectively if sampling procedures were rigorous and questionnaire construction was systematic; second, he emphasized that quantitative measures could be paired with qualitative ones such as participant observation; third, he stressed, a theoretical conception rooted in various social sciences could become a seedbed of serendipitous empirical findings; last but not least, he knew, schemes and procedures recommended on the basis of social-science research (such as the "merit points" scheme for discharge from the Army after cessation of hostilities) had been enormously popular with the soldiers. All this related to the work of the Research Branch of the War Department's Information and Education Division under the directorship of Samuel Stouffer.[125]

Last, *production of military equipment and consumer goods* had been balanced through the Bureau of Research and Statistics, in their program masterminded through the Supply Priorities and Application Board.[126] He argued that in the United States, production and labor-market decisions had been grounded in advice from social science frequently based on research carefully ascertaining the balance between individual self-realization and national emergency. In contrast, in Nazi Germany decisions on the procurement and distribution of goods, services, and labor had been command-like in their coercive *Wehrwirtschaft*, involving force, fraud, and even murder.

At the end of his memorandum, he returned to the then-immediate present. He added to the list of areas of research denoting "war work" one that directly benefited the nation at the time of his writing. On January 1, 1948, the European

---

[122] Ibid., p. 55; the next quote is from the same page.

[123] As elsewhere in the memorandum, he addressed American politicians through the metaphor, "practical men."

[124] Parsons, "Social Science – A Basic National Resource, 1948," pp. 55–61.

[125] The Harvard Department of Social Relations of which Stouffer was a member had been founded in 1946, an outcome of the war work, as has been pointed out, among other things, by Barry V. Johnston, "Contemporary Crisis and the Social Relations Department at Harvard: A Case Study in Hegemony and Disintegration," *American Sociologist*, vol. 29, 1998, pp. 26–42.

[126] Parsons, "Social Science – A Basic National Resource, 1948," pp. 61–63.

Recovery Program (ERP) had started.[127] He referred to ERP in order to emphasize how important social scientists, such as economists, could be for devising and setting up a particular policy. He hastened to add, however, that such influence should never be dictatorial in any way.

"Under the pressure of war – as to a lesser degree that of depression in the New Deal period – the practical men were to a high degree, though not without many contests, ready to listen to the advice of the economists," he declared, when "practical men" were to him politicians as contrasted with social scientists. He added, "It is not surprising that when that pressure was released there was a strong reaction. On the whole the rapid abandonment of the system of economic controls was at the instance of the practical men against the advice of the economists. Nevertheless it seems to be difficult to keep them permanently out of the picture."[128]

It was on the note of the value of economists as social scientists that Parsons referred to ERP. This program, on which hinged the reconstruction of Europe as newly important player in the postwar world economy, had been proposed by economists when it was introduced as part of a new policy apparently originating in the State Department. The policy and program of the Marshall Plan, then only recently introduced, were enormously successful eventually, representing the epitome of beneficial influence of U.S. foreign policy, in the particular context remedying Europe's postwar economic slump.[129]

As a last attempt at persuasion, Parsons sought to promote the cause of social science by endorsing the support of one leading figure in the debate for establishment of NSF, Harvard President Conant (an eminent chemist). He sought to enlist Conant's support via a personal reference. To persuade Conant that he, Conant, had been in favor of social science all along, he used a quotation from Conant which suited him, Parsons, beautifully. In April 1948, as he quoted, Conant had said before the New York–based Community Service Society: "We need to put to use what has already been learned by scientists concerned with the study of man."[130] Did the study of man not evidently include the social sciences?

---

[127] The European Recovery Program, which was first announced in a speech at Harvard by Secretary of State George C. Marshall, on June 5, 1947, has also become known under the name of the Secretary as the Marshall Plan.

[128] Parsons, "Social Science – A Basic National Resource, 1948," p. 63. "Practical men," or politicians, in this context, were the Truman administration who abandoned price and wage controls after the end of World War II (although Truman attempted to stall when Congress demanded return to a market economy).

[129] For more details, see, for instance, Charles P. Kindleberger, *Marshall Plan Days* (Boulder, Colo.: Westview, 1989) as well as Kindleberger, *Life of an Economist* (Cambridge, Mass.: MIT Press, 1991). Kindleberger, an economist who after 1948 taught economic history at the Massachusetts Institute of Technology, belonged to the group of economists who had originally proposed the program and later elaborated the details of ERP; see Michael Hogan, *The Marshall Plan: America, Britain, and the Reconstruction of Western Europe, 1947–1952* (Cambridge: Cambridge University Press, 1987). Previously, as mentioned above, Kindleberger, together with Walt W. Rostow as his deputy, had directed the Division of German and Austrian Affairs (GA) in the State Department, which had been instrumental for policies concerning German economic reconstruction starting in June 1945.

[130] "Social Science – A Basic National Resource, 1948," p. 75.

He ended his memorandum for the SSRC on a deliberately modest note. His closing statement warned of unrealistically high expectations, while still recommending strong support for the social sciences: "The contribution of social science to the solution of our social problems... will not satisfy those who want a sovereign formula of radical reconstruction.... It is sober, pedestrian, undramatic. But at its best it can get a great deal done. For aid in the gradual development of an intelligent human order of social life it is too important a resource to be neglected."[131]

The memorandum, though commissioned by and written for the SSRC, was not well received by SSRC when it was delivered in July 1948. Indeed, when the memorandum drew heavy criticism from most of the sixty-nine (!) reviewers who were asked for comments, Parsons was advised to revise it thoroughly. This he did with the help of his junior colleague, John W. Riley, Jr.

The Second Memorandum, an Unpublished Book
A Story of Revisions

The revision, produced with the assistance of John W. Riley, Jr., was entitled "Social Science – A National Resource." It was submitted to the SSRC in early 1950. Indeed, the genesis of the second memorandum was outlined by Pendleton Herring, president of SSRC, in the introduction to what, in the event, was the draft version:

> In 1946, Talcott Parsons... undertook to prepare... an analysis of the social sciences as a national resource. His report was submitted to the Council... in 1948. Many helpful suggestions were made at that time which the author subsequently undertook to use in reworking his manuscript. Meanwhile, in the spring of 1949, John Riley, Professor of Sociology at Rutgers University, at the request of Donald Marquis prepared a memorandum surveying the social sciences to assist the advisory committee studying the program of the Ford Foundation. The statistics and factual data gathered by Dr. Riley and the draft manuscript prepared by Dr. Parsons provided the basis for collaborative effort by the two authors. Accordingly, in the summer of 1949, the present book was outlined as a joint effort under the auspices of the Social Science Research Council. Dr. Parsons worked on the manuscript during the summer and Dr. Riley, beginning in September 1949, brought the manuscript to completion soon after the first of the year.[132]

The first chapter, which was devoted to "The Nature of the Social Sciences," contained, as its first part, a section entitled "The Social Sciences and Society." It began with a statement which listed the subject area of the social sciences, cautioning against the difficulty that despite the mundane nature of their topics

---

[131] Ibid., p. 76. In the published version, p. 111 in Klausner and Lidz, eds., *The Nationalization of the Social Sciences*, this read as follows: "The contribution of social science to solving our social problems... will not satisfy people who want a sovereign formula of radical reconstruction.... It is sober, pedestrian, undramatic. But at its best it can accomplish a great deal. For aid in the gradual development of an intelligent, humane order of social life, it is too important a resource to be neglected."

[132] Talcott Parsons and John Riley, "Social Science. A National Resource" (draft version), cit. "Foreword," by Pendleton Herring, p. i; Parsons papers, HUG(FP) – 15.70, box 2.

they nevertheless had to be scientific in their methods when they tackled such seemingly unscientific themes as economic prosperity or world peace:

> Ideas can be turned into knowledge once they have been proved. Thus the social scientist quite legitimately attempts to test even such hypotheses[133] as that economic prosperity can be maintained through the introduction of certain types of social controls, or that world peace can be guaranteed through certain types of world government. In dealing with these questions he may be motivated by his own wishful thinking and what he *wants* to find to be true, but this in no sense necessarily vitiates his scientific analysis of the ideas themselves. He is, *qua* scientist, concerned with them solely for the purpose of determining what particular aspects of the ideas and their interrelations may be translated into knowledge. He is, consequently, in his scientific role much more limited in his handling of ideas than the intellectual non-scientist.[134]

To clarify this for the sociologist, Parsons and Riley made two points. For one, they endorsed value neutrality in the Weberian sense, which allowed the sociologist as a citizen to take part in the life of his community and take sides as a citizen, and nevertheless analyze society as a scientist. In this, they clarified, the model of the type society mattered which the sociologist analyzed, on the background that ideas were important. They maintained that the social scientist could not remain neutral, but was an observer who had to take a stance vis-à-vis the type of society which he analyzed. Under the subheading of "Social science vs. a controlled society," they had this to say,

> In the background of many of the currents of thought in which social science has been rooted, have been systems of ideas which purported to diagnose a single source of the ills of society and to base thereon a program for the *total* reconstruction of society. The most familiar example, of course, is Marxism. Undoubtedly many of the particular conceptual elements and insights of such movements have been built into the body of modern social science. But the spirit of such a movement, as a total system, is foreign to that of the social scientist.[135]

Elucidating what role therefore befitted social science in modern society, they invoked the model of the physician whose task was to diagnose and, on the basis of proven knowledge, help rectify malfunctioning, where at all feasible. What, in this vein, was the spirit in which acted the social scientist?

> He is, in terms of the relation between theory and practice, more akin to the physician. No doubt the total body of scientific knowledge underlying medical practice heads up in some sense to a single "theory of the human organism." It does not, however, fix on one source of what is wrong with man in general, nor does it set up a formula for procuring an "ideal body." It deals with particular problems of functioning of the organism. It diagnoses particular modes of malfunctioning and gives a foundation in scientific knowledge for specific measures to deal with such situations. Similarly the physical sciences in their engineering applications

---

[133] An alternative reading which Parsons crossed out by hand read "to test the hypothesis."
[134] Riley and Parsons, "Social Science. A National Resource," p. I–3 (the five chapters were each paginated separately); italics original.
[135] Ibid., pp. I–14–15; italics original.

do not give a formula for reforming nature in general – they deal with particular problems in which man has a practical interest. This is the general spirit of modern social science.[136]

The memorandum had five chapters: After having dealt with the nature of the social sciences, the problem was utilization and application of the social sciences, with regard to five venues, namely everyday life, business and industry, the federal government with respect to its need for "statistical intelligence," and the two sides of "The War-time Record," namely "The Military Fronts," and "The Home Front"; then followed a chapter on techniques and theories in science in general and the social sciences in particular, leading up to a chapter dealing with "Professional Needs and Problems" which discussed "The Problem of Professionalization," "The Personnel Back-log," and other topics crowned by "The Financing of Research." Eventually, a conclusion entitled "Prospects" considered "The Prospect for the Future."

This memorandum which amounted to a book on the function and accomplishment of social science in the context of American society, particularly in the decade of the 1940s, did not meet with the approval of SSRC when it was submitted in the spring of 1950. Herring, in his foreword to this draft version, praised it, although his praise to the two authors rang curiously ambivalent. About Parsons he wrote, when he named the authors separately, "Social scientists feel indebted to Dr. Parsons for his initiative when the range of problems discussed in this report were first considered by the Council several years ago, and to his continuing interest," and about Riley, "We are all grateful to Dr. Riley for the major responsibility that he has borne in carrying through to completion a project that has been a common concern of the social sciences over a period of years."[137] In the event, the memorandum was not approved for publication by SSRC. Parsons and Riley undertook to revise it yet another time, intent on meeting the criteria set for the project by the commissioning agency, the SSRC.

The SSRC's indecisive reaction to the first memorandum and unfavorable response to the second might have been influenced by outside events. For one, Congress in 1949 passed the legislation based on the Kilgore Bill, and the NSF was established with no provision for social-science research. Also, the rapid development of the Cold War (leading up to the Korean War in the spring of 1950) presumably influenced the expectations which the SSRC now wished realized in the memorandum, putting into the forefront of the memorandum's mandatory achievements other ideas than originally had been agreed upon in the meetings of the Council in September 1945 and November 1946.

Three letters dating between August 1950 and March 1951 preserved in the Harvard Archives document how, eventually, the project was abandoned unfinished. When the revised version of the second memorandum was again not accepted for publication by SSRC, the two authors who had invested enormous work and considerable patience to meet the agency's expectations backed out of their commitment.

---

[136] Ibid., p. I–15.
[137] Ibid., pp. i–ii.

On August 2, 1950, Parsons wrote to Herring, sending along a set of "corrections of the Riley-Parsons manuscript," offering to gladly come to New York to discuss them if need be, admitting, "If you need me don't hesitate to call on me, but I am much pressed with other things and much prefer not to have to come."[138] On November 8, Herring wrote to Parsons informing him that he had had a long conversation with Riley when they had dealt with the comments by the readers whom the SSRC had commissioned to evaluate the memorandum. "To go into details in a letter would be much to [sic] lengthy a process. It is enough to report that Jack now has a notion of the various lines of revision that seem called for and he has agreed to set forth in writing the changes that he is prepared to make. Several readers have contributed helpful suggestions and I brought the sum of these comments to Jack's attention," wrote Herring.[139]

Eventually, on March 16, 1951, Parsons addressed to Herring a five-page letter which brought to light what problems he discerned. They were, first, that the two relatively divergent original manuscripts, his own 1948 memorandum and Riley's Ford Foundation report, had not been entirely merged into one and the same framework; second, that the position taken was different from what even most social scientists were willing to acknowledge regarding "theory-oriented research."[140] Though he (and obviously Riley also) thought applicability of findings important, they believed in "the role of theory in science which is at the root of the enormous importance of 'pure' scientific research." "I personally, and I think Jack will agree with me, have no apology to make to this pure science – theory-orientation emphasis."[141] This led to a remark on what apparently was the crux of the difficulty in getting the report accepted by SSRC.

> In large perspective I think there would be rather general agreement that the greatest weakness of American science had been its reluctance to give sufficiently serious attention to theory. The relation of this to the "pragmatic" atmosphere of American life is obvious. It is precisely this which may make some of our emphasis unrepresentative of this public opinion of the relevant professional groups. But I think we would feel that a document such as ours ought not to be simply a reflection of the public opinion of the profession, but ought to try to present a serious diagnosis of the problems faced by the profession and to point the way to levels of achievement and of self-knowledge beyond its present state.

He pointed out in some detail the conspicuous lack of progress in, for example, theory in political science and also economics of the last twenty years. The majority

---

[138] Letter, Parsons to Herring, August 2, 1950; Parsons papers, HUG(FP) – 42.8.4, box 19. He had received funding for the first half of the academic year of 1950 to bring together the group of discussants mainly from the Department of Social Relations that resulted in the volume co-edited with Shils, *Toward a General Theory of Action*. It was published, in 1951, as companion volume to *The Social System*. The latter book, it appears, was finished during the winter or spring of 1951, with preparatory work done in 1949 and 1950, at the time when Parsons and Riley revised the memorandum on social science at least twice.

[139] Letter, Herring to Parsons, November 8, 1950; Parsons papers, HUG(FP) – 42.8.4, box 19.

[140] Letter, Parsons to Herring, March 15, 1951; Parsons papers, HUG(FP) – 42.8.4, box 19, p. 2; the next quote is from the same page.

[141] Ibid., p. 3; the next quote is from the same page.

of approaches had clung to conceptions long obsolete and superceded by, in the case of economics, "the Keynesian version," although admittedly "a few rather recent developments in such places as the Cowles Commission and in Leontief's work" had also used up-to-date conceptual approaches. On the whole, a majority of current theory and research was behind the times, and protagonists of bygone thought might be the SSRC reviewers who (had) rejected Parsons's (Riley and Parsons's) theory-laden empirical account of the role of social science for the nation. On this note, both he and Riley were not willing to go back to what might appear a desirable approach to authors of comments commissioned by SSRC. "If we are to go farther with the project," he concluded, Riley would be first author in a prospective publication and he, Parsons, took a "smaller share." The letter asked Herring that he, Parsons, be excused from major further revision(s): "I certainly do not wish to convey an impression of intransigence. But you suggested that I state what, from my point of view, was the 'philosophy' of the document and I have tried to do so."[142]

The work of Riley and Parsons entitled "Social Science – A National Resource" never appeared in print. It was revised at least twice at about the time of the writing of *The Social System*, and its argument and use of empirical evidence may be compared with the sequel, which became a world classic.

The Argument in the Book

On the whole, the first chapter in the revised version of the rewritten "Social Science (.) A National Resource" recapitulated the first memorandum that had shown social science as a basic national resource. The point of origin of the entire endeavor to elucidate the function of social science for the nation, the memorandum stated, was the achievement of nuclear physics. "Our control over the forces of nature, so much further advanced than in any other known civilization, is obvious.... [T]he harnessing of the energy of the atom is but the most recent chapter in a long history extending over centuries."[143]

Science, whether concerned with nature or society, distinguished itself from thinking in wishful categories or practical knowledge through systematic method. "The criteria lie in the way in which these subject matters are investigated. It lies simply in the systematic search for objective knowledge and truth."[144] The social sciences, still in their early stage of development, far behind the degree of systematization reached by the natural sciences, had been making immense progress since the seventeenth century after the Renaissance had made freedom of thought a motor for scientific enquiry. "It is certainly true that social science has, in any technical sense, started later than has natural science, has developed more slowly, and has not yet reached comparable levels."[145]

---

[142] Ibid., p. 5.
[143] John W. Riley, Jr. and Talcott Parsons, "Social Science. A National Resource," p. 1–1; Parsons papers, HUG(FP) – 42.41, box 3; again, pages were numbered by individual chapters, now through Arabic numerals.
[144] Ibid., p. 1–4.
[145] Ibid., p. 1–11.

The Second Memo, an Unpublished Book 165

From this vantage point, as achievements were obvious, the need was clear:

> [T]he statistical intelligence provided by the federal government, and in daily use by Congress, the judiciary, farmers, business men, labor leaders, educators and ordinary citizens, is a product of social science.... Perhaps the most dramatic record of the social sciences, however, has been written during the crisis of war. Social scientists attached to the Army developed techniques for predicting non-battle casualties, determined the "consumer acceptance" of all kinds of military equipment, solved serious problems of morale deterioration, and developed the point system which was used for demobilization. Similar teams wrestled successfully with the knotty problems on the domestic front of informational policies, the allocation of scarce materials and the rationing of civilian goods. But however impressive this total record of practical accomplishments may be, it clearly could never have been written had it not been for the available reservoir of technical and theoretical resources. Nor has the task of building up this fund of knowledge and skills been an easy one. It is the slow, laborious, and unglamorous process of scientific research.[146]

From this, they derived the most important problems of the future, which were, for one, to safeguard sufficient and sufficiently qualified personnel for research, and "[a]nother highly important key to the future lies in the organizational and financial support accorded social research – and particularly research which may be properly classified as basic."[147]

Parsons's core interest was Part III. Under the inconspicuous title of "The Development of Techniques and Theories," starting with a chapter on "Science and Common Sense," he elaborated that two types of research existed, namely one ascertaining facts within a taken-for-granted theoretical framework ("fact-centered research"), and one taking a theoretical perspective to the empirical world, thereby making visible new or hitherto unknown aspects of its inner structure ("theory-centered research"). He clarified the latter:

> At one pole research is predominantly "theory-oriented." The problems it attempts to solve – by theoretical reasoning, by empirical verification or more usually a combination of the two – are those which are involved in the major logical structure of a body of theory. Above all such research is meant to verify inferences drawn by theoretical reasoning or to produce empirical evidence for a decision between theoretically possible alternatives. At the other pole, research is primarily "fact-finding" ... outside the structure of theory itself.[148]

To concretize what were studies that were "theory-oriented," he referred to, among other work, Thomas and Znaniecki's *The Polish Peasant in Europe and America*, of which he emphasized that the construct of "definition of the situation" had been its seminal conceptual achievement tested in empirical comparison. The "definition of the situation," in Thomas and Znaniecki's work, had proved unanalyzable through the distinction between "egoistic" versus "altruistic" motives. Only when distinguishing between self-interest as of a business man and the professional interest of a physician (whose self-interest it was "to conform to good

---

[146] Ibid., p. 2–3.
[147] Ibid., p. 2–4.
[148] Ibid., pp. 8–9/10.

professional conduct, ... to serve the 'welfare of the patient,' "[149]), Thomas and Znaniecki could understand "differences between the *roles* of 'physician' and of 'business man,' as determined by the definition of the situation." They thus could elucidate the wealth of the empirical data collected. Likewise, Durkheim's *Suicide* witnessed how his theory of social structure had been the motor for his seeking evidence in the statistical data available on the subject of suicides. (Parsons briefly referred to Weber, whom he cited together with Durkheim, stressing in regard to both, "Using as its principal point of reference the conception of a social system, specific structures may now be carefully described and dynamic processes of social behavior analyzed in relation to them.")[150] He emphasized how Durkheim had proceeded in his research:

> From other sources, particularly his critique of Spencer's concept of contractual relations, he had developed a *theoretical* basis for questioning the adequacy of explanations of many uniformities of social behavior in terms of their immediate motives in this sense. He had come to the conclusion that an important set of factors lay in variations in the types and degrees of integration of individuals with the social groups of which they were members. He deliberately selected the problem of suicide as a field in which to test the empirical validity of his reasoning. He was therefore *looking* for facts which might be incompatible with the "motivation" type of explanation.[151]

Accordingly, for Parsons, theory had a stake in research beyond the ominous divide between facts and ideas. However, at the same time, he cautioned, not only was there no uncontroversial authoritative theory in sociology which could be converted into research hypotheses, but neither could there be one at the present time due to the fact that sociology in regard to the state of development of theory was far behind other branches of social science such as economics or psychology. In this situation, when even the most basic lines of reasoning had to be reassessed to approximate a network of concepts whose enunciation still lay in the future, the only way out was to formulate, for the time being, a frame of reference from which to start. He packed this diagnosis of the state of sociological theory into a consideration comparing various social sciences:

> [M]uch theoretically oriented research has been pushed forward in such fields as social structure, economic analysis, human motivation, and cultural variability. The conceptual schemes which are emerging from such efforts are, to be sure, being made more and more explicit but the development has been uneven. At some points it appears to be hardly more than a frame of reference; at others, however, such as in some branches of economic and psychological theory, it has proceeded far beyond in producing analytic and conceptual tools of considerable power.[152]

---

[149] Ibid., p. 9–26; the next two quotes are from the same page; emphasis original.
[150] Ibid., p. 9–27.
[151] Ibid., p. 9–28.
[152] Ibid., p. 9–1.

In the event, in *The Social System* written concomitantly with the second version of the (second) memorandum, Parsons declared his theory of society as social system an approach grounded in a frame of reference, stating clearly that it was Weber's theory of social action.

The Third Attempt

The story told of the two unsuccessful memoranda, the truth is that the only long-term effect of Parsons's engagement analyzing the nation's war effort in regard to sociology's postwar accomplishments was his *The Social System*.

Obviously, though not ostentatiously, *The Social System* profited from the many themes which he had tackled during the war period. The book became a worthy sequel to his attempts in the two ill-fated memoranda to sum up and evaluate the war work. *The Social System*, a world classic despite the fact that it lacked a bibliography, benefited from more than ten years' analysis of empirical subjects such as Nazi Germany contrasted with democracy in the Anglo-Saxon world. Parsons's attempt to evaluate the results of wartime research, and his continuous effort to ascertain what sociology as a science could do to further the goals of a democratized modern society, were thus not in vain. He introduced into *The Social System*, though not in conspicuous fashion, most of the themes which had had priority during the war and remained high in priority in the postwar world. These were, for instance, the question of the role of science as an agent of societal progress, or whether the Soviet Union was an enemy in the Cold War comparable to Nazi Germany in World War II.

Medical Practice, Epitome of Social System

One of the topics discussed among positive outcomes of the war work and again tackled in *The Social System* was the nature of psychiatry as a social science, involving certain insights on the issues of health and illness but also medical practice.[153] Chapter X of *The Social System* was devoted entirely to the doctor-patient system of medical practice. Its aim was to elucidate that psychiatric (psychosomatic) aspects helped to understand medicine as well as illness and health in modern society, thus building on the wartime insight that psychiatry was a social science. In this vein, he surmised that all medical practice had a psychiatric, or rather psychotherapeutic side to it, due to the fact that illness meant regression to a child-like state of dependency out of which therapy would lead, playing on the unconscious motivation to deviance underlying sickness in general. He spoke of "unconscious psychotherapy" which constituted any type of medical care, allowing for a

---

[153] Parsons devoted a research project to action orientations in medical practice already in the 1930s. At the time, he focused on some psychosomatic issues concerning physicians' professionalism, but not psychiatry. He did not, before 1951, except in the memorandum of 1948, address psychiatry as a social science.

four-stage social-control process of recovery.[154] To reject any incredulity on the side of physicians in his time regarding this unusual thesis, he cautioned, "Psychotherapy to the militantly anti-psychiatric organic physician is like theory to the militantly anti-theoretical empirical scientist. In both cases he practices it whether he knows it or wants to or not. He may indeed do it very effectively just as one can use a language well without even knowing it has a grammatical structure."[155]

The background to this analysis was a picture of the concatenated roles of physician and patient integrated into a pattern which hinged on shared value-orientations. Both roles, he showed, embodied norms of universalism, affective neutrality, functional specificity, achievement, and collectivity orientation. Indeed, as he pointed out at the outset of the chapter, he took medicine as a paradigm for the social system:

> It will perhaps help the reader to appreciate the empirical relevance of the abstract analysis we have developed if, in addition to the illustrative material which has been introduced bearing on many particular points, we attempt to bring together many if not most of the threads of the foregoing discussion in a more extensive analysis of some strategic features of an important sub-system of modern Western society. For this purpose we have chosen modern medical practice.[156]

Deviance, in Perspective of Type of Society

Illness, no doubt, was deviance. More on the topic of deviance, including its sociological counterpart of social control (which included therapy as one type, coercion as another, as he had explained also in "Propaganda and Social Control"), filled chapter VII. The chapter, entitled "Deviant Behavior and the Mechanisms of Social Control," related to the ideas developed in connection with the war effort, particularly in the two subchapters devoted to "The Direction of Deviant Orientation" and "The Social Structure of Deviant Behavior Tendencies." What were the main points?

Locating different directions of deviance, particularly inasmuch as deviance differed from as well as overlapped with conformity, he used some of the types introduced in Robert Merton's classic essay, "Social Structure and Anomie."[157] Merton had analyzed situational conditions in the social structure of deviance

---

[154] He elaborated further on this in an essay with Renée Fox, "Illness, Therapy, and the Modern Urban Family," *Journal of Social Issues*, vol. 8, 1952, pp. 31–44. The four stages, which were the general process pattern of social control, were permissiveness, support, denial of reciprocity, and manipulation of rewards. Another locale where he would subsequently elaborate on this more fully was, in conjunction with younger collaborators, *Working Papers on the Theory of Action*, where he would elaborate on the same four-stage process nature of socialization, therapy, and social control in general. See Parsons, Robert F. Bales, and Edward A. Shils, *Working Papers in the Theory of Action* (New York: Free Press, 1953).

[155] Parsons, *The Social System* (Glencoe, Ill.: Free Press, 1951; paperback edition, New York: Free Press, 1964), p. 462.

[156] Ibid., p. 428.

[157] Robert Merton, "Social Structure and Anomie," *American Sociological Review*, vol. 3, 1938, pp. 672–682.

which he had addressed as anomie; among other types, he had introduced ritualism (which resembled somewhat Fromm's idea of "automaton conformity"[158]) and innovation, which equaled crime. These Parsons merged into a kind of deviance representing conformity, which he labeled "compulsory comformity," clarifying "Merton's 'innovation' and 'ritualism' are our two compulsively conformative types, while 'rebellion' and 'retreatism' are clearly the two alienative types."[159]

This allowed Parsons to identify elements in the criminal (totalitarian) society as deviant inasmuch as they *were* conformist, and it was the compulsiveness attached to such conformity that denoted its alienating nature. This was then further elaborated in the context of the social structure of deviance. What interested Parsons was the functioning of "a group which is genuinely solidary" of organized alienation.[160] Such type group was an arena of, as it were, "alienative need-disposition"[161] allowing for compulsory conformity: "The compulsive quality of the need to conform ... may have an important bearing on various features of such delinquent sub-culture groups such as the extreme concern with loyalty to the group and the violence of the condemnation of 'ratting.'"[162]

When the criminal destructiveness was political, in other words, the "primary alienative orientation ... directed against normative patterns as such,"[163] and when a criminal subculture had arisen or had taken over an entire society, he realized, compulsive conformity became the dominant feature in a culture of deviance. "Certain features of the dynamics of group prejudice seem to fit here,"[164] he stated, and then he explained anti-Semitism, with Nazi Germany as the extreme case, as the deviation from universalism which posed as pseudo-universalism by means of the scapegoat mechanism. He suggested that crime and racial anti-Semitism relied on the same mechanism. The only difference was that the delinquent gang member was motivated "against" mainstream society, whereas the anti-Semite displaced his alienative needs onto a scapegoat outgroup while he "belonged" to mainstream (fascist) society:

> The hypothesis that the displacement of aggression on the Jew as a scapegoat object plays a part in anti-Semitism has become almost a commonplace of social science. But from the point of view of the Gentile group this constitutes deviant behavior since the Jew is by the main value-pattern entitled to the same universalistically tolerant behavior as any fellow Gentile. Hence there is a strong pressure to "rationalize" his special treatment by such allegations as that he "does not compete fairly," and that he cannot be counted upon to be honest or loyal.

---

[158] Erich Fromm, *Escape From Freedom* (New York: Holt, Rinehart, and Winston, 1941) had used this term explicitly when earlier he had introduced a similar idea using the label of "authoritarian character," in the exiled Frankfurt Institute of Social Research's report on a series of empirical studies, *Studien über Autorität und Familie* (Paris: Félix Alcan, 1936), with which Merton was familiar.
[159] *The Social System*, p. 258.
[160] Ibid., p. 287.
[161] Ibid., p. 286.
[162] Ibid., pp. 286–287.
[163] Ibid., p. 288.
[164] Ibid., p. 289.

Discrimination against him is thereby subsumed under the universalistic value system. So long as this type of legitimation is accepted and mutually reinforced within the Gentile group, or a sub-collectivity within it, we can have a reinforced pattern of deviant behavior without any individual having to accept the normal price of deviance in the form of overt break with his institutionalized role and the risk of negative sanctions. Indeed, if the process goes far enough it is the person who conforms with the main value-pattern who is subject to negative sanctions.[165]

From this vantage point, he discussed the chances that society could be taken over by its deviant groups. Considering the claims to moral or political legitimation and supremacy by ideological or religious (including political) groups, he warned that "[t]he deviant sub-group which is making the most of its claims to legitimacy"[166] would tend to lie about the "radicality of [its members'] differences from the main value-system." This, he realized, might even go together with "declaring [society's] ... value-orientations to be illegitimate in its own terms."

Whereas at this point he assured his reader that rarely would a revolutionary movement be successful that denounced or threatened to destroy a society's value orientations, he could not help admitting that occasionally a deviant mass movement could win over. In the light of the postwar situation, since the Nazi régime had been crushed, evidently, he resorted to another example. Parsons pointed out how deviant groups harbored ambivalent motivational structures, which could go either way. While they took advantage of their surrounding liberal society, they expressed violent aggression against those whose recognition they sought. This could be seen in Weimar-Germans but also American Communists who at the same time denounced and used the liberties of their democratic societies: "For example the Communists certainly often quite self-consciously exploit the patterns of freedom of speech and the like in liberal societies, but certainly in the rank and file there is widespread feeling that in justice they have a right to expect every 'consideration' from the law. But at the same time that they insist on this right they indulge in wholesale denunciation of the 'system' of which it is an institutionalized part."

Pattern Variables Considered

Parsons made explicit mention of Nazism in Chapter V. Under the title of "The Structure of Social Systems III: Empirical Differentiation and Variation in the Structure of Societies," he explored a matrix of four types of societal structures combining the value orientation tendencies of universalism or particularism, and achievement orientation or ascription valuation. The model types, he cautioned, were of course mere empirical abstractions but could be envisaged through four paradigmatic historical societies. They were, for the "Universalistic-Achievement Pattern" the United States, and the "Universalistic-Ascription Pattern" pre-Nazi

---

[165] Ibid., p. 290.
[166] Ibid., p. 294; the next three quotes are from the same page.

Germany but also, conspicuously, Nazism.[167] What mattered about these types, he emphasized, was how much strain was in the particular combination of predominant value orientations in a culture or society, and what mitigating or stalling mechanisms were therefore needed to guarantee a certain level of stability in the social system.

Major structural dissimilarity divided the universalistic-achievement pattern from the universalistic-ascription one, when he emphasized for the latter, "The universalistic element has the same order of consequences here as in the above case [i.e., the universalistically oriented achieving society, Anglosaxon type], but its combination with ascription gives it a different twist."[168]

This had two sides, he clarified. First, in the universalism-ascription type pattern there was a tension between the universalistically defined ideal state and the existing reality that was categorized in terms of approximation to the ideal; this, he said, invoked "a strong tendency ... to drawing a sharply absolute distinction between conformity with the ideal and deviation from it, and in action terms, being 'for it' or 'against it.'" The dualism might express itself through contrasting an idealized future against a corrupt present – which the Nazis had done during the Weimar Republic.

Second, three elements could mitigate the tension. They were that universalism in the occupational world was paired with ascription, engendering categories of "*status*" "where the accent is on what a given actor *is* rather than on *what he has done*";[169] "collectivism," facilitated by the fact that "it is easy to make the transition from an ideal state to be achieved, to the ascription of ideal qualities to the collectivity"; and "authoritarianism" developed "in that the clear conception of what is ideal for all makes it natural for those who have roles enjoining collective responsibility to 'see to it' that everyone lives up to the ideal, either directly, or in making the proper contribution to the collective achievement."

What, in the scenario of universalism-ascription, was the ideal so enforced? "Nazism," he explained, "projected the ideal state into a political future ideal, conceived to be an emanation of the mystically ideal qualities of the German *Volk*."[170] Thus was produced an all-pervasive politicization of the society such that internal opposition was thoroughly repressed. This repression itself spurred aggression directed against designated "outside" enemies. "The combination of this politicism and universalism have something to do with the tendency to aggressiveness of such societies,"[171] he observed, clarifying that such aggressiveness was of the type of "free floating aggression."[172]

---

[167] The other two types, namely a "Particularistic-Achievement Pattern" as in China or a "Particularistic-Ascription Pattern" as in certain Spanish-American cultures were of less sociological relevance, he found.

[168] *The Social System*, p. 191; the next quote is from the same page.

[169] Ibid., p. 192; the next two quotes are from the same page.

[170] Ibid., p. 193.

[171] Ibid., p. 194; the next quote is from the same page.

[172] He thus incorporated Lasswell's thesis originally introduced in 1934 (or 1933, respectively), suitably amended, as he had done, in the period of World War II in his explanation of fascist movements,

At this point in his argument, Nazism was not the only type system which he mentioned as universalistic-ascriptive, although it had been all too conspicuous. The other example, for him, was the Soviet Union, which also cultivated a utopian political future ideal that was held out against empirical realities, using coercive force. He ventured, "There are also certain respects in which Soviet Russia approximates this type. Communism is a utopian ideal state of affairs to be realized by collective action. The primary status-focus revolves about the Party as the elite vanguard of the realization of the ideal."[173]

What About Science?

In Chapter VIII, Parsons addressed the issues of science. Science, he ventured there, both benefited from but also promoted progress epitomized in freedom of inquiry, but it could be held hostage to political power through corruption by ideology in authoritarian societies. The topic of this first of two chapters dealing with "principal components of a cultural tradition" were "systems of beliefs or ideas" (the other topic was "systems of expressive symbols," discussed in Chapter IX).[174]

When the cultural significance of value-orientations was taken for granted, he began, the relationship "of belief systems to social action processes"[175] needed attention. Beliefs, to be sure, had an "integrative function" in society as a whole in the guise of "*existential beliefs*, ... empirical and non-empirical"[176] – which relied on evidence provided by ideas (ideologies) ranging from philosophy and religion to science. The truth of "existential empirical beliefs,"[177] undoubtedly, lay in science. The institutionalization of scientific investigation was of enormous importance not only for the society whose welfare might hinge on utilization in applied science. But the advancement of knowledge depended on continuous adherence to the ideal cultivating the basic "norms of scientific knowledge." "The basic norms of scientific knowledge are perhaps four, empirical validity, logical clarity or precision of the particular proposition, logical consistency of the mutual implications of propositions, and generality of the 'principles' involved, which may perhaps be interpreted to mean range of mutually verified implications."[178]

This opened up a perspective on why the universities, harbingers of occidental civilization, were mediators for competent professionalism in the wider society:

> In so far as the doctrine is upheld that in general the "leading men" of the society should be educated men in the modern sense, their elite status carries with

and in his analysis of aggressiveness in Western-type societies published in 1947. His image of National Socialism implied that "free-floating aggression" was both more widespread and more intensive in totalitarian dictatorships than Western-type democracies.

[173] *The Social System*, pp. 193–194.
[174] These characterizations are from ibid., p. 23.
[175] Ibid., p. 327.
[176] Ibid., p. 328.
[177] Ibid., pp. 332 ff.
[178] Ibid., p. 335.

it commitment to a value-system of which the values of the scientist, and the valuation of his activities and their results, form an integral part. This integration of science, both with the wider cultural tradition of the society, and with its institutional structure, constitutes the *primary* basis of the institutionalization of scientific investigation as part of the social structure. ... The occupational role which the scientist occupies, with its center of gravity in the university, is an integral part of the general occupational system. ... The fact that it shares the pattern elements of universalism, affective neutrality, specificity and achievement orientation with the occupational system in general does not require special comment here. But it is worth while to call attention to the fact that as a professional role it is institutionalized predominantly in terms of collectivity–rather than self-orientation.[179]

Two dangers thus became obvious: "One is the implication of the saying 'knowledge is power,' "[180] making for undue arrogance instead of heightened "other-orientation";[181] the other was the "idea that 'a scientist's theory is his castle,' " making for undue reluctance to acknowledge the achievements of professional colleagues and develop sufficient collectivity-orientation vis-à-vis the public. (This, he insisted, applied equally to 'pure' and applied science.) In the latter vein of proper embeddedness of science in the value-orientations of a social system, one problem was the institutionalization of ideologies. What was an ideology, as distinguished from a system of knowledge warranting acceptance?

> To constitute an ideology there must exist the ... feature that there is some level of evaluative commitment to the belief as an aspect of membership in the collectivity, subscription to the belief system is institutionalized as part of the role of collectivity membership. There is a great variation in the mode of this institutionalization as well as its degree. It may be completely informal, or it may be formally enforced as subscription to a specified text with sanctions for deviance enforced by a specific agency. But as distinguished from a primarily cognitive interest in ideas, in the case of an ideology, there must be an obligation to accept its tenets as the basis of action. As distinguished from a purely instrumental belief, there must be involvement of an idea that the welfare of the collectivity and not merely attainment of a particular goal hinges on the implementation of the belief system.[182]

It was in the latter guise that deviance, in the extreme case totalitarianism, entered into the topic realm of "The Problem of the 'Role of Ideas.' "[183]

Dynamics of Systems Change

Last but not least, when in Chapter XI Parsons dealt with social change, insights derived from his wartime work and its postwar sequels again entered the picture.

---

[179] Ibid., pp. 342–343.
[180] Ibid., pp. 343–344.
[181] Ibid., p. 344; the next quote is from the same page.
[182] Ibid., pp. 349–350.
[183] This latter expression was the subtitle of Chapter VIII.

Analyzing "[t]he general nature of change in social systems,"[184] he felt, could only be a tentative venture.

Two sets of contradictory forces had to be taken into account. One was the "vested interests" prevailing in every society that might work for or against change inasmuch as "change is never just 'alteration of pattern' but alteration *by the overcoming of resistance*."[185] The other was whether strains and reactions to them produced a countervailing tendency nullifying the change, such that a return to the previous equilibrium became either possible or unavoidable.

In this vein, he felt, the direction of social change could be in two opposite directions. It could either mean, in Weberian terms, a "process of rationalization,"[186] which aimed to increase or improve modernization in an already rational-legal type society, such as, for instance, the universalistic-achievement type system in the Anglo-Saxon democracies. Or, conversely, the change could go in the opposite direction, tending toward less rather than more rationalization. "We have seen repeatedly that in social systems a very large class of obstacles may operate to block the process of rationalization," he cautioned.[187]

In a Weberian framework, he knew, this could only mean reduction of "the level of rationalization of a social system"[188] through a charismatic movement. On the surface of it, he felt, Weber had explained evolutionary progress in history through "the introduction of new energy into the system from outside," which usually, in Weber's view, involved charisma:

> By thus reducing the general level of rationalization of the system, the process of rationalization could, as it were, get a new start. Indeed in Weber's view this was the primary reason why, in spite of the place he gave to the process of rationalization, a generally linear conception of the evolution of social systems could not be upheld. Of course similar considerations will apply to an independent directional trend in the field of expressive symbolism, so far as this can be demonstrated.[189]

In this context, charismatic rule was that kind of social change, that is, change of type of régime in a society, which needed attention in two respects. One was how a regression or change from a rational-legal type society to charismatic-type rule could occur. The other were processes of routinization of charisma as envisaged by Weber as the social change converting a charismatic into a traditionalism régime.

Regarding the first of the two directions of change, he chose the transition from the Weimar Republic to Nazism in Germany as a paradigm and demonstration topic. He outlined four stages of such transition, exemplifying them in a masterly

[184] Ibid., p. 490 ff.
[185] Ibid., p. 491.
[186] Ibid., p. 499.
[187] Ibid., p. 501.
[188] Ibid., p. 502; the next two quotes are from the same page.
[189] In a footnote hinged on the sentence preceding the quotation, Parsons pointed at Weber's understanding of charisma: "In Max Weber's scheme this, we may infer, was one of the theoretical functions of the concept of *charisma*, to serve as the conceptualization of the source of new orientations on which the process of rationalization was then conceived to operate."

sketch of the history of Weimar Germany:

1. Widespread alienative motivation was present in the population and, moreover, "the alienative motivation will cluster about particular points of strain"[190] such as, for instance, the loss of Germany's national integrity in the wake of the First World War;
2. A deviant group emerged which exploited the alienative motivations; and
3. Its "ideology – or set of religious beliefs – ... can successfully put forward a claim to legitimacy in terms of at least some of the symbols of the main institutionalized ideology."[191] This, however, would only lead to revolutionary change in a system where "the organization of the power system, with particular reference to the state"[192] was hierarchical, centralized, and dominated by an élite. For Germany, he asserted, this had meant patriotic anti-Republicanism. Yet the political assassinations in the first years of the Weimar Republic had set a climate of instability which the Nazi movement had made use of within the German military and authoritarian tradition. Hitler's appeal to nationalism as well as "socialism" then served as a reservoir for an immensely successful mass movement while liberalism remained "considerably weaker in Germany than in the rest of the Western world."[193]
4. "Finally," he added, "the treatment of Germany by the victorious allies was notably indecisive and vacillating. It is highly probable that this was more important than either severity or generosity; it created a situation where agitation for revisionism had an excellent chance in Germany, and the elements in power were highly vulnerable to such agitation."[194]

At this point in his argument, before going on to discuss routinization of charisma for which, he felt, the Soviet Union was a better example than Nazi Germany, Parsons made what may be taken as a near-personal statement. He said about the successful conversion of Germany back to the rational-legal type of democratic society subsequent to military defeat in World War II, "Whatever new combination of the ingredients which went into the Nazi movement may come about in the future, it is unlikely that just the same kind of movement will arise in Germany again. The above has been an exceedingly bare sketch, but it is sufficient to indicate some of the principal ways in which the factors abstractly dealt with in this work [i.e., *The Social System*] operated to make the ascendancy of the Nazi movement possible."

Nazi empowerment, he found, stood out as social change from rational-legal to charismatic authority. But routinization of charisma that meant change from

---

[190] Ibid., p. 521.
[191] Ibid., p. 522.
[192] Ibid., p. 523.
[193] Ibid., p. 524.
[194] Ibid., p. 525; the next quote is from the same page.

charismatic to traditional rule, an ongoing inner development in totalitarian régimes, might best not be envisaged through Nazism. The process of routinization of charisma, he stated, had not been completed in Germany. Germany's regression to traditionalism had been halted by defeat in World War II.[195]

In the last section of the chapter, he epitomized the routinization of charisma using another charismatic régime, the Soviet Union. "The Adaptive Transformation of a Revolutionary Movement" meant that, in the type case, conservative tendencies such as provision for acceptable living standards or a limited range of opportunities within the scope of possibilities had a "mitigating" effect on the dominant ideology. Despite the fact that the victorious revolutionary group had to "discipline" not only its followers but the entire population, "mitigating" influences could compel the régime to make compromises. In the case of the Soviet Union, he diagnosed, a conspicuous change had taken place in policy rather than ideology, in the early period of the régime after the Revolution:

> The abandonment of the immediate abolition of coercion came very early, indeed, the semi-military organization of the party and its discipline was carried over more or less intact into the new regime. But in the early part of the Revolution there was certainly a widespread expectation that men now at last were "free" and could quite literally do what they pleased. Perhaps the most crucial step came after the attempt on Lenin's life, which became the occasion for the institution of the Terror as a deliberate policy which has never been relaxed since. It may perhaps be held that the tension between the drastic evaluative repudiation of coercion in the ideal state and the drastic way in which the regime has employed it for its own ends is in certain ways the deepest source of long-run tension in Russian Communism.[196]

In the long run, however, he felt, the hold on the population could not be maintained. He came to think, as he studied the particular kind of routinization of the charismatic régime in the Soviet Union, that this totalitarian system would not last. "If the regime itself does not fall apart [over the problem of succession of Stalin] it is certain that a very complex process of adjustment will have to occur in the next generation or two in the relation between the ideology and the realities of the social system," he stated when he added a personal confession, "This particular sociologist's prediction is that 'communism' will not be realized and that the increasing realization that there is no prospect of its realization will force far-reaching modifications in the ideology. Indeed, it is difficult to see how once the phase of dynamic expansionism, internally and externally ... is over, the ... system can hold up."[197] In other words, it appeared likely to Parsons in light of the discrepancy between an idealistic belief system and utterly coercive practices of control of the intelligentsia, that the Soviet Union would not last. "What the outcome of this dilemma is likely to be will have to be

---

[195] The reason he felt that Germany's Nazism was not the best example for routinization of charisma, he stated, was that "the relevant development in Nazi Germany was cut off short" (pp. 525–526).
[196] Ibid., p. 530.
[197] Ibid., pp. 532–533.

left for future analysis – or the event – to decide,"[198] was all he was prepared to actually say.

To conclude my brief recapitulation of *The Social System*, the various analytical observations which Parsons made in his magnum opus, some somewhat hidden in one or another subchapter, some commanding the main line of argument in entire chapters, documented his interest in the problems of embattled democracy. In the context of World War II and its immediate postwar followup, he had devoted his energy to sociological theory but also its practical applications. The war effort of social science at Harvard and elsewhere, realized as it was not only by Parsons but also many of his colleagues, went into the themes tackled in *The Social System*. The book that was to be labeled abstract theory was indeed related to the sociohistorical situation of the day.

He thereby located himself far removed from the proverbial "incurable theorist," whom he often has been portrayed in secondary literature assessing the rationale of *The Social System*. His self-reference as an "incurable theorist" in the dedication of *The Social System* to his wife, Helen, should not be taken as a true self-image, let alone generalizing statement about his deepest objectives as a sociologist.

Summary

The Social System has frequently been mistaken for abstract theory, far removed from the exigencies and characteristics of concrete contemporary societies. My argument is that, on the contrary, *The Social System* had a rich background of sociohistorical concern. On the one side, the Harvard social-science war effort, including the work of some of Parsons's colleagues there, inspired *The Social System*. It could be called a late product of his effort at repeated stock-taking on behalf of the Social Science Research Council of the contribution of social science to the nation's cause during World War II. On the other hand, the book took notice of the importance of science for modern society, concentrating on the role of social science (sociology) in the postwar period. In this endeavor, the prospect was to help preserve peace and prevent World War III, in the wake of the deployment of the atom bomb.

In the effort leading up to *The Social System*, defense of democracy in Parsons's work took a different form than in *The Structure of Social Action* and differed also from his activist cum analytical stance taken between 1938 and 1945. He came to focus on the scope of democracy as social system. Defense of democracy took into account that processes of regression from democracy to dictatorship could happen, as could the reverse, namely social change overcoming totalitarianism through modernization (and also, as in the United States, modernization of a modern society through "institutionalized rationalization").

From the perspective of democracy as advanced social system, he deemed charismatic régimes such as National Socialism or Soviet Communism undeniably doomed to failure sooner or later. His new focus was understanding sociologically

---

[198] Ibid., p. 533.

how the social system, as integrated structure of action, functioned. This theme, crowning work on many agendas of more than a decade, underlay *The Social System*.

Postscript: Becoming Politically Embattled Personally

In the years to follow, but also at a much later point in time, two events in the period of writing and immediate success of *The Social System* left Parsons vulnerable to accusations of political deviance, from opposite quarters. In June 1948, he traveled to Germany on his way to Austria, where he taught at the Salzburg Seminar for Social Studies organized by the Harvard Student Union. The journey became a nightmare, so to speak, posthumously: He was accused, in the late 1980s, of alleged sympathies for at least one notorious Nazi collaborator. The other issue was McCarthyism. He was accused of disloyalty to the nation. The charge engulfed him personally in the year 1954, at the end of which he undertook to explain McCarthyism sociologically.

A Nazi Sympathizer?

Some forty years after the period in his life culminating in *The Social System*, he was accused of harboring sympathies for Nazi Germany, even committing Nazism-prone acts in the years 1948 and/or 1949.

The issue belongs in an intellectual biography of Parsons because of the blatantly obvious misconstructions of his life and work, to redress the balance where false accusations were made. The story has two facets. One is the tale told, and the other is what actually happened (inasmuch as details can be learned from various sources).

Regarding the former: In 1989, an article in *The Nation* charged Parsons with having shepherded into the United States a former Nazi employee who was also a Russian emigré. A historian-journalist accused Parsons of, between June 1948 and early 1949, having helped a Nazi collaborator enter the United States with the assistance of the Russian Research Center (RRC) to whose Executive Board he belonged. The accusation made a stir when it was preceded by an article in *The Harvard Crimson* refuting the accusation.[199] The wider context was a Ph.D. dissertation delivered at UCLA in 1990, targeting the RRC for alleged intelligence work directed against Communists (and benefiting ex-Nazis) in postwar Europe, with Parsons a foremost protagonist.[200]

The main suspicions concerned ten letters of Parsons written to Kluckhohn during the three-week trip and preserved among the papers of political scientist

---

[199] See Ron Wiener, "Talcott Parsons' role: Bringing Nazi sympathizers to the U.S.," *The Nation* (March 1989), pp. 306–309; and Joseph R. Palmore, "Parsons Allegations Challenged by Professors. Colleagues Say Scholar Did Not Knowingly Recruit Collaborators," *The Harvard Crimson*, February 23, 1989, pp. 1–2.

[200] Charles Thomas O'Connell, "Social Structure and Science: Soviet Studies at Harvard." Ph.D. dissertation, University of California at Los Angeles. Department of History, 1990 (unpublished).

Merle Fainsod in the Harvard University Archives. These letters were suspected to contain secret intelligence information when, among many other subjects, they reported back to Kluckhohn on contacts and conversations of Parsons as he met military government personnel as well as Russian emigrés (the latter often living in the underground in postwar Germany, in fear of being repatriated and sent to the Gulag). In the context of the emerging Cold War, Parsons supposedly had been an envoy in the service of one or another government agency (allegedly the State Department and/or the then recently founded CIA). The accusation was: In a semi-official mission of anti-Communist intelligence, Parsons had arranged for an ex-Nazi to be allowed into the United States using false identification (which indeed the person in question had done).

The upshot: Since at an earlier time in the 1980s the letters had been removed from the Harvard Archives by Fainsod's heirs, it appeared impossible when the accusation was made in the late 1980s to refute the charge that Parsons had shepherded a Nazi sympathizer into the United States. That person supposedly had been introduced to Kluckhohn in the letters preserved among the Fainsod papers.

In actual fact, however, there was no wrongdoing on Parsons's part. His ten letters, originally handwritten, were typed at the RRC on his own request (he received a set of flimsies, as did Kluckhohn and Fainsod, for that matter). The letters at the time were addressed to Kluckhohn as Director of RRC, since Parsons had agreed to procure on occasion of his visit to Germany, a large amount of information concerning location of libraries, special bookstores or books, experts on Russia, and related issues. Fainsod received one batch of copies of the letters since he was director of a research project planned by the RRC, for which Parsons also supplied material from Germany (the project was to analyze personality structures of refugees, so-called Displaced Persons now living in the Western zones of Germany, a large number of whom came from Communist countries). During his trip, as documented in the RRC Executive Council minutes of June 7, 1948, he was to contact people whom he met on behalf of his colleagues, among them one ex-Russian linguist who now lived under an assumed name given him by British intelligence, Poppe. During the preparatory Executive Council meeting, Parsons noted the different tasks he was to fulfill on behalf of various colleagues during his three weeks in Germany: This is how his various tasks in Germany on behalf of RRC colleagues can now be reconstructed.[201] In his correspondence to Kluckhohn, mention was made of Poppe (the Nazi sympathizer in question) in one single letter only. It seems that Parsons never met the man at all. It appears that Poppe, subsequent to Parsons's talking to a military government official about him, was considered unsuitable for the one-year appointment as consultant in a refugee

---

[201] Raymond Bauer's requests concerned, for instance, "German-American experience with Russians. Germans in the Russian army. Germans with experience in occupied Russia." Alex Inkeles's wishes concerned "Questioning of DP's on condition in Russia." Fainsod asked for "Interviews with Dudins about Party etc. Mrs. Fischer – Munich – Karpovich or Nikolaevsky (;) Literature on Communist parties – ." Parsons, handwritten notes, undated (presumably June 1948), starting "Bauer Question of DP's"; Parsons papers, HUG(FP) – 42.45.4, box 1.

study offered him by RRC (in April of 1948).[202] As it went, the RRC's invitation to Poppe was withdrawn, in October of that year. However, Poppe immigrated into the United States, presumably because Columbia University economist Karl Menges eventually secured him an appointment at Washington University, Seattle. Fifty years later, Parsons was charged with a role in this, when he had had none. Dennis Wrong, eventually recollecting and evaluating the accusation against Parsons, labeled this tell-tale example of political slander "left-wing McCarthyism."[203]

An Ex-Communist?

In the academic year 1953–1954, Parsons accepted an invitation to Cambridge, England. During his sojourn abroad, McCarthyism became an ardent concern for him when it affected his colleague and collaborator Stouffer, and a major problem personally when he was accused of disloyalty.

To recount the facts: From England, early in 1954, he applied for a visa to go to France for a UNESCO Conference in April; to his astonishment, his passport was withheld and he was sent a fingerprint chart which he was supposed to complete and submit. The enigma became a scandal when he learned that Stouffer had been charged by the Eastern Industrial Personnel Security Board, for collaborating with Parsons who, it was stated, had been a member of the Communist Party and had openly supported Communist organizations such as, for instance, the "American Committee for Spanish Freedom" in the 1930s and the Harvard branch of the John Reed Society in the 1940s.

Parsons was horrified. He swore an affidavit on behalf of Stouffer on February 23. There, among other refutations, he declared unequivocally his political stance:

> My political opinions have always been in support of free democracy and opposed to totalitarianism of any sort whether of the left or of the right. In addition to my acceptance of such a position as natural and obvious for a loyal American citizen I have long felt that I had a strong professional interest in it as a social scientist. It could not fail to be evident to one of my profession that freedom for the scientific study of social problems was drastically curtailed under any totalitarian system. Experience as a student of Pre-Nazi Germany made me particularly sensitive to

[202] The text in the letter #3, of June 30, 1948, from Berlin, ran as follows: "Secondly thru CJ I met one of the men in intelligence. ... He told me that the British have collected most of the Nazis' German experts on Russia in a hotel ... Finally he (...) came up with the name of our friend Poppe. He told me that P. was under the protection of the British Intelligence people but they want to get him to the United States. He is hot for them because he is explicitly wanted by the Russians – quite recently there was another request for him. On this I saw a British Intelligence man named Rhodes who confirmed the story. The dossier he had on his desk on P. was by the way marked Top Secret. He told me that when Gen. Walsh (Chief of Intelligence in EUCOM) was in Washington this spring he tried to get the State Dept. to admit P. but failed and felt he was lucky that they consented to keep the case open. (If he can get into U.S. the British will take care of letting him out of Germany.) What the story is, I don't know but these facts may help if you want to try to do anything." The acronym CJ stood for Carl J. Friedrich. I wish to thank Victor Lidz for making the letter accessible to me.

[203] Dennis Wrong, "Truth, Misinterpretation, or Left-Wing McCarthyism?," *Sociological Forum*, vol. 11, 1996, pp. 613–621.

this feature of the Nazi regime, and I have been highly conscious that essentially the same kind of conditions if not worse prevailed in Soviet Russia.[204]

In early March, despite support from many quarters, Stouffer lost his case before the Eastern Industrial Personnel Security Board in New York; henceforth, he would be denied access to classified materials in government agencies, a serious handicap for the devoted researcher he was. However, Parsons was to be targeted personally. On May 6, he received by Registered Mail Return Receipt Requested, an interrogatory demanding "explanation or answer to the derogatory information."[205] The charges were, apart from that he had been a member of the Communist Party, and others, that he had been associated with Harlow Shapley, a Communist Party member, had been associated with Communist organizations as specified by the Special Committee on Un-American Acitivites (such as the John Reed Clubs of the United States), had been a leader in opposing the prosecution of Alger Hiss, and, low and behold, that his son at a party at home in approximately 1949 had cited Karl Marx's "Communist Manifesto." Parsons, in a affidavit sworn at the London Embassy on May 23, refuted all accusations. On the latter slight, concerning his son Charles, he had this to say, among more detailed rebuttal, "That my son's alleged interest in Marx could be construed as evidence of my own acceptance of Marxism, which he allegedly got from me, is completely out of the question because I have always been in radical disagreement with Marx's theories; which perhaps has a special significance in my case because much of their subject-matter falls within my own professional field."[206]

On his attitude regarding communism, he made a passionate statement rejecting any system of repression, endorsing American democracy:

> I am strongly opposed to Soviet Communism and its influence in the United States and elsewhere for four main reasons. First, the Communist Party advocates and works for revolution by violence and refuses to accept the legal procedures of Constitutional Democracy as it is practiced in the United States and other countries like England. Second, it works by conspiratorial methods which are incompatible with the requirement of a democracy that differences of political opinion, which we treat as legitimate within a considerable range, should be openly threshed out before the forum of public opinion and decided by constitutional processes. Third, the Communist Party in the United States is known to be controlled by the Russian Party and not to be an independent movement of free Americans. The fourth reason is that I do not like the Communist ideal and where they have gained ascendancy, their practice, of what a society should be. Above all I abhor

---

[204] "Before the *Eastern Industrial Personnel Security Board, Matter of Samuel Andrew Stouffer*." Sworn statement, signed Talcott Parsons, Great Britain and Northern Ireland, London, England, Embassy of the United States of America, dated Twenty-third day of February, 1954, p. 2; Parsons papers, HUG(FP), 42.8.4, box 13.

[205] Letter, Pierce J. Gerety, Chairman, International Organizations Employees Loyalty Board, by J. Paul Fairbank, Executive Secretary, on behalf of United States Civil Service Commission Washington 25, D.C., to Parsons, dated May 6, 1954; Parsons papers, HUG(FP) – 42.8.4, box 13.

[206] "Interrogatory. Mr Talcott Parsons, International Organizations Employeess Loyalty Board, Washington, D.C.," Part VII-5; Parsons papers, HUG(FP) – 42.8.4, box 13.

their ruthless suppression of the freedom of the individual. I subscribe to these views, which I understand to be taken for granted by all loyal American citizens, without reservation.[207]

On the other side of the Atlantic, Stouffer, who remained a friend despite the loss incurred through his relation with Parsons, sat down to write in a letter dated May 21, 1954, "Dear Talcott: O tempores! When a guest in one's home, identity forever unknown, can inform the secret police that the 15-year-old son of the host is familiar with the Communist Manifesto, and such information is produced to deny the country of the host's services – this is terrifying."[208]

Parsons, in a letter to Dean McGeorge Bundy, analyzed the danger to the very fabric of democracy in the United States involved in McCarthyism:

> I am proud of Harvard for its fine defensive stand in relation to the Congressional investigations which has, I think, been critical in stemming the tide of the direct attack on the universities as such. But I do not think the universities or the academic profession can afford only to defend this "home" position. They must defend their rights to serve their own government and international organizations within their fields of competence on reasonable terms and without the insidious prior presumption of disloyalty which is now so universally operative. Much of the country and not only the profession is, I think, at stake.[209]

Further thought on the issue resulted in a manuscript, originally entitled " 'McCarthyism' and American Foreign Relations: A Sociologist's View." It was published under a slightly different title in the winter issue of *Yale Review*.[210] Parsons argued that the United States had fallen into the persecutory tendency of McCarthyism as a reaction to their unaccustomed role in world politics subsequent to World War II. When William Langer read the article, he thanked Parsons in a letter written in early January, stating: "I certainly think that articles of this sort are very useful in putting things into something like the proper perspective."[211]

In January 1955, Parsons was cleared of all charges raised against him. The letter from the United States Civil Service Commission ran: "It has been determined that, on all the evidence, there is no reasonable doubt as to the loyalty of this person to the Government of the United States."[212]

With his name cleared, however, the matter was not over yet for Parsons. When the American Association of University Professors, in the fall of 1955, established a Special Committee on Academic Freedom and Tenure attached to its Committee A to investigate each case of dismissal or sanctions against a faculty member at

---

[207] Ibid., Part VII–6/7.
[208] Letter, Stouffer to Parsons, May 21, 1954; Parsons papers, HUG(FP) – 42.8.4, box 13.
[209] Letter, Parsons to McGeorge Bundy, undated (presumably May 1954), p. 2; Parsons papers, HUG(FP) – 42.8.4, box 13.
[210] Parsons, "McCarthyism and American Social Tension: A Sociologist's View," *Yale Review*, vol. 44, 1954–1955, pp. 226–255; the original manuscript is preserved among the Parsons papers, HUG(FP) – 15.70, box 2.
[211] Letter, William L. Langer to Parsons, dated January 6, 1955; Parsons papers, HUG(FP) – 42.8.4, box 13.
[212] Letter, Gerety to Parsons, dated January 19, 1955; Parsons papers, HUG(FP) – 42.8.4, box 13.

any U.S. university investigated by the Special Committee on Un-American Activities, Parsons volunteered to serve on the Committee. For the best part of four years, only interrupted by his one-year sojourn as a fellow of the Center for Advanced Study in the Behavioral Sciences at Stanford University, he was occupied with the AAUP work of investigating the decisions taken and measures executed under McCarthyism.[213]

It was on the basis of the latter painstaking work that Ellen Schrecker, analyzing the impact of McCarthyism on American universities in her book published in the 1980s, had only praise for the responsible work done by Parsons in the context of alleviating the aftermath of McCarthyism.[214]

---

[213] Material documenting Parsons's heavy workload in Committee A of AAUP Committee on Special Freedom and Tenure Cases during the 1950s is preserved among the Parsons papers, HUG(FP) – 42.8.4, box 2; the work continued into the early 1960s.

[214] Ellen Schrecker, *No Ivory Tower: McCarthyism and the Universities* (New York: Oxford University Press, 1986).

4
A New Agenda for Citizenship: Parsons's Theory and American Society in the 1960s

Introduction

Harvard historian Arthur Schlesinger, Jr., first insider-analyst of the presidency of John F. Kennedy[1] and later chronicler of *Robert Kennedy and His Times*,[2] failed to mention Harvard social science when he honored the many contributions from Harvard scholars toward the seminal politics changing American society in the Kennedy era and until 1968.

A recent account taking notice of the merits of social science and also Parsons mainly in the 1960s, Stephen Graubard's retrospect of forty years of *Daedalus*, the journal of the American Academy of Arts and Sciences, published in 1999,[3] does take account of Parsons's achievements. But Parsons, for Graubard, is only one among a larger group of sociologists who contributed to the success of the Academy and its journal, helping to safeguard the role of science as guardian of cultural knowledge in our civilization. The particular accomplishment of Parsons as a social theorist in the 1960s deserves yet more special mention.

Polemics such as Alvin Gouldner's *The Coming Crisis of Western Sociology*[4] which charged Harvard sociology, and particularly Parsons, with mechanistic thinking, even lack of analytical reflexivity, have unduly clouded recognition of Parsons's "late" oeuvre.

My thesis is that in the course of the 1960s, urged on by the liberal progressivism of the Kennedy administration, he thoroughly reformulated his systems theory. His main insight, I suppose, took the then-current changes of scope and structure of societal organization on a national as well as international scale as indicators of major developments in the history of modern democracy. Pluralist democracy in the United States, from his point of view, was undergoing seminal reorganization which made it, yet again, a world leader in an ongoing process of modernization.

---

[1] Arthur Schlesinger, Jr., *A Thousand Days: John F. Kennedy in the White House* (Boston: Houghton Mifflin, 1965).
[2] Schlesinger, *Robert Kennedy and His Times* (New York: Ballantine, 1978).
[3] Stephen Graubard, "Forty Years On," *Daedalus*, Supplement to vol. 128, 1999 (entire issue).
[4] Alvin Gouldner, *The Coming Crisis of Western Sociology* (London: Heinemann 1970).

In his own present, he took notice of the strain toward equality in American society spurred by the Supreme Court legislation in the 1950s regarding civil rights, involving defiance of the law on the part of Southern states and eventual opening up of the educational and occupational markets for minorities, when in his analysis he created new conceptual perspectives to adequately take into account these new chances for citizenship. He analyzed these changes when he also recognized the dangers of reversal of modernization by way of fundamentalist "revolutions" fostering antidemocratic tendencies. Even in the less than violent guise of movements such as McCarthyism, he never ceased to perceive a danger of reversal of modernization.

In this endeavor, Parsons contradicted the sociological approaches of many of his contemporaries, which he felt were inadequate for the scientific understanding of the developments of the 1960s. What he found particularly unacceptable were, for one, Marxism which to him appeared as an approach mirroring the historical and scientific problems of the nineteenth century (and only that), and, in addition, revivals of utilitarianism and behaviorism clad in approaches analyzing elementary structures of social life such as, in the 1960s, so-called exchange theory and also conflict theory: Both, he felt, suffered from defaults which he, in the 1930s, had meant to eradicate through *Structure*.

The new phase in his thinking, going beyond his *The Social System*, I would suggest, originated in his having revisited the Weberian thesis of economy and society in the mid-1950s. That he had developed the four-function scheme of system dynamics helped him understand the generalized symbolic media. His original idea had been to revisit Weber on economy and society, suitably taking as scenario the 1950s. He had come to realize that cultural orientations defining rationality in economic activities were the nonutilitarian aspect of economic knowledge which, since the 1930s, had made Keynes's idea of the modern economy into dominant theory (which, to be sure, had long replaced the marginal-utility economics that had been the dominant theory in Weber's lifetime).

His first conceptual achievement, which opened up a new perspective on power and the polity involving the modern development of democracy, was that he refuted what he named the "zero-sum" notion of power. He proposed, instead, that power had a variable quality of extension and concentration, when in the polity prevailed two separate interaction media, political power and influence; in addition, a fourth medium, value-commitments, was also modeled after money as a symbolic device. He also made suggestions on the sum total of media quantity in a society, depending on the type of authority, in Weberian terms.

Parsons's second conceptual achievement was that he explained democracy through processes of integration into one system of diverse elements in differentiated, pluralist (sub)systems; these, on principle, were equal though distinct, suggesting the newly introduced construct of societal community.

When he recapitulated, in 1976, in his "Afterword" to the re-issue of Max Black's collection entitled *The Social Theories of Talcott Parsons*, that his theory had advanced immensely since the early 1960s when he had written his original "The Point of View of the Author," he remarked that at that time he had only begun what now was far more advanced. He remembered that then "a major line of development was barely beginning," and he announced to his readers that "a major development of the theory" had taken place since.[5]

Among the many scholarly accounts that have stated and restated his intellectual achievements in the last decade and a half, surprisingly few have appreciated the salience of his theory of societal community, the empirical nucleus of his revised approach. Interestingly, the very first attempt at reappraisal other than critical reconstruction, Robert Holton and Bryan S. Turner's *Talcott Parsons on Economy and Society* (1986), came nearer appreciation than many later accounts, although Holton and Turner did not apprehend the whole story. They realized that Parsons had new things to say on the integration of Blacks in American society, but overlooked the serendipity of his theory of citizenship. They rightly credited him with transcending both utopian optimism that centered around the nineteenth-century ideal of *Gemeinschaft* and cultural pessimism that endorsed twentieth-century skepticism against presumably individualistic *Gesellschaft*.[6] But they failed to comment on the fact that Parsons had welded together the twin concepts of *Gemeinschaft* and *Gesellschaft* into one groundbreaking notion – namely, societal community. Prior to Holton and Turner, an earlier reconstruction originally published in Parsons's lifetime, François Bourricaud's *The Sociology of Talcott Parsons*, first in French in 1977, had acknowledged his use of cybernetics in the works of his later life and understood the importance of his analysis of interaction media and polity, but failed to recognize the serendipity of the discovery of societal community.[7] In recent years, two authors have reversed the trend to a certain extent, namely Jeffrey Alexander in his reformulation of the notion of civil society in his so-called Neo-Functionalism, and Richard Münch analyzing the problem of order in today's globalized society in his contribution to our recent volume celebrating the achievement of *The Structure of Social Action*.[8]

I hope to accomplish two things through my account in this chapter. For one, I wish to elucidate the major conceptual instruments of sociological analysis contained in Parsons's theory of democracy in the 1960s, highlighting two phenomena, interaction media and societal community. I wish to show that he envisaged these as bipolar phenomena, varying between one pole of anomie and de-differentiation, on the one side, and one of integration and pluralist differentiation, on the other. (It is certain that he envisaged the variation in a bipolar structure of the interaction media; it is somewhat uncertain, however, as will be discussed later, whether societal community varies between a pole of anomie and one of integration, or is

---

[5] Parsons, "Afterword," in Max Black, ed., *The Social Theories of Talcott Parsons* (London/Amsterdam: Feffer & Simons, 1976), p. 367.

[6] Robert J. Holton and Bryan S. Turner, *Talcott Parsons on Economy and Society* (London: Routledge and Kegan Paul, 1986), p. 232.

[7] Francois Bourricaud, *The Sociology of Talcott Parsons*. Translated by Arthur Goldhammer (Chicago: University of Chicago Press, 1981).

[8] Jeffrey C. Alexander, "Citizen and Enemy as Symbolic Classification: On the Polarizing Discourse of Civil Society," in Alexander, ed., *Real Civil Societies: Dilemmas of Institutionalization* (London: Sage, 1998), pp. 96–114; Richard Münch, "The Problem of Social Order, Sixty Years after *The Structure of Social Action*," in Bernard Barber and Uta Gerhardt, eds., *Agenda for Sociology: Classic Sources and Current Uses of Talcott Parsons's Work* (Baden-Baden: Nomos, 1999), pp. 211–232.

itself the pole of integration which can be attained in a democratic structure.) In this, I will take account of his relation to other authors wherever feasible: Contemporaries who drew criticism from him when their theses were unsatisfactory were, for instance, C. Wright Mills in *The Power Elite*, or, less outspokenly, George Homans in *Social Behavior: Its Elementary Forms*; or, alternatively, he found convincing, for instance, Robert Bellah's concept of civil religion and T. H. Marshall's idea of the threefold nature of citizenship.

My second theme: I am convinced that many of Parsons's essays throughout the period between the middle 1950s and the early 1970s were written when events in the society called for a particular problem or situation to be thought through sociologically. My conjecture is that he frequently sought his themes, particularly those in his historical-analytical essays, with practical problems in mind as they required sociological expertise to understand them in their context. To give three examples: When Senator McCarthy had been censured in Congress in spring 1954 and consequently McCarthyism began to relent, Parsons immediately devised a sociological rationale for the episode of intolerance and witch hunting in postwar American history. When the essay was reprinted in 1962, he insisted that he should add a comparison between McCarthyism and the white supremacism of the John Birch Society, which had then recently gained prominence.[9] When the Supreme Court under Chief Justice Earl Warren made school segregation illegal and barred segregation in public places including transportation, as historian Schlesinger would remark later, the third issue that had not yet been dealt with but needed urgent attention was the issue of voting of Blacks, in the South but also elsewhere.[10] Precisely at that point in time, Parsons decided to analyze voting in his paper entitled "'Voting' and the Equilibrium of the American Political System."[11] Or, to give another example, when violence erupted in (mostly) Northern cities subsequent to enactment of the first Civil Rights Bill in 1964, he convinced the *American Academy of Arts and Sciences*, backed by the Ford Foundation, that a major analytic effort was called for, which was to start a series of conferences and eventually led to two groundbreaking issues of *Daedalus*, which, in 1966, became the volume with a foreword by President Johnson, *The Negro American*.[12]

This chapter has three parts. The first one deals with interaction media and how they fitted into the analytical program which Parsons had first outlined in *The Structure of Social Action*. The second part deals with his theory of societal community and how this theory of society allowed for citizenship as the core of a genuinely modern democracy. Both these parts explain his tenet that cybernetics

---

[9] Letter, Parsons to Daniel Bell, January 11, 1962: "I think I would like to add a brief piece on the relation of McCarthyism to the newly emergent movements. I think there are some important differences." A newspaper clipping preserved among the Parsons papers (from the *Sunday Republican*, Springfield, Mass., March 31, 1963) contained the judgment: "The efforts of these radicals – from the lunatic fringe to the thoughtful conservatives – have been to resist the tide of progress, mainly because they don't understand social change." Parsons papers, HUG(FP) – 15.4, box 4.

[10] Arthur Schlesinger, Jr., *Robert Kennedy and His Times*, p. 287.

[11] Reprinted in *Politics and Social Structure*, pp. 204–240. See also below.

[12] See below.

be introduced into social theory. The third part, a postscriptum, discusses how he related to three political issues of the 1960s in his professional and personal activities, namely the civil-rights movement, university unrest, and the war in Vietnam.

The New Perspective on Power and the Polity
Understanding Distribution of Power in the United States

Mills's *The Power Elite* maintained that American society was dominated by a hermetic circle of the top business executives, the military establishment, and what he called the political directorate. According to Mills, this power elite, secluded from the mass of the population, monopolizing decisions that involved power over the lives of millions, was posited against a mass society of citizens who were denied power or influence to actively shape their own fate. The middle level of the democratically elected legislative and members of the executive or administration were utterly dependent on the stratagems of the truly powerful (Mills said nothing about the judicative branch of government): "If the top is unprecedentedly powerful and increasingly unified and willful; if the middle zones are increasingly a semiorganized stalemate – in what shape is the bottom, in what condition is the public at large? The rise of the power elite . . . rests upon, and in some ways is part of, the transformation of the publics of America into a mass society."[13]

Mills's concern was to point out that the political reality in the United States was irreconcilable with the ideal of a knowledgable public able to judge the issues on which they voted. Instead, total power supposedly was with an elite who had no sense of responsibility to those whose lives in an age of potential nuclear war lay in their hands. The prospects were gloomy: "Status, no longer rooted primarily in local communities, follows the big hierarchies, which are on a national scale. Status follows the big money, even if it has a touch of the gangster about it. Status follows power, even if it be without background. . . . The American elite is not composed of representative men whose conduct and character constitute models for American imitation and aspiration.[14]

The book, an instant success, was not destroyed in the reviews it received. In *Social Forces*, Robert Agger, who taught at North Carolina, commented about Mills's book: "It . . . is important in the sense of being the sort of focus so desperately needed by political reformers today."[15] In the *American Sociological Review*, Leonard Reissman from Tulane University conceded, "The judgment to be made of Mills is never that what he says is true but unimportant, as can be said for much of the reporting in the social sciences."[16] One critic, Peter Rossi from the University of Chicago, in the *American Journal of Sociology* charged Mills with simplifying the issue of power, "There is little doubt that the bare facts upon which Mills has built his thesis are correct. However, around them he weaves a web of implications for which little evidence is given."[17]

---

[13] C. Wright Mills, *The Power Elite* (New York: Oxford University Press, 1956), p. 297.
[14] Ibid., pp. 357 and 360.
[15] Book review of *The Power Elite*, *Social Forces*, vol. 35, 1956/7, p. 288.
[16] Book review of *The Power Elite*, *American Sociological Review*, vol. 21, 1956, p. 514.
[17] Book review of *The Power Elite*, *American Journal of Sociology*, vol. 62, 1956/7, p. 232.

Parsons, however, could not let it stand at that. He embarked upon a thorough criticism of Mills in a review for *World Politics*.[18] He charged Mills with two oversights; first, to seriously misconstrue the structure and process of modern Western societies when he overlooked "the dynamic of a maturing industrial society,"[19] in the American case one whose world position had been redefined by "a variety of exogenous changes, including the relative decline of the Western European powers, the rise of Soviet Russia, and the break-up of the 'colonial' organization of much of the non-white world." The other charge was that Mills misunderstood the nature of power itself.

Regarding American society, Parsons made three analytical statements on contemporary empirical phenomena. One was that power no longer was the only dimension of stratification – let alone a skewed distribution of power/status such as was the target of Mills. Differentiation ranging in the market economy from replacement of the kinship-based family farm by an industrial production system in the nineteenth century to, in due course, further differentiation between property and management as foci of influence in the twentieth century, was a fact which could not be explained away. Power and prestige, in the middle twentieth century, had become separate dimensions of social stratification: "The most striking case is the relatively high position of the professions relative to executive roles in business, as revealed by the famous North-Hatt data. Physicians as a group do not exercise great power, but there is no reason to question their very high prestige, which has been demonstrated in study after study."[20]

The second point was that control, including that of the military over economic or political decisions, was subject to checks and balances within the American system, a tradition which Mills seemed to overlook. What Parsons conceded to Mills was that in the post–World War II decade, the United States had found it difficult to assume the role of world leadership bestowed upon it through changes in the relative impact of Europe as compared with the Soviet Union, and "the higher military officers have tended to fill a vacuum in the field of national decision-making."[21] But this certainly did not warrant a diagnosis of power elite dominating over the public degraded to mass society.

The third point Parsons put in the form of a rhetorical question: What was Mills missing out on? For one, Mills misunderstood that in the alleged mass society,

---

[18] Parsons, "The Distribution of Power in American Society," first published in *World Politics*, vol. 10, 1957, pp. 123–143, republished as Chapter 6 in *Structure and Process in Modern Societies* (New York: Free Press, 1960), and again in *Politics and Social Structure* (New York: Free Press, 1969), pp. 185–203.

[19] Ibid., p. 190; the next quote is from the same page. The argument highlighting the changed role of America, now a world superpower, after World War II had been Parsons's explanation for McCarthyism in 1954.

[20] Ibid., p. 194; the findings he referred to were published as, among other works, National Opinion Research Center, "Jobs and Occupations: A Popular Evaluation," *Opinion News*, IX (September 1, 1947), pp. 3–13; Paul K. Hatt, "Stratification in the Mass Society," *American Sociological Review*, vol. 15, 1950, pp. 210–216; and, with collaborators Otis Dudley Duncan, Paul K. Hatt, Cecil C. North, and Albert J. Reiss, Jr, *Occupation and Social Status* (New York: Free Press, 1961; reprint, New York: Arno Press, 1977).

[21] *Politics and Social Structure*, p. 196.

structural elements did matter which he, Mills, tended to dismiss, such as kinship and the family, religion, or associational activities and relationships. Furthermore, Mills entirely overlooked the positive role of science and learning for modern democracy, thus failing to note that professionals who were university-trained could prove able to withstand temptations or pressures of power. Finally, Mills overlooked the function of lawyers, and the judicial branch of government in particular, which "seems to be a most biased appraisal of the role of the courts. Not to speak of the longer-run record, the initiative taken by the courts in the matter of racial segregation and in the reassertion of civil liberties after the miasma of McCarthyism does not appear to me to be compatible with Mills' views."[22]

The theoretical crux was that Mills misconstrued the nature of power, as for him, Mills, "power is not a facility for the performance of function in, and on behalf of, the society as a system, but is interpreted exclusively as a facility for getting what one group, the holders of power, wants by preventing another group, the 'outs,' from getting what it wants."[23]

Thus reigned a "zero-sum" concept of power,[24] a concept that Parsons found widespread in contemporary political science approaches. This kind of thinking falsely presumed that power vested in one person or group would necessarily have to be withheld from, taken away from, or denied, another. Instead, he ventured,

> Power is a generalized facility or resource in the society. It has to be divided or allocated, but it also has to be produced and it has collective as well as distributive functions. It is the capacity to mobilize the resources of the society for the attainment of goals for which a general "public" commitment has been made or may be made. It is mobilization, above all, of the action of persons and groups, which is *binding* on them by virtue of their position in the society.[25]

From this vantage point, he dismissed Mills's "individualistic utopianism."[26] Mills himself had rejected "liberal" advocacy of Jeffersonianism deemed inadequate to modern society, and "capitalist" endorsement of the liberty of the entrepreneur conducting his business as he pleased, primarily production-oriented. Mills, though, stood for "socialist" politics against capitalism when he advocated state control over the economy, presupposing a "popular will" that would forestall

---

[22] Ibid., p. 199; the next quote is from the same page.

[23] One background notion, which Parsons criticized not only in Mills's view, apart from Marxism, was that of Lasswell, *Politics: Who Gets What, When, How* (Glencoe, Ill.: Free Press, 1951). That book started out with, "The study of politics is the study of influence and the influential.... The influential are those who get the most of what there is to get.... Those who get the most are *elite*; the rest are *mass*" (p. 13).

[24] In lecture notes, dated April 29, 1960 and destined for Dartmouth College, whose topic was "Power in Social Systems," he charged that the zero-sum concept saw power lodged with the unit (or actor) but not the collectivity of the society ("state of system"): "Zero-sum concept – essentially *unit* power vv other units distinguished from state of system." The argument, it appears, saw the political-science view of power (which, for him, presupposed a zero-sum quality) replicate what he had called the "utilitarian dilemma" in his writings of the 1930s. See "Dartmouth. *Power in Social Systems*[.] April 29, '60," p. 1; Parsons papers, HUG(FP) – 15.4, box 19.

[25] "The Distribution of Power," p. 200.

[26] Ibid., p. 201 f.

misuse of power. In Parsons's view, all three types of utopianism were unacceptable. The reason was, as he unambiguously clarified, that "power, while of course subject to abuses and in need of many controls, is an essential and desirable component of a highly organized society."[27]

Mills neither accepted the criticism nor agreed that power was a positive component of the modern world. He denounced Parsons's approach as "Grand Theory" in *The Sociological Imagination*, where he deliberately disregarded Parsons's alternative view on power and also the fact that Parsons's oeuvre had progressed beyond *The Social System*.[28] Mills, like other critics of the late 1950s such as Ralf Dahrendorf, failed to as much as take notice of the fact that Parsons's theory had gone beyond his earlier writings.

Unperturbed, Parsons broadened and sharpened his understanding of the political structure. A striking piece was a chapter he contributed to *American Voting Behavior*, a book originally planned in 1957 and eventually published in 1959.[29] The essay reinterpreted the data collected by a major study whose main investigator had been Bernard R. Berelsen, conducted in conjunction with Columbia University's Bureau of Applied Social Research (whose director was Lazarsfeld).[30] This study, which had been a sequel to the classic *The People's Choice* that had analyzed the Roosevelt-Willkie election in Erie County, Ohio, in 1940,[31] reported on the Truman-Dewey contest in Elmira, a small town in upstate New York. Berelsen and his collaborators provided data which Parsons used as evidence to prove that his new concept of power, and of political system derived therefrom, made sense empirically.

What was the evidence, what the theory? Berelson et al. established what were the demographic and party preferences background in Elmira, before they looked at the role of labor unions and other organizations, the impact of socioeconomic and ethnic status, the role played by groups setting voting norms, but also the dynamics of personal discussion and the effect of the campaign on how voting tendencies changed. They further analyzed the structure and impact of local party chapters, the candidates' impression made on the electorate based on their stand on issues, and also the role of the mass media. Summing up the 149 propositions derived from their

---

[27] Ibid., p. 202.

[28] See C. Wright Mills, *The Sociological Imagination* (New York: Oxford University Press, 1959). In the chapter "Grand Theory" Mills ridiculed Parsons by "translating the contents of *The Social System* into English" (p. 207). He charged, "The basic cause of grand theory is the initial choice of level of thinking so general that its practitioners cannot logically get down to observation" (p. 33). The rift never healed. Parsons even persuaded Lazarsfeld to have Mills excluded from the list of speakers proposed by the American Program Committee for the Sixth World Congress of Sociology, which was to take place in Washington, D.C. in 1962. See correspondence between Lazarsfeld and Parsons, dated May 22 and June 5, 1961; Parsons papers, HUG(FP) – 15.4, box 11.

[29] Parsons, "'Voting' and the Equilibrium of the American Political System," in Eugene Burdick and Arthur Brodbeck, eds., *American Voting Behavior* (New York: Free Press, 1959), reprinted in *Politics and Social Structure*, pp. 204–240.

[30] Bernard B. Berelson, Paul F. Lazarsfeld, and William N. McPhee, *Voting: A Study of Opinion Formation in a Presidential Campaign* (Chicago: University of Chicago Press, 1954).

[31] Paul F. Lazarsfeld, Bernard Berelson, and Hazel Gaudet, *The People's Choice: How the Voter Makes Up His Mind in a Presidential Campaign* (New York: Columbia University Press, 1948).

findings which they explicated in ten chapters and subchapters, Berelson et al.'s conclusion found it difficult to explicate their study: "A sociological proposition involves properties of groups; a sociological interpretation explains findings in terms which include interactions between group members."[32] Eventually, they cited French psychologist Gabriel Tarde before settling down with a statement of allegiance, "Our study unquestionably contains data which deal with systems of individuals and, to this extent, fits in with one tradition of sociology."[33]

Parsons, in his re-analysis, provided the rationale which Berelson et al. had unsuccessfully sought for their study, making sense of their excellent data and fine report. In this endeavor, he applied to the empirical evidence accumulated by Berelson et al. the four-function analytical scheme which, earlier in the decade, he had developed mainly together with two collaborators, Robert F. Bales and Neil Smelser. This reconciliation between data and analytical scheme chose voting as concretized in the results of Berelson et al., as a theme for interpretation which avoided deductive reasoning that would merely apply a model. The aim was twofold. For one, he conceptualized the importance of voting in the American political system – if only in the wake of recent Supreme Court jurisdiction. On the other hand, he wanted to see whether his concepts of system analysis, purporting the four-function scheme developed subsequent to *The Social System*, would hold out as an analytical approach accounting for the empirical facts.

After a brief inquiry into the nature of choice in the dominant two-party system, he proceeded to reinterpret Berelson et al.'s findings. He identified four dichotomies of problems which he related to the four functions a system had to solve in order to perpetuate itself. In this vein, he made four discoveries. First, the apparent contradiction between the often irrational traditionalism of any single voter and the rationality of eventual allegiance to the elected President turned out to disappear when group involvement (as shown by Berelson et al.) was taken into account. Thus was revealed give and take between the polity and the public "as belonging to the pattern-maintenance subsystem."[34]

Second, the frequent shift of political allegiance in the course of an electoral campaign of which Berelson et al. had made so much, Parsons explained, signaled the element of flexibility in the system of stability, guaranteeing the latter while enabling the system to attain its goal when the outcome was legitimate government.

Third was "the problem of 'polarization,' or what Berelson et al. speak of as the balance between consensus and cleavage."[35] He argued (as he made a short aside regarding the "pathology" of a "a certain type of 'charismatic' appeal, to extremism and emotionalism" such as then-recent McCarthyism[36]):

> The pressure of political cleavage – by activating ties of solidarity at the more differentiated structural levels that cut across the line of cleavage – tends automatically to bring countervailing forces into play. The point of view of an individual

---

[32] Berelson et al., p. 298.
[33] Ibid., p. 301.
[34] "'Voting'," p. 238.
[35] Ibid., p. 221.
[36] Ibid., p. 225.

voter is likely to be, "My fellow union member (lodge member, coreligionist, office colleague, and so forth) who is intending to vote Republican (Democratic) is in general a pretty decent guy. I just can't see how all people who hold his views can be as bad as they're made out to be." Awareness that this type of sentiment will be activated may put a certain restraint on extremism in the campaign.[37]

This realm of functioning, obviously, secured integration, particularly when subsequent to an election citizens had to get on with their lives beyond party rivalries.

The last problem concerned a mechanism for mediation of "the processes of adaptation to structural change in a rapidly evolving society,"[38] solving tension between progress on the one side and conservation on the other. It was here that the image of the Republican Party as conservative and the Democrats as reform-prone mattered to the electorate. He added that, interestingly, reforms such as the New Deal measures bitterly fought over during their enactment had subsequently been adopted and even enlarged by a Republican President. This, no doubt, served the adaptation function in the political cum social system.

The four requirements for structure and process were thus fully met, he recapitulated. The structure of voting allowed for stability *and* dynamism, enabling a system "relatively stable... that can integrate multifarious pluralistic interests and yet adapt to changing conditions."[39] In detail, the balances between involvement and indifference and stability and flexibility were met, and, likewise, those between consensus and cleavage, and progress and conservation. (A fifth balance, between individualism and collectivism, he admitted, lay on another plane). "I organized my more detailed review of the relevant findings of *Voting* about the relation between my four propositions," he summarized when he emphasized:

> What is important in the present connection is rather the *fit* of these findings and conclusions with a more generalized conceptual scheme. This fit strengthens the impression from the authors' own exposition that there is an important *internal consistency* in the main structure of their findings and interpretations. In the light of the above discussion it seems to me inconceivable that the facts should be just a random collection of discrete items with no essential connection with each other.[40]

Thus he proved two things. For one, the general theory of action had progressed beyond what had been, in the earlier 1950s, the target of the Department of Social Relations' multiple-authored *Toward a General Theory of Action*, now incorporating the accomplishments of *Working Papers in the Theory of Action*.[41] *Economy and Society*, co-authored with Smelser, had proposed that the four-function scheme of system analysis fitted economic processes, and further application using contemporary data was now feasible for the political system (or,

---

[37] Ibid., p. 224.
[38] Ibid., p. 235.
[39] Ibid., p. 234.
[40] Ibid., p. 235.
[41] The main accomplishment of *Working Papers* was that the four-function scheme which conceptualized social process as a succession of the stages of – using their acronyms – A, G, I, and L, and also social control (including socialization) as the reverse-order succession of the stages of L, I, G, and A, could now be applied to the social-historical world, revealing its empirical dynamics.

rather, an important realm thereof).[42] In this vein, he wrote in a letter in April 1960, putting his interpretation of the Berelson et al. data into perspective, "I think it is the most advanced theoretical thing yet."[43]

The other proof was factual. He knew now that the four-function matrix helped understand the functioning of one important sphere of the polity of contemporary America.

Authority Vis-à-Vis Force

In June 1960, John F. Kennedy, on the occasion of his being nominated by the Democratic Party as candidate for the election, crowning his triumph at the Democratic Convention in Los Angeles, addressed a crowd of eighty thousand in the Los Angeles Coliseum:

> For the world is changing. The old era is ending. The old ways will not do. Abroad, the balance of power is shifting.... The world has been close to war before – but now man, who has survived all previous threats to his existence, has taken into his mortal hands the power to exterminate the entire species some seven times over.... The new frontier of which I speak is ... a set of challenges.... Beyond that frontier are ... unsolved problems of peace and war, unconquered pockets of ignorance and prejudice, unanswered questions of poverty and surplus.... [T]he times demand invention, innovation, imagination, decision.[44]

Some six and a half months later, in his inauguration address on the occasion of taking his oath of office in a ceremony in front of the Capitol in Washington, D.C., Kennedy pleaded, "Let us begin anew, – remembering on both sides that civility is not a sign of weakness, and sincerity is always subject to proof. Let us never negotiate out of fear. But let us never fear to negotiate."[45]

The double focus of such concept of power which Kennedy's speeches suggested in masterly fashion and whose legacy the American public accepted as a pledge for the future, Parsons analyzed in two essays. One had been written for a symposium inaugurated by Friedrich in 1955 and published eventually in 1958, and the other was destined for a conference on the topic of *Internal War* in August 1961, whose proceedings appeared in 1964. The former dealt with authority, the latter with force.

Authority, he started out in his analysis of "Authority, Legitimation, and Political Action," was a type of relationship extending beyond the political realm. Since it involved goal attainment, however, it accomplished a system function typically lodged with the polity.[46] The important feature was that authority embodied social

---

[42] To be sure, the "zero-sum" notion of power was the obverse, as Parsons came to realize in the course of his conceptualizing the new approach, of the thought of such eminent political scientists as Lasswell, or Robert A. Dahl, *Who Governs? Democracy and Power in an American City* (New Haven and London: Yale University Press, 1961).

[43] Letter, Parsons to R. J. Apthorne, dated April 6, 1960; Parsons papers, HUG(FP) – 15.4, box 1.

[44] Cit., Arthur Schlesinger, Jr., *A Thousand Days*, pp. 59–61.

[45] Cit., ibid., p. 4.

[46] Parsons, "Authority, Legitimation, and Political Action," in Joachim C. Friedrich, ed., *Authority* (Cambridge, Mass.: Cambridge University Press, 1958), reprinted in *Structure and Process in Modern Societies* (New York: Free Press of Glencoe, 1960), pp. 170–198.

values which in turn formed orientational frames for legitimate action. Values, to the actor, had to be "'grounded' in three main directions: first, his *existential beliefs* about the world, second in his own *motivational needs* as a personality, and third in his relations to others in the society."[47] It was the actor who legitimated authority when his orientations did, or did not, allow for acceptance of an authority relationship in which he felt obliged to act, "Legitimation . . . is the set of criteria by reference to which 'adherence' to a pattern of values is translated *by the individual* into implementing action – it is, that is to say, the *action* rather than the values themselves, which is legitimated."[48]

Institutionalization, which was the counterpart of, when it also limited legitimation, concerned the system of the society as a whole. He clarified, "Authority, for my particular purposes, I shall define as a category of institutionalization, not one of legitimation"[49] – which allowed him to focus on an institution such as property as comparable with authority, the former structurally being lodged with the economy, the latter with the polity.

Why was an analogy with the economy important? The economy as an institutional sphere meant production and consumption in the service of growth and well-being in the societal system as a collectivity or community, not for the benefit of individual actors alone. Property, to be sure, safeguarded the economic system, establishing secure relationships of exchange and entitlement. Authority, in turn, safeguarded the effectiveness of a group or organization as a whole, benefiting, in the ideal case, the totality of citizens rather than merely an elite or an oligarchic caste.

This concept of authority contained an option for a democratic structure of the society. That he anchored authority in the support from members for a political structure or person in office, stating that collective goals were reconciled with citizens' voluntary commitment, established a notion of authority which was not merely descriptive but intrinsically opted for a maximum reciprocity type of mutual relationship. The concept of authority, stated in this way, involved an idea of the polity that went beyond reductionist realism as in positivism. Support given a leader by the collectivity of citizens on a voluntary basis made for authority as conceptual phenomenon: "Authority, from this point of view, is the institutionalization of given modes and levels of integration of the collectivity so far as these are essential conditions of effective and legitimized collective action. It is the institutionalization of the rights of 'leaders' to expect *support* from the members of the collectivity."[50]

From this vantage point, four dimensions of authority applied to every empirical system, namely, "(1) legitimation in terms of the general values of the society, (2) status in the system of roles or collectivities to which it is applied, (3) the type of situation with which authority-bearers are expected to be faced, and (4) the sanctions which, on the one hand, are at their disposal, on the other hand, can be brought to bear by others in relation to their action."[51]

---

[47] Ibid., p. 174.
[48] Ibid., p. 176.
[49] Ibid., p. 178.
[50] Ibid., p. 186.
[51] Ibid., p. 187.

"It is important to note that Max Weber's famous classification dealt with only *one* of them, namely, the bearing of the general values of the society through the processes I have called those of legitimation,"[52] he determined as good reason to now fit in the other three variables.

Weber, in addition, epitomizing "rational-legal" authority, had given him the keyword to emphasize another point. The law, which itself was an institution, stressed Parsons, served as a safeguard for the normative use of power through authority as it embodied adequate functioning of institutions in modern society – which, to be sure, presupposed that a division of power existed where rule of law prevailed. Another prerequisite became thereby visible, namely that pluralism, a high level of functional differentiation, evolved: "The legal definition of the content and limits of authority becomes an imperative necessity in a society in which functional differentiation has reached high levels."[53]

The obverse form of power was addressed in "Some Reflections on the Place of Force in Social Process."[54] He defined force as violence, when he used as a basic model the idea that an alter was being made to do something by an ego, given little leeway other than to comply. Physical force involved took three forms. First, force could be a deterrent to restrain an alter in one imperative way prescribed by ego, second, force could be a punishment, or, third, force could be a demonstration by ego that he meant what he said, that is, demonstrating "capacity to act."[55] All three were intended to create fear or anxiety as a motivation, making an alter unconditionally comply with an ego's demands. The emotional side was crucial, namely that ego's force (or threat of force) created in alter fear or anguish. Parsons distinguished between compulsion and coercion, to further elucidate that variables were involved:

> [E]go may attempt to deter alter by acting so as to make his carrying out undesired intentions realistically impossible – or nearly so. We would refer to this behavior as *compulsion*. A classic example would be the arrest and imprisonment of persons whose future action is feared, without giving them any choice in the matter. The alternative to compulsion in this respect is *coercion*. By this term, we mean "threatening" to use force *if* alter carries through the presumed undesired (by ego) intentions. If alter then disregards the threat and carries out his act, the use of force against him becomes a punishment, although the primary intention of ego may still be deterrence and he may be deeply regretful at having to carry out his threats and actually to resort to force.[56]

---

[52] Ibid., p. 188.
[53] Ibid., p. 191.
[54] "Some Reflections on the Place of Force in Social Process," in Harry Eckstein, ed., *Internal War: Basic Problems and Approaches*. (New York: Free Press of Glencoe, 1964), pp. 33–70.
[55] Ibid., p. 35.
[56] Ibid., p. 36. A case in point might have been, for compulsion, the arrest of Reverend Martin Luther King, Jr., in the fall of 1960 on charges of a minor violation, in Mississippi, to keep him from carrying the campaign for the right to vote of Blacks into this Southern state. (The original refusal to accept bail for King was reversed only when presidential candidate John Kennedy made a personal telephone call to the prisoner, assuring him of unconditional support.) A case in point exemplifying coercion might be when, in October 1962, entrance into the University of Oxford, Mississippi, of

In generalized theoretical terms, the distinctions belonged in a matrix of social control. Such matrix, a four-type table, involved two dimensions, namely high or low leeway for an alter to submit to ego's commands, and positive or negative sanctions. The four types of social control were, respectively, inducement, coercion, suggestion, and appeal to moral integrity. "Each of these types can – with respect to the time left open to alter to make a decision, ego's 'tolerance' of his position and hence willingness to hear this case, etc. – be 'foreshortened' in the same basic sense in which compulsion, as we have discussed it, foreshortens coercion."[57] This, then, revealed force as the opposite of persuasion, and a "hard-core" version of each type of social control could be contrasted with an optimal-leeway version, a minimum type with a maximum one of interactive reciprocity.

All four involved a compulsive version. They were, first, inducement that became tightened into the "*gift*... which leaves no option of refusal open"; second, coercion that was tightened into compulsion; third, suggestion which became enforcement of compliance on "good reasons" clad into threats that "'we such-and-suches *do* so and so' with the clear implication that, if you do not, you are not 'really' a such-and-such";[58] and, fourth, appeals to moral integrity in terms of presumptively shared standards of right action such as were perverted into blackmail in a totalitarian regime threatening to incarcerate family members of one allowed to travel abroad, "unless he complies with their wishes."

What were the relationships between sanctions and force when the four types of social control each allowed for a mild and a compulsive version?

> Physical force may be an important instrument in the enforcement of *any* deprivation. It is, however, intrinsic in the deprivation itself, particularly in deprivations of liberty. Although fines and taxation are backed by force, for example, the process of implementing such sanctions by taking over financial assets is ordinarily not a forcible one. If, however, an act of enforcement is challenged, the question of what to do in case of refusal to comply arises. This question can always lead to the problem of force, for resistance can be made effective by alter, through such physical means as leaving the field commanded by ego or removing assets from it. The ultimate preventive of such evasion is force. Hence in a very broad sense we conclude that force is an "end-of-the-line" conception of a type of negative sanction that can be effective – in the context of deterrence, please note – when milder measures fail.[59]

From this vantage point, the fluidity of the power phenomenon, of which force was one polar expression, was only too obvious. To be sure, this variability epitomized the double face of political power. In his explanations, he understood that

---

its first Black student, Meredith, had to be secured by the National Guard. The troops faced a mob of protesters and an inactive local police unable or unwilling to come to the rescue of Meredith. He was, however, surrounded by envoys from the Department of Justice sent by then Attorney General Robert Kennedy, who were also attacked. The small group confronted a violent mob threatening their lives during a long and dangerous night, until the National Guard at last moved in at dawn of the next day.

[57] "Some Reflections on the Place of Force," p. 39; the next quote is from the same page.
[58] Ibid., p. 40; the next quote is from the same page.
[59] Ibid., p. 42.

power – as force – was not a one-way street between a government and a presumably mass-like public (power in the form of authority surely was a two-way passage anyway).

Power that legitimized authority, he noted, could also be withheld when parts of the population refused to trust a given government or leader – with varying consequences: "[T]otal noncontingent withdrawal through unannounced resignation is of course a case of compulsion. The strike is a clear case of coercion through contingent withdrawal. On the other side, deterrence by withdrawal may well call into play at least the contingency of coercive countermeasures, in that cooperation is obligatory in more than a 'moral' sense and there are negative sanctions for failure to comply."[60]

Concluding his paper, he came back to the theme of "internal war" when he invoked "the makings of a revolutionary situation."[61] He sketched a situation in which a government was challenged to meet fully and at once all its "presumptively legitimate obligations,"[62] which of course was impossible. In any such highly charged atmosphere of demands on a government to satisfy all or a large range of far-reaching needs of the population, when the government was unable or unwilling to fulfill its promises, and the population failed to scale down demands, major tensions (bordering on internal war) could ensue. Dissatisfactions could abound in both directions. Between an embattled government and impatient righteous groups fighting for their just causes, a "vicious circle" of action and counter-action could develop.

The Power Bank and the United Nations

The economy was an exemplary field to epitomize how power was hinged on situational givens in an environment. Money as medium enabled commodity production and consumption; its function could be more or less extensive, that is more or less "liquid" in terms of monetary resources. Through banking, these resources could be "lent" to firms engaging in production in a market economy, and so forth. Or, monetary means could be scaled down to the restrictive terms of the "gold standard," which severely restricted the amount of money available, production feasible, employment possible, and so on. "This argument is not merely a gratuitous digression into the commonplaces of economics," Parsons pleaded as he broached the topic in his paper on the place of force in social process. "It is presented in order to demonstrate an exact parallel between money and power."[63]

Money was a symbol for commodities (regarding their production as well as consumption), distributed either equally or unequally, making for affluence or poverty, and, similarly, power could be vested in many who in turn entrusted selected persons with leadership for limited periods in office, or usurped by a dictator or oligarchic caste.

One theme in the essay written for *Internal War* was "The Monopoly of Force and the 'Power Bank.'" The focus was the hiatus in differentiation between the

[60] Ibid., p. 47.
[61] Ibid., p. 66.
[62] Ibid., p. 69.
[63] Ibid., p. 46.

socialist-type and capitalist-type economy, rendering the latter vastly better able to serve the needs of the population: "The 'ultimate' basis of the value of its money then is the productivity of the economy."[64] What was it that accounted for the ability of capitalism to produce affluence in a highly developed economy, communism to afford only a much lower-level living standard in a much less developed economy? The reference was to the nature of government in the two system types. The role of government in the United States and USSR was different inasmuch as the two type systems allowed for different scope of stimulation of economic growth through political process. Whereas democratic government guaranteed that civil rights and political participation involved much more leeway for individual freedom in economic life, thus spurring economic growth as in the U.S. type system, the hierarchical political control in Communist-type countries imposed hermetic reins on free enterprise which, in turn, dampened economic growth and prosperity.

Western-type government which "lent" empowerment as economic subjects to its citizens and received "deposits" from them in the guise of being voted into office, he pictured after the model of a "power bank." "[T]he existence and prominence in advanced political systems of a political analogy of the bank, which we may call, in appropriate quotation marks, the 'power bank'" meant that investments would be made into the leadership by citizens, and also vice versa. In the system which spread citizenship rights widely, in the manner of a bank issuing credit, trust that allowed for enormously enlarged leeway of every single individual could make possible a differentiated pluralist world.

Trust and leeway, by contrast, were less obvious in the less differentiated, more "fundamentalist" type society. He summarized,

> That there is a distributive aspect of power is almost obvious and is clearly implied by our comparison with money. We wish, however, to extend the parallel to the point where we postulate a set of mechanisms of expansion and contraction of the total as a function of forces operating on the level of the system as a whole, which is parallel to the phenomenon of credit in the case of money. We think that these considerations are highly relevant to the problems of the place of force and constitute some of the reasons why the complexity of the relations between power and force that we have outlined is so important.[65]

Parsons said more about this in an article which was never published. The article "The Power Bank: Notes on the Problem of World Order" was written, presumably in late 1963, for a journal *Disarmament and Arms Control* which obviously ceased publication after the galley proofs had been sent to Parsons. Subsequently, Bartholomew Landheer, editor of *International Journal of Comparative Sociology*, apparently offered to publish the piece in that journal, but nothing appears to have come of this.[66]

---

[64] Ibid., p. 59; the next quote is from the same page.
[65] Ibid., p. 61.
[66] See letter, Wayland Young to Parsons, April 9, 1964 as well as letter, Robert Maxwell to Parsons, April 23, 1964; Parsons papers, HUG(FP) – 42.41, box 4. Landheer was known to Parsons from their planning together during World War II a study on countries occupied by Nazi Germany. See above, Chapter 2.

The power bank analogy now targeted international politics: "The conception of a pluralistic international community, in certain respects analogous to the internal structure of stable democratic societies, is fundamental to the analysis,"[67] – a conception against which the actual world situation could be held as an approximation of varying adequacy: "The international power-system is relatively weak because of the 'locking' of so much power in national units and in their actual and potential antagonistic relations to each other. This means that the ratio of physical force to the other aspects of power is kept unnecessarily high."[68]

Parsons used the banking analogy to describe what were the power problems that could be solved in a way analogous to the money-market institutionalization in the modern economy:

> In the economic case growth operates, above all, through the mechanism of investment. The assets invested may come from direct savings of the investing unit; they may also be collected from a variety of primary savers and put to productive disposal. There are, certainly, important analogies of both these processes in the power field.... There is, however, another mechanism...: namely, the creation of new money as credit through the banking operation.... [T]he result of creating money can be an increased level of production.

The latter was the mechanism that counted. Through the bank's extending credit to more and more individual units who each used it for producing goods and thereby entering an ever-increasing market, an extension of economic activity ensued. The argument concerning power held that not only did power relations become more extensive ("pluralist") but also the economy was stimulated in a more democratic polity. In a lecture at the University of Hermosillo in Mexico in November 1962, Parsons expressed this in his notes thus: "'Solutions' at broadly political integrative levels are prerequisites of massive economic development."[69]

In his essay on "Power-banking," after he had also considered "The Banker's reputation" (to account for the importance of trust in the fiduciary transactions involved), he turned to "Applications," where his prominent examples were national governments and the United Nations:

> [N]ational governments are in this sense power-bankers, both internally and externally.... Internally, government "promotes" the development of power-units which eventually are expected to become independent.... Externally, commitment through treaties and assumption of membership in international organizations are the type case.... The case of the international organization comes closer to the ideal type. To take the UN as an example... there is a considerable range within which action can be taken which does not require the detailed specific commitment of each participating government but where, on the other hand, majorities... can commit the organization to risks.... The most striking

---

[67] Parsons, Abstract: "The Power Bank: Notes on the Problem of World Government"; Parsons papers HUG(FP) – 42.41, box 4 (typed sheet).

[68] "The Power Bank: Notes on the Problem of World Order," p. galley 35; Parsons papers, HUG(FP) – 42.41, box 4; the next quote is from the same page.

[69] Lecture notes, handwritten, entitled "Hermosillo," dated "Nov. 13, 62"; Parsons papers, HUG (FP) – 15.4, box 12.

examples of UN power-lending are, of course, cases like the Gulf of Aquiba or the Congo, where the initiative of the Secretary-General has been decisive.[70]

In an earlier essay, he had defined what was the emergent world order seen to hinge on the United Nations, despite then-obvious polarization between East and West.[71] His sensational thesis: The very fact of polarization "between the so-called free world and the Communist bloc"[72] locked in apparently unsolvable conflict involving "the danger of general war," meant that an emergent world-political community had already begun to exist: "It would be my contention that the very fact of polarization itself implies such an element or order." Although the ideological contrast was clearly enormous, he contended that, all the same, "[a]n ideological conflict presumes that there is a common frame of reference in terms of which the ideological difference makes sense."

The four elements of order that both sides had in common, albeit in different degree and distinction, were: First, economic productivity was given a high value on both sides of the Iron Curtain; second, the values of personal as well as political autonomy of the individual were appreciated by both the West and the East; third, equality was a principle for justice in both system types; and, fourth, education was given high regard as a means to achieve these valued objectives. Since these four elements were present in the "'imperialist' and the 'people's democratic' nations,"[73] it appeared conceivable that between East and West there could be something other than "inevitable 'war,' whether military or economic." The sociologist's task was "identifying the mechanisms by which this integrative process can take place."

Four realms exemplified rudimentary communality between the polarized megasystems. They were, first, "a common set of values"[74] that included economic prosperity and political liberty (although these values were incorporated with different

---

[70] "The Power Bank," pp. galley 38–39. The example case of Congo was that, in the fall of 1960, a UN force had interfered when this country appeared to be on the verge of being taken over by a Communist government shortly after having achieved independence from colonial rule, in the name of (re)establishing parliamentary democracy there. A more recent example might be the UN taking responsibility for the security of the newly constituted democratic government of Cambodia after the overthrow of the terrorist "Khmer Rouge," or, in the 1990s, UN intervention in Bosnia, Croatia, and also Kosovo. Interestingly, Parsons failed to mention the Korean War, which had been called by the Secretary-General on behalf of the Security Council of the UN.

[71] Parsons, "Polarization and the Problem of International Order," *Berkeley Journal of Sociology*, vol. 6, 1961, pp. 115–134; reprinted as "Polarization of the World and International Order," in Quincy Wright, William E. Evan, and Morton Deutsch, eds., *Preventing World War III: Some Proposals* (New York: Simon and Schuster 1962), pp. 310–331; see also Parsons, "Order and Community in the International Social System," in James A. Rosenau, ed., *International Politics and Foreign Policy* (New York: Free Press, 1961), pp. 120–129, reprinted in *Politics and Social Structure*, pp. 292–310. The suggestion to write about the problem of war threat and peace prospects was first made to Parsons by James Rosenau in September 1959, and he reported to have finished a first rough draft for the Rosenau volume in mid-June 1960 to Deutsch, one of the editors of *Preventing World War III*. See letter, Rosenau to Parsons, September 17, 1959; Parsons papers, HUG(FP) – 15.4, box 15, and letter, Parsons to Deutsch, June 15, 1960; Parsons papers, HUG(FP) – 15.4, box 6.

[72] "Polarization," p. 115; the following three quotes are from the same page.

[73] Ibid., p. 118; the following two quotes are from the same page.

[74] Ibid., p. 121.

emphasis on actual practice in the beliefs and doctrines in the oppositional systems); second, norms that involved shared orientations of action such as in international law, and the United Nations was an organization of such norm realization: "[T]he central characteristic ... is the establishment of consensus at the *procedural* level"[75] – with special attention paid to the scope of enforceable sanctions against violators of mutual agreements: "[T]he UN is a forum short of a court of law in which there is an obligation ... to hearing the opposition's objections to the case as stated. The very fact of participation in it implies, at some level, recognition of the legitimacy of judgment by 'world opinion.'"[76]

Third, interests were there, although expressed either in the monolithic hierarchical system or the multiplicity of pluralist (sub)systems sustaining crisscrossing loyalties between different parties, associations, and the like. The fourth realm, namely ideology, could be virulent as coercive imposition of a "definition of the situation," but also in less oppressive, more diversified forms when freedom of expression and assembly were granted. The central issue was, he found, that both hemispheres were equally indebted to "the great traditions of all Western culture."[77] The latter included not only "[p]rocedural norms and the pluralistic differentiation of interests" but also "another very important resource, namely the development of social science."

Parsons's interest in the United Nations as a "Power Bank" for international politics, I propose, had two rationales. One was theoretical. He expressed it in the revised version of the essay on polarization which he eventually included in *Politics and Social Structure*, namely that the central focus in the concept of international order was viable despite duality of totalitarianism versus democracy. In this vein, he wished to "identify the principal elements of normative order that are present in contemporary international relations, and to suggest their potentialities and limitations for being strengthened at cultural levels and for meeting the basic conditions of minimal institutionalization."[78] In his article on "The Power Bank" he clad this theoretical zeal into a statement on the necessity to avoid Nazi-like backlash reactions during progressive modernization of the world order:

> There is an immense gap between even relatively full commitment to values as morally desirable, and their institutionalization in stable social structure. They must be spelled out at the level of norms ... Collectivities must be adjusted to the normative framework ... Then the relevant commitments of individuals must be integrated sufficiently at the level of the structure of roles so as, above all, relatively to minimize alienation from the newer normative order – alienation of the type that Nazi-inspired German Nationalism exhibited relative to the order between the wars. Finally, not least is the overcoming of the vested interests in an older, more partial order.[79]

---

[75] Ibid., p. 125; italics are in the original.
[76] Ibid., p. 126.
[77] Ibid., p. 132; the following two quotes are from the same page.
[78] Parsons, "Order and Community in the International Social System," in *International Politics and Foreign Policy*, edited by James A. Rosenau, p. 121; see *Politics and Social Structure*, p. 295.
[79] "The Power Bank," p. galley 34.

The other than merely theoretical rationale, in my view, concerned the United Nations' role in world politics at the time, of which Parsons took notice. In April 1960, at the U.N. General Assembly, Soviet General Secretary of the Communist Party and Prime Minister, Nikita Krushtshev, staged an éclat when he demanded that the Western Allies abandon Berlin to exclusively Soviet-Russian control.[80] In June 1960, Parsons reported to Deutsch that he had finished a draft of his article on the topic, responding to the request by Rosenau but also Deutsch (who had first written to him in January of that year).[81] In June 1961, a summit between Kennedy and Krushchev in Vienna failed to end the crisis which, for the time being, ended with the construction of the Berlin Wall in August 1961, followed slightly more than a year later by the Cuban Missile Crisis. (Parsons rewrote and republished his essay on polarization in international politics twice during this time period.) Eventually, the two superpowers (in conjunction with the United Nations) signed the first Nuclear Test Ban Treaty in the summer of 1963. In April 1963, Parsons participated in a one-day miniconference whose topic was "The Behavioral Scientist and Human Survival," at the annual convention of the American Society of Orthopsychiatry who, in their announcement, proposed to focus on the threat of annihilation of humankind through nuclear warfare (he spoke on "The Role of the Behavioral Scientist in the International Situation").[82]

Political Power Vis-à-Vis Influence

In a letter, commenting on a manuscript of Friedrich in October 1962, Parsons stressed how much he was in agreement with Friedrich when they both opposed "the current pseudo-realistic theorizing in this whole area these days," specifying, "I particularly like your grounding of authority in something of the order of reason and the conception therefore that it must have a firm cultural base." But he confirmed that he saw a major difference, "over your treatment of the concept of power": "[I]t does not seem to me to be necessary ... to go as far as you do in spreading the concept analytically to include the whole range of influence."[83]

In the essay on the place of force in social process, he had dealt with the difference under the headline, "Money, Power, and Influence" when he stressed that the analogy of money extended beyond the realm of power.

Max Weber had advocated that the state should not use the power, let alone force, whose monopoly it held, and Parsons, in faithful Weberian manner endorsing such restraint, clarified that state "authority ... in a liberal society ... is normally

---

[80] See, for analysis of the world crisis at the end of the 1950s, John L. Snell, *Dilemma Over Germany* (New Orleans: Hauser, 1959), and Hans Speier, *Divided Berlin: The Anatomy of Soviet Political Blackmail* (New York: Frederick A. Praeger, 1960).

[81] Later in the year, he asked permission from Rosenau to also see his essay published in the *Berkeley Journal of Sociology* in early 1961, where it appeared before it was published in the two book versions in 1961 and 1962.

[82] See "The Role of the Behavioral Scientist in the International Situation," unpublished manuscript; Parsons papers, HUG(FP) – 42.8.6, box 1.

[83] Letter, Parsons to Friedrich, October 23, 1962; Parsons papers, HUG(FP) – 15.4, box 7.

confined to monetary resources (taxation) and physical resources (eminent domain)."[84] But this left the government curiously ineffectual unless its leadership could be based on something other than political power. The crucial aspect of democracy, to be sure, was the support system, and he ventured that it contained a medium of exchange other than political power when he defined influence through persuasion:

> The mode of control in this case is persuasion. We have defined "persuasion" as an offer of good reasons why alter should, in his own interest, act in accord with ego's wishes. The contingent positive sanction attached to persuasion is *acceptance*, which is an attitudinal as distinct from a situational sanction. We may speak of influence then as generalized capacity to persuade through the offer of contingent acceptance.... To persuade, in our technical sense, is then to give alter the status of shared membership, to treat him as "one of us." ... The contingent bases of acceptability may be summed up under the heading of conformity with the *norms* governing the operation of the collectivity.... Persuasion will involve a normative reference defining the sense in which the reasons offered are "good"; this reference may be called the *justification* of their acceptance by alter.[85]

"Influence may then be thought of as a medium that links the power aspect of social control with the structure of norms in the society," he stated: "[G]roups must not only have access to power, but their position must be 'justified' ... within an institutionalized system of norms – for example (but not exclusively) at the legal level."[86]

In 1962, on the occasion of the American Association for Public Opinion Research's annual conference, he clarified these thoughts further. Indeed, "The Concept of Influence"[87] was so successful as a presentation that a number of participants requested offprints long before Parsons (who had spoken from notes) had even written up the article which appeared in print in *Public Opinion Quarterly* in the spring issue of 1963.[88]

To elucidate the theme, he now borrowed from linguistics. In 1960 he and Harvard linguist Roman Jakobson had considered planning a book together.[89]

---

[84] "Some Reflections on the Place of Force in Social Process," p. 53. The latter formula, evidently, referred back to Max Weber's assertion, at the end of his memorandum on value-neutrality in the economic and sociological sciences (as Weber phrased the title of his essay), condemning syndicalism and praising sociology's refusal to endorse political utopias on the grounds of science. Weber, in the concluding paragraph of this essay, endorsed the state's monopoly on physical force when he, Weber, said that he self-evidently expected the Prussian-German state to refuse to use its most blatant means of enforcement. See also above.

[85] "Some Reflections," pp. 54–55.

[86] Ibid., pp. 55–56.

[87] Parsons, "On the Concept of Influence," *The Public Opinion Quarterly*, vol. 27, 1963, pp. 37–62; reprinted in *Politics and Social Structure*, pp. 405–429.

[88] A stack of postcards collected among the Parsons archival material bear witness to such demand from participants of the conference. See Parsons papers, HUG(FP) – 42.8.6, box 2.

[89] Letters, Thomas J. Wilson of Harvard University Press to Jakobson and Parsons, February 3, 1961, and Parsons to Wilson, February 13, 1961: Wilson reported on a conversation with Jakobson and enthusiastically accepted the offer made that the two authors would produce a symposium, "the plan that the two of you have for a symposium by linguists, sociologists, anthropologists, and practitioners of related disciplines to result in the first really significant book on the general subject

Jakobson, whose special field was phonetics, had proved that language on the featural level of spoken English had distinct, recognizably systematic elements. Symbolizing objects in the world through their communication which spurred mutually meaningful activities, speakers and listeners were engaged in interpretive exercises recognizable as opposition and contrast, message and code, and ellipsis and explicitness, Jakobson found. The upshot, from the perspective of Parsons trying to understand, for example, influence, was that a code existed which neatly patterned messages in an intersubjectively recognizable, systematic fashion.

Jakobson explained, "If the listener receives a message in a language he knows, he correlates it with the code at hand and this code includes all the distinctive features to be manipulated, all their admissible combinations into bundles of concurrent features termed *phonemes*, and all the rules of concatenating phonemes into *sequences* – briefly, all the distinctive vehicles serving primarily to differentiate morphemes and whole words."[90] From this point, Parsons took the structure of language (i.e., spoken English) to epitomize a scheme depicting the nature of exchange in interactional relationships more generally. He likened influence to money when he related both to language, adopting Jakobson's findings:

> In the well-known formulation of Jacobson [sic] and Halle, a language must be understood to involve two aspects: on the one hand, the use of language is a process of emitting and transmitting messages, combinations of linguistic components that have specific reference to particular situations; on the other hand, language is a *code* in terms of which the particular symbols constituting any particular message "have meaning." In these terms, a message can be meaningful and hence understood only by those who "know the language," that is, the code, and accept its "conventions."[91]

"Language consists of a variety of mechanisms for controlling, by means of codes, the regular emission of messages," concluded François Bourricaud, interpreting this tenet of Parsons.[92]

Applying Jakobson's conception of language as communication medium, Parsons now likened both money and influence to language, recognizing that both were a "generalized medium of communication": "[F]or my purposes, I would like to say not merely that money resembles language, but that it *is* a very specialized language, i.e. a generalized medium of communication through the use

---

of the Sociology of Language." Parsons replied, "The terms you suggest sound very favorable. However, since Jakobson has already gone to the West Coast, and since our plans are still far from fully worked out, I think we best postpone a decision until he and I can go over the problems carefully together." Parsons papers, HUG(FP) – 15.4, box 20.

[90] Roman Jakobson and Morris Halle, *Fundamentals of Language* (S-Gravenhage: Mouton & Co., 1956), p. 5.

[91] Parsons, "On the Concept of Influence," in *Politics and Social Structure*, p. 406.

[92] François Bourricaud, *The Sociology of Talcott Parsons* (Chicago: University of Chicago Press, 1981), p. 174. Bourricaud, interpreting Parsons using a citation from another book of Jakobson's, explained that codes secured "a fixed transformation, usually term by term, by means of which a set of information units is converted into a sequence of phonemes and vice versa," p. 175, quoting Roman Jakobson, *Essais de linguistique générale* (Paris: Editions de Minuit), p. 91.

of symbols given meaning within a code. I shall therefore treat influence as a generalized medium which in turn I interpret to mean a specialized language."[93]

Influence, in this vein, was a medium of communication which yielded courses of action in a recipient. Influence – as a source of authority – differed from Weber's classic idea of chance of an actor to find obedience of another in a framework of legitimate superordination/subordination, in that it was a "symbolic medium of persuasion":[94] "[Influence] is bringing about a decision on alter's part to act in a certain way because it is felt to be 'a good thing' *for him*, on the one hand independently of contingent or otherwise imposed changes in his situation, on the other hand for positive reasons, not because of the obligations he would violate through noncompliance."[95]

Influence invoked prestige. That is, the source of influence was that someone had the prestige which by itself made him a person to be turned to as a source of authority, a resource for others in what he did or said or thought. Since influence as a symbolic medium signified persuasion, the point was that the status of a "giver" of influence rendered him automatically able to be persuasive in the eyes of a "taker": "[In the realm of information] must be some basis on which alter considers ego to be a trustworthy source of information and 'believes' him even though he is not in a position to verify the information independently – or does not want to take the trouble."[96] Prestige, which was the quality derived from influence, marked a noneconomic and nonpolitical dimension of equality/inequality, an intrinsically democratic force in society.[97]

Parsons, in "The Power Bank," when he spoke of "media of integration,"[98] suggested that a hierarchy of media could be constructed, reaching from money that signified the lowest level of cybernetic control to power and eventually to "the capacity to persuade":[99]

> The medium next above political power in the societal hierarchy is what I call *influence*.... Influence in this sense... operates as a medium in cases where

---

[93] "On the Concept of Influence," p. 407.
[94] Ibid., p. 415.
[95] Ibid.; emphasis original.
[96] Ibid., p. 416.
[97] A first comprehensive documentation of research and theory that showed that economic ("class") and political ("power") differences were only part of the reality of social inequality, and had to be supplemented by a third dimension, as discussed since the early 1940s, was Reinhard Bendix and Seymour Martin Lipset, eds., *Class, Status, and Power: Social Stratification in Comparative Perspective* (New York: Free Press, 1953; 2d ed., 1966). The title of their collection suggested what they substantiated through the contributions to the volume, that class which stood for money as a medium and suggested an economic dimension of societies, and power which stood for the political structures, were to be supplemented by a third medium which had come to be used as the preferred dimension on which social status was measured in empirical studies, namely prestige as apparently noneconomic, nonpolitical dimension of social structures. The first to use prestige as an indicator of social status had been W. Lloyd Warner in the series investigating the social structure of a "typical" American town termed Yankeetown (Newport), in the so-called Yankeetown series of studies whose first volume appeared in 1941.
[98] "The Power Bank," p. galley 35.
[99] Ibid., p. 36; the next quote is from the same page.

intrinsic persuasiveness is not sufficient: for example, where the object of persuasion is not technically competent to understand reasons. Hence a "reputation" must be involved in which there is some sort of confidence that accepting "advice" on X's reputation as, for example, a competent physician will bring desirable consequences of the ensuing action, i.e. an improvement of health.

On the level of societies as entire systems, influence found its institutional order in the realm of public opinion, an institution vastly relevant for democratic societies.[100]

Its egalitarianizing quality made influence, on principle, available for everyone vis-à-vis anyone. In this vein, Parsons asked the rhetorical question, "Is influence a fixed quantity in a social system?" whose answer invited another refutation of the "zero-sum" model. The non-"zero-sum" nature of influence was analogous to how money was a medium spurring credit through banking, he suggested. Increase of the overall amount of money circulating at any point in time (including assets and liabilities from the "nonliquid" credit, etc.) characterized a functioning financial market. Likewise, the amount of power in the polity increased with the sum total of citizens' rights in a democratic society, and "[i]n the field of influence, the analogy with banking and credit seems most obvious in connection with the allocation of loyalties.... My suggestion is that the principal way in which this is done in a society like the American is through voluntary associations.... Such associations may thus be considered to be a kind of 'influence bank.'"[101]

Influence, in this perspective, was vested with prestige lodged in social status, its institutionalized form. In influence which involved the authority derived from prestige, trust was invested in, for example, a professional such as a physician. In a society as a whole, when influence abounded as a symbolic medium, public opinion dominated the political process. Four types of influence could be distinguished, namely, "(1) 'political' influence, (2) 'fiduciary' influence, (3) influence through appeal to differential loyalties, and (4) influence oriented to the interpretation of norms."[102]

An open question was whether influence, similar to money and political power, was also a variable. Did influence oscillate between a form of minimal extension, the contracted type of deflated persuasiveness, and, at the other end of the spectrum, a maximum amount of mutual acceptance of competence? Would a situation appear likely where influence could deteriorate or disappear, affecting the high status enjoyed by, for instance, a professional but also a person in high office, or, for that matter, the Army?

It was not until he finalized the manuscript for publication that Parsons found the answer to this question. He made an addendum to the original paper which

---

[100] An earlier treatise on public opinion had been, elucidating American democracy during World War II, Carl J. Friedrich, *The New Belief in the Common Man* (Boston: Little, Brown & Co., 1942). *Public Opinion Quarterly*, founded in 1937, and indeed the American Association of Public Opinion Research whose journal it was, owed their existence not least to the impact of the 1936 Gallup poll that had correctly predicted against all odds Roosevelt's re-election victory – thus establishing widespread awareness of the reality of public opinion.

[101] "On the Concept of Influence," p. 428.

[102] Ibid., p. 419.

dealt with exactly this point. The addendum, in an insert to the galley proofs,[103] invoked McCarthyism when the theme was influence which commanded loyalty.[104] McCarthyism in the history of U.S. society, he ventured, appeared as a "deflationary episode entering into the influence field, which at its culmination approached panic proportions: the demand for 'absolute loyalty' was analogous to the demand for a return to the gold standard in the financial area."[105]

Power – The Concept

In his own opinion, the paper originally presented at the 1962 fall meeting of the American Philosophical Association,[106] "On the Concept of Political Power,"[107] was the culmination of his explaining the new notion of the polity.[108] Power, he clarified conclusively, was analyzed from three perspectives which were all new. One was reformulation of political theory inasmuch as, from Thomas Hobbes in the 1600s to Robert Dahl in the 1960s, power had been conceptualized not as a relational quality in interpersonal exchange but an achievement of persons in office issuing more or less coercive orders. The second was that power was lodged in consensus between equals, and the traditional notion invoking conflict or hierarchy was but a partial understanding of a much wider phenomenon. The third was the idea of a network of all-encompassing collective efforts at effectiveness, with an ever-widening arena for – to use the money analogy – credit that spurred productivity, replacing the "zero-sum" model.

The issue on which hinged the integrative pole of political power was voluntary participation, and only at the other end of the spectrum lay coercion. Both together, under the perspective that social theory took the perspective of developmental direction of the phenomenon which it analyzed (rather than merely "pseudo-realistic theorizing," as his phrase went in the letter to Friedrich[109]), yielded the following definition. Power was the "generalized capacity to secure the performance of binding obligations by units in a system of collective organization when the obligations

---

[103] The insert attached to the draft version of the essay, typed on yellow legal-size paper, has been preserved among the Parsons papers, HUG(FP) – 42.8.6, box 1.

[104] It might be mentioned in passing that Parsons, in his postscript to his essay on McCarthyism for Daniel Bell's *The Radical Right*, drew attention to the fact that McCarthyism was only one among various forms of coercive intolerance – although he judged that the John Birch Society was less dangerous than McCarthyism, due to its rightist extremism.

[105] "On the Concept of Influence," p. 429. The perspective invoking deflationary tendencies owed much to the economic theory of Keynes, evidently. Since the 1930s Parsons had been convinced that Keynes's economics mirrored the modern situation better than (most) other economic theories. See also above, Chapter 1, and also Chapter 3.

[106] The original presentation was a twenty-minute affair. But he was free to give his paper any length he deemed necessary when he wrote it for publication.

[107] Parsons, "On the Concept of Political Power," *Proceedings of the American Philosophical Society*, vol. 107, 1963, pp. 232–262; reprinted in *Politics and Social Structure*, pp. 352–404.

[108] In *Politics and Social Structure*, where the paper on power appeared before the one on influence, he dated the two papers, giving a publication date of "Spring, 1963" for the influence paper, and "June, 1963" for the essay on power.

[109] See above, fn. 83.

are legitimized with reference to their bearing on collective goals and where in case of recalcitrance there is a presumption of enforcement by negative situational sanctions – whatever the actual agency of that enforcement."[110]

The thrill was that power, so to speak, was limitless. It implied that though everybody could have it, no "War of All Against All" would necessarily result from equal distribution. That this was possible was due to the fact that power was a "symbolic" medium inasmuch as it constituted merely a "capacity to secure compliance"[111] from others in a network of mutual relationships, the sum total of which formed a community (e.g., a group, party, or nation).

As regarded legitimation, he used the money analogy: "Legitimation is, ... in power systems, the factor that is parallel to confidence in mutual acceptability and stability of the monetary unit in monetary systems."

As regarded "Power and Equality of Opportunity," crediting Yale political scientist Karl W. Deutsch[112] with the suggestion, he again used the monetary analogy proposing that force was the "gold-standard" "fundamentalist" form to which power was in danger of reverting in times of crisis:

> I spoke above of the "grounding" of the value of money in the commodity value of the monetary metal, and suggested that there is a corresponding relation of the "value," i.e. the effectiveness of power, to the intrinsic effectiveness of physical force as a means of coercion and, in the limiting case, compulsion.... Force ... is in the first instance important as the "ultimate" deterrent.... Willingness to impose negative sanctions is, seen in this light, simply the carrying out of the implication of treating commitments as binding, and the agent invoking them "meaning it" or being prepared to insist.[113]

When he addressed the situation of political crisis when force was being considered, he spoke of a "deflationary spiral." It could set in when a government was unable to handle pressures under which an overall political scenario posed it. His example, interestingly, was again McCarthyism, seen as a reaction to an all-too-demanding world situation:

> [U]nder unusual pressures, even highly responsible leadership can be put in situations where a "deflationary" spiral sets in, in a pattern analogous to that of a financial panic. I interpret, for instance, McCarthyism as such a deflationary spiral in the political field. The focus of the commitments in which the widest extension had taken place was in the international field – the United States had very rapidly come into the position of bearing the largest share of responsibility for maintenance of world political order against an expansionist Communist

---

[110] "On the Concept of Political Power," in *Politics and Social Structure*, p. 361.

[111] Ibid., p. 362; the next quote is from the same page.

[112] Deutsch in *The Nerves of Government* published in 1963, acknowledged (in the introduction) his indebtedness to Parsons, as a representative of what Deutsch called an innovative view. The latter, for him, was equally put forward by Harold Lasswell, David Easton, and others (a view which Parsons surely failed to share). Deutsch devoted a subchapter to Parsons's approach to interchange between systems, praising it for dynamic conceptualizing of the contemporary political arena.

[113] "On the Concept of Political Power" pp. 365–366. At the same time, he referred to the opposite alternative, "On the other hand, there are areas in interaction systems where there is a range of alternatives, choice among which is optional."

movement.... The McCarthy definition of the situation was ... that virtually anyone in a position of significant responsibility ... should explicitly renounce all other loyalties that might conceivably compete with that to the nation.... It tended to "deflate" the power system by undermining the essential basis of trust on which the influence of many elements bearing formal and informal leadership responsibilities, and which in turn sustained "power-credit," necessarily rested. Perhaps the most striking case was the allegation of communist infiltration and hence widespread "disloyalty" in the army.[114]

Focusing on the relationship between influence as the "more integrative" medium, challenged in the event of McCarthyism, and power, which was the topic he discussed, Parsons invoked the cybernetic hierarchy of control: "The focus of the McCarthy disturbance may be said to have been in the influence system, in the relation between integrative and pattern-maintenance functions in the society.... Since, however, in the hierarchy of control the influence system is superordinate to the power system, deflation in the former is necessarily propagated to the latter."[115]

"On the Concept of Power," in his own opinion, was a conclusive statement. He included it in various of his collections of essays henceforth, and permitted that it be incorporated into the second edition of Bendix and Lipset's *Class, Status, and Power* and a number of other textbooks, himself citing the paper in his subsequent writings as the breakthrough.[116]

Understanding Value-Commitments

In the spring of 1968, in Europe, French students staged their short-lived, spectacular rebellion against universities and the de Gaulle government, provoking the French president's resignation, and Czech reform Communist leader Alexander Dubcek initiated equally short-lived, immensely popular parliamentary socialism termed "The Prague Spring." Parsons at that time undertook to analyze value-commitments.[117]

The Fourth Communication Medium

Power and influence, as he had maintained earlier, were linked to the two system functions of goal attainment (through the pursuit of collective effectiveness), and

---

[114] Ibid. pp. 392–393.

[115] Ibid., p. 393.

[116] Other essays following on from the new conception of power were, for example, "The Political Aspect of Social Structure and Process," originally in David Easton, ed., *Varieties in Political Theories* (Englewood Cliffs, N. J.: Prentice Hall, 1966), and "Theoretical Orientations on Modern Societies," in *Politics and Social Structure* (Chapter 2). In "Polity and Society," p. 486 in *Politics and Social Structure*, in a footnote hinged on explicating his non-"zero-sum" notion, he had this to say about his power concept of the 1960s, as contrasted with that expounded in *The Social System*: "From the author's personal point of view this constitutes an explicit change of opinion."

[117] Parsons, "On the Concept of Value-Commitments," *Sociological Inquiry*, vol. 38, 1968, pp. 135–160, reprinted in *Politics and Social Structure*, pp. 439–472.

integration, respectively (through service epitomizing welfare of, in effect, the community). A fourth "symbolic medium," again resembling money, he now felt, needed attention urgently. He began, "In this paper, I will take up a long-standing commitment (!) to 'round out' the analytical scheme for the four generalized symbolic media of interchange that operate within *societal* systems, as distinguished from the general action system and from the other three primary subsystems of action. The three societal media besides value-commitments are money, political power, and influence."[118]

Parsons clarified in advance two specifics, guarding against misunderstandings. For one, he disengaged from "the 'Chicago' approach" in sociology, thereby rejecting that value-commitments were due to forces of normative control external to the actor which in the so-called labeling approach were being analyzed as how society impinged on the individual.[119] The other approach which he dismissed was "the 'Chicago' tradition" in political science, which meant Lasswell and also David Easton, whose approach he viewed critically: "The crucial difficulty with this concept lies in its identification of the distinction with the actor-object (or situation) dichotomy as *concretely* conceived."[120] In other words, these approaches signified for him what in his letter to Friedrich he had called "pseudo-realistic theorizing."[121] Against these, he held "a view that derives, I think, mainly on the one hand from Max Weber, and on the other from American anthropology, especially Clyde Kluckhohn."[122]

Weber, to be sure, had distinguished value rationality from means-end rationality. In the context of Parsons's discussion of value-commitments, his reference to Weber was general, centering around the two types of ethics, *Gesinnungsethik* versus *Verantwortungsethik*. The reference to Kluckhohn, however, was specific. Parsons referred to Kluckhohn as far back as 1950/1951, citing a text from *Toward a General Theory of Action* where Kluckhohn had ventured a particular notion of culture (which Kluckhohn had later abandoned). Values, Parsons stated with

---

[118] Ibid., p. 439. The other three primary subsystems of the system of action were culture, personality, and organism.

[119] Ibid., p. 440; he cited, and guarded himself against, the Blumer explication of symbolic interactionism as said to be lodged in the work of Thomas/Znaniecki of 1918/1920, in an account originally written in 1937, namely Herbert Blumer, "An Appraisal of Thomas and Znaniecki's *The Polish Peasant in Europe and America*" (New York: A Social Science Research Council Monograph, 1939). For a juxtaposition of Parsonian and symbolic-interactionism (labeling) explanations, exposing the latter's thesis of external control of behavior through societal expectations (labeling, stigma), see, taking illness as a topic of interest, Gerhardt, "Stress and Stigma Explanations of Illness," in Gerhardt and Michael E. J. Wadsworth, eds., *Stress and Stigma. Explanation and Evidence in the Sociology of Crime and Illness* (London: Macmillan, 1985), pp. 161–204, and *Ideas About Illness* (New York: New York University Press, 1990), esp. pp. 1–177.

[120] "On the Concept of Value-Commitments," p. 440.

[121] See above, fn. 83.

[122] "On the Concept of Value Commitment," p. 440; his reference was to Kluckhohn's contribution to *Toward a General Theory of Action* (1951). Kluckhohn, who had died in 1960, had been a participant in the intensive discussions in the winter of 1950 of a group from four disciplines who on the basis of these discussions had contributed their understandings to the compendium aiming at unified, advanced "general theory of action."

reference to Kluckhohn, were "conceptions of the desirable"[123] (not necessarily identical, he warned, with the empirically desired by the majority of the population[124]) in the sense, concretized by Kluckhohn, that they were "'patterns' at the cultural level," relevant for actors as "conceptions of the desirable *type of society* held by the members of the society of reference and applied to the particular society of which they are members."

He clarified, "A value-pattern... defines a *direction* of choice, and consequent commitment to action."[125]

In value-commitment, linkage between institutionalization and internalization was crucial. A society's conceptions of the positively valued, of what was normative in the guise of moral ideas, images, conditions, or patterns of action built into institutions had to be firmly ingrained in individuals' taken-for-granted action orientations. Indeed, their personalities and conceptions of moral integrity had to function accordingly. Only such links bound commitment through motivation to action. His object of study, then, was clear: "Our master conception under that of value-pattern here is that of *commitment*. Regardless of what other value-commitments an acting unit may have, our concern is with his or its commitments to implement value-patterns in his capacity as a member of one or more social systems."[126]

To be sure, the issue was not what values existed that characterized the desirable in a society. The aim was to epitomize the double face of value-commitment as a "symbolic medium" of societal exchange, similar to the three other media already analyzed.

Integration, Charisma, Inflation–Deflation

With regard to the symbolic medium, the dynamics between the two poles needed clarification. At the one extreme pole, all citizens were highly committed to the values that epitomized the democratic, integrated society: "In the ideal-type case,

---

[123] "On the Concept of Value Commitment," p. 441; all quotes in the remaining paragraph are from this same page.

[124] In 1964, on the occasion of concretizing his stance vis-à-vis Homans, he dismissed Homans's utilitarianism on the ground that value orientation would not center around what individuals *desired*, as Homans held. Instead, the only acceptable view was to concentrate on the morally desirable image of the self in the society. The criterion of value-commitments was not utilitarian. He criticized that, "Homans' concept of value being clearly confined to the desired," no allowance was made to the symbolic when the emphasis were material processes to govern the human condition. (He whimsically referred to the work of James Olds to make the point that even laboratory rats had been shown experimentally to act on symbolic rather than merely material rewards.) He wrote, "I believe with Homans that there are elementary principles that govern the behavior of organisms in general, and that govern the behavior of 'men as men,' if one understands by that formula creatures which are not only organically human but which live in systems of complex social relationships organized in relation to *cultural* symbolic codes and norms. I do not believe that the two are the same, because [of] the *cultural* level of organization of living systems." Parsons, "Levels of Organization and the Mediation of Social Integration," *Sociological Inquiry*, vol. 34, 1964, cit. pp. 215 and 217.

[125] "On the Concept of Value-Commitments," p. 441.

[126] Ibid., p. 442.

generally, commitment to a highly general value-pattern is shared by all units of the social system in which it is institutionalized."[127]

The highest form of representation of value-commitments was that ego and alter, any two actors in an exchange relationship, defined each other in moral communality of mutual respect for each other. "When we speak of *an ego activating an alter's commitments*, we mean that, through symbolic communication, ego helps alter 'define the situation' for alter's exercise of his moral freedom,"[128] when each actor was given "the freedom to make his own decisions of legitimacy."[129]

This, certainly, introduced pluralism accomplishing modernity: "In a social system characterized by pluralism, from the roles of individuals through many levels of collective organization, loyalties must be balanced within a manifold of claims. This is to say that, in becoming committed, e.g., to an association, a member unit does not 'spend' its *whole* stock of commitments, but reserves some of it for other channels in which commitment may take place, including other associational solidarities."[130]

And:

> Even if the overall value-pattern is stable, structural changes occur continually and at many different levels in all parts of a society. Relative to subvalues, exigencies are continually undergoing change, thereby necessitating reevaluation of the legitimacy of different modes of coping with them. . . . It is the *combination of this differentiated and specified complexity with the exposure to change* – much of which is unpredictable in advance – *that makes commitments as a generalized symbolic medium essential* to the functioning of a society.[131]

The metaphor of "commitment banking" helped to explicate that the individual who took "moral responsibility for the collective interest"[132] would extend his obligations to more and more spheres. The spiritual side of social relations, involving an orientational image of the desirable society, which with respect to the economy Weber had called the "spirit of capitalism," suggested a moral dimension that could sustain an ever-increasing network of loyalties. Associational loyalties, in such an expanding network of social exchanges, tended to overlap but needed not necessarily clash, as he illustrated using an example not far from home: "Harvard University is a 'member' of the local communities of Cambridge and metropolitan Boston, the Commonwealth of Massachusetts, the United States and, in some sense, 'world society.' It is also 'involved' in – or 'with' – innumerable other associations, such as different levels of government, the complicated world of the organization of scholarly interests, the readership of the publications of its faculty members, etc."[133]

All the same, "The problem is complicated by the fact, noted above, that the exigencies that govern the value-implementative effectiveness of commitments

---

[127] Ibid., p. 451.
[128] Ibid., p. 456.
[129] Ibid., p. 455.
[130] Ibid., p. 458.
[131] Ibid., p. 455.
[132] Ibid., p. 459.
[133] Ibid., p. 462; the next quote is from the same page.

cannot be assumed to be stable. In a sense directly analogous with a firm's need continually to adjust to changing market conditions, the value-implementing unit must stand ready to adapt the allocation of its commitments to changes in the exigencies of implementation."

"The societal community, the integrative system"[134] provided opportunities for security in the community: "Here, commitments are specified to a context of 'valued association'; in terms of combinatorial logic, this involves the acceptance of the normatively-primary *social* (as distinguished from political and economic) conditions of effective value-implementation. The individual unit no longer 'goes it alone' but adopts associational status, which gives him expectations of solidarity with fellow-members of the community or collectivity in question."

Approaching the other end of the spectrum, two issues mattered. One was "'intensity' of commitment," the other was "moral leadership."

The former meant that "persons in the requisite statuses are *more or less* intensively committed, as personality systems, to the implementation of the value patterns institutionalized in their respective statuses."[135] The other issue was that individuals defined each other in terms of moral superiority or inferiority, a tendency which invoked "moral leadership," usually that of some kind of charismatic leader. For his followers, the latter was an epitome of value incarnation, which, in strictly Weberian terms, could mean that "deficiency in duty," in other words, lack of allegiance and denial of followership, could allow for coercive punishment. Parsons, referring to Weber, focused on the fact that the charismatic forces in value-commitments could facilitate that a charismatic leader usurped power: "The predestined 'Saints' of early Calvinism and the Communist Party have in some respect been similar elites of moral leadership, both treating political power as on the whole an *instrument* for implementing their moral commitments.... Weber, among many others, emphasized the tension between moral leadership and political power."[136]

"Commitment 'banking,'" which varied between a "credit" and a "gold-standard" pole, could involve either the large network of "credit" relations in value-commitments, or a reduction of transactions to hard and fast allegiance or alignment. The latter was the type of "gold-standard" low, the "moral leadership" of a charismatic leader. Though the latter would mostly promise a radically 'new' moral order, "failure of success,"[137] Parsons warned, could undermine any kind of trust in the system; mass "withdrawal" of citizens' willingness to put their commitment into any kind of "bank" of state authority could ensue:

> Probably the most generalized formulation of the role of the "commitment banker" in sociological thought is Weber's concept of charismatic leadership. The charismatic leader imposes compliance with his 'demands' as a *moral duty*, not as enhancement of self-interest.... One of the more difficult problems in interpreting Weber's conception of charismatic "breakthrough" concerns the degree of "totality" of the break.... If breaks were as drastically radical as ideologists

[134] Ibid., p. 461; the next quote is from the same page.
[135] Ibid., p. 454.
[136] Ibid., p. 452.
[137] Ibid., p. 469.

often hold them to be, it is difficult to see how their movements could avoid occasioning, almost immediate "runs" on the "commitment banking" system, so that commitment-creation through the charismatic type of process would be impossible.... The answer lies, I think, in the conception of the *institutionalization* of value innovations. A charismatic commitment-expansion will be noninflationary insofar as it represents a first step in a process of institutionalization.[138]

Parsons addressed two processes of pathology of value-commitments, both leading away from the pluralism type of social order, "Inflation and Deflation of Commitments." The inflation-deflation image was borrowed from Keynes's theory of the monetary system, "The inflationary case involves what is frequently called *over-commitment* at least in the value-implementation context. It occurs when a unit has made so many, so diverse, and such 'serious' commitments that its capacity to implement them effectively must reasonably be called into question.... The deflationary tendency is a disposition toward unwillingness to 'honor' the commitments that units are willing to make."[139] Instead of allowing individuals the freedom to choose their own commitments, in a situation of "deflationary tendency" "some outside agency, e.g., the 'law'" would frequently replace individuals' own judgment of right or wrong, imposing on them what were binding commitments. This, he added, could lead to a "vicious circle" between increase of coercion and decrease of voluntary norm compliance: "Major movements in this direction... have the familiar consequence of purchasing 'security' at the expense of benefits which may accrue from greater freedom for autonomous responsibility."

The Generalized Symbolic Media and the Theory of Society

In his entry "Social Systems" in the *International Encyclopedia of the Social Sciences*, Parsons took together the four dimensions of social action as they related to the symbolic media and likened them to language in terms of communication "of the special normative sort":

> The "monetary system" is a *code*.... Political power is certainly another.... A third generalized symbolic medium is influence..., the capacity to achieve "consensuus" [sic] with other members of an associated group through persuasion.... Fourth is the medium of generalized *commitments* to the implementation of cultural values, at the level of the social system as such. It is the most difficult to conceptualize, and the least can be said about it.[140]

This suggested a matrix of media which varied, each individually and all together. A handwritten note preserved among Parsons's papers in the Harvard Archives depicted clearly the variable structure of the four generalized symbolic media. In a comprehensive view, the note put together – in the top row – what were the four institutionalized elements in a democratic (integrated) society, as

---

[138] Ibid., pp. 467–469.
[139] Ibid., p. 463; the next three quotes are from the same page.
[140] "Social Systems," in *International Encyclopedia of the Social Sciences*, vol. xx (New York: Free Press, 1968), reprinted in *Social Systems and the Evolution of Action Theory*, cit. pp. 198–199.

contrasted with – in the bottom row – the four states of media realization that verged on change of type of society and/or complete loss of social order. In between, in the lower middle row, were listed four issues characteristic of pathology.[141]

Property	Authority	Status	Pattern
Money	Power	Influence	Commitments
Panic	Riot	Deviance	Sectarianism?
Craze	Revolution	Normative Reorganization	Charismatic Movement

In the chart, property, authority, and status, but also pattern (if in a somewhat different context) stood for institutionalization. At the other extreme were listed forms of utmost insecurity, negations of institutionalized order (all of them invoking apparent change of type of social structure). The four forms of pathology embodied social process that tended toward anomie. The diagram (obviously never used nor meant for use in a publication) pulled the generalized media together into one fourfold matrix which (tentatively) pictured their variation between an integrated and an anomie form.

Variation, indeed, explained the arrangement of columns as well as rows in the diagram. On a vertical axis, the four generalized symbolic media varied between an integrated and an anomie pole. On a horizontal axis, the four rows, particularly that at the top and bottom end of the diagram, signified types of social structures – in ideal-type fashion, in terms of realization of the generalized media, superseding the four-function scheme and also the pattern-variable combinations which in Chapter V of *The Social System* had illustrated the opposite cases of Anglo-Saxon democracies and Nazi- or Soviet-type totalitarianism.

The diagram was also compatible with the two types of social dynamics, epitomized in the "banking" and "vicious circles" metaphors. (Both suggested ways to proceed from one type of structure to another, either differentiation, etc., which would move upward from a bottom-row to a top-row type form or structure, or disorganization, or vice versa.)

Each of the media, in turn, involved an analogy to "banking," elucidating how social forms varied between a "credit" pole and a "gold-standard" one. Likewise, the metaphor of "vicious circles" could be used to elucidate the dynamics of how entire societies could change from a structure of more or less accomplished social integration to "totalitarianism" (as rose their level of conflict that, in essence, signaled anomie).

In all this, the generalized media became a core of Parsons's general idea of society. It was obvious that the media provided a fruitful conceptual framework to analyze contemporary society in the 1960s, an analysis one focus of which was social stratification.

A Media Theorem of Stratification

One use made of interaction media in the theory of society, analyzing American society in the 1960s, concerned stratification. The theory of the media thus became

---

[141] One-page diagram, untitled, undated; Parsons papers, HUG(FP) – 42.45.4, box 5.

an innovative perspective re-interpreting the dilemma between inequality and equality in modern "postindustrial" society.[142]

In his sixty-page essay, "Equality and Inequality in Modern Society," Parsons clarified how the conception of the media helped understand how inequality was intimately linked with equality in the four realms of interaction mediation, in modern "postindustrial" society. Traditionally, he began, there had been four foci of inequality that had been connected with ascription (ethnicity, religion, territorial location, and social class); but only social class – at the end of the 1960s – was still a source of apparent inequality in contemporary America.[143] Nevertheless, Leon Mayhew had argued in 1968[144] that new sources of ascription had arisen, through taking advantage of equality of opportunity in unequal fashion as family background boosted capacity for achievement, thereby partly negating the accomplishments of universalism in modern America. Parsons concluded, accordingly, "that equality versus inequality and ascription versus achievement should be treated as independently variable."[145]

The new perspective resulting therefrom hinged on the four generalized media. For one, since equality of occupational opportunity had not eradicated poverty, despite the fact that it generated access to income, some hitherto undervalued mechanism was at work, namely that relative deprivation took the place of abject want: "As Rainwater (1969) in particular has made clear, the essential answer to the nondisappearance of the problem in the face of increasing general productivity lies in *relative deprivation*."[146] Inequality with respect to power, in due course, meant that, despite equality of opportunity to attain positions of authority, an ostentatious "gap" existed between comparatively high amounts of power given to, for instance, holders of office in industry or government as compared with, on the other side, individual workers or voters. Interestingly, he hastened to point out, such asymmetry hinged on office, not the person – but that it existed

---

[142] Parsons, in 1949 and again 1960, had tackled the topic of stratification. At the end of the 1960s, after having developed the theory of generalized symbolic media, he added a twist to the discussion that was entirely groundbreaking. Work on stratification in the "early" Parsonian tradition was Bernard Barber, *Social Stratification* (New York: Harcourt, Brace, 1957). Work analyzing the scenario of the "late" Parsonian view was Daniel Bell, *The Coming of Postindustrial Society* (New York: Basic Books, 1973; reissued 1999). Parsons, however, would not adopt the idea of "postindustrial" society when he was aware of seminal social change in the 1960s. The latter, as he mentioned in lecture notes for Amherst in 1965, entitled "Academic Profession in the U.S.," rendered even more important than previously, the "academic profession as the 'core' of an (word unreadable) professional complex emerging into a new prominence in modern society.... *As* key profession, the spearhead of what is probably a new society." Lecture notes, "Amherst. Academic Profession in the U.S. March 1, 1965"; Parsons papers, HUG(FP) – 15.4, box 3.

[143] Parsons, "Equality and Inequality in Modern Society, or Social Stratification Revisited," *Sociological Inquiry*, vol. 40, 1970, pp. 13–72, reprinted in *Social Systems and the Evolution of Action Theory* (New York: Free Press, 1977), cit. p. 330.

[144] Leon Mayhew, "Ascription in Modern Societies," *Sociological Inquiry*, vol. 38, 1968, pp. 105–120. Mayhew had been a research assistant to Parsons in the earlier 1960s.

[145] "Equality and Inequality," p. 333.

[146] Ibid., p. 337. The reference was to Rainwater's essay, "The Problem of Lower-Class Culture and Poverty War Strategy," which was a contribution to Patrick Daniel Moynihan, ed., *On Understanding Poverty* (New York: Basic Books, 1969).

had its prerequisite in the equality of chances institutionalized in the society in general.

Another field where similar structures could be found was culture. There, egalitarianism went far when mass consumption of cultural goods had become the basis of the spectacular commercialization of popular entertainment. However, unquestioned egalitarianism could also generate ressentiment inducing anti-intellectualism (clearly a danger threatening the modern university): "Indeed one source of modern 'anti-intellectualism' seems to be a sense of inferiority, and hence of being, if not 'exploited' – certainly not in the strictly economic sense – 'put upon' by the superiorities of those who have enjoyed superior access to cultural resources."[147] In this realm, therefore, whereas inequality was being superimposed on equality (of opportunity), the duality was not sufficiently institutionalized.

In all, the point was that only presupposing institutionalization of equality of opportunity in all four generalized symbolic realms – money (equal opportunities in the employment sector), political power (through voting, etc.), influence (through civil rights, etc.), and value-commitments (through cultural pursuits) – would inequality evolve.

That inequality (as superimposed on equality) allowed for structures to function did not apply in the same way as in the other three in the realm of influence. Civil rights, making for the basic equality of citizens before the law, with respect to legislation as well as jurisdiction, could not be graded in a superimposed inequality lest democracy be jeopardized. In addition, however, fiduciary authority which characterized jurisdiction or medical care meant inequality when it alone safeguarded professional competence that, as it did, fulfilled citizens' needs in regard to justice or health. Last but not least, culture was concentrated in institutions such as universities, such that inequality vis-à-vis the mass of citizens with regard to pursuing scientific inquiry was a guarantee for preserving the heritage of Western civilization.

"[I]n normative terms, the pattern-maintenance 'base' of the modern societal community is essentially egalitarian"[148] – which required, for inequality to be institutionalized, that a justification be established: "[T]he burden of proof is shifted to the side of justifying inequalities." In this vein, justifications for inequality were not all equally acceptable to citizens who had internalized the values of equality; some, in principle, were more convincing, but most precarious were those that concerned influence.

Parsons observed, presupposing the hierarchy of symbolic media, that in democracy the lowest-level generalized control medium was money. In contradistinction, political power and, in turn, influence were higher-order media (less clearly, value-commitments were fitted in, though they were not addressed as highest cybernetic medium in the hierarchy). In the cybernetic order, "seen in the stratification context, a primary function of influence is to justify functionally necessary forms of *in*equality." In other words, competence and excellence in structures grounded

---

[147] "Equality and Inequality," p. 345.
[148] Ibid., p. 346; the next three quotes are from the same page.

in achievement accounted for and justified surplus of influence. Indeed, such justification could legitimize the "competence gap" which, between the doctor and patient in modern society for example, was the condition for effectiveness of medical practice: "It is clear that, though the factor of competence makes for a critical element of inequality – with fiduciary responsibility – it also puts a premium on capacity independent of ascriptively particularistic considerations and hence enhances the general societal stress on equality of opportunity."[149]

General Theory

That the idea of generalized media belonged in a general theory of society did not yield a treatise à la *The Structure of Social Action* or *The Social System*. The general theory which Parsons developed mainly between the middle 1950s and 1970 did not show in Parsons's published oeuvre in like manner as the earlier stages of his sociological theory. In "On Building Social System Theory," written in 1969, he did not look back on the 1960s as a time of foregone further advancement of his thought, however. He mentioned, under the title of "Media of Interchange and Social Process," that he had refuted the logic of the "zero-sum" conceptual framework, but did not highlight the interaction media as a newly developed theme in his theory:

> The monetary dynamics referred to is clearly that incompatible with the idea that money is a "zero-sum" phenomenon. Credit expansion and contraction are, of course, central features of monetary inflation and deflation. Political theorists, however, have been predominantly of the opinion that power should be treated in zero-sum terms. Hence, to make money and power comparable in this vital respect, it has been necessary to investigate the basis of this contention and to show that it was untenable for my purposes.[150]

Instead of the interaction media, in this intellectual autobiography he referred to the four-media structure of functional institutions (economy, polity, etc.), and the four-system idea of society as the latter was in constant interchange with its environment (the social system bordering on, and entertaining input-output exchange with, culture, personality, and organism).

Handwritten notes and a little known text, however, give evidence of how the interaction media were the focus of general theory in the 1960s (and 1970s) not only in the wake of *The Social System*, but also *The Structure of Social Action*.

The three pages of handwritten notes carried the title, "Status + Problems of General Theory."[151] These notes provided a link between the idea of generalized interaction media and the knowledge interest that utilitarianism was methodologically unsatisfactory, an idea that had pervaded as it did already *Structure* in the 1930s.

---

[149] Ibid., p. 343.
[150] "On Building Social System Theory: A Personal History," in *Social Systems and the Evolution of Action Theory*, p. 47.
[151] "Status + Problems of General Theory," handwritten, p. 1; Parsons papers, HUG(FP) – 15.4, box 19.

At the outset, the notes turned against Homans "and partly Blau,"[152] accusing both of reviving utilitarianism, "the problem [that] will not down,"

> Problem will not down – witness status of own work – now also Homans and partly Blau.
> Ramifications into neighboring disciplines + philosophy of science.
> At what levels do (words unreadable) general theory? T.P. vs. G.C.H.
> (words unreadable) involve something short of the logical- (two words unreadable)
> but much more comprehensive in its application, and more "concrete"
> ...
>
> categorization of comparative (incl. evolutionary) dimensions
> and technical analysis of processes –
> including generalized media.
> Beware of sense in which "elementary."[153]

From this vantage point of returning to his criticism of individualistic utilititarianism, "the problem (that) will not down," against Homans and also Blau who in their recent work had invoked "elementary forms" of social behavior modeled after marginal utility economics, he had to state his own cause as against such theory, "including generalized media." Interestingly, as he had done in the 1930s, he returned to biology when the issue was what kind of evolution to assume. He recapitulated three models of biological theory and that "[s]ociology must be placed in broader *theoretical* context – vv economics and politic – 'culture' theory at social level – more difficult." He then stated what were "certain general societal processes,"[154] which generated sociology's knowledge interest: "a) Solidarity[,] b) Normative conformity[.] Partly 'deviance + social control'[.] Equilibrating processes." He outlined three problem areas for solidarity and normative conformity as "articulation of the social system with other action systems," namely religion, personality, and "organism, physical world, technology." From this, returning to the methodologically crucial issue that sociology could not be positivist but needed a frame of reference for conceptual adequacy, he drew a line of evolutionary theory and stated that it marked the very essence of modernization of society itself. Starting out from the relationship of the social system with its three "environment" systems, he now noted:[155]

> For each: frame of reference – structure of system – major processes (theory) – then problem-solving + facts.
>
> We have some really new resources –
>
> Focus on integrative subsystem of societies.
> Evolutionary dimension of *any* theory of social change of sufficient generality.

---

[152] The reference presumably was, Peter Blau, *Power and Exchange* (New York: Wiley, 1964).
[153] "Status + Problems," p. 1; the next four quotes are from the same page.
[154] Ibid., p. 2; the next three quotes are from the same page.
[155] Ibid., pp. 2–3.

Continuity with biological theory
Natural selection takes account of failures, malintegrations, etc.
Also there are "niches" of survival.
But there *is* a "main line."

The technical problems of the processes + sources of variation + selection.

Paradigm of institutionalization –

Three references in these notes were crucial. One was that he postulated progress in the modern society where "some really new resources" had emerged, rendering society truly more democratic than previously, allowing for integration and thereby leading away from anomie as a general development. Second, he focused on the evolutionary dimension in theory which had to match that in the social world, emulating that of biological theory – invoking a progress of knowledge as much as of society against all odds ("but there *is* a 'main line'"). Third, he stated that on the background of the evolution of society as well as theory (as he had proved in *Structure*), the technical problems of society could be solved.

The conclusion was the culmination. He postulated that general theory and general methodology were one. That this meant no return to positivism he secured by demanding that variation of "contributions" (supposedly historical events or structural features) be acknowledged and history honored:[156]

General theory + general methodology.
Bound to meet, but independent variation of of [sic] contributions.
"History" the matrix
    Quantification
    Comparative formalization
    Temporal [formalization]

On a separate page, he noted names for relevant literature, namely Coser, Lazarsfeld, and Zelditch, adding the name of "Adams, etc." and, to concretize why the latter apparently was important, "real + basic – H. vs E.," and "Not same society after integration."

That these notes resumed his knowledge interest from *Structure* was borne out by a text written also in the middle 1960s, unpublished in English.[157] It was entitled, as had been suggested to him in the letter of invitation, "The Theory of Society."[158]

---

[156] Ibid., p. 3. Instead of writing the word "formalization" twice, in the last line, he used a sign customary only in German. The word that otherwise he would have repeated, he replaced by the sign ,,. This sign, in German usage, can be written underneath a word thus duplicated, which is what Parsons did! (Thus behaved, I should say, the true Weberian.)

[157] The text was prepared on request of Edouard Morot-Sir, Cultural Counselor and Representative of French Universities in the United States, for a special issue of *Les Études Philosophiques* whose deadline was March 15, 1964. The text never appeared in English but was translated into French and published, "La théorie de la société," *Les Etudes philosophiques, perspectives sur la philosophie nord-américaine*, vol. 3, 1964, pp. 537–549. The name of the special issue is cited from letters, Morot-Sir to Parsons, dated October 21, 1963 and December 31, 1963; Parsons papers, HUG(FP) – 15.4, box 19; French journal specifics are from the bibliography in *Action Theory and the Human Condition*.

[158] "The Theory of Society"; Parsons papers, HUG(FP) – 15.4, box 19.

He had been asked to put his theory of society into a comparative context with others, but – and he apologized for doing so – he only focused on his own work. His topic was "a conceptual scheme on which I personally have been working for a period of years," a scheme which was

> grounded in the converging tradition of Western thought in these matters, as certain trends crystallized in the generation spanning the turn from the 19th to the 20th centuries. Certain aspects of English utilitarian thought at least, as exemplified by Alfred Marshall, contributed to this convergence. With Vilfredo Pareto building a very important bridge between economic theory and sociology, the most important specific figures were certainly Emile Durkheim and Max Weber.[159]

Parsons then reviewed some fallacies of utilitarianism that could not solve the contradiction between ethically postulated individual freedom and public welfare. His next point was that heredity and environment frequently had been seen as diametrically opposed to each other, in biological thought after Darwin as well as in Marxism.[160] The latter, he charged, could not get beyond their "dilemma of the relation between 'ideal' and 'material' factors in the determination of social phenomena"[161] dissociating so-called material "substructures" from presumably dependent cultural "superstructures." This posed the problem anew, which Darwinism and Marxism had addressed using their "false dilemma." An explanation had to be supplied which accounted for the "acceleration" of the world but also science in the past two decades – a problem which "information theory and cybernetics" involving the symbolic media of human action systems, could solve.

> A way of resolving it for the specific phenomena of human societies, has been in course of developing along the lines I have indicated. This has, however, been enormously reinforced and accelerated in the past twenty years or so by a much more general development in science, into which the sociological movement fits very closely. This is the general conception that nature, both those aspects of it which have spontaneously evolved, and those which have been contrived by man, is characterized by a system of hierarchies of control. In one context the most generalized formulations have been in information theory and cybernetics. . . . The connection between these very general developments and the theory of society lies in the involvement of cultural elements in human action systems. It has gradually become clear that cultural systems are organized about patterns of meaning at symbolic levels; there is a sense in which language is the prototypical example of such a system. There had, however, been a tendency to dissociate these cultural systems from social and individual "substructures." The new perspective consists in better understanding of the ways in which far from being dissociated they are intricately interwoven and interdependent.[162]

---

[159] Ibid., p. 1.
[160] In the discussion of the 1960s, following the lead of, presumably, Margeret Mead whose research in the South Seas had become the basis of strong scientific emphasis on environment (culture) as opposed to heredity after World War II, the Nazi variety was as much as forgotten that, in the 1930s in so-called eugenics in Germany (termed "Racial Hygiene"), environment had been addressed as just the other side to heredity – with no alternative left. See also above, Chapter 1.
[161] Ibid., p. 3.
[162] Ibid., p. 4.

From this he continued: "Whatever may be the case with subhuman social organization, human society is clearly the most deeply penetrated with cultural components. It is not simply an aggregate of interbehaving 'animal' organism, directly similar to social insects, but it is above all characterized by cultural belief and commitment systems (e.g., 'religion'), by values and norms and by intricate linguistically formed mechanisms of communication."[163]

As he explained this, he embedded the interaction media into another hierarchy of control which invoked cybernetics. It involved, indeed, three hierarchies, which he explained briefly. One rendered "cultural elements in human action systems"[164] a higher-order controlling force than "interests in the economic, political or composite Marxian sense."[165] Another made for realms not governed by interests as were, for instance, religion and also the law (legal system) as superimposed upon, or at least not to be subsumed under, economic structures of behavior (which, as he pointed out, referred back to Weber). A third was in the fourfold structural components of society – from highest to lowest levels – values, norms, collectivities, and roles: "This set of structural components is deliberately selected in order to emphasize both cybernetic hierarchy and the analytical distinctness of the social system from both cultural and personality or psychological systems."[166] Values were the most inclusive of the four. To illustrate how they functioned in U.S. society, thus embodying "American values," he pictured them as "conceptions of the desirable type of system . . . which are held by its members."[167] "Empirically values in this sense are, for modern societies, most directly observable in the highest level 'canonical' statements about the society, e.g. for the current American case the Declaration of Independence, Preamble to the Constitution, Bill of Rights, etc., and certain memorable statements by preeminent public figures like Lincoln, Woodrow Wilson, indeed Kennedy."

"The Theory of Society," an overview of his theory as it had come to incorporate not only the generalized media but also the idea of cybernetic control, both used to understand modern democracy, was a crucial text. It proved that in the 1960s he still considered his theory solving the same problem as in the 1930s, a problem then posed in the succession of theoretical findings of Marshall, but also Pareto, leading up to the solutions elaborated by Durkheim and Weber. For him, now, the media and cybernetics were the solutions that solved the problem, which in the 1930s he had addressed using Weber's theory of action structure, adequately amended by Durkheim's conception of ritual.

In a similar vein, the unsatisfactory state of theory as in individualistic utilitarianism and positivism, against which his newly reformulated approach was an antidote, was the target of criticism, in his handwritten notes entitled "Status + Problems of General Theory."

---

[163] Ibid., p. 5.
[164] Ibid., p. 4.
[165] Ibid., p. 6.
[166] Ibid., p. 8.
[167] Ibid., p. 9; the next quote is from the same page.

Regarding Dedifferentiation

I have argued above that *Structure* proposed a two-pronged image of society, one oscillating between two types of social structure, integration and anomie – when a "main line" of societal evolution tended toward integration but anomie signaled the ever-present threat of loss of modernization.

One explication of the media, which was only elaborated in the last of the essays analyzing the generalized media, dealing with value-commitments, further elucidated how the two-pronged concept inspired Parsons's work of the 1960s.

Resuming, from the previous part of the paper, the topic of charisma, redefining it as a "loan" by citizens to an entrepreneur-like charismatic figure, Parsons saw "commitment-capacity" in "moral leadership." Charismatic authority, he clarified, allowed a "focus of a process of *dedifferentiation* relative to the historical background."[168] In the concentration on the one agent, the charismatic leader, of political power as well as influence and also commitments, institutionalizations in social exchange were delegitimized, thus establishing fundamentalist, coercion-type control:

> Responsibilities focusing in other "normally" obligatory areas may be neglected or, if the tension rises sufficiently, explicitly repudiated to the point of being declared specifically illegitimate. Thus a very large sector of common Western liberal socio-political values were repudiated by the Communist movement, especially in its Stalinist phase. The values of free speech, orderly procedure in reaching collective decisions, and many other aspects of "civil liberties" have been downgraded..., with the fundamentalist implication that those who share the values, but insist on retaining a broader pattern for allocating rights, are "enemies" of the innovative movement.

Parsons found that the reversal through dedifferentiation of a more democratic into a more coercive régime implied, in Weber's terms, a reversal from the more advanced state of *Verantwortungsethik* to predominant *Gesinnungsethik*.[169]

This said, in 1968, he offered a tableau of options open to present-day society between the scylla of revolution and the charybdis of stagnation. He outlined these options, of whom the first two were comparatively unproblematic, namely that (1) more or less "exotic" sectarian movements emerged which had little impact on a society as a whole, or (2) "mildly revolutionary" movements developed as, for instance, in the early history of modern physics when utterly novel knowledge had temporarily provoked coercive intolerance, particularly on the part of the Church as it used Inquisition, but these "mildly revolutionary" events had subsequently contributed to further successful differentiation when science in society had become an autonomous institution.

---

[168] "On the Concept of Value-Commitments," p. 470; the next quote is from the same page.

[169] Weber, to be sure, explained these two types of individual ethical orientation in modern societies through, on the one hand, syndicalism, a radical world view involving admiration of, and willingness to resort to, state violence (as in Mussolini fascism in Italy after 1922, but in Weber's lifetime propagated by his erstwhile student and friend, Robert Michels), or a more moderate view denying the state a basis in violence despite the modern monopoly of means of force rendered to the state (as in Imperial Germany and, even more prominently but beginning only after Weber had published his essay, the Weimar Republic).

The third alternative was that (3) major schisms split a world or even *the* world into blocs of apparently irreconcilable régimes, along axes of economic or political system, or religion, or ideology. He remarked, on this note, that in the era of the Cold War, "The Communist movement has also divided on an East-West axis, broadly between the more fully 'industrialized' societies and those to the East of the European center, which are in 'need' of more basic economic development," and added, "The more 'revolutionary' alternative may now make the 'road back' to reintegration exceedingly difficult."[170]

Only the fourth form of social change, spelling modernization, to him appeared adequate, namely that (4) reformation overcame the dilemma between innovation safeguarding progress and regression due to charismatic movements. Only pluralism was an answer to the question of reconciliation between tradition and progress.

He concluded with a personal confession, invoking engagement of the sociologist in the service of making the world understood, in the at once troubled and eventful year of 1968,[171] "[W]e must ask which is most important: (1) fundamentalist regression to more primitive levels, (2) schismatic revolutionary outcomes, which will tend to maximize conflict, or (3) institutionalization of new levels of generality in value systems? Sociology has a grave responsibility to help clarify the understanding of what is going on and of what lies at stake in the balance among these possibilities."[172]

The New Perspective on Integration and Democracy

In the 1950s, Lewis Coser, in *The Functions of Social Conflict*, criticized Parsons for his alleged inability to analyze conflict, and, in his book review of the first edition of *Essays in Social Theory Pure and Applied*, castigated Parsons for alleged inability to analyze social change. He was wrong both times.[173] Parsons's ideas on modern societies in the 1960s witnessed how much Coser – and others who shared his criticism – missed the mark.

Modernization in Modern Society

That social change was to be distinguished from social process – something which Coser apparently failed to notice – occupied Parsons in an essay and a working paper in the early 1960s. Social process, as he defined it, meant the functioning of a societal structure as it had evolved in the course of time, with neither differentiation nor dedifferentiation. (He gave his book, published in 1960, dealing with American

---

[170] "On the Concept of Value-Commitments," p. 471.
[171] For a an endeavor to put together the strands of chaos and euphoria woven into the one year of 1968, see Charles Kaiser, *1968 in America: Music, Politics, Chaos, Counterculture, and the Shaping of a Generation* (New York: Grove Press, 1988).
[172] "On the Concept of Value-Commitments," p. 472.
[173] Lewis Coser, *The Functions of Social Conflict* (New York: Free Press of Glencoe, 1956) and Book review, "Essays in Sociological Theory Pure and Applied. By Talcott Parsons," *American Journal of Sociology*, vol. 55, 1950, pp. 502–504. In this book review, Coser charged Parsons with "defense of total systems, even to the extent of condoning and advocating manipulation" (p. 504).

society in the 1950s when no major restructuring had occurred, the title *Structure and Process in Modern Societies*)[174]. Social change, in contrast, involved gradual or abrupt reordering, revolution or reformation of the structure. In American society, the issue was differentiation to more specialized systems of social organization, modeled on Durkheim's organic solidarity.

The latter topic, modernization of modern society, as he addressed it in the early 1960s, involved two foci, namely differentiation which he analyzed as historical development such as had occurred in the wake of the industrial revolution in the nineteenth century, and integration, which could involve social conflict when an ongoing change was not yet complete.

An article in *Rural Sociology* analyzed how the rural world of the family farm had been drawn into the urbanized arena of industrial production. The outcome meant splitting a "residual" family that persisted as an institution but lost most of its economic functions to the now dominant industrial sector that came to organize employment,[175] from the occupational world typically lodged outside the home. This involved social change, namely "a process by which facilities, previously ascribed to less differentiated units, are freed from this ascription and are made available through suitable adaptive mechanisms for the utilization of the higher-order new class of units that are emerging."[176]

Differentiation in terms of the interaction media meant that each main institutional order (economy, polity, etc.) branched out into systems of more specialized interchange with the other institutional orders, and also more specialized subsystems were established, for example, in the money realm an arena for power, or a supervisory agency that functioned as guarantor for norms of moral integrity in financial transactions, and so on; likewise, in the polity, arenas emerged involving especially money, influence, and/or value-commitments. Parsons depicted the complicated scenario thus emerging in a succession of diagrams, appendix to his essays on the concept of political power, and on stratification.[177]

Democratization Through Differentiation Plus Inclusion

In a memorandum entitled "Notes on the Process of Inclusion," one of the preparatory papers for his major essay on Black Americans ("Full Citizenship for the Negro American?"), Parsons elucidated for the economy and polity what he knew was democratization through differentiation.

> The more differentiated the economy the more allocation of the factors of production ought to be governed by market considerations. By the same token, the more differentiated the polity, the more disposable ought services to be, on both

---

[174] *Structure and Process in Modern Societies* (New York: Free Press of Glencoe, 1960).
[175] Parsons, "Some Considerations on the Theory of Social Change," *Rural Sociology*, vol. 26, 1961, pp. 219–239.
[176] Ibid., p. 235.
[177] See the diagrams at the end of the article on the concept of political power, in *Politics and Social Structure*, pp. 397–404, and in "Equality and Inequality in Modern Society, in *Social Systems and the Evolution of Action Theory*, pp. 366–367.

sides of the exchange relationship – i.e. the freer the performer of service should be to determine the context of that performance, which comes down to choice of employment and autonomy within the employing organization[,] and the freer the employer of service should be in choosing among possible performers of service for him. This mutual freedom is optimized if not maximized when both parties have a maximum of power compatible with its articulation with other factors in their respective situations. The power of the performer is his freedom of choice in employment and his autonomy within the employing organization, always assuming that he is concerned with implementation of the common values.[178]

He added at the end of this paragraph, handwritten into the typed draft, the words which he put in brackets, "(factors of generalization on both sides.)." This referred to his, for him, self-evident hypothesis that increase of differentiation in the realm of the "employing organization" but also "freedom of choice in employment" for the "performer" meant, in both cases, *development* from a less participatory to a more democratic, therefore more modern, society. He then focused on the North and South before and after the Civil War, to clarify the developmental perspective:

In this respect the basic difference between Northern and Southern societies lay in the fact that these components [i.e., the legal and the political components in T. H. Marshall's sense] had developed much further in the North. In particular universal adult suffrage had been attained. Here again the Women's Suffrage Amendment was a landmark. The analogy between women and minority groups has often been remarked.... Of course, in all this, the Southern position was progressively weakened by the actual social changes in the South itself, i.e. the ones usually associated with the concepts of industrialization and urbanization.[179]

On the occasion of using the metaphor of "Power Bank" for understanding modern politics, a paper which he had written about a year earlier than "Notes on the Process of Inclusion," he presupposed that a social order was partial when it was less modern such as had been Nazism. Therefore, for the postwar world, he had invoked progress facilitated by the United Nations, "not least is the overcoming of the vested interests in an older, more partial order."[180] In this way, he had identified the less differentiated type of social order that meant "alienation of the type that Nazi-inspired German Nationalism exhibited" as "partial" – less general in the sense of less democratic, evidently less differentiated.

His "Memorandum: The Problem of Polarization on the Axis of Color" dealt with inclusion of more and more categories of members of a society into the system of action, incorporating the most diverse parts of the population into mainstream society. In this vein, in the Reformation, as he explained, laity had been made full-fledged members in the divine community of "God's children," equal to their priests or pastors; in post–civil war England, Catholics had become equal to Protestants through *habeas corpus* that rendered them protected subjects under the crown; or, in the American case, the "Puritan" modifications of Protestantism had eventuated

---

[178] Parsons, "Notes on the Process of Inclusion," p. 10; Parsons papers, HUG(FP) – 42.45.4, box 4.
[179] Ibid., pp. 8–9.
[180] "The Power Bank: Notes on the Problem of World Order," p. galley – 34; Parsons papers, HUG(FP) – 42.41, box 4; the next two quotes are from the same page.

that "[t]he 'invisible' church ceased to be a 'two-class' system and became an association of presumptive equals, in principle open to all who would join."[181] Political processes, he ascertained, followed a rationale similar to religious ones – establishing equal chances for all parties, associations, and so on in the polity. The American and also the French Revolutions had established the principle of citizenship, inviting "all who would join" under the banner of nation to take part in the political life of the community.

In his essay "Full Citizenship for the Negro American?" Parsons spelled out in some detail that the processes of differentiation cum inclusion were involved in the civil-rights movement, leading toward rights for Black Americans equal to those of any other citizen. Evidently, he admitted, nationalism as the modern form of solidarity in the "New Nations," among which the United States could be counted a forerunner,[182] in the eighteenth century had shaped the struggle for political independence when "the core was surely white, Anglo-Saxon, and Protestant (WASP). The Negroes, most of whom were slaves, were not included."[183] Among the white population, subsequently, denominational diversity guaranteed in the Constitution, originally between various Protestant churches, in time benefited Jewish or Catholic immigrants from Russia, Italy, or Ireland. However, whereas the Black population had been excluded from most of the inclusive processes that eventually would bring about a genuinely pluralistic society, when sketching American history between the Civil War and the 1960s, the present,

> [T]he trend of American development has been toward increasing pluralism . . . and, hence, increasing looseness in the connections among the components of total social status. This trend has one particularly important implication for our purposes, namely, that it is essential to make a clear distinction between *inclusion* and *assimilation*. . . . However, because the United States was originally primarily a white Protestant society, it was often thought that inclusion was synonymous with becoming Protestant or as similar as possible to the Anglo-Saxon tradition. . . . I shall argue that it need not and probably will not be so for the Negro. Full inclusion and multiple role participation are compatible with the maintenance of distinctive ethnic and/or religious identity.[184]

Restructuring American Society

This suggested a sociological link between the topics of unity and conflict, one that Parsons explored in a lecture at McGill University in January 1965.[185] His notes cautioned that there was not yet a generalized comparative theory that he could outline, but there were insights regarding "religion, ethnicity, race" which could specify the features of each. He noted, starting out with religion,

---

[181] Parsons, "Memorandum: The Problem of Polarization on the Axis of Color," p. 9 (unpublished); HUG(FP) – Talcott Parsons – 42.45.4, box 4.
[182] The reference was to Seymour M. Lipset, *The First New Nation* (New York: Basic Books, 1963).
[183] "Full Citizenship for the Nego American?," *Daedalus*, vol. 94, 1965, p. 1011 (*The Negro American*, p. 711).
[184] Ibid., pp. 1015–1016 (pp. 715–716, respectively).
[185] Parsons, "McGill[.] *Unity + Conflict*[.] Jan. 28, '65"; Parsons papers, HUG(FP) – 15.4, box 12.

Religion. Higher-order + deeper than ethnicity. Divisive if 'columnar' (Nation-state is a column.)
Also step to higher order-integration – (Herberg)...
Now an interfaith society...

Higher-order system the 'Oecumenical world'. Separation of Church + state left U.S. open to it.

Back to race – the toughest of all the U.S. problems.
Started to "come unstuck" with W.W. I but really going in last decade.
Migration, vote, economic pressures

Also continuing cultural pressure translated into
a) constitutional
b) legal at lower levels.
Role of Supreme Court.

General conditions
Openness to differentiating + upgrading processes at "private" levels.
Breaking up of blocks – negro migration
Industrialization of South.
Standard of living, communication, education.[186]

Analyzing the relationship between unity and conflict, and how the polarization of American society on the axis of color could be overcome in the course of civil-rights changes, he resumed his interest in how superiority-inferiority relationships between categories of citizens could be converted into genuine equality – a knowledge interest which he, in his analysis of value-commitments, would direct against dedifferentiation in "moral leadership" and which he, in his memorandum on polarization on the axis of color, had directed against the "partial" type society as in Nazi-type nationalism. He (had) clarified, in the introduction to the memorandum,

> Very generally, relations between polarized components include a dimension of superiority-inferiority, which in certain circumstances became dominant over other dimensions. I am particularly interested in the case in which the superior component – as judged by some relevant institutional criterion – comes eventually to include the inferior component in an integrated societal (or other forms of social) community on grounds of fundamental equality in some basic sense.[187]

He pledged himself to the knowledge interest in his draft paper, "Notes on the Problem of Inclusion." Although there was the question of equal achievement capacity in a category of citizens such as Blacks, most of whom had been excluded categorically from participation in education, voting, and so on, the prospect was that generalization of achievement chances meant justice: "The Negro is, we have argued, the symbol of inferiority.... The allegation of inferiority is inseparable from the question of the potentiality of the Negro AS RESOURCE FOR implementing

---

[186] Ibid., pp. 4–5.
[187] "Memorandum: The Problem of Polarization on the Axis of Color," p. 2; the memorandum was originally written, presumably, in 1961.

achievement values. The obverse of the inferiority status is that the Negro constitutes the most important unused resource in our society – the whole complex of deploring waste can be mobilized here, reinforcing the theme of justice."[188]

His concluding statement was, "It is the general theme of the whole citizenship (societal community) complex that in this basic respect there is no legitimate status of inferiority. The racial problem in the United States as of now has become the test case in this area."

Integration was therefore crucial. Inclusion, as he emphasized when he stressed the special position of the legal system guaranteeing equality of (civil) rights (in his lecture notes for McGill), meant that "inclusion not same as 'assimilation.' "[189] He postulated in "Considerations on the Theory of Social Change," the essay that dealt with industrialization in the nineteenth century (replacing rural organization) as a paradigm for differentiation in the social structure, that "normative components of structure . . . [be] reorganized as part of a process of differentiation. . . . The prototype here for large-scale and highly differentiated social systems is the system of legal norms . . . Standards of performance or achievement, of technical adequacy, and the like are also involved."[190]

One other knowledge interest was that he wished to avoid to inadvertently endorse cultural pessimism. He remarked, in a "General Statement" attached to his "Notes on the Process of Inclusion," that "particularly marked pessimism"[191] was widespread, as rightly had been castigated in the spring issue of *Daedalus* of that year. But he noted – himself proposing an "antidote to this tendency":

> Not only has much progress toward full inclusion [of Blacks in the United States] actually been made, but for the first time the genuine possibility of its successful accomplishment is in sight. Moreover social science knowledge gives us a considerably better understanding of what has been taking place than we have had before, and of the conditions it will be necessary to fulfill in order to carry the process to completion. My object is to mobilize a certain amount of that understanding to make these conditions more widely known and thereby in a small way to help promote the process itself.

Another line of his thinking concerned the role of sociology in the active restructuring of contemporary American society, promoting full citizenship for Black Americans. The academic system was the arena of the last of the "three 'revolutions' that have underlain the emergence of modern society – the industrial revolution, the democratic revolution, and the educational revolution. Indeed, it is the focus of the present phase of the educational revolution," he wrote, in 1968, in an article on the academic system in the United States.[192]

---

[188] "Notes on the Process of Inclusion," p. 12; capital letters are original; the next quote is from the same page.
[189] "McGill," p. 3.
[190] "Some Considerations on the Theory of Social Change," p. 236.
[191] "General Statement," attached to "Notes on the Problem of Inclusion"; Parsons papers, HUG(FP) – 42.45.4, box 4; the next two quotes are from the same one-page statement.
[192] Parsons, "The Academic System: A Sociologist's View," reprinted in Daniel Bell and Irving Kristol, eds., *Confrontation: The Student Rebellion and the Universities* (New York: Basic Books, 1969), p. 181.

In a handwritten comment entitled "Columbia Affair," he aligned sociology to the educational revolution that, he postulated, had followed the democratic revolution – thus sociology became an epitome of democracy extending beyond the political into the societal structure and process of today,

> 3 Revolutions.
> Industrial – Economics was "king"
> Democratic – Political science
> Educational – Sociology[193]

Introducing Societal Community
A Lesson from History

Parsons's first account of societal community was in his work on the historical evolution of (premodern) societies, crowning the work of Shmuel N. Eisenstadt on empires. Eisenstadt, in 1963, constructed a Parsonian theory of emergence and decay of empires, highlighting differentiation and dedifferentiation. He showed how universalism, if frequently locally checked, had replaced particularism, and achievement, if often hindered by stratification, had overcome ascription, in the development of diversified political systems in practically all known cultures. He ventured,

> [D]ifferentiation in the major institutional spheres... was manifested by a relatively high degree of development, in the major institutional fields of the society, of varied specific organizations, of "producer" roles, and, to a much smaller extent, of "consumer" roles. In all these spheres, this differentiation created different types of free-floating resources. This limited but pervasive differentiation constituted those "external" conditions which, according to our hypothesis, were necessary for the institutionalization of the major features of the political systems of the societies examined here – i.e., a centralized polity of bureaucratic administration, channels of political struggle, and differentiated political activities.[194]

Parsons further developed the idea of how universalism as a main value orientation had replaced particularism, and achievement had overcome ascription, first in an article on "Evolutionary Universals in Society,"[195] and subsequently, *Societies*.[196] In this slim book, he contrasted, for instance, the Egyptian and

---

[193] "Columbia affair" (handwritten notes); Parsons papers, HUG(FP) – 42.45.4, box 5 (presumably written in 1968).

[194] S. N. Eisenstadt, *The Political Systems of Empires* (London: Free Press of Glencoe/Collier Macmillan, 1963), pp. 94–95.

[195] Parsons, "Evolutionary Universals in Society," *American Sociological Review* 29 (1964): 339–357.

[196] On the request of Alex Inkeles, series editor of *Foundations of Modern Sociology* and long-time colleague and collaborator, Parsons had signed the contract in 1961 and begun work on a book that soon became a projected two books, the first of which was written in 1963–1964. Intending to explain how differentiation and integration fitted together in historical perspective, he dealt with archaic and ancient classic societies in *Societies: Evolutionary and Comparative Perspectives* (Indianapolis: Bobbs Merrill, 1966). The second was *The System of Modern Societies* (Indianapolis: Bobbs Merrill, 1971), and a third was a collection of readings, edited together with Victor Lidz, *Readings on Pre-Modern Societies* (Englewood Cliffs, N.J.: Prentice Hall, 1972). In 1977, Jackson Toby combined the two books by Parsons into one volume, entitled *The Evoluton of Societies* (Englewood Cliffs, N.J.: Prentice Hall).

Mesopotamian cultures among ancient societies. His hypothesis was that the stability of ancient Egypt, but also its inability to develop, had been due to the fact that the political and the religious in that society had been literally fused into one and the same institutional structure, rendering the pharaoh a veritable god. This meant that no legal system existed as guarantor of individuals' rights, because differentiation between religion and the polity had not yet taken place. In contradistinction, in Mesopotamia, religious and political authority had been differentiated to a certain extent, and a legal system of degrees had developed concomitantly, although further differentiation and consolidation of institutional spheres had been hindered by the fact that "a unified conception of the grounding of the meanings of the obligations" did not develop. This latter achievement, however, had been reached as it was in Ancient Greece, creating the idea of *polis*.[197]

The book was the first to introduce societal community. What, in this first attempt, was societal community? Parsons outlined four action systems within a functioning society, using the four-function scheme of AGIL (adaptation – goal attainment – integration – latency). Among them, representing the function of integration, was the societal community. "The Concept of Society," chapter two in *Societies*, delineating societal community, rejected the idea that cause-and-effect sequences of motivated behavior were the elementary forms of society. Instead, action systems including the societal community as core social system were hinged on cultural tradition and spiritual worlds, constituting "the 'ultimate reality' with which we are ultimately concerned in grappling with what Weber called the 'problems of meaning' – e.g., evil and suffering, the temporal limitations of human life, and the like. 'Ideas' in this area, as cultural objects, are in some sense symbolic 'representations' (e.g., conceptions of gods, totems, the supernatural) of the ultimate realities, but are not themselves such realities."[198]

Societal community functioned in an environment of three other action systems, namely culture, personality, and the organism when there were interchange relations establishing that the societal community had a *sui-generis* reality. As such, it was a collectivity in the sense suggestive of Durkheim's *conscience collective*. The important point which he wished to emphasize was self-sufficiency:

> A society must constitute a societal *community* that has an adequate level of integration or solidarity and a distinctive membership status.... This community must be the "bearer" of a cultural system sufficiently generalized and integrated to legitimize normative order. Such legitimation requires a system of constitutive symbolism which grounds the identity and solidarity of the community, as well as beliefs, rituals, and other cultural components which embody such symbolism.... A society's self-sufficiency in this context... involves its institutionalizing a sufficient range of cultural components to meet its *societal* exigencies tolerably well.... Self-sufficiency by no means requires that *all* the role-involvements of all members be carried on within the society.... Finally, self-sufficiency implies adequate control over the economic-technological complex so that the physical environment can be utilized as a resource base in a

---

[197] *Societies*, ch. 4, pp. 51–68, cit. p. 67. To be sure, Parsons in 1942 had invoked the idea of *polis* when he cited Weber to hold democracy against Nazism in the then "contemporary crisis," war that endangered Western civilization. See above, Chapter 2.

[198] *Societies*, p. 8.

Introducing Societal Community   233

purposeful and balanced way. This control is intertwined with political control of territory and with control of membership in relation to the residence-kinship complex.[199]

Self-sufficiency, apparently, was a synonym for cybernetic control capacity lodged with the societal community. Compared with and in relation to the other three, from the standpoint of the sociologist explaining how a democratic society functioned, societal community – suggesting self-sufficiency – was a considerably advanced system of self-regulating action orientation. The cybernetic control capacity, in turn, enabled individuals to have their cultural identity which, strengthened by legislation and jurisdiction, safeguarded their voluntary, morally significant interactional activities.

"The Principal Structures of Community"

Parsons's earliest text on the topic, which dealt with community when he had not yet created the idea of societal community, was published in 1959. Friedrich, under the umbrella of the American Society for Political and Legal Philosophy he had founded in 1955, held yearly gatherings in Cambridge, the second of which dealt with Community. Parsons participated and later also contributed to the volume in the series, *Nomos*.[200]

"The Principal Structures of Community: A Sociologists's View"[201] addressed community when he used neither Werner Sombart's antimodernist concept of *Gemeinschaft* nor Ferdinand Tönnies' counterpart to *Gesellschaft*. He wished to understand community as the here and now active substrate of solidarity in contemporary America. He abandoned the trodden paths when he found new, indeed interestingly dated, ground on which to stand. He turned to Robert MacIver's *Community: A Sociological Study*, published in 1917:[202]

---

[199] "The Concept of Society," reprinted in *Politics and Social Structure*, cit. pp. 19–20.

[200] In the years 1958–1964 alone, the series *Nomos* addressed the serendipitous topics Authority (1958), Community (1959), Responsibility (1962), and Justice (1964), among others.

[201] Other contributions to the volume, Carl J. Friedrich, ed., *Community* (New York: Liberal Arts Press, 1959), were, among others, William Y. Elliott, "The Co-Organic Concept of Community Applied to Legal Analysis: Constitutional and Totalitarian Systems Compared," pp. 50–64; Benjamin Nelson, "Community – Dream and Reality," pp. 135–151; and Lon L. Fuller, "Governmental Secrecy and the Forms of Social Order," pp. 256–268.

[202] Robert MacIver, *Community: A Sociological Study* (London: Macmillan, 1917). MacIver's main objective was to provide a sociological view that rejected positivism (Spencerian as much as Durkheimian) when it explained social fact as well as social law and also the place of sociology among the sciences, overcoming what MacIver termed "False Perspectives of Community" (pp. 67 ff.). In this vein, when he discussed the elements and structures of community, MacIver named as one source of unity in a community "territorial boundaries" (p. 107), supplemented by complexes of common interests or associations related to specific interests as the other two sources. He found, thus contradicting Spencer, that institutions were "forms of order established within social life by some common will" (p. 150). Then he progressed to formulate three laws of communal development which owed nothing to Spencer's idea of natural selection or deterministic progress, but everything instead to emphasis on associations and indeed the benefit to modern society of a multitude of associations catering for economic, cultural, and a host of other common interests in a community.

> By the term community I would... designate one aspect of every concrete social collectivity or structure.... [S]ince MacIver's book... emphasis has been placed on the relation of community to territorial location. I would thus give a tentative working definition of community as that aspect of the structure of social systems which is referable to the territorial location of persons... and their activities. When I say "referable to" I... mean... observable and analyzable with reference to location as a focus of attention (and of course a partial determinant). In this respect the study of community structures comes close to what an important group of sociologists (centering in the University of Chicago and, later, of Michigan) have called the "ecological approach" to the study of social phenomena.... The full formula... comprises... persons acting in relation to other persons in respect to the territorial locations of both parties. The *population*, then, is just as much a focus of the study of community as is the territorial location.[203]

Regarding "the principal categories of meaning of territorial location to persons in roles, and how... all these [are] related to each other," knowing that "a territorial location is always significant as a 'place where' something socially significant has happened or may be expected to happen,"[204] he identified four foci of such spatial, boundary-prone identification. These were residential location, occupation and work premises, jurisdiction, and "the communicative complex."

About these: *Residential location* meant that segregation frequently hinged on residential distinctions. The nuclear family, the unit of immediate belonging and source of social-class membership, had "a tendency to relative uniformity of residential neighborhoods" making "for the 'better' neighborhoods to segregate out from the 'less desirable' ones": "This in turn is an important set of reference points for the class structure of the society."[205]

Occupational and work premises were spatially segregated. In short, "it is usual for... a role to have some kind of home base... from which the incumbent goes out and to which he returns,"[206] which, by implication, separated out temporary residents such as guests in a hotel.

Jurisdiction was organized on a territorial basis although constitutional rights and duties were guaranteed through the federal government of the United States. This double-layer structure related to "obligations which are imposed on categories of persons by some process of decision-making where the ultimately relevant agency is held to have legitimate authority under a system of normative order."[207]

---

[203] "The Principal Structures of Community: A Sociological View," in Friedrich, ed., *Community*, cit. pp. 152–153; the reference to the Chicago or Michigan approach was to, in one instance, Otis Dudley Duncan who, in 1958, had outlined the ecological approach in a programmatic article later republished in the compendium volume, Seymour Martin Lipset and Neil Smelser, *Sociology: The Progress of a Decade. A Collection* (Englewood Cliffs, N.J.: Prentice Hall, 1961), pp. 311–325 (Duncan and Leo F. Schnore, "Cultural, Behavioral, and Ecological Perspectives in the Study of Social Organization").

[204] "The Principal Structures," p. 153.

[205] Ibid., p. 156.

[206] Ibid., p. 159. He would later transfer this distinction to that between citizens of a country, evidently a territorial unit, and foreigners who received protection of property rights, but were not full-fledged members. See his "Theoretical Orientations on Modern Societies"; see also below.

[207] "The Principal Structures," p. 160.

The important point was access to or use of coercion, or physical force. Since 1957, even the governors of some Southern states had ostentatiously disobeyed Supreme Court jurisdiction, barring desegregation when violence erupted in the struggle for constitutional rights. Parsons saw that "the strategic role of physical force rests on... a 'regression scale' of punishment," cautioning "that while there are critical limits on the effectiveness of force or the threat of force in motivation of positive action, in the prevention of feared or disapproved action, force is the ultimate sanction."[208]

Although the higher-order control agency was the federal government, Parsons warned that "the boundaries of integrated societal systems have a strong tendency to coincide with the territorial jurisdictions of their political systems."[209] Nevertheless, although not all "political obligations are the 'highest' human obligations,"[210] he cautioned, "no society can be effectively integrated which permits other jurisdictional claims to take precedence over those of its governmentally sanctioned legal system." He declared, "[P]olitical jurisdiction is paramount, and no society can be effectively politically organized if a claim of other jurisdictions to supersede that of the law is successfully put through."[211]

The fourth, the "*communicative complex*," concerning "persons-in-places,"[212] regulated informational content (structuring interactions). Cognitive content, intentionality in the direction toward others, acceptance or rejection of influence involved, and commonality of common culture were the four preconditions of effective communication. "What, now, are the modes of involvement of physical persons in physical locations in processes of communication?"[213] Communication required physical media such as speech, often transported through technology of communication, but the language aspect was not the condition of interpersonal relations. The media of communication, especially their symbolic substrate, meant territoriality inasmuch as property typically belonged to, for instance, a local person in a context (economic, cultural, residential, etc.), and was patterned accordingly. "The upshot of this discussion of communication is to make it clear that not only must activities of members of a social system be spatially located, and hence their distribution patterned, but the physical aspects of the processes of interaction between social units must be definitely patterned."[214]

The target, undoubtedly, was American society. The insight that societal community hinged on territoriality convinced another author in the *Community* volume whose contribution followed that of Parsons. Thomas A. Cowan, a lawyer, complimented Parsons, "I had thought of community as a quest pursued largely in the realm of human thought," he recalled as he introduced his own piece. "Parsons says, on the contrary, 'study the ground under your feet.' And begin no farther away

---

[208] Ibid., p. 161.
[209] Ibid., p. 163.
[210] Ibid., p. 165; the next quote is from the same page.
[211] Ibid., p. 167.
[212] Ibid.
[213] Ibid., p. 170.
[214] Ibid., p. 175.

than home."²¹⁵ By choosing an unusual theme, territoriality, Cowan felt, Parsons had discovered or, rather, rediscovered an undeniably crucial theme in the theory of law.

He then made a suggestion which was on the mark of Parsons's own ideas. (Indeed, Parsons, as he came to analyze influence and political power subsequently, in the early 1960s, might haven taken up Cowan's thought.) "I should like to see the present one-dimensional view of the nature of 'community space' expanded into a polar system," wrote Cowan.

> Professor Parsons has suggested that the principal structures of community are home, work, jurisdiction, and communication. I should like to look at these structures as including a set of polar opposites. For example, in the case of jurisdiction we could look upon our structure as combining forces that tend either toward or away from jurisdictional space. Still keeping our major focus on space (and time as well, I suppose, since Parsons' systems are all teleological) we could view the forces as centripetal to or centrifugal from the space in question.²¹⁶

The legal system, Cowan explained, was centripetal inasmuch as it imposed sanctions on human beings to regulate their conduct. Not all sanctions were negative, though, as one could learn from Parsons himself, Cowan felt. Parsons, he thought, preferred affirmative sanctions over punishments.²¹⁷ Cowan invoked America's role in international politics, to point at obvious centripetal or integrative tendencies, "The new American imperialism is in the form of 'foreign aid' in exchange for military bases and ideological loyalties. Not alone are our own citizens demanding affirmative governmental services but a great part of the world itself is eager to put itself under American 'jurisdiction.'"²¹⁸

Citizenship by Legal System

"Full Citizenship for the Negro American?" started out from a designation that Blacks were "second-class citizens" in the United States, invoking T. H. Marshall's understanding of three dimensions of citizenship.²¹⁹ Marshall's aspects of citizenship, that is, civil or legal rights supplemented by the political and the social (economic) side of equality and social justice, Parsons explained, were indeed crucial for understanding how "colored" Americans could become citizens like everybody else. However, Marshall's idea needed grounding regarding the dynamics of how

---

[215] Thomas A. Cowan, "The Principal Structures of Community Reviewed," in Friedrich, ed., *Community*, pp. 180–181.
[216] Ibid., p. 185.
[217] This, presumably, referred to *The Social System* which had elaborated, especially in Chapter VI and VII, on positive mechanisms of ascertaining conformity in democratic societies (such as socialization or therapy as forms of social control), with negative sanctions as only a second-tier layer of social order.
[218] Cowan, "The Principal Structures," p. 186.
[219] See T. H. Marshall, *Class, Citizenship, and Social Development* (Garden City, N.Y.: Doubleday, 1964). The original book which was republished in the 1960s had appeared in London in 1950, a collection of essays some of which had been written during World War II.

such tripartite citizenship evolved. "The concept of citizenship, as used here," he clarified in his introduction, "refers to full membership in what I shall call the *societal community*. This term refers to that aspect of the total society as a system, which forms a *Gemeinschaft*, which is the focus of solidarity or mutual loyalty of its members, and which constitutes the consensual base underlying its political integration."[220]

From a perspective of the individual citizen, he saw that "societal community is a category of the commitment of members of the collectivity in which they are associated, and of the members to each other."[221] He thus endorsed the kind of equality of rights which, in terms then recently explicated by John Rawls, made distributive justice imperative among otherwise certainly unequal individuals.

In "The Concept of Society," he anchored the societal community in the legal system, on the basis of its accomplishing three tasks: It distinguished between members and nonmembers; it sustained a sense of solidarity which gave citizens a common, meaningful identity; and, last but not least, it represented a society's self-sufficiency, both territorial and political, the viable basis for an empire's, city-state's, or nation's economy and polity.

Less than modern societies had forerunners of a legal system in their religious world. But the full-fledged differentiated societal community that entailed institutionalization of the law existed only in modern democracy. "The differentiation between cultural and societal systems is, in its earlier stages, most conspicuous in the field of religion, becoming evident as greater 'distance' emerges between the gods and the human condition" he ventured,[222] and, "The development of autonomous legal systems is perhaps the most important indicator of differentiation between the societal integrative system, focusing about the societal community, and the polity, which is concerned with the selection, ordering, and attainment of collective goals rather than the maintenance of solidarity (including order) as such."

The law was crucial; "As we shall see, Roman law of the Imperial period came by far the closest, among premodern systems, to meeting the more 'formal' aspects of these requirements – and, of course, it made essential contributions to the later emergence of fully modern systems."[223]

Chapter Two of *The System of Modern Societies*, the sequel of *Societies* that focused explicitly on the evolution of the modern world, carried this much further.[224] He now presented an elaborate view of, in long-term perspective, how Western democracy had reached its most advanced state, present-day America.

---

[220] "Full Citizenship for the Negro American?" in *The Negro American*, co-edited with Kenneth Clark (Boston: Houghton Mifflin, 1966), pp. 709–710.

[221] Ibid., p. 710, citing John Rawls, "Constitutional Liberty and the Concept of Justice," in C. J. Friedrich and John W. Chapman, eds., *Justice* (Nomos VI) (New York: Atherton, 1963), pp. 98–125.

[222] "The Concept of Society," in *Politics and Social Structure*, p. 28; the next quote is from the same page.

[223] Ibid., pp. 31–32; Weber's sociology of law had been recently translated then; Max Rheinstein, ed., *Max Weber on Law in Economy and Society* (Cambridge, Mass.: Harvard University Press, 1954).

[224] Prepublished as "Theoretical Orientations on Modern Societies," *Politics and Social Structure*, pp. 34–57.

Differentiation, he reiterated, constituted pluralist societies. Division between the legislative, executive, and judicial branches of government, and equally the economy, the polity, and the various realms which formed "society" (which were the law and medicine, among others), and also culture, the fourth realm, were seminal achievements. In "society," the core realm for integration, three spheres fulfilled the fiduciary functions that held the social order together as they allowed for competence in the service of the citizen. They were higher learning that safeguarded culture and science, the legal system that safeguarded civil rights and regulated contractual relations, and so forth, and professional practice that safeguarded health (e.g., in the guise of medicine). These main centripetal forces, among them prominently the legal system that allowed for toleration of diversity among citizens,[225] produced loyalty.

> Our core category is... the component centering about the definition of obligations of *loyalty* to the societal collectivity, both in the capacity of membership as such and in various categories of differentiated status and role within the society... Loyalty is a readiness to respond to properly "justified" appeals to the collective or "public" interest or need. The normative problem concerns the definition of occasions when such a response constitutes an obligation. Particularly important are the relations between sub-groups' and individual's loyalties to the societal collectivity and their loyalties to other collectivities of which they are members.[226]

The legal system, an arena for integrative tendencies, catered to nonparticularistic, nonascriptive rules and roles, a universal framework for justice. The highest authority in the orientational coordination of legal and, indeed, jurisdictional justice was the Constitution.

> Some aspects of legality are literally given in constitutionally defined terms. Insofar as this is a variable component..., the most important agency of variation seems to be judicial decision or its equivalent.... The Constitution itself... is by no means only an assertion of value-commitments. It states many rather specific *norms* concerning the conduct of government itself and the relations of its various agencies to units in the private sector.[227]

Some implications were explored by a colleague of Parsons, Harvard Law Professor Archibald Cox, in his lecture, "Direct Action, Civil Disobedience, and the Constitution."[228] His was the rhetorical question, "If direct action, disobedience of local authorities, and like techniques of the civil rights movement have at last produced a measure of reform in race relations, will they not lead us still closer to the goal in that area and also promote long-overdue reforms in other segments of

---

[225] See also next section below.
[226] "Theoretical Orientations," p. 41.
[227] "Polity and Society," in *Politics and Social Structure*, p. 481.
[228] See Archibald Cox, Mard DeWolfe Howe, J. R. Wiggins, *Civil Rights, the Constitution, and the Courts* (Cambridge, Mass.: Harvard University Press, 1967). The three papers collected in the book were originally a series of evening lectures organized by the Massachusetts Historical Society in the winter term of 1965–1966.

society?"²²⁹ For one, demonstrations demanding freedom of speech and liberty to assemble, facing local police authorities barring such demonstration, were entirely legal: "Such action involves no civil disobedience – no violation of law in the ultimate sense – because the only orders that are violated are nullities (that is, not law at all) being unconstitutional."²³⁰ On the other hand, for instance, obstructing railroad tracks at an Army base to demand greater equality for Blacks was illegal: "Not one of the great events in the civil rights movement has involved this kind of disobedience to law on the part of the Negroes involved."²³¹

A third category involved disobedience in "cases in which all one can say at the time of the demonstration is that it goes to the outer boundaries of and perhaps exceeds any constitutional right." This was where jurisdiction needed to interpret the Constitution, "When there is doubt, the demonstrator takes his chance upon the ultimate decision of the highest court which will hear his case and to which he has the means and perseverance to carry it. If the court sustains the constitutional claim, he will go free; otherwise he will suffer the penalty." This made jurisdiction societal procedure, though not an instrument of utilitarian pursuit, Cox asserted,

> Society would disintegrate if demonstrations and direct action widely replaced reason and civility as methods of resolving questions of public policy. Repeated resort to such tactics is also likely to lessen their usefulness when truly needed. Nevertheless, when the cause is just, when there is urgency, and when other channels are closed, we should defend the social and moral right to disobey a law that one sincerely believes will be held unconstitutional, even though he turns out to be wrong. Whatever harm is done to the principle of consent is balanced by the need to conform the law to the demands of conscience.²³²

Parsons wrote as he analzed the problem of social order, "I regard the constitutional doctrine that has been so prominent in recent Supreme Court decisions, that every citizen is entitled to equal protection of the laws, as a fundamental statement of values about the desirable type of society in which we live."²³³

The moral yardstick was the American Bill of Rights. Moral principles were the protection from disenfranchisement and exploitation, assured to each citizen on the assumption that he contributed to the effectiveness of the nation.²³⁴

Civil Religion

One arena for pluralism established through the American Constitution was religious practice. Handwritten notes entitled "Religious and Social Pluralism"

---

[229] Archibald Cox, "Direct Action, Civil Disobedience, and the Constitution," in *Civil Rights, Civil Disobedience, and the Courts*, p. 3.
[230] Ibid., p. 9.
[231] Ibid., p. 10; the next two quotes are from the same page.
[232] Ibid., pp. 26–27.
[233] Parsons, "Order as a Sociological Problem," in Paul G. Kuntz, ed., *The Concept of Order* (Seattle and London: Grinnell College, University of Washington Press, 1968), p. 376.
[234] "Theoretical Orientations," p. 44.

explored in what way, in American society in the 1960s, religion (separated from the state) was a moral resource which helped integrate Americans into a world of toleration and diversity:

> Main outline of religious pluralism is familiar – importance of continuance.
> Constitutional separation – not controversial (Millis).
> Religious freedom and toleration.
> Denominational pluralism (neither church nor sect à la Troeltsch).
> Revivalism and democratization of churches.
> Negative toleration of Catholics and Jews.
>
> Secularization of higher education a major step, private and public.
> Relative insulation of fundamentalism
> Conservative reaction to the new immigration
> Beginning inclusion only after WW I
>   Klan of 1920's
>   1928 election
>   Antisemitism of 1930's
> All signs of strain
>
> Now –
> Herberg
> Far greater entry into general life.
> Catholicism
>   The Kennedy story
>   Cushing's position
>   Pope John and the Council
>   The "civic" religion
> United religious front for Civil Rights
>
> Pluralization of secular society
> Broadly a familiar syndrome
> Urbanization – metropolis
> Industrialization
> Isolation of nuclear family
> Educational upgrading
>
> The "middle class" society.
> Plural involvements of one *same* people
>
> A "secular city" in a new sense.
> Religion enormously privatized
> but also extended in relevance
>
> Many problems – social and theological
> but on whole organized religion had fared better than in Europe.
>
> Basic situation culmination of a deeply rooted trend.[235]

---

[235] Handwritten notes, "Religious and Social Pluralism," Parsons papers, HUG(FP) – 15.4, box 16; emphasis original.

Four sources mentioned in these notes can be identified: One was *Protestant-Catholic-Jew*,[236] written by a Jewish theologian in the middle 1950s. Herberg had argued that when the United States had evolved through immigration from ethnically, culturally, and religiously different countries, mainly from Europe, Russia, and the Near East, the would-be Americans had been identified by their origin for a time to come when they also were integrated into a world of multiple ethnic, cultural, and religious identities. "To be a Protestant, a Catholic, or a Jew are today the alternative ways of being an American," wrote Herberg,

> This religious normality implies a certain religious unity in terms of a common "American religion" of which each of the three great religious communions is regarded as an equi-legitimate expression. Each on his part – the Protestant, the Catholic, the Jew – may regard his own "faith" as the best or even the truest, but unless he is a theologian or affected with a special theological interest, he will quite "naturally" look upon the other two as sharing with his communion a common "spiritual" foundation of basic "ideals and values" – the chief of these being religion itself. America thus has its underlying culture-religion – best understood as the religious apect of the American Way of Life – of which the three conventional religions are somehow felt to be appropriate manifestations and expressions.[237]

Another reference was to Catholicism, and, among the four issues there was "The Kennedy story." The source that Parsons had in mind might have been a three-page note of his, presumably written on the occasion of Kennedy's funeral, clarifying what the theoretical salience was:

> Kennedy was the first Roman Catholic to be elected to the Presidency of the United States, and his election has been a major event in the inclusion of the nonWASP elements in full membership in the societal community. That *he*, of all recent presidents, should be assassinated, combined with his youth cast a special air of tragedy and martyrdom on the event. The funeral was unquestionably a crucially important symbolization of the new ecumenical status of the American community in its relations to the religious affiliations of its members.... It was taken for granted that he should have a Catholic funeral... For the first time,... the implications of the American system of denominational pluralism, and the peculiar balance between the public and private status of religion in our society, came to the sharpest symbolic focus. At the funeral, which was seen by millions on television, the Cardinal symbolized this situation.... Given the Protestant background of American society, it was new and crucially important that a Catholic priest should assume the latter role – as a Rabbi may well do some time in the future.[238]

Another reference, interestingly also subsumed under "Catholicism," was to "civic" religion. This undoubtedly invoked Robert Bellah's concept of civil religion, first introduced at a conference of the American Academy of Arts and Sciences late in 1965. Bellah, citing Kennedy's inaugural address, invoked references

---

[236] Will Herberg, *Protestant-Catholic-Jew: An Essay in American Religious Sociology* (Garden City, N.Y.: Doubleday, 1955).
[237] Herberg, p. 274.
[238] Untitled manuscript, starting with "We have put our principal emphasis...," p. 3; HUG(FP) – 42.45.1, box 1.

to the Almighty whose blessings were asked for the nation, assuring that "the rights of men have come not from the generosity of the state, but from the hand of God."[239] He asked what the meaning was of such apparent reverence to God when doctrines neither of Protestantism nor Catholicism nor Judaism were as much as referred to. The answer lay in a specific modern form of transdenominational religion, addressed as civil. Bellah explained,

> The American civil religion was never anticlerical or militantly secular. On the contrary, it borrowed selectively from the religious tradition in such a way that the average American saw no conflict between the two. In this way, the civil religion was able to build up without any bitter struggle with the church powerful symbols of national solidarity and to mobilize deep levels of personal motivation for the attainment of national goals.[240]

American civil religion dignified the celebrations of the Constitution and the memorial tribute to the war dead, Bellah found, and he assured, "American civil religion is still very much alive. Just three years ago we participated in a vivid reenactment of the sacrifice theme in connection with the funeral of our assassinated President." He also found, "The American Israel theme is clearly behind both Kennedy's New Frontier and Johnson's Great Society."

The fourth source that was a background to Parsons's notes was Christian theologian Harvey Cox's *The Secular City*.[241] He had argued for modern urban culture in light of the fact that cities were favored places for today's population; there, religion was anchored in intellectual pursuits rather than doctrinaire gospel interpretation. This suggested genuinely modern ways of honoring Christian faith other than through orthodoxy, superceding the false choice between fundamentalism and atheism.

In his notes, as he reconciled pluralism and unity regarding religion, Parsons welded these four sources together, amidst a wide array of other materials. He arrived at a comprehensive appreciation of civil religion, an integrative force in the societal community. Civil religion was shared by individuals of diverse beliefs, Jews or Christians as much as (possibly) atheists, who all joined the "united religious front for Civil Rights" (as he phrased it in his notes). The message was that pluralism embraced both differentiation (religious toleration) and integration (religious freedom by right, as a civil right). "[P]luralization ... has a double implication. One aspect concerns ... the principles of toleration.... The other aspect is that the community itself must be grounded in a moral consensus. Groups within a community who differ on the explicit religious level not only are to be 'permitted' to go their varying ways but must be held to have a *moral right* to do so – the difference is crucial...."[242]

---

[239] Robert Bellah, "Civil Religion in America," in *Beyond Belief: Essays on Religion in a Post-Traditionalist World* (Berkeley: University of California Press, 1970), cit. p. 171; originally, the essay appeared in *Daedalus* in winter, 1967.

[240] Ibid., pp. 180–181; the next two quotes are from the latter page.

[241] Harvey Cox, *The Secular City: Secularization and Urbanization in Theological Perspective* (New York: Macmillan, 1966).

[242] Parsons, "The Nature of American Pluralism," in Theodore R. Sizer, ed., *Religion and Public Education* (Boston: Houghton Mifflin, 1967), p. 253 (emphasis original).

The Academic Profession, Higher Learning, Sociology

In a paper entitled, "The Role of the Behavioral Scientist in the Internation[al] Situation,"[243] in the spring of 1963, he wrote:

> [A] word should be said about the great strategic importance of the universities in our modern situation. The universities are the primary organizational trustees of the great intellectual traditions of the Western world. They must be the primary seed-bed, in which the most important new developments are cultivated. I do not wish to under-estimate the contributions which can be made by various types of free-lance people outside such organizational settings or by those in research institutes, government agencies and so on. Nevertheless the universities seem to be the crucial node at which the most important threads of conditions of the development of these new sciences come together. The fact that the first responsibility of the university professor is the advancement of knowledge in his field and the training of his successors as professional experts in it, seems to me the most important single guarantee that the balance will not tip too far in the direction of sacrificing the potential of the future to the urgencies of the present.[244]

In the early 1960s, when Parsons was chairman of Committee C of the American Association of University Professors (AAUP), which was devoted to problems of university structure, he devised the first of his three studies on the academic profession.[245] In a short proposal submitted to the Carnegie Foundation he explained that he expected to explore the role of science for society in general:

> [T]he most important structural change in American society... during the present century has been the development of the higher intellectual disciplines.... The center of this development has been in the sciences.... This century has also seen the rise of the behavioral and socio-cultural sciences to a level not approached before.... The importance of the complex as a whole is so great that I should not wish to isolate the sciences from the other disciplines, namely the traditonal applied professions of law and divinity and the core humanities as these are represented in the typical university organization.[246]

The essay, "The Academic System: A Sociologist's View" (written in 1968)[247] clarified the particular structural features which made the university an organization

---

[243] The paper had originally been a contribution to the one-day meeting of the American Orthopsychiatric Association, held on March 7, 1963, on the theme, "The Behavioral Scientist and Human Survival." Parsons spoke from notes but later wrote a rough draft of a paper which, in a letter to the editor of the *American Journal of Orthopsychiatry*, he offered to elaborate into a full-fledged paper, if this would be requested of him, which obviously it was not. See the correspondence, conference program, handwritten notes, and the draft paper in the Parsons papers, HUG(FP) – 42.8.6, box 1.

[244] Ibid., pp. 18–19.

[245] Research proposal, submitted to the Carnegie Foundation, "A Study of the Place of the Professions in the Current and Prospective Development of American Society, for a period from July 1, 1961, to July 1, 1964 (three years)," dated January 25, 1961. HUG(FP) – 15.4, box 2. Material on the study during its phase until 1964 is preserved in the Harvard Archives under the same call number. Subsequently, a second project lasted from 1965 to 1967, and a third followed, all leading up to *The American University*, co-authored with Gerald Platt (Cambridge, Mass.: Harvard University Press, 1973).

[246] "A Study of the Place," p. 2.

[247] "The Academic System: A Sociologist's View," *The Public Interest*, vol. 13, 1968, pp. 173–197.

whose specifics, "associational" diffuse distribution of power and autonomous control over its economic resources, were of pivotal importance in regard to science apt for modernity. He elucidated: The organizational specifics of the American academic system had been fought over between the middle nineteenth and the early twentieth century, and a major crisis had erupted which had only been solved by the then newly founded AAUP. In the 1930s, anti-intellectualism had targeted New Deal supporters, and in the 1950s alleged sympathizers of Communism had been harassed. In the 1960s, a new threat now came from the left, but was no different a menace. What was at stake was the collegial structure, the safeguard of the historical-cultural function of the American university.

"Cognitive Rationality," the raison d'être of the academic system, was jeopardized, and the responsibility of the university members was undermined which centered around research free from political control in its range of inquiry. Academic teaching, Parsons held, including undergraduate teaching, hinged on the values of competence and integrity derived from cognitive rationality. The "'Collegial' Pattern," he insisted, was the organizational form for realization of cognitive rationality in the spirit of academic freedom. The differentiated structure of the university was to be preserved in the interest of intellectual excellence.

On these grounds, as it united diversity and integrated responsibility, the academic system was "An 'Engine of Change.'" He warned, "[A] strong and prominent academic system is by no means a bulwark of the status quo, but very much a source, through many channels, of impetus to societal change.... Indeed, it is the focus of the present phase of the educational revolution."[248]

Academic teaching and research, the cultivation of values of knowledge, rendered an indispensable service to the welfare of modern America as such. In this function lay the fate of democracy itself, he explained. An example of how this function had been left unfulfilled, he knew, were the faculties in Germany not having protected their members' academic freedom against encroachment by the Nazi state: "[U]niversities can legitimately act, collectively, to defend themselves from a political movement or regime that threatens their autonomy or the academic freedom of their members. It is widely felt, retrospectively, that the German universities corporately – not just the members of their faculties individually – should have fought much more vigorously against the threat of the Nazi movement in the early 1930's."[249]

The concomitance of diversity and unity which was the landmark of institutions belonging in the societal community, reconciling pluralism and inclusion, differentiation and integration, held universities together. Despite their "spirit of tentativeness," their granting "unusual tolerance" when the binding forces were predominantly procedural rules, they were the harbingers of democratic culture. "[A]cademic discussion, in the classroom, the seminar, or the department or faculty meeting is governed on the whole by the same kind of procedural rules that govern parliamentary procedure – though they do not usually have to be so highly

---

[248] Ibid., p. 195.
[249] Ibid., p. 190.

formalized.... The basic spirit of tentativeness, therefore, as contrasted with 'commitment,' must be granted unusual tolerance.... The academic way of dealing with... conflicts is discussion under procedural rules, not 'confrontation.'"[250]

If this was the particular structure and process which the academic system was to preserve lest democracy suffer, what was the role of the sociologist in this scenario?

Sociology, he suggested, was one of the learned professions that had "begun to replace business entrepreneurship as the most strategic sector of modern society."[251] This process, he assured, had "gone farther in the United States than anywhere else." As such an academic profession, sociology had developed impressively, not just quantitatively: "It has been increasingly assuming a new strategic position in the world of intellectual disciplines and the professional groups involved."

Theory of Integration
Integration, A Variable

The entry in the *International Encyclopedia of Social Sciences* on "Integration," by Robert Cooley Angell, listed as an accomplishment of Parsons a type of "normative integration": "According to his theory, such integration is achieved when the focal elements in the cultural system – the society's common values – are institutionalized in structural elements of the social system. This occurs at three levels [categories of persons, collectivities, and roles]."[252] In line with such understanding, Angell pictured Parsons as a theorist of one allegedly unsophisticated type of integration. He went on, "There is evidence... that normative integration of large systems is not supported exclusively by normative integration of their subsystems," – citing as proof Shils and Janowitz's study on the German Wehrmacht.[253]

Such a mechanistic image was not Parsons's own, evidently, as he practiced what Angell could not even see him preaching.

Parsons no longer spoke of normative integration as such. For him, the societal community was "the integrative subsystem of a society as a social system."[254] For him, under the aegis of integration, this made the societal community into "the primary focus of articulation between a system of values and norms, deriving from the cultural system of general action, and the motivational attachments to social collectivities and to the normative system, relating to personality systems in particular."

---

[250] Ibid., pp. 188, 196.
[251] Letter, Parsons to Elaine Vitcha at Western Reserve University, December 6, 1965, giving brief synopses of two presentations which he planned there in the week; Parsons papers, HUG(FP) – 15.4, box 21.
[252] Robert Cooley Angell, "Social Integration," *International Encyclopedia of the Social Sciences*, edited by David Sills, Vol. 7 (New York: Macmillan and Free Press, 1968), p. 382.
[253] Ibid., citing Edward Shils and Morris Janowitz, "Cohesion and Disintegration in the Wehrmacht in World War II," *Public Opinion Quarterly*, vol. 11, 1948, pp. 280–315.
[254] Parsons, "Some Problems of General Theory in Sociology" (originally, 1970), reprinted in *Social Systems and the Evolution of Action Theory*, cit. p. 250. He went on to say there, "Durkheim was undoubtedly the classic theorist of the institutionalization of the normative component." The next quote is from the same page.

The two levels of theory – values related to culture and motivation related to norms – he diagnosed, belonged together when frequently they were separated. A large number of studies existed on only "the motivational side" of community-prone action. "There has, of course, been a great deal of work done on deviant behavior, and on the alienation which underlies phenomena ranging from vague and diffuse discontent to violent protest and militant movements for change; but an adequate basis of generalization seems to be lacking."[255]

Parsons wished to provide the theory which reconciled the culture-society interchange (when analyzing values) with the personality-society interchange (through analyzing "the motivational attachments to social collectivities to the normative system").

In this endeavor, he no longer felt a structural functionalist. The label of structural-functionalism, given his systems theory and widely used even until today, no longer fitted the nature of his theory, he protested: "It has become my increasing conviction that this is not a proper designation. The concept *function* is not correlative with *structure*, but is the master concept of the framework for the relations between any living system and its environment. Functions are performed, or functional requirements met, by a combination of structures *and* processes."[256]

The new epithet for his approach, as he announced at the 62nd Annual Meeting of the American Sociological Association in 1967, was "cybernetic-evolutionary." He delineated his new theory of integration, analyzing large-scale societies such as the United States in a paper presented at the 1967 Annual Conference of the ASA, in a session whose topic was "Macrosociology." This paper united the three elements of his (new) theory of integration when it ended on the confession, as he phrased it in his handwritten notes, "Why I'm no longer a structural-functional theorist."

The first of the three elements was the evolutionary perspective. It reconciled the dynamics of differentiation with the goal of universalistic citizenship, and invoked the possibility of de-differentiation and regression. He jotted down in his notes the following outline:[257]

> Structure –
> Primitive undifferentiatedness ...
>
> Two basic modes of differentiation internally
> Hierarchical – stratification – archaic divine legitimation
> Affinal – associational (.) Basically Durkheimian
> Political – religious stress or combination ...
>
> Modern society, like man has evolved from *one* source (Weber)
> [Cultural system transcends society]
> Basic, new level differentiation of culture, society (unreadable) Christianity ...

---

[255] Ibid., p. 251.
[256] Ibid., p. 236.
[257] Lecture notes, "Macrosociology(.) San Francisco(,) Aug. 27. '65," pp. (1, unpaginated)-M2; Parsons papers, HUG(FP) – 15.20, box 4. The items in square brackets are written on the margin of the text.

> Church (.) Monastic Orders.
> Intermediary [17ᵗʰ century] ...
>
> Basic universalistic institutions [*System* of Modern societies]
> Associational societal community
> working toward citizenship.
>
> Universalistic independent law
> Bureaucracy
> Money and markets
> Secular cultural institutions. ...
>
> Over against more "conservative" old-regimish societies.
> *Relative* distinction
>
> Paradigm of *progressive* change
> vs. all sorts of failures and regressions
> – also creative dedifferentiation

The second element was the particular nature of inclusion, which was *not* assimilation. Under the headlines of "Differentiation," he highlighted equality through citizenship, under that of "Inclusion – extension," pluralism, and that of "Upgrading," progress.[258]

> *Differentiation*
> Household + employing org.
> Government + societal community through citizenship
>
> *Inclusion* – extension
> Inclusion of previous "lower" classes – equality aspect of citizenship.
> Inclusion of "new elements" – religious + ethnic in U.S.
>
> *Upgrading*
> Economic development
> Knowledge + Education
>
> Value generalization – Moral consensus vs. religious Particularism

Third, he tied this new perspective in with the theory of the media, as variable in double focus:[259]

> Role in process of
> a) Generalized media
>   money, power, influence
> b) "Credit" creation –
>   from banking to Charisma

Here, his lecture notes ended on the sentence

> Why I'm no longer a structural-functional theorist

---

[258] Ibid., p. M4 (italics original).
[259] Ibid., p. M5.

In his letter to Amitai Etzioni agreeing to participate in the session on Macrosociology (which Etzioni organized, with Lazarsfeld as another speaker), Parsons acknowledged: "The topic appeals to me very much since it is really right in the center of my current and I should write a paper along somewhat the line of the large scale society as a social system."[260]

The analysis, then, was "cybernetic-evolutionary" as he called the new perspective, tentatively.[261]

He outlined "Macrosociology" as he explained the "large scale society" using his analytical trias – differentiation, inclusion (extension), upgrading. These three were dimensions of social change. Taken together, they constituted integration. Integration, especially as lodged with the societal community, was not only an abstract principle but also a concrete accomplishment.

The gist of the analysis was that his lecture notes, which focused on development from primitive to modern societies, culminated in U.S. society particularly in the 1960s. He drew a line from "17th Century," epitomized as "Intermediary (:) Monarchy – aristocracy(,) Ethnic nationality(,) focalistic economy," to "System of Modern societies." The latter he elucidated as "Basic universalistic institutions. Associational societal communities working toward citizenship" – which, no doubt, invoked the reality of what he saw his own society achieve, in the 1960s.[262]

In "On Building Social System Theory," Parsons came to attribute his interest in integration in the 1960s to his re-reading Durkheim on the occasion of the latter's one hundredth birthday in 1958.[263] In the *International Encyclopedia of the Social Sciences*, he credited Durkheim with taking into account the apories of both utilitarianism and Rousseau's and Locke's idea of commonality of interests before he, Durkheim, had conceptualized social order as a variable. "The most important step that Durkheim took beyond his predecessors, however, was to treat solidarity and with it, presumably, the *conscience collective*, not simply as given, but as variable entities. He made a distinction, therefore, between organic solidarity and mechanical solidarity."[264]

"It seems to have been Durkheim's view, a strongly defensible one," he explained there, "that the more primitive the society and the culture, the less differentiated they are from each other. He extensively analyzed the case of the Australian aborigines on the strength of this theory ... Beyond this, Durkheim established the

---

[260] Letter, Parsons to Etzioni, January 20, 1967; Parsons papers, HUG(FP) – 15.20, box 4.
[261] His lecture notes ended on the sentence, "Why I'm no longer a structural-functionalist theorist" (p. M5), which he might have explained further personally to his audience at the San Francisco ASA meetings. The beginning part of his lecture notes included his referring to "the organic world + biological theory" (p. 1, unpaginated), where he noted "structural-functional vs. Cybernetic-evolutionary" and mentioned "genes as now (unreadable) + culture" as he expressed as his point of departure that even biology – denoting definite progress – had abandoned mechanistic thinking.
[262] Lecture notes, "Macrosociology," p. M3.
[263] See Parsons, "Durkheim's Contribution to the Theory of Integration of Social Systems," in Kurt H. Wolff, ed., *Essay on Sociology and Philosophy by Emile Durkheim et al. with appraisals of his life and thought* (New York: Harper and Row, 1959), pp. 118–153.
[264] Parsons, "Durkheim, Émile," in *International Encyclopedia of the Social Sciences*, Vol. 4 (New York: Free Press, 1968), p. 314.

groundwork for an exceedingly valuable conception of the morphology of social development – the conception of processes of structural differentiation and of attendant new, more general levels of integration"[265] – which Durkheim had achieved, Parsons demonstrated, in three realms, namely in his analysis of religion, value judgments, and, eventually, suicide rates that were an indicator of societal anomie.

A Societal Community Conceptualization of Stratification and Ethnicity

That integrative functions in the large-scale society were bundled in the societal community allowed for envisaging new developments in the process of ongoing social change. The two arenas for triple dynamics in the emergence of the societal community were stratification and ethnicity.

Regarding stratification, "Equality and Inequality in Modern Society" started out with the thought that equality in (civil) rights transcended social-class differences but inequality arose out of taking responsibility in roles defined through office. Parsons then turned to the societal community in "two particularly significant contexts of value specification."[266] These were, "first... the *fiduciary* complex," and second, the generalized media of interchange (above all, he discussed the relative preponderance of influence in the modern, i.e., democratic, society).

With regard to the fiduciary complex, he highlighted that the "modern professions" were of first-rate importance. They signaled inequality not based on power but competence; their typical social organization was not hierarchical but collegial; they indeed epitomized the "educational revolution" which enabled the modern world to literally lower the level of domination while reconciling authority and competence.

> The "educational revolution"... has above all created a new basis of solidarity, cross-cutting the traditional divisions between such spheres as those of "government" and "business." Hence the professional complex, as I am calling it, has the potential not only of a powerful instrumental influence in societal functioning but also as a focus of integrative mechanisms. These can operate above all through a process of balancing the necessary differentiations based on competence and authority, with patterns of equality.[267]

The other dynamic, again in the vein of pluralism which reconciled differentiation and inclusion, had been addressed in the slogan "Integration not same as 'assimilation'" which he had used in his lecture notes for McGill in 1965.[268] "Some Theoretical Considerations on the Nature and Trends of Change of Ethnicity," first written in 1972, came to elaborate on the theme.

In the course of the decade since the Civil Rights movement when legislation had in effect begun, he realized in the first half of the 1970s, the significance of

---

[265] Ibid., pp. 317–318.
[266] "Equality and Inequality," in *Social Systems and the Evolution of Action Theory*, p. 342; the next two quotes are from the same page.
[267] Ibid., p. 344.
[268] See above.

race (now labeled ethnicity) had changed. Parsons now delineated two aspects of ethnicity that had become visible only through the seminal changes since the 1960s.

For one, ethnicity was *pluralist*: Far from being a biological given, race or culture or origin (which could each be called ethnicity) had long become an achieved identity. Most Americans were of multicultural or, indeed, multi-ethnic origin, he realized. At the time, Parsons cited David Schneider, who had maintained for kinship relations in the United States that ethnic origin was far from 'one and only.' More recently, in a similar vein, David Hollinger reminded his audience that Alex Haley, author of *Roots*, had had a father who was Irish.[269] The point was that "the American societal community is no longer in the older sense of its own history and of the classical pattern of the national state an ethnic community.... The most salient point, however, is that it is an ethnically pluralistic community where even the previous vague and informal stratificiation of ethnic subgroups has ceased to have its previous importance."[270]

The other issue in ethnicity was a development which he named "desocialization." It had come to prevail in the wake of "ethnic pluralism in American society": "[E]thnic groups... have been 'desocialized' and transformed into primarily cultural-symbolic groups.... [M]embers of such groups may crystallize their solidarities, for example, about political interests, but... there is an element of voluntary selectivity."[271]

In other words, ethnicity became a "privatized" characteristic of the person – usually one chosen from a range of different ethnic/cultural/origin categories attainable. Ethnicity thereby lost its previous role of criteria for discrimination or exclusion from educational, occupational, or other market chances.

These two intensely modern achievements, Parsons knew, were precarious when they signaled highest-degree democracy yet. The new modernity in the societal community of the United States reached approximate levels, but was by no means definitive yet. Nevertheless, these American ventures held out prospects for the future which were encouraging for Europe, Africa, and the world in general. "There are... powerful incentives toward commitment to ethnically pluralistic national societal communities in a sense which involves at least some resemblances to the problem of the evolution of a type of community like the recently emerged America."[272]

Democracy, he explained, meant integration through the triple dynamic of differentiation – inclusion – upgrading. However, evolution was no one-way street, and developmental vicissitudes made integration a *variable*, not a static given. On this note, he warned against the many self-declared revolutionary movements in the world of the 1960s when all sorts of seemingly progressive doctrines raised their

---

[269] See David Schneider, *American Kindship: A Cultural Account* (Englewood Cliffs, N.J.: Prentice Hall, 1968) and also David A. Hollinger, *Postethnic America* (New York: Basic Books, 1995).

[270] Parsons, "Some Theoretical Considerations on the Nature and Trends of Change of Ethnicity" (originally published, 1975), reprinted in *Social Systems and the Evolution of Action Theory*, p. 389.

[271] Ibid., p. 391.

[272] Ibid., p. 403–404.

heads to claim rights and undermine traditions. These, he felt, could all the same be "the obverse of the desocialization of ethnic solidarity and identification."[273] For instance, Protestant Fundamentalist groups could incite a dangerously antimodern revival of faith, or "the militant right-wing Jewish group led by Rabbi Kahane should not be left out of the picture." Their doctrinaire stances, invoking "intensification of 'groupism,'" spelled a danger of "anomic social disorganization and alienation" in times of rapid social change, he warned.

It is obvious that in the guise of discussing stratification and ethnicity in their newly developing, highly promising forms of pluralist egalitarianism, Parsons resumed his lifelong topic of democracy versus antidemocratic crisis. He concentrated on democracy now, focusing in great detail on the "large scale society as a social system," predominantly for him the present-day America of the 1960s.

But he never forgot that the danger of reversal of integration, namely regression, was perpetually given. "I have found it useful to refer to this ... as 'de-differentiation,'" he remarked in the essay on change of ethnicity. "Its nature and significance should be seen against the background of the very powerful incidence, in recent developments of social structure, of universalistic standards of mobility and of the development of relatively enhanced freedoms, which, however, can easily turn over in anomic directions."[274]

Two Episodes of Anomie in American Postwar History

An unfinished book is being preserved in the Harvard University Archives. Its working title was *The American Societal Community* (it contains ten partly incomplete chapters). The introductory chapter of *The American Societal Community* wished to familiarize the reader with the idea of societal community using two "cases" from recent American history. They were the Watergate scandal ("The Crisis of Executive Leadership") and, epitomized by the events in 1968–1969 at Columbia and Harvard Universities, the "student revolt" ("The Crisis in Higher Education").

Contrary to their usual image signaling destabilization, both "'keynote' cases" epitomized "that American society has considerable integrative capacity, for both might easily have escalated into much more severe social conflicts than they did."[275] Of course, the book was written in the mid-1970s, and its judgment on the two "cases" took place not during but after the events, when the turmoil had subsided and a conclusion could be drawn. The conclusion was that some mechanisms were visible in the societal community as they preserved integration and helped reverse disintegrative tendencies.

In the Nixon "case," he recollected, the buildup was during Nixon's first term in office of President when a small clique was entrusted with power, and the wider public and party were disregarded. The 1972 election campaign made it obvious

---

[273] Ibid., p. 393; the next three quotes are from the same page.
[274] Ibid., pp. 393–394.
[275] "The American Societal Community. Introduction," p. 5; Parsons papers, HUG(FP) – 42.45.1, box 1.

that legitimate institutions were disowned when the president relied on a group of partly criminal persons (an organization named CREEP) rather than the Republican Party Committee, to secure re-election. The Watergate break-in was not brought to court until the election. When it was, however, an avalanche of reactions against the deviance of the president and his group set in, which gripped the nation. One level on which the Nixon group was vulnerable and failed to remain undetected was, Parsons clarified, hinged on legality related to morality.

> [D]uring the second Nixon administration, the storms began to gather and finally broke in full force. This not only made clear, especially as revealed by the Senate committee of investigation chaired by Senator Ervin of North Carolina, that with connivance and/or direction in or very close to the White House, a complicated series of definitely illegal acts had been carried out. There is, then, an important connection between legality and morality, and the opposition raised readily passed from the one to the other.[276]

The other level concerned loyalty. "The second field in which this deviant enterprise was vulnerable in the longer run concerned the problem of loyalty, with its close connections to political support.... It is of course significant that towards the end of the road, notably under the pressure of the investigative operations of the House Judiciary Committee, even loyal Republican Party supporters began to desert the Nixon group."[277]

Although a pluralistic system tended toward considerable leeway for a deviant group in government positions, when the crisis escalated, two fields within the social community were main arenas for the public's reaction, Parsons analyzed. One was the press, in the guise of two major newspapers entering into some kind of competition in "ferreting out facts about the Watergate story," and, "then the electronic media, notably CBS, soon joined in the chase."[278] The other sphere was the legal system. To be sure, it was part of government and nevertheless initially sanctioned the cover-up reactions: The attorney general and vice attorney general resigned after Nixon had sacked the Special Council appointed by the Judiciary Committee of the House of Representatives, and eventually the Supreme Court held unlawful the president's actions (which forced him to turn over the acrimonious tapes), Parsons explained:

> It seems to us highly significant that the mobilization of counteraction to the Nixon deviant faction came to focus at the level of the legitimation of political action on the part of office holders. This reaction would have been far less likely, and if some of it had occurred, far less effective, if it had not been backed by a genuine movement of public opinion activated by the press and the broadcast networks.... More than any other agencies, two Congressional committees brought the pressure to a point which, for the President, proved to be unbearable.[279]

In the universities "case," two developments had come together since the 1950s. These were, on the one hand, a remarkable increase of the number of students in

[276] Ibid., p. 17.
[277] Ibid., pp. 17–18.
[278] Ibid., p. 19.
[279] Ibid., pp. 21–22.

higher education which exacerbated competition at colleges and universities, and, on the other hand, decrease of the social prestige of the academic or professional in society. In the wake of the "educational revolution," Parsons understood, parts of the population were incorporated into the system of higher learning who were not familiar with the frustrations in the pursuit of knowledge "for its own sake." At the same time, the importance of research, and scientific knowledge in general, had risen dramatically. These tensions built up without most academics – Parsons explicitly mentioned himself – expecting trouble:

> It was a typical "revolution of rising expectations." Perhaps the most important factor bearing on the affected students... was the competitive situation in which they were placed, and about which they complained vociferously.... The revolt was against "the system," not alleged unfairness in administration of it.... More popularly, the symbols of complaint were, in addition to competition, particularly impersonality and "dehumanization." Put a little differently, "the system" tended to put a heavy stress on rationality. It was hence understandable that it should be reacted to in the name of something like "expressiveness."[280]

Eventually, in mid-1971, when none of the grievances had been definitively remedied, the turmoil nevertheless subsided, Parsons observed. It was, however, true that the universities, by and large, had made only some concessions when they were careful sometimes even to withdraw measures that were "too seriously damaging to the main institutional pattern":[281]

> Within this framework the social aspect of the problem seems to have been "handled" – with rather minimal concerted planning – by processes analogous to psychotherapy. With a few exceptions, such as the police actions which were so bitterly resented..., the tendency of university administrations and trustees and faculties, has been on the whole one of permissiveness and support.... [B]y and large the standard of professional competence as manifested in research performance has continued to prevail.[282]

The two "cases" illustrating the fabric of "American Societal Community" showed that a range of mechanisms for preservation of integration in the societal community existed. He suggested that they sufficed to deal with even the different types of crises. In the Nixon "case," the crisis had affected the moral substrate of the American polity, and the legal system (including the respective sphere of government) and the press in conjunction with the public had proved a bulwark against disintegration in the longer run. In the academic system "case," the crisis had been one of "growth" in inclusion and extension of cognitive rationality, and the reintegrative process involved the university and also the wider society in that the values of cognitive rationality were eventually reestablished, if they had lost their salience at all.

From this vantage point, Parsons concluded, there was no reason whatsoever to see evidence in American society of a "'fascistoid trend' "[283] witnessed in "the

---

[280] Ibid., pp. 26–27.
[281] Ibid., p. 30.
[282] Ibid., pp. 30–31.
[283] Ibid., p. 31; the next two quotes are from the same page.

whole 'Nixon phenomenon,'" nor one, which was being discussed at the time, "in this respect being linked to McCarthyism, to the status of the 'military-industrial complex' and the like." Likewise, since those who lamented most against the student revolt were the political right, who campaigned openly against intellectuals, the solution to the university crisis spelled reassurance. In all, Parsons felt, there was reason to believe that the American societal community was strong enough to preserve integration, or develop re-integrative tendencies in "cases" of crisis.

"The Integrative Process"

Under the subtitle of "The Integrative Process," in "Full Citizenship for the Negro American?" Parsons raised the question how behavior could be social when it was not coerced and constituted a genuinely voluntary motivational side in the societal community (under the proviso of equality of opportunity and civil rights). This, to be sure, invoked his criticism of elementary forms of social behavior which were apparently utilitarian. He emphasized reciprocity instead.

In his reply to James Coleman who had commented on "On the Concept of Influence," Parsons juxtaposed two notions of action: "[T]he basic conceptual scheme with which I have been working attempts consistently to think in terms of reciprocal interaction and not of a one-way schema of one actor 'having an effect on' others."[284] The latter he found not only in Coleman but also Homans. He criticized both for their assuming in social behavior a baseline of hedonism.

Such one-way conceptual approaches, he clarified, presupposed that social organization could be traced to actors or actors' actions as elementary units, and that larger entities presumptively were composed of these elementary units – presuppositions which Parsons had castigated already in the 1930s. Since then, his rejection of "methodological individualism" had lost nothing of its acumen.

One corrollary of such "methodological individualism," for which he now charged Coleman, was surreptitious return to utilitarianism – with its unavoidable implications of denial of integration and/or acceptance of coercion in social relations. Coleman, he charged, could conceptualize influence – in Parsons's view a variable medium of interaction – only as a one-sided phenomenon, "'the major weapon of interest groups.'"[285] Along those lines, Coleman could not comprehend the cybernetic nature of action analysis, as he, Parsons, developed it in "On the Concept of Influence." He stated, "Coleman imputes to me the view or implication that 'all rewards are monetary, and all punishments are power.' I certainly said no such thing and very much challenge that I implied it."[286]

In other words, approaches of the 1960s that claimed to analyze the basic structure, even elements, of empirical societies were on the wrong track. Using a conceptual scheme made plausible through nothing but the use of examples when they professed empirical realism, Parsons chided, they could not prove their own

---

[284] Parsons, "Rejoinder to Bauer and Coleman," *Public Opinion Quarterly*, vol. 27, 1963, p. 87.
[285] Ibid., p. 88.
[286] Ibid., p. 89.

underlying theoretical assumptions. These assumptions took for granted that a presumptively presupposition-less description of the social world (often mistaken for explanation) was possible. But, as Parsons insisted on making clear, these approaches were far from free from presuppositions when they had their own – frequently unnoticed – images of man and society. These images envisaged a "mind your own business" type of modern man, reminding the thoughtful sociologist of the doctrines of Sumner and Spencer. These approaches could not serve as viable alternatives to Parsons's system theory.

His lifelong criticism of positivism never relented. Seemingly objective reseachers or theorists who failed to understand their own perspectivism could never gain his approval. Weber, who had been conscious of the problem that a methodological position would necessarily be taken in any sociological analysis, Parsons knew, had solved the problem in his own way: He had proposed the methodologically specious ideal type. Weber had thereby introduced a conceptual tool that helped understand and thus explain whatever given phenomenon.

Parsons, first in *Structure*, had refrained from following Weber in this one respect. In his own methodological perspective, he had endorsed the warning of "fallacy of misplaced concreteness" issued by, above all, Alfred N. Whitehead, suitably amended by the philosophy of science of Lawrence Henderson, and (to a certain extent) that of John Dewey.

Parsons's position in the 1930s and 1940s had been: A model of the social was even in concepts, not merely their use. Weber, for one, had stated, "Action is social in so far as, by virtue of the subjective meaning attached to it by the acting individual (or individuals), it takes account of the behavior of others and is thereby oriented in its course."[287] Weber had distinguished between three types of action orientation vis-à-vis others, by virtue of objective meaning, namely rational, traditional, and affectual. Parsons had adopted Weber's pledge for rational action, fused with Durkheim's concept of anomie, in a two-pronged idea of the structure of social action.

Parsons wholeheartedly subscribed to Weber's tenet that the reciprocity relationship between two actors in their mutual orientation to each other accomplishing meaning was the elementary unit. No sociology could go beyond or below it, so to speak.

As a true follower of Weber's methodological caveats, in the opening chapter of *The Social System*, Parsons ostentatiously backed the Weberian conceptual approach. He made it a frame of reference for the analysis he undertook (i.e., the "action frame of reference" was the perspective under which the social system was to be analyzed). On this background stood his stance of the 1960s, firmly. The developments of European science from the early utilitarianism of, as major figures, Thomas Hobbes and David Ricardo, through Malthusianism and eventually Marxism as representatives of "economic utilitarianism," as one stream of history

---

[287] Max Weber, *The Theory of Social and Economic Organization*, edited with an introduction by Talcott Parsons (New York: Free Press, 1964; originally translated by A. M. Henderson and Talcott Parsons, New York: Oxford University Press, 1947), p. 88.

of thought, and from the idealism of Kant and Hegel through to late nineteenth-century German philosophy culminating in *Kulturwissenschaften*, as the other major stream of thought, he recapitulated in 1964, were antecedents to the seminal achievements of Weber. In "Unity and Diversity in the Modern Intellectual Disciplines: The Role of the Social Sciences," an expanded version of the paper which he presented at the workshop connected with the German *Soziologentag* in Heidelberg celebrating Weber's one-hundredth anniversary, he pictured these two lines of thought against which Weber's sociology stood out authoritatively.

Utilitarianism had been developed in economics and biology, he recounted, "[i]t seems best to call the movement 'utilitarian' in a sense close to Halévy's term, 'philosophical radicalism,' applying to early nineteenth century. From it grew, first and perhaps with the most solid grounding, the main outline of the science of economics."[288] The other tradition, idealism, he noted, had introduced the notion of *Geist* and thereby allowed for the development of *Wissenschaft* (he used the German word).[289]

Only Weber (and concomitantly Durkheim), he emphasized, had transcended the dichotomy between the natural and the culture sciences, between "the atomistic and holistic trends."[290] Weber (and Durkheim) had reconciled the utilitarian and the idealist-historicist traditions, making understood the genuinely independent third direction of science, namely social science. When he aimed to understand economic processes, being himself trained as a lawyer, as Parsons explained, Weber had found in economic phenomena that they were not solely "material." Rather, "materialistic" forces were accompanied by spiritual ones in the "definition of the situation": "The crucial point is that Weber's analysis, the core of which is the Protestant Ethic thesis, bridged the theoretical gap between 'want' in the economic-psychological sense and 'cultural patterns' in the idealistic senses."[291]

From this vantage point, emphasizing the seminal achievement of Weber, Parsons came to reconcile cultural patterns of meaning and the personality of the individual. On the basis of taken-for-granted freedom of choice for the individual in society, he could explain "The Integrative Process" as one involving motivation when it involved values. ("The basic question is why, having freedom of choice, people in fact opt for one, not some other, personal goal and means of attaining it."):[292]

> To put it simply and radically, Weber's solution was that, once cultural patterns of meaning have been internalized in the personality of an individual, they define the situation for the structuring of motives. Therefore questions of how action (including the acceptance of the goals toward which it is oriented) makes sense

---

[288] Parsons, "Unity and Diversity in the Modern Intellectual Disciplines: The Role of the Social Science," *Daedalus*, vol. 94, 1965, pp. 39–65, cit. p. 44. In the article, not only did he cite a recent re-edition of Hobbes's *Leviathan*, but he also referred to Halévy's *The Growth of Philosophical Radicalism*, republished in 1960.
[289] Ibid., p. 48.
[290] Ibid., p. 49.
[291] Ibid., p. 57.
[292] Ibid., p. 53.

must be answered by reference to the meaning-system defining the situation of action. Weber then postulated, not given wants, but given cultural definitions of the situation (the human condition) which make commitment to the satisfaction of certain classes of wants intelligible.[293]

He complemented this praise for Weber's methodological perspectivism, based as it was on the ubiquity of meaning systems as the subject matter of humanistic-cultural study, with a reference to Durkheim. Durkheim, he added, had realized what Weber had nearly missed out on. Weber had presumed the tendency toward rationality in historical evolution all-pervasive, but Durkheim had known all along that it could be halted or negated by anomie: "The basic theme of internalization of the normative patterns defining situations had, as noted, been partially worked out by Weber. It was considerably further analyzed by Durkheim in his studies of suicide and education – his famous concept of *anomie*."[294]

This concept, to be sure, linked personality, culture, and the social order: "[A]*nomie* was a name for the failure of this relation to become stabilized in the relation of a normative system to the personality of the individual. In this basic respect Durkheim converged impressively with Freud and the American social psychologists . . . , particularly George Herbert Mead."

As he reread Durkheim during the "late" oeuvre, as he described in "On Building Social System Theory," Parsons realized how much Durkheim had emphasized the imperatives of social integration. For Durkheim, the crisis of the modern world had resulted from the difficulties in modern society to counteract overly expansive division of labor. He was impressed, Parsons reported in this "Personal History," by the fact that confirmed his own conceptual achievement in the 1960s, that Durkheim had conceptualized social entities – among them *conscience collective* – as *variables*.

Parsons postulated a bipolar social structure between integration and anomie throughout his life. He now realized how both were variables. He had, in *Structure*, welded Durkheim's and Weber's work into the dichotomy between anomie (signaling "War of All Against All") and integrated social order. In *The Social System*, he had analyzed integration on the background of societies stalling it such as National Socialism, which was a deviant type of system. In the 1950s, he had conceived of value orientation in terms of variables ("Pattern Variables"), for typification of social relations as well as entire societies. He had also introduced the action-process scheme consisting of four stages which were system functions (A-G-I-L) when the reverse order of process stages mirrored socialization and social-control processes (L-I-G-A), a particularly interesting variant of the idea of variables.

In the 1960s, he created the tableau of interaction media, which evidently were variables. He crowned his analytical scheme by the idea of societal community. Inasmuch as it represented a centripetal force that counteracted centrifugal tendencies of differentiation, could it itself be seen as some kind of variable phenomenon?

---

[293] Ibid., p. 57.
[294] Ibid., p. 61; the next quote is from the same page.

Could it really? The evidence which he procured pointed in two distinct directions.

Societies where he first used the concept of societal community compared the ancient societies of Egypt, Mesopotamia, and Greece. He used the term of societal community for the Greek *polis* despite the fact that categories of members such as slaves or women were excluded from the unity that constituted equality among its members. Likewise, he spoke of the societal community established through the Constitution of the United States of America despite the fact that Blacks were being excluded from a broad range of constitutional rights as late as the 1960s. In a similar vein, he spoke of the nation in general as a societal community, despite the fact that nations, nearly everywhere in the world, frequently distinguished between parts of the population that were privileged and others discriminated against.

When he analyzed the social change spurred by the Kennedy administration, at last establishing the jurisdictional basis for equal rights for all citizens, he hailed the advent of societal community in the United States. At last, all citizens were being offered citizenship, he clarified. This could mean that he tended to think that until the early 1960s no societal community existed yet. The question was: Did a societal community exist before incorporation into mainstream American society of Blacks who had been a part of the population since at least the eighteenth century?

The two conceptions appear in his oeuvre side by side, I find. It seems that the former conceptualization makes societal community a category but not a variable, whereas the latter does make it one.

To recapitulate the evidence inasmuch as Parsons himself contributed to solving the problem: The societal community, in Parsons's conception of society, signaled integration. Integration, in turn, throughout his oeuvre, signaled democracy, as contrasted with dictatorship (ranging from totalitarianism to traditionalism). Integration (parallel to differentiation) meant modernization, as contrasted with either regression or underdevelopment. Inasmuch as the societal community epitomized democracy, it was a variable as it signaled the presence of integrative forces that varied between democratic and dictatorial régimes. "The Integrative Process," in his "Full Citizenship for the Negro American?" addressed societal community through actors' reciprocal orientations. The idea was that Blacks as well as Whites (or others, for that matter) became the more important as individuals, the more democratic a society was. The outcome was humanism, even in a confusing social reality. He declared in his essay on the nature and trends of change of ethnicity, "The more complex and pluralistic a society becomes... the more dependent its functioning comes to be on freedom of unit decision and on generalized mechanisms which facilitate and guide those decisions."[295]

On this note, what mattered were action orientations that were reciprocal as opposed to utilitarian. In his criticism against Homans which was a sequel to his credo, stated in 1935, that the actor was an "active, creative, evaluative creature,"[296] he endorsed pluralism which suggested individuality. Together with Winston

---

[295] "Equality and Inequality," p. 355.
[296] See the opening paragraph of "The Place of Ultimate Values in Sociological Theory," *International Journal of Ethics*, vol. 45, 1935, p. 282.

White, in the early 1960s, when he undertook to criticize David Riesman's *Lonely Crowd*, he raised the same point. He insisted that choice was a boon rather than a burden in modern social life.[297] He opposed Riesman's cultural pessimism that deplored the disappearance in the modern world of the type of self-sufficient "inner-directed" individual; Parsons held against Riesman that freedom of choice prevailed in modern America, signifying progress over the less accommodating culture of the nineteenth century.

The "Integrative Process" denoting societal community in modern America, therefore, had a backdrop of pluralism and produced a climate of diversity. However, whatever constituted "The Integrative Process," emotional ties were part of it, producing identifications. Identity in the social community, certainly, required identification. With regard to how the societal community spurred integration of Blacks, Parsons gave "precedence to the category of *affect* because of its *inter*personal integrative significance... and at the same time its 'access' to the more primordial motivational components, notably the erotic at the organic level."[298]

He realized that psychological forces were behind the social ties that commanded or facilitated the integrative process (constituting the societal community). He came to understand that identification and internalization, two personality correlates of social bonds, spurred the experience to belong and to be related:

> This means two primary things. The first is what we call *identification* in the sense of motivational "acceptance" – at levels of "deep" motivational "commitment" – of membership in collective systems, most notably the society itself, which essentially is what we mean by solidarity, when seen from the point of view of function for the collective system, and, secondly, internalization of some kind of priority system which structures the manifold of membership expectations for the individual – and somewhat differently for collective units.[299]

Both psychological processes, identification and internalization, to be sure, had first been discovered by Freud. (He had analyzed identification in respect of, as one societal phenomenon, crowd formation.)[300] Parsons had re-analyzed Freud in the 1950s when he adapted psychoanalytic notions to the exigencies of understanding socialization and the relationship between individual and society in general.[301]

---

[297] For the appreciation of the pivotal role of choice, cf. Parsons and Winston White, "The Link Between Character and Social Structure," in Seymour M. Lipset and Leo Lowenthal, eds., *Culture and Social Character: The Work of David Riesman Reviewed* (New York: Free Press, 1961), pp. 89–135.

[298] "Equality and Inequality," p. 355.

[299] Ibid., p. 356.

[300] See, for instance, Sigmund Freud, *Massenpsychologie und Ichanalyse* (Vienna: Internationaler Psychoanalytischer Verlag, 1921), translated: *Crowd Psychology and Group Analysis* (London: Hogarth Press, 1925). Freud, in this essay, had analyzed ego-transcending identification processes as they prevailed in mass organizations such as the Army or Church. The superego could exist as truncated version of an idealizing psychological agent securing conformity, he ventured; but it could also become the locale of identification that benefited both person and society. Internalization, in this view, could occur as an individualizing process. Parsons followed Freud only partially, when he adopted the notions of identification and internalization as harbingers of social community in individual actors.

[301] His *Personality and Social Structure* (New York: Free Press, 1964) was a collection of some of these essays, mostly written in the 1950s.

His notion of identification differed from that of Freud – and became the focus of a critical review in the 1961 volume, *The Social Theories of Talcott Parsons*.[302] He now merged identification and internalization into personality correlates of the social world. Thus he found the link between the individual who acted voluntarily in the service of others in the differentiated society and the society that allowed for disinterestedness in the action orientation of its members. The latter functioned through a societal community. In it, actors realized themselves in and through institutions, inasmuch as they could and would accept these as their own.

Summary

Parsons's "late" theory of the 1960s has not yet received its due appreciation in many circles. This chapter reconstructs the two theoretical models he proposed in the course of the decade (venturing into the 1970s). He aimed to understand modern democracy in its most developed form, envisaging that the United States underwent a historical breakthrough of structural social change equivalent to revolution.

The first model centered around the four interaction (generalized symbolization) media. The model explained variation between dictatorship and democracy, in two different respects. For one, democracy allowed for expansion of media participation such that every citizen could have an income, vote, and so on. But dictatorship (or its potential predecessor movements such as, for instance, McCarthyism) tended to confine access to media possession to a few, analogous to a "gold-standard" deflationary economy. Furthermore, the four media formed a hierarchy of cybernetic control. This hierarchy would superimpose political power over money, influence over political power – denoting loss of level of cybernetic control in cases of societal regression (such as occurred, for instance, in McCarthyism). Eventually, he used the generalized media theory to revisit the problem of stratification, clarifying the dialectics between equality and inequality in an egalitarian achievement society.

The second model centered around the dynamics of differentiation and dedifferentiation. It saw the core of social organization in societal community. The latter concept, first developed in an evolutionary explanatory context, became the nucleus of a new theory of citizenship, grounded in Marshall's triple focus. He explained that differentiation, inclusion, and upgrading formed a flexible schema for analysis in "Macrosociology." He used issues denoting "nation, ethnicity, race" as well as religion to elucidate how his theory fitted the events of the 1960s. The culmination was that identification engendered voluntary commitment, which in turn produced loyalty – the latter a noncoercive force of allegiance in a nonhierarchical community. He reconceptualized stratification as it invoked professional responsibility for fiduciary services, but also ethnicity in the wake of "desocialization" that engendered 'new' achievement (choice) categories.

In defense of democracy, Parsons opened up a novel perspective on some of sociology's most intractable problems. Not only could he reconcile stratification and ethnicity with equal rights in a democracy. But he could also prove that a

---

[302] Urie Bronfenbrenner, "Parsons's Theory of Identification," in Max Black, ed., *The Social Theories of Talcott Parsons*, pp. 191–213.

tendency toward progress loomed large in the troubled times of his day: A cybernetic hierarchy inhered in the evolving of pluralism through differentiation. In this way, a sociological rationale became visible in the credo of the American nation, *E Pluribus Unum*.

Postscript: The Three Arenas for Change and Crisis

As a postscript, I should like to link Parsons's sociological analysis with his personal engagement in three realms of contemporary events. They were, originally, for him one agenda for social change: Civil rights, the "New Left" (university unrest), and American involvement in the war in Vietnam as an apparently anti-Communist campaign in the era of Cold War.

His introductory essay to *The Negro American*, entitled "Why 'Freedom Now,' Not Yesterday?" remarked on the problem of race, signaling unacceptable lack of equal opportunity: It was the root cause also for two other arenas for crisis in the middle 1960s. The civil rights movement, he began,

> has certainly been a direct agent for bringing about certain specific changes, such as the desegregation of schools, lunch counters, and bus stations. However, its more important function has been symbolic; it has dramatized the moral issue in terms which make concrete continuance of the old practices morally intolerable.... (T)he movement has been... contributi(ng) to the current moral "reenergizing" of American society.... Here we have an important example of the generalization of movements for social change, ... such as civil rights.... [T]he so-called "New Left"... [is] centering on youth and the salience of civil rights... as... embodied first in CORE and then more radically in SNCC[.] [T]he most important point here is that the same groups, by and large, have now taken up protest in two other important contexts, namely, higher education (most conspicuously at Berkeley) and the American involvement in the war in Viet-Nam.[303]

The three arenas, from his theoretical point of view, belonged to one and the same movement. The issue was expansion of citizenship in American society but the fervor of the civil-rights struggle carried over to the forum of university unrest (as in the "New Left") and the anti-Vietnam activism. "The racial issue had been generating pressure for a considerable time," he analyzed the spurs in the 1960s when the Kennedy era unleashed a remarkable willingness to risk more democracy. "The first major break came with the 1954 Supreme Court decision; then occurred Little Rock with its dramatization not only of Southern resistance, but of the federal government's passivity. With the election of a liberal Democratic administration in 1960, expectations began to mount rapidly."[304]

He was convinced that the three movements had the same origin, and indeed only separated out possibly after Kennedy's assassination. How did he personally relate to the three movements which, as he judged, came from the same source, an agenda for citizenship?

---

[303] Parsons, "Introduction: Why 'Freedom Now,' Not Yesterday?" in *The Negro American*, ed. Parsons and Kenneth B. Clark (Boston: Houghton Mifflin, 1966), pp. xxv–xxvii. The acronym CORE stood for *Congress of Racial Equality*, and SNCC *Student Nonviolent Coordinating Committee*.
[304] Ibid., p. xxiii.

Civil Rights

Sociology had tackled problems of race and racism since the 1930s. Under the Works Program Administration (WPA) during the New Deal, the American Youth Commission had conducted groundbreaking studies on the life situation and chances of young Blacks, many of which were reprinted now in the 1960s: W. Lloyd Warner and his collaborators had investigated the effect of color on personality development among the ghetto population of Chicago's South Side,[305] and John Dollard had published two excellent research reports, namely *Caste and Class in a Southern Town*[306] and, with Allison Davis, *Children of Bondage*,[307] to name but two out of many. Their main analytical point had been that Blacks were in effect locked into a system of caste, with little chance to blend into mainstream society.[308] Gunnar Myrdal was entrusted with the study published as *An American Dilemma*, which pictured impoverishment and disenfranchisement.[309] In 1962, Philip M. Hauser concluded from the census data of the year 1960 that the national median income for the nonwhite population was only 54 percent of that of whites – with a median of 43.4 percent in the South and 70 percent in the rest of the country.[310]

In 1963, when Seymour Martin Lipset summed up prospects and pitfalls of democratization in "new nations" in Africa or Asia, he had this to say about the United States:

> American egalitarianism is, of course, for white men only. The treatment of the Negro makes a mockery of this value now as it has in the past. During the early nineteenth century, when European leftists and liberals were pointing to the United States as a nation which demonstrated the viability of equality and democracy, America was also the land of slavery. The trauma of slavery is deeply rooted in the American psyche. The contradiction between the American value system and the way in which the Negro has been treated has, if anything, forced many Americans to think even more harshly of the Negro than they might if they lived in a more explicitly ascriptive culture. There is no justification in an egalitarian society to repress a group such as the Negro unless they are defined as a congenitally inferior race.[311]

---

[305] W. Lloyd Warner, Buford H. Junker, and Walter A. Adams, *Color and Human Nature: Negro Personality Development in a Northern City* (New York: Harper and Row, 1941), reprinted by the same publisher in 1969 on behalf of the American Council of Education, Washington, D.C.

[306] John Dollard, *Caste and Class in a Southern Town* (New Haven, Conn.: Yale University Press, 1937; reprinted Garden City, N.Y.: Doubleday, 1957).

[307] Allison Davis and John Dollard, *Children of Bondage: The Personality Development of Negro Youth in the Urban South* (New York: Harper and Row, 1940).

[308] See, for instance, W. Lloyd Warner, "American Caste and Class," *American Journal of Sociology*, vol. 42, 1936, pp. 234–237.

[309] Gunnar Myrdal, *An American Dilemma: The Negro Problem and the Modern Democracy* (New York: Harper and Brothers, 1944; republished by Harper and Row, 1962); see also Obie Clayton, ed., *An American Dilemma Revisited* (New York: Russell Sage Foundation, 1996).

[310] Philip M. Hauser, "More From the Census of 1960," *Scientific American*, vol. 207, 1962 (Oct.), p. 37. Parsons was present at the conference in 1960 when the original data were being discussed.

[311] Seymour Martin Lipset, *The First New Nation: The United States in Historical and Comparative Perspective* (New York: Basic Books, 1963), p. 330.

Postscript: Three Arenas for Change and Crisis 263

This was the background against which was set the initiative suggested by Parsons and masterminded by the American Academy of Arts and Sciences to convene a conference on Poverty and Race, under the joint leadership of Parsons and social psychologist Kenneth B. Clark, Director of the Social Dynamics Research Institute and Professor of Psychology at the City College of the City University of New York, who was Black.[312] Parsons's own contribution was "Full Citizenship for the Negro American? A Sociological Problem."[313]

His theme was that Blacks were second-class citizens, and how this could be effectively changed: "In this succession, the Negro stands at the 'end of the line.' His is the most serious (hence in some respects, the most plausible) basis of exclusion, namely, his inherent inferiority. The relatively satisfactory – it will not in our time ever be fully so – resolution of the problem of Negro inclusion will certainly be one of the greatest achievements of American society."[314] He interpreted Marshall's notion of citizenship as a pledge, not descriptive yet of American society. "It is a very long step from the constitutional and legal enactment of these rights to their effective implementation, and this process is still going on in many sectors of American society":[315] "[D]iscrimination may be abolished or minimized across a whole range of opportunities, particularly in employment. But even absence of discrimination is 'empty' if remediable handicaps continue to prevail."[316]

He concretized that what mattered were not slogans but clearcut normative procedural rules: "In Little Rock, Governor Faubus was defying not only the 'decent opinion of mankind,' but also a specific order of a duly constituted federal court."[317]

"The American Record on Inclusion Processes," nevertheless, was good despite the fact that its blotch of shame was indeed America's Black citizens, and despite various episodes of regression:

> The problem of absorption of Jews and Catholics resulted in a genuine crisis of the American community; it was probably one of the major foci of social tension and disturbance in this century. The Immigration Act of 1924, with its system of quotas based on the composition of the population by national origin in 1890, was one striking symptom of this strain.... The substantial disturbances and anxieties over the presence of such large "foreign" groups in our midst and their relations to the fears of "un-American" influence and of Communism – from the Palmer Raids and the Sacco-Vanzetti case of the 1920's to the McCarthy episode on the early 1950's – must be understood in this context.[318]

---

[312] The eventual publication of the proceedings, which first appeared as two issues of *Daedalus*, contained contributions, among many others, by Philip Hauser on "Demographic Factors in the Integration of the Negro," Daniel Patrick Moynihan who shortly before had resigned from his post of Assistant Secretary of Labor in the Johnson administration on "Employment, Income, and the Ordeal of the Negro Family" (an account which Parsons found notably instructive), and Thomas Pettigrew on "Complexity and Change in American Racial Patterns: A Social Psychological View."
[313] Parsons, "Full Citizenship for the Negro American? A Sociological Problem," in Parsons and Clark, eds., *The Negro American*, pp. 709–754.
[314] Ibid., p. 748.
[315] Ibid., p. 717.
[316] Ibid., p. 718.
[317] Ibid., p. 720.
[318] Ibid., p. 725.

However, "The Negro Case" could not just mean inclusion of another ethnic group in the ongoing process of "pluralization": "In this context skin color symbolizes inferiority in the sense that it is purported to justify placing Negroes as a category so radically at the bottom of the scale as to be only equivocally inside the system at all."[319]

The almost intractable problem was that race and poverty formed an unholy alliance. Low income and low education overwhelmingly reinforced each other, and both were most typical for poor urban neighborhoods with high crime rates, high rates of school dropouts, and poor levels of ability to make the most of whatever resources there were: "Behind this... is... the 'slum.' The central concern is the vicious circle of the factors of *actual* inferior capacity for valued performance, in which poverty, bad health, low educational standards, family disorganization, delinquency, and other anti-social phenomena are mutually reinforcing. This is where the structure of the urban community itself becomes a salient problem focus."[320]

The goal was clear when reaching it was yet a struggle, "The United States now seems to be well into a third phase. Perhaps its most important feature has been the shift in concern from welfare in the narrower sense to health, education, and the nature of the urban community, focusing most acutely so far upon housing."[321]

From this he proceeded to analyze the inclusion process, culminating in his astute observation, "The presence of Catholic nuns among the demonstrators in Selma was a new note having a significance scarcely to be overestimated."[322]

"We are in the midst of a process of social change in which these components [of values and norms], and not only the interests, are changing,"[323] was his understanding of the historical importance of the civil-rights movement.[324] To substantiate his interpretation of the historic importance of the changes, Parsons wrote an article for *The Washington Post*.[325]

In December 1968, Harvard's Faculty of Arts and Sciences decided to establish an Afro-American Studies Program. Colored students who were organized in the Association of African and Afro-American Students at Harvard and Radcliffe were to have a say as elected members of the Standing Committee (Afro-American Studies Committee) which, especially through the Afro-American Search Committee, was to decide upon the rules under which the Search Committee would work, and find candidates for the staff positions envisaged. Parsons became chairman of the Search Committee when Henry Rosovsky chaired the Standing Committee. Parsons drafted a number of rules which he thought indispensable for avoiding an

---

[319] Ibid., p. 734.
[320] Ibid., p. 738.
[321] Ibid., p. 737.
[322] Ibid., p. 740. He referred to the five-day march of three thousand people under the leadership of Martin Luther King, Jr., to Selma, Mississippi, to support voting rights of Blacks there, one of the most dramatic events in the Civil Rights movement, in the spring of 1965.
[323] Ibid., p. 742.
[324] Ibid., p. 750.
[325] "The Negro American as Citizen" (draft of an article for the *Washington Post*, written in 1965 but apparently never printed), HUG(FP) – Talcott Parsons – 42.41, box 4.

impression that the Afro-American Studies Program was academically inferior to other parts of the university. He noted, under the headline, "Questions on Search Committee," the items which he felt (and had discussed in the session) would help to make Afro-American Studies equal to other Harvard subjects:

1. Membership on General Administrative Committee?
2. No Student Veto
3. Competence takes precedence over race in qualification. No requirement of all-black staff....
5. If chairman black, must all other staff be?
6. How many slots in what ranks etc. ?
7. No. of committee members [.] 4 faculty 1 white student? Rosovsky's suggestion.[326]

After April 10, 1969, when militant students occupied University Hall and forced faculty and administrators to vacate the building, one complaint was that Harvard did not provide adequately for the need in Afro-American Studies. One subsequent proposal for reorganization of the Afro-American Studies Committee vented feelings of being disregarded by the university, based on the observation that on April 7, 1969, "a meeting for potential concentrators in the field was held.... It has been 'rumored' that a change in the proposal of the Standing Committee has occurred. There has been no official communications with any black students concerning this change. This flagrant disregard for black student opinion has continued. We demand an end to this disregard."[327]

Rosovsky resigned in the aftermath of the events at Harvard, but Parsons did not relent in his efforts to make the Afro-American Program a success. In a meeting on April 16 after the Search Committee had discussed in detail fifteen potential candidates, "considerable discussion" concerned "the status of Standing Committee and of this committee," as the minutes documented. The minutes continued, "Prof. Parsons pointed out that if, in tomorrow's faculty meeting, a motion to dispose of the Standing Comm. passes, this would disband the Search Committee. After this statement, the three students stepped outside to confer. When they returned, Craig Watson said that the Black Students wanted to propose in the faculty meeting that the Search Committee remain even if the Standing Comm. is disbanded."[328] Parsons, evidently, invested admirable energy into the work of the Search Committee, earning the students' (even militant students') respect for it.

Despite the turmoil, he continued his attempts as chairman of the Search Committee to find academically well-established colleagues for Harvard's program. During the next three months, he contacted more than twenty scholars, inviting them to join Harvard's faculty, among them Kenneth Clark, St. Clair Drake, John Hope Franklin, James Gibb, Charles Hamilton, and Franklin Edwards, to name

---

[326] "Questions on Search Committee"; Parsons papers, HUG(FP) – 15.10, box 1 (question 4 in this list was, "Leave of absence in fall," concerning Parsons's own plans at the time).

[327] Four-page typed text, beginning with "We would like to preface our proposal"; Parsons papers, HUG(FP) – 15.10, box 1.

[328] "Minutes of the Afro-American Search Committee, 4/16/69," p. 3; Parsons papers, HUG(FP) – 15.10, box 5.

but a few, in addition to candidates who had done work in related fields, such as Richard Cloward or William Labov. None of his urgent requests were honored, however, when most of those whom he contacted informed him that they felt they did not wish to move away from their present universities.

Parsons resigned on August 5, to take a sabbatical in the fall after he had gone on the half-pay program offered by Harvard for professors over age sixty, on July 1. On this occasion, one of the student members of the Search Committee wrote to the Dean, expressing gratitude and appreciation for Parsons's work there.

To conclude: Corroborating his analysis that civil rights for Blacks were the most urgent agenda for social change in the 1960s, Parsons not only preached that Blacks warranted full citizenship but within Harvard participated with immense involvement in the establishment of an Afro-American Studies Program, the predecessor in 1968–1969 of what was to become the Department of Afro-American Studies. (Indeed, one of the eventually successful candidates originally considered by the Committee was Orlando Patterson, who was to become Professor and Chair of Sociology.)

University Unrest

Throughout the 1950s, the theme of academic freedom had occupied sociology. At Columbia University, the American Academic Freedom Project under the directorship of Robert M. MacIver had yielded major studies investigating the history and condition of American Higher Education.[329] MacIver had addressed in his comprehensive report the dangers of McCarthyism, stating in his introductory chapter, "The mode in which at the present time charges of communist infiltration are being leveled against our leading colleges and universities is a case in point.... Under the guise of patriotism the makers of these charges arouse the primitive emotions that lurk in the hearts of men, the unreason that hates difference and demands conformity, the superstition that shuns the light of truth, the fear that in its blindness confuses enemy and friend."[330]

Another study carried the problem further. Financed through the Fund for the Republic, Lazarsfeld investigated in the spring of 1955 how far the threat of dismissal or denial of promotion based on allegation of lack of loyalty (had) intimidated college professors, to a degree influencing their personality or their style or subject of teaching.[331] Using a long and carefully constructed questionnaire, he

---

[329] After, in 1952, a collection of classic texts had been a forerunner, three studies appeared simultaneously in 1955. They were Richard Hofstadter's *Academic Freedom in the Age of the College* (New York: Columbia University Press, 1955), which dealt with the early history of college education; Hofstadter and Wolfgang Metzger's *The Development of Academic Freedom in the United States* (New York: Columbia University Press, 1955), which stressed the roots of the American university in the principles of academic freedom (as they had been adapted from the famous *Lehrfreiheit* and *Lernfreiheit* of German universities in the early 1900s); and, last but by no means least, Robert MacIver's *Academic Freedom in Our Time* (New York: Columbia University Press, 1955).

[330] MacIver, *Academic Freedom*, pp. 30–31, 32.

[331] Paul F. Lazarsfeld and Wagner Thielens, Jr., with a field report by David Riesman, *The Academic Mind: Social Scientists in a Time of Crisis* (Glencoe, Ill.: The Free Press, 1958).

measured respondents' tendency toward worry and caution, built an index of apprehension on which one-half of the professors had low scores but one-third scored medium, and one-sixth scored high. He found that apprehensive college professors were not less but more activist, which made him discuss "cautious activism." He eventually came to judge the professorial mind as, on principle, highly permissive, that is, inclined toward liberalism endorsing civil liberties and opposing control over political views. However, caution could develop from apprehension which easily became grounded once a so-called event or incident of accusation or censure had occurred. Calling McCarthyism "the difficult years," Lazarsfeld (in 1958) warned that "the effective scope of higher education in America was threatened."[332]

Whereas this research concentrated on professors, other studies investigated the rapidly changing type and mentality of students. One project found a high degree of idealism at the beginning and end of medical school but obvious ennui and pragmatism in the extended middle phase.[333] Another project, originally carried out at Vassar College and supplemented by a reader, *The American College*,[334] analyzed the college as a subculture and being a student as an experience which changed the personality of the student, not only the level of his/her professional knowledge.[335]

After unrest had erupted in Berkeley in 1964, some sociological accounts were partisan, supporting what they saw as just cause of the militant students, while others were more guarded. A collection of journalistic as well as analytical texts supplemented by activists' statements and other first-hand material, entitled *The Berkeley Student Revolt*,[336] invoked Max Weber to make sense of the events:

> If students are defined as socially irresponsible, they are also encouraged to be idealistic. Value-transmitting agencies such as the family, church, and school, tend to present morality in absolute, right or wrong terms. The famed German sociologist Max Weber observed that youth has a tendency to follow "a pure ethic of absolute ends," while mature men tend to espouse an "ethic of responsibility." ... University students, though well educated, have generally not established a sense of close involvement with adult institutions; experience has not hardened them to imperfection.[337]

Opposite positions were taken, in the same volume, by sociologists Nathan Glazer and Philip Selznick, together illustrating the pro and con positions taken

---

[332] Ibid., p. 264.
[333] Howard Becker, Blanche Geer, Everett Hughes and Anselm Strauss, *Boys in White: Student Culture in Medical School* (Chicago: University of Chicago Press, 1961).
[334] Nevitt Sanford, ed., *The American College: A Psychological and Social Interpretation of the Higher Learning* (New York: Wiley, 1962).
[335] David Riesman and Christopher Jencks, "The Viability of the American College," and Christopher Jencks and David Riesman, "Patterns of Residential Education: A Case Study of Harvard," in Sanford, ed., *The American College*, pp. 74–192, and pp. 731–773.
[336] Seymour Martin Lipset and Sheldon S. Wolin, eds., *The Berkeley Student Revolt: Facts and Interpretations* (Garden City, N.Y.: Anchor [Doubleday], 1965).
[337] Seymour Martin Lipset, "Students and Politics," in Lipset, ed., *The Berkeley Student Revolt*, p. 3.

in the conflict. Glazer voiced the opinion that the most unfortunate outcome of the student action was that an irredeemable weakness of the university administration had revealed the fragility of the institution itself. Selznick felt that "much of what the students did was clearly necessary if we were to be made to *really listen*. I think they accomplished that. And considerably more."[338] He condemned policies of "law and order." "Legality is a two-way street. He who insists on obedience to rules should be ready to justify the rules themselves.... I was deeply impressed by the earnestness, dedication, and basic moral enlightenment of most of the student supporters, I encountered."[339] Glazer replied to Selznick, "Unquestionably the knowledge that the students in the FSM were also involved in the larger fight for justice and equality for Negroes made many faculty members hesitant in judging their actions... But no movement in this world is immune from the threat of distortion and corruption, even a movement for the good and the just."[340]

In all, student protest against style or contents of academic teaching remained minor in comparison with politics that opposed the war in Vietnam or demanded changes in admission standards or procedures, with intent to enforce access to universities for hitherto discriminated minorities, predominantly Afro-Americans (as they were now being called). At Columbia University, in the summer of 1968, and at Harvard, in April 1969, a standoff between students and the university administration led to the president's calling the police on campus.

The Public Interest, a journal whose editor was Daniel Bell, published a special issue on the universities, soon to be converted into a book, *Confrontation: The Student Rebellion and the Universities*.[341] Parsons contributed an essay, at last putting into perspective how anomie resulting from student militancy (aggravated by faculty complicity or complacency) held grave dangers for the university as an institution of academic learning in the modern pluralist society.

Students, he understood, were not members of the institution, the collegial body of professors who represented the tradition of research and teaching rooted in standards of excellence of inquiry. The student militants, therefore, intent on equalizing influence for students with faculty, threatened the very heart of the academic endeavor: "Student power cannot supercede faculty power. Without a faculty, and its autonomous core position, a university is nothing."[342]

Obstruction of classes and pressure on faculty to adopt selective political views or teach on topics like Marxism, or even to privilege Blacks regarding judgment of their academic achievement, as demanded by some student militants, inadvertently endangered the academic system itself.

---

[338] Philip Selznick, "Reply to Glazer," in Lipset and Wolin, eds., *The Berkeley Student Revolt*, p. 303.
[339] Ibid., pp. 310–311.
[340] Glazer, "Reply to Selznick," in Lipset and Wolin, eds., p. 315; the acronym of FSM stood for Free Speech Movement – a self-styled name of militant students for their movement urging the university to allow political demonstrations on campus.
[341] Daniel Bell and Irving Kristol, eds., *Confrontation: The Student Rebellion and the Universities* (New York: Basic Books, 1969).
[342] Parsons, "The Academic System: A Sociologist's View," *The Public Interest*, vol. 13, 1968, p. 187.

Parsons objected to student militancy because he felt, contrary to these students' own perception, that their aims were antimodern and their opposition to pluralism revealed their inability to allow for the new agenda for an integrated society. Pluralism needed strengthening, even against an onslaught made in the name of freedom of opinion. He pleaded that institutionalized tolerance combined with excellence be preserved in the American university, firmly lodged there for the last eighty years, lest the current tendency of "absolutizing" selective world views or commitments undermine the democratic fabric itself.

His reasoning used the conceptual framework of the interaction media: He hypothesized that the level of generality of values in the moral community was lowered, that is, more particularistic values – demanding political partisanship instead of freedom of thought – were being promoted:

> [P]olarization of commitment takes the form of "absolutizing" a selective value... The effect is to lower the *level of generality* in the definition of the value pattern to which a commitment is demanded and exclude from the "moral community" those who share the implicit source – e.g., the valuation of basic equality – but who are unwilling to make such an exclusive commitment to *one* – however important – and not to others.... [T]he academic system *as such* cannot be committed to such exclusive positions on the level of its own self-definition without betraying its larger trust as the guardian of the main cultural tradition of our society.[343]

Handwritten notes with the title "Columbia Affair" document in no uncertain terms that Parsons deemed the student movement societally regressive. He charged that it was a revolt against the educational revolution, opposing the mainstay of modernizing civil society. He challenged their argument made against the educational revolution that the promises of the democratic revolution had not been fulfilled yet. He criticized that the parallel between students and the proletariat was true in a way different from what militant students maintained: The proletariat had been created by the Industrial Revolution, rather than being a victim of it; likewise, the student movement was a consequence of the educational revolution, and should not pose as its critic. Lastly, he accused the militant student leaders of feeling cut out from academic leadership, feeling ressentiment which made them debunk academia. He ventured,

> Columbia affair – Regressive in sense of focussing on themes of democratic revolution and as such a revolt against the educational revolution. Assertion prerequisites have not been fulfilled. – Parallel to case of working class v.v. industrial revolution. Generated by latter's success. – Is there a parallel in that industrial revolution created new leadership echelons which educational has also done, raising acute questions of seclusion?[344]

Elsewhere, in another handwritten memo, putting the "educational revolution" into a wider perspective and contrasting the more traditional regimes both of capitalism or socialism with what he tentatively addressed as "postindustrial society,"

---

[343] Ibid., p. 197.
[344] Handwritten notes, starting with "Columbia affair"; Parsons papers, HUG(FP) – 42.45.4, box 5.

he explored the issue in a more general sense. He characterized the type of deviance in "politization." He diagnosed that in the situation of extension of universalistic standards to more categories of citizens and differentiation of academic values to more disciplines, resistance against such changes could mount. Such resistance against modernization had occured in the 1950s through McCarthyism (taking the Korean war as a pretext for an increase of anti-Communist loyalty demands), and in the 1960s the same kind of antimodernism turned against war as such, in the guise of opposition to American involvement in Vietnam:

> *Theoretical* significance of higher education: Capitalism-Socialism vs the "Post-industrial" society. – General problem of *Wertbeziehung*.... – Activistic deviance through "politization". Passive-regressive through withdrawal. – Pressure of universalistic standards and differentiation of academic values: competition + success. – Korea triggered a disturbance on the right: focus McCarthyism. Communism as symbol. – Viet Nam has triggered one on the left, the "New Left", only vaguely pro-anything but violently anti. Probably war as such the primary negative symbol. Anarchistic overtones.[345]

In 1976, when he participated in a symposium in *The American Scholar* which had been triggered by an article by Robert Nisbet, "Knowledge Dethroned," Parsons referred to *The American University* authored with Gerald Platt when he invoked his theory of the media, in its dedifferentiation variant to account for the university unrest of the recent decade.

> Our thesis... is that there had been a long inflationary background behind the exceedingly rapid growth... in academia, especially since the end of the Second World War. We interpreted the student disturbances... as symptoms of a deflationary turn that had followed this rapid growth... We make clear that we... mean inflation... of intellectual or cognitive growth and expansion.... An expansionary-inflationary period... is generally expected to be followed by a reaction that bears the earmarks of deflation and recession.... [W]e think that a very important aspect of the disenchantment that Nisbet speaks of can be characterized as a deflationary reaction to a previous inflationary period with its attendant recessionary characteristic of a diminution of confidence.[346]

On this note, he pleaded not to throw all disciplines into the same lot. The task was not only to see the obvious differences between natural and social sciences, but also that the latter could not be expected to yield the "massive practical benefits that a few of their less cautious proponents and many outsiders have expected."

The latter remark gave him an opportunity to discuss briefly not only the public's allegedly pejorative opinion about contemporary (social) scientific knowledge but also that many in the academic profession today worked extremely hard (referring

---

[345] Handwritten notes, starting with "*Theoretical* significance of higher education"; Parsons papers, HUG(FP) – 42.45.4, box 5. The epithet of " 'Postindustrial' society," no doubt, stood for Parsons's own image of the desirable modern society, beyond both capitalism and socialism – a view which he had cherished since the early 1930s. In the course of time, he had adopted different names that were to capture as best he could his projected image.

[346] Parsons, "Social Science: The Public Disenchantment," *The American Scholar*, Autumn 1976, pp. 580–581; the next two quotes are from the latter page.

to his empirical data material as yet unpublished). "Whatever disenchantment has been characteristic of the general public outside these groups, the profession itself remains substantially committed, and there is evidence that a corresponding level of commitment is being satisfactorily transmitted to students, particularly at graduate levels."

In November 1969, standing by the academic profession worldwide as it was an important resource for societal progress, together with three colleagues who were presidents of a Scientific Association, Parsons sent the following telegram to President Nixon warning against resumption of loyalty checks interfering with international intellectual exchange:

> Acting personally and as individuals, the undersigned respectfully urge that you maintain longstanding practice keeping admission of visiting foreign scholars to United States under full de facto control of State Department as favored by Secretary Rogers. Waivers by Justice Department should continue to be granted routinely. Best interests of United States, including its image abroad, require that international intellectual exchanges be not – repeat not – subject to police veto or climate of intimidation. (Signed) Karl W. Deutsch, President, American Political Science Association; C. Vann Woodward, President, American Historical Association; Wassily Leontief, President-Elect, American Economic Association; Talcott Parsons, President, American Academy of Arts and Sciences.[347]

Vietnam

The third arena in the 1960s was the war in Vietnam. Historical and political analyses have tackled the problem of why and how the United States became entangled, originally aiding a presumably embattled South Vietnamese government and during the Johnson presidency launching a major campaign. Sociological analysis of American commitment in Southeast Asia so far is rare. Neither Parsons nor others published on the topic of that war. Parsons's attitude toward American involvement can be assessed, if indirectly, from evidence preserved in the Harvard Archives. Four occasions may show his concern for the plight of the nation. As a scholar and private citizen he was extremely worried about peace in Vietnam.

In the summer of 1967, sixteen Harvard professors took an initiative (similar to others at other Ivy League universities such as, for instance, Yale). On August 3, 1967, they wrote a letter to President Johnson requesting that their fears be taken seriously by policymakers. They wrote to the president:

> We first wish to express our understanding of the extreme pressures you have been under to prosecute the war on a much greater scale, and our appreciation of the fact that you have resisted these pressures.... It is enough for us to say that as we see it the cost of the war (in all senses) now exceeds any foreseeable gains and that no increase in commitment is likely to improve the situation.... Although as individuals we have opinions as to possible desirable steps, our main purpose is to ask if there is anything we can do, now or in the future, which will make it easier for you to forward the cause of peace in Vietnam?[348]

---

[347] "Telegram Sent to President Richard M. Nixon, The White House, Washington D.C., Sunday, November 30, 1969"; Parsons papers, HUG(FP) – 15.10, box 3.

[348] Letter to the president, dated August 3, 1967, pp. 1–2; Parsons papers HUG(FP) – 15.10, box 3.

The letter was signed by Dean Franklin Ford, Roger Revelle, Edward Purcell, Parsons, and E. Bright Wilson Jr.

Parsons prepared himself for the occasion of the encounter with the president by collecting material that put into perspective what was propaganda on behalf of the Viet Cong alleging American total warfare, and what crimes had indeed been committed against civilians in the local population. His handwritten notes contained the following thoughts:

> Central danger of Viet-nam may be parallel to that leading up to Civil War. Are we attempting a kind of "Reconstruction." Ominous view of Defense Dept.... Extension of *our* community pattern without adequate institutional basis.... Viet Cong can organize *intermediate* types of structure – particularistic solidarities *under* central political control. Generate *national* collectivity – political effectiveness.... Even with military ascendency problem of longer-run integration....
>
> Cost of Viet-nam policy. 1) Strain on internal integration because of distortion of focus from internal problems – Financial yes, but secondary to community integrative costs – esp. Negro- and political aspects (Breakdown of the 1964 Consensus).
> 2) Strain on international relations
>   a) Placing of U.S. in position of spokesman of the "Reaction" against the "revolutionary" movements of development. (cf. Soviet position at Pugwash.) Tragic repetition of British position vv. French Revolution.
>   b) Repercussions on world intellectual (cultural) system. Constant defensive – and of course political.
>
> Importance of the political settlement. Is South Vietnam *really* consolidating as a societal entity?
>
> Two possibly tolerable alternatives.
>   a) Let Ho take over. Certainly heavy cost to U.S. – but somewhat like Algeria for France. Great uncertainties about what would result.
>   b) Some kind of settlement on coalition basis. It is still à la Poland + Czechoslovakia impossible to protect a constitutional regime from totalitarian take-over.
>
> Are there measures which are tolerable short of early peace? E.g.
>   a) No bombing north of 20th parallel,
>   b) Withdrawal of line Southward.[349]

On September 26, a group of fourteen Harvard professors were received by Johnson as well as Robert McNamara, a Harvard man now Secretary of Defense. However, the outcome was disappointing, as voiced clearly by various of the members of the delegation: They felt that their concern had been dismissed as apparently irrelevant to the nation's political establishment. In another letter to the president, signed by Dean Ford, they expressed their thanks for the time given them by the president and other officials in Washington but also repeated their serious concern with peace in Vietnam:

---

[349] Handwritten notes; Parsons papers, HUG(FP) – 15.10, box 3. The reference to Poland and Czechoslovakia related to the totalitarian take over by Nazi Germany, in 1939 at the outset of World War II.

Above all, we hold more strongly than ever to our belief that the solution cannot be strictly, or even primarily, a military one, that the greatest attention and the best thought should be directed toward formulating constructive conditions for a political settlement in Southeast Asia and that, to this end, every effort must be made to elaborate something better and more realistic than the Government's now apparently narrowing range of options.[350]

On February 14, 1968, Parsons as president of the American Academy of Arts and Sciences invited British political scientist Sir Denis Brogan to speak on the war in Vietnam in an internal seminar. Brogan, whose paper was entitled "The Illusion of American Omnipotence – Reconsidered," argued that the United States was in a war with an ally entirely unreliable, a dictatorial régime, in the unfortunate position neither to be able to withdraw nor check on the apparent totalitarianism of the Saigon government.[351] Parsons in his letter of thanks felt in complete agreement with Brogan: "The subject was very timely indeed and you said some much needed things. The note of sympathetic understanding of the American problem was, of course, very welcome but I for one am very glad that it was combined with unequivocal criticism."[352]

On April 7, 1968, the *Washington Post* carried an advertisement signed by over five hundred members of the American Academy of Arts and Sciences, whose president was Parsons, or the American Philosophical Association (among them were, to name but a very few, Hannah Arendt, Kenneth Burke, Wassily Leontief, Lionel Trilling, and Carl F. Voegelin), demanding a peace settlement in Vietnam to contain the immense danger of nuclear war. The text said,

> The undersigned ... deem it their duty as citizens and students of domestic and international affairs to state their conviction that the vital national interest of the United States requires a rapid settlement in Vietnam based on meaningful mutual accommodations with those Vietnamese now opposing politically and militarily the present Saigon regime. Social and political stability cannot be attained without active participation of all significant elements of the Vietnamese people, including the N.L.F., in the Government of South Vietnam.
>
> Continuation of our present course is bound to lead to rapid further deterioration of the economic, political and diplomatic position of the United States, as well as ever greater devastation of a people we are seeking to help. Moreover, it increases day by day the chance of an uncontrollable escalation of a major, but still limited conflict into a world-wide nuclear war.[353]

In April 1968, the American Academy of Arts and Sciences decided to embark on a research project, "A Study of the Vietnam Conflict," for which a study group

---

[350] Letter to the president, dated October 13, 1967, signed by Franklin Ford; Parsons papers, HUG(FP) – 15.10, box 3.

[351] American Academy of Arts and Sciences, The 148th Stated Meeting, February 14th, 1968, "The Illusion of American Omnipotence – Reconsidered," Sir Denis Brogan; Parsons papers, HUG(FP) – 15.25, box 7. Brogan had been an analyst of U.S. policy and mentality already during the 1940s when he published his *The American Character* (New York: Knopf, 1944).

[352] Letter, Parsons to Sir Denis Brogan, February 23, 1968; Parsons papers, HUG(FP) – 15.25, box 7.

[353] "A Statement on U.S. Policy in Vietnam," *The Washington Post*, Sunday, April 7, 1968 (newspaper clipping); Parsons papers, HUG(FP) – 15.25, box 9.

was established and $20,000 funding obtained (assured to Mr. Kistiakowsky) and a steering committee founded. Suggested participants of the latter were, for the Summer Study Group, Dan Ellsberg, Carl Kaysen, Paul Kekskemeti, Henry Kissinger, Thomas Schelling, and Adam Yarmolinsky, among others. (Kissinger, Harvard Professor of Political Science, signaled his willingness to serve in a letter dated April 23). The purpose was strictly within the range of scientific study, to address "the question: Negotiations in Vietnam: What is the range of possible results?"

In good Parsonian fashion, emulating the stance already taken during World War II, the working paper stated for the Vietnam Steering Committee that the aim was to understand the situation before judging it – thereby overcoming being influenced by ideologies rather than information:

> Purpose: To enrich public discussion of the forthcoming negotiations by describing and analyzing the variety of conceivable compromises that lies between the polar positions of Washington and Hanoi. It was agreed that this polarization of views is dangerous and likely to continue until the availability and meaning of the alternatives are made clear. The paper published by this study group would not argue the desirability of this or that alternative but would examine them all.[354]

The 18th Pugwash Symposium, which took place in April 1968, had the working title suggested by Parsons (as president of the American Academy), "Control of Peaceful Uses of Atomic Energy with particular reference to non-proliferation."[355] As Parsons described in a Letter to Francis X. Sutton, president of the Ford Foundation, in September 1968 when he requested a sizable grant to support future Pugwash Conferences, "Pugwash is a particularly valuable channel of communication with Soviet scientists: it is the only series of international scientific meetings which they can regularly attend without special permission for each session; it is regarded by the Soviet Academy as their principal point of general contact with world scientists and thus its delegation is led by the executive vice president of the Soviet Academy, M. D. Millionshcheikov."[356] He went on to point out, when immediately upon his taking office as president of the American Academy in 1967 he had developed as he did the American input into the Pugwash Conferences into a major axis of East-West scientific exchange, that major devastating effects of the Vietnam war had been contained so far.

> Indeed it is likely that such important projects as the Joint Study Group on Arms Control would have been completely abandoned by the Soviets because of the Vietnamese conflict without this avenue of communication. Anyone who has dealt with the Soviets, and the East Europeans, knows how important such continuing contacts can be for promoting informal, off-the-record exchanges and for organizing serious, substantive discussions in study groups and symposia.

---

[354] American Academy of Arts and Sciences, "Vietnam Steering Committee. Brief Outline for Summer Study Group," May 3rd, 1968; Parsons papers, HUG(FP) – 15.25, box 9.

[355] 18th Pugwash Conference: The conference, which took place yearly (since 1950), had its name from a small town in Newfoundland, the original venue of the meetings of (mainly, so far) nuclear physicists from both sides of the Iron Curtain.

[356] Letter, Parsons to Francis X. Sutton, The Ford Foundation, September 9, 1969, p. 2; Parsons papers, HUG(FP) – 15.25, box 7; the next quote is from the same source.

Two years later, when Nixon had accelerated the war in Southeast Asia and American-Soviet scientific relations had suffered from virtual breakdown, he renewed the exchange on the occasion of the 7th World Congress of Sociology in Varna, Bulgaria, and wrote subsequently to the new vice president of the Soviet Academy of Sciences, Rumiantsev:

> I am writing you mainly in my capacity as chairman of the American Sociological Association Committee on relations with Soviet Sociologists. . . . I think we would propose a conference . . . in this country. Alternatively, of course, . . . we would be glad to consider a proposal to hold a meeting in the Soviet Union . . . I think Professor Osipov's suggestion of something having to do with problems of peace could be fruitful. . . . As I suggested in our discussion at Varna perhaps it would be possible to use some of the outstanding findings which our respective sociologists have worked out about their own societies, in order to discuss some problems bearing of differences and similarities on the relation of the two societies to each other at the level of international politics.[357]

---

[357] Letter, Parsons to Academician Aleksei M. Rumiantsev, Vice President Presidium, Soviet Academy of Sciences, Leninskii prospekt, 14, Moscow, dated October 9, 1970, p. 2; Parsons papers, HUG(FP) – 15.25, box 7.

Epilogue:
A Life of Scholarship for Democracy

Parsons in many a secondary account has been deemed a prototypical Harvard professor – aloof from everyday life in supposedly single-minded concern for abstract theory, disengaged from political life as either apolitical or a dreamer à la *Brave New World*. This book has revealed both accusations as mere fabrications. Appreciation of Parsons as due him has been the rationale for this intellectual portrait.

This intellectual biography, using material from published and unpublished sources, has meant to reverse judgments that stigmatize this greatest of American sociologists. The sum total of Parsons's intellectual biography is how devoted he was to the defense of democracy, both in his scholarship and personal politics.

At the end of this book, let me cite the abundant evidence once more, documenting how in his scholarship and politics, he defended democracy in its most advanced stage yet, American society.

In his earliest work, culminating in *The Structure of Social Action*, Parsons's aim was to understand how sociology, through the works of four European writers, had contributed to analyzing the empirical salience of democracy – in a world troubled by political conflict with Nazi totalitarianism, then urgent menace to the contemporary world. He analyzed anomie that signaled insecurity as much as coercion, as the obverse of integration that fostered reciprocity and involved rationality in the essential Weberian sense. The work opposed Spencerian positivism when its message was voluntarism refined by methodology. It embraced the Weberian principle of *"Wertfreiheit"* when its baseline was to establish sociology beyond surreptitious advocacy of authoritarianism.

In the so-called "middle phase" of his oeuvre, analyzing National Socialism, and American society as its obverse in the first part of the 1940s, he had democracy on his mind. During the period between 1938 and 1945, as Chapter 2 argues, he unhesitatingly identified democracy, epitome of humane society, with the United States. Though his Memorandum prepared for the Council for Democracy cautioned his readers against relenting on social reform, he left no doubts open that U.S. society was a model to be emulated by lesser developed societies of

Europe and elsewhere – even those democratic. Germany under re-education in the wake of World War II benefited greatly from Parsons's understanding American democracy: His idea of controlled institutional change helped remodel the German nation on the economic-occupational system.

Subsequent to World War II, Parsons's main focus was now how the social system worked – a social system that not only had proved victorious over the less stable German Nazi type régime, but harbored mechanisms of integration that deserved close scrutiny. His world classic, *The Social System*, undertook to analyze what made the democratic (integrated) type organization both more resilient and more humane, compared with the totalitarian (anomic) type. In a succession of three book-length manuscripts, whose first two were to-be-left-unpublished memoranda for the Social Science Research Council and whose third version became a bestseller worldwide, he explored the nature of democracy as epitomized in the United States. In the years of immediate success of *The Social System*, however, he became targeted as an alleged ex-Communist under McCarthyism.

In the 1960s, his scholarship took a leap, due to changes in U.S. society which he perceived happening. He started more or less afresh. He proposed two analytical models to capture the dynamics of the modernization of modern democracy which took place in the United States in the 1960s. One model analyzed societal functions through a fourfold scheme of interaction media, yielding an array of differentiating subsystems that organized interfaces between the various media in institutional settings. He now conceptualized anomie as media representation analogous to a "gold-standard"-like fundamentalism. Democratization was the obverse. Truly democratic society and polity functioned beyond the "zero-sum" idea of media distribution. It proliferated reciprocal relationships defined in terms of financial standing, empowerment, influence, and cultural (moral) commitments.

The other analytical model focused on social integration. Parsons envisaged triple dynamics of differentiation, pluralism, and upgrading. This suggested his "evolutionist-cybernetic" conception of society. He sketched an anomie-type image of society in dedifferentiation as one important process of regression. His main interest was with signs and symptoms of progress in society that helped understand the crises of the 1960s as a step toward a better life for more people. The gist of modernity was equal legal rights, with the legal system (along with medicine as well as higher learning) an apex of societal community. He analyzed stratification but also ethnicity as focal arenas for serendipitous change in American social structure.

But he would also involve himself personally in the politics of the day, from the 1930s to the 1960s. His personal politics were an arena where he would actively practice what in his sociological theory he aptly preached. He was not the tell-tale academic who would hide away in the ivory tower of Harvard. From his student days onward, he voiced his political opinions in print or through actively taking part in whatever political group matched his interests. No doubt, he most openly was an activist during the period of Nazi rule in World War II. But he also involved himself in antinuclear armament concerns, and promoted civil rights for Blacks, among many other causes.

In the 1930s, for one, by filing an affidavit for some of the exiles from Germany and Austria, he assured their entrance to the United States, where they eventually found university employment. Two about whom this is known were political scientist Eric Voegelin and sociologist Hans Speier.

In the first half of the 1940s, Parsons campaigned for the Committee for Militant Aid for Britain, joined the Harvard Group of American Defense (where he chaired the Committee of National Morale), became a member of the Council for Democracy (where he belonged to the Committee of Correspondence), participated in the Conference of Science, Philosophy and Religion in Their Relation with the Democratic Way of Life, to name but a few. He volunteered to shoulder a hefty teaching load at the Harvard School of Overseas Administration, instructing future military government personnel for Europe and the Far East. He even secured a position as consultant in the government agency responsible for immediate postwar planning for Germany under military government – in the interest of "controlled institutional change" there.

In the 1950s, one side of his politics was that he opposed Soviet Russia. This nation had revealed itself an imperialist totalitarian power in the wake of victory in World War II. Parsons came to judge Russia an industrial society, albeit backward in modernization. After 1945, he opposed nuclear armament, joining the Association of Atomic Scientists as well as the American Association for the Advancement of Science, for the purpose of making his voice as a sociologist heard. Long before McCarthyism hit Harvard University, he revived the Harvard AAUP chapter in the years 1946–1948, an anticipatory bulwark that could spare his university, if only for a limited period of time, the ordeal of being investigated. He devoted the best part of four years to the AAUP's effort at rehabilitation of those unjustly treated by the Committee on Un-American Activities.

In the 1960s, he involved himself – if indirectly – in the Kennedy era's political zest. During the Johnson administration, he participated in the interuniversity initiative to influence policy related to the Vietnam war, among other activities. As president of the American Academy of Arts and Sciences, he initiated highly successful contacts with the Soviet Academy of Sciences – indeed, one of the successes of the 1968 18th Pugwash Conference, to the chagrin of the Kremlin, was that Soviet physicist Andrew Sacharov published a proposal for world peace in the *New York Times*. He also made the American Academy sponsor conferences in different parts of the country, discussing University Goals and Governance – a viable alley to the moderate reforms of higher learning in the 1970s, which coped with the increase in numbers of students and opened up sensibly equal opportunities in higher education for minorities.

As for his party politics, Parsons never was a Republican. During the 1930s and beyond, he ardently supported Roosevelt. He was a staunch believer in Kennedy, whom he recognized as a potential leader when he became Senator of Massachusetts in 1952. After Kennedy's assassination, he very nearly despaired of national politics in the face of American support for the undemocratic régime in Saigon. Eventually, in 1972, he campaigned for Nixon's unsuccessful challenger,

Senator Eugene McCarthy. He analyzed Watergate as a threat to American democracy, equally dangerous as McCarthyism. Nixon, for Parsons, was as close to a fascist as an American president could get.

His activism, even after retirement, never relented. In 1975, he joined a number of colleagues sending a telegram to Yugoslav dictator Jossip Tito, protesting unlawful incarceration of a dissident in that country.

What was so special about his defense of democracy? My judgment is that, for him, democracy was never merely a type of political organization. Rather, democracy was a structure of social action, denoting voluntary commitment of citizens to their community. He saw democracy mirrored in the *attitudes* of the actors. That is, for him, discrimination mattered for sociological analysis as much as disenfranchisement. The realm of "definition of the situation" contained two opposite provinces of meaning. They were prejudice, on the one end, and reciprocity patterns representing democratic orientations, on the other.

In this vein, for him, society was more than mere social structures organized in systems. Society incorporated what people felt and thought about each other – their patterns of action mirrored their world views in the economic as well as many other fields of life. That interaction media – generalized symbolic media for interactive reciprocity – eventually entered his sociological imagination was no accidental discovery. He had followed Weber all his life. Now he emulated Weber when he relied on the latter's definition of social action as characterized by *Sinnkonstruktion*, construction of mutually understandable meaning. Parsons's notion of democracy involved the actor as a rational *and* emotional (and also judgmental) being when he followed Weber's classic conception of social action.

What made him sustain the effort? He was convinced that sociology had a mission to fulfill – namely, understanding the very nature of the dynamics of society. In his correspondence with Louis Wirth in 1939, defending his methodological realism in *The Structure of Social Action*, he distinguished three social science disciplines with realms of their own – economics, political science, and sociology. Wirth, interestingly, had doubted that a separate realm carved out for sociology existed; but Parsons made it clear that autonomy suited this emergent science, due to the structure of the social world, couched in the tradition of Weber.

Toward the end of World War II, he pursued his sociological expertise through seeking employment with the government agency responsible for planning for postwar Germany. As a consultant, he convinced the experts in the agency that Morgenthau's "plan," though logically sound and politically correct, was impractable. His sociological advice in this unlikely arena proved right subsequently.

Never in his lifetime could he sit back and regard the job done securing sociology's mission. At the end of an article co-authored with Bernard Barber in 1948, Parsons expressed his usual attitude of optimism: "As a professional group we are committed to a venture which is in many ways without precedent and which, indeed, the pessimists freely predict to be impossible. It is a challenge worthy of the finest traditions of the American spirit of enterprise."

Epilogue

Twenty years later, in 1968, he would say about sociology – still a venture for the self-styled, "incurable theorist" when sociology's reputation as a science had become all but firmly established,

> [W]e must ask which is more important: (1) fundamentalist regression to more primitive levels, (2) schismatic revolutionary outcomes, which will tend to maximize conflicts, or (3) institutionalization of new levels of generality in value systems? Sociology has a grave responsibility to clarify the understanding of what is going on and of what lies at stake in the balance among these possibilities.

Bibliography

Parsons – Important Writings

Parsons, Talcott. "Society." *Encyclopedia of the Social Sciences* (1934), reprinted *in Early Essays*. Chicago: University of Chicago Press, 1991, pp. 109–121.

"The Place of Ultimate Values in Sociological Theory," *International Journal of Ethics* 45 (1935): 282–316.

The Structure of Social Action. A Study in Social Theory with Special Reference to a Group of Recent European Writers. New York: MacGraw Hill, 1937. 2d ed., 1949, reprinted in paperback New York: Free Press, 1968.

"Max Weber and the Contemporary Political Crisis." *The Review of Politics* 4 (1942): 61–76, and 155–172; reprinted in *Talcott Parsons on National Socialism*, edited and with an introduction by Uta Gerhardt. New York: Aldine de Gruyter, 1993, pp. 159–187.

"The Problem of Controlled Institutional Change: An Essay in Applied Social Science." *Psychiatry* 8 (1945): 79–101; reprinted in *Talcott Parsons on National Socialism*, pp. 291–324.

Parsons, Talcott, and Bernard Barber. "Sociology, 1941–1946," *American Journal of Sociology* 53 (1948): 245–257.

Parsons, Talcott. *The Social System*. New York: Free Press, 1951.

Parsons, Talcott, and Edward A. Shils. *Toward a General Theory of Action*. Cambridge, Mass.: Harvard University Press, 1951.

Parsons, Talcott, Robert F. Bales, and Edward A. Shils, eds., *Working Papers in the Theory of Action*. New York: Free Press, 1953.

Parsons, Talcott, and Neil J. Smelser. *Economy and Society*. New York: Free Press, 1956.

Parsons, Talcott. "Durkheim's Contribution to the Theory of Integration of Social Systems," in Kurt H. Wolff, ed., *Essay on Sociology and Philosophy by Emile Durkheim et al. with Appraisals of His Life and Thought*. New York: Harper and Row, 1959, pp. 118–153.

Parsons, Talcott. "The Principal Structures of Community: A Sociological View," in Carl J. Friedrich, ed., *Community*. New York: The Liberal Arts Press, 1959, pp. 152–153.

Structure and Process in Modern Societies. New York: Free Press of Glencoe, 1960.

"Polarization of the World and International Order," in Quincy William Wright, E. Evan, Morton Deutsch, eds., *Preventing World War III: Some Proposals*. New York: Simon and Schuster, 1962, pp. 310–331.

"On the Concept of Influence." *The Public Opinion Quarterly* 27 (1963): 37–62; reprinted in *Politics and Social Structure*, pp. 405–430 (Postscript, pp. 431–438).

"On the Concept of Political Power." *Proceedings of the American Philosophical Society* 107 (1963), pp. 232–262; reprinted in *Politics and Social Structure*, pp. 352–404.

"Some Reflections on the Place of Force in Social Process," in Harry Eckstein, ed., *Internal War: Basic Problems and Approaches*. New York: Free Press of Glencoe 1964, pp. 33–70.

Personality and Social Structure. New York: Free Press, 1964.

Parsons, Talcott, and Kenneth B. Clark, eds., *The Negro American*. Boston: Houghton Mifflin, 1966.

Parsons, Talcott. *Societies: Evolutionary and Comparative Perspectives*. Indianapolis: Bobbs Merrill, 1966.

"The Nature of American Pluralism," in Theodore R. Sizer, ed., *Religion and Public Education*. Boston: Houghton Mifflin, 1967.

"On the Concept of Value-Commitments," *Sociological Inquiry* 38 (1968): 135–160; reprinted in *Politics and Social Structure*, pp. 439–472.

Politics and Social Structure. New York: Free Press, 1969.

"On the Building of Social System Theory: A Personal History." *Daedalus* 99 (1970): 828–830; reprinted in *Social Systems and the Evolution of Action Theory*, pp. 22–76.

The System of Modern Societies. Indianapolis: Bobbs Merrill, 1971.

Lidz, Victor, and Talcott Parsons, eds., *Readings on Premodern Societies*. Englewood Cliffs, N.J.: Prentice-Hall, 1972.

Parsons, Talcott. "Some Theoretical Considerations on the Nature and Trends of Change of Ethnicity," in Nathan Glazer and Daniel P. Moynihan, eds., *Ethnicity: Theory and Experience*. Cambridge: Harvard University Press, 1975; reprinted in *Social Systems and the Evolution of Action Theory*, pp. 381–404.

Parsons, Talcott. *Social Systems and the Evolution of Action Theory*. New York: Free Press, 1977.

Secondary Literature on Parsons

Alexander, Jeffrey C. *The Modern Reconstruction of Classical Thought: Talcott Parsons*. Berkeley: University of California Press, 1983.

Twenty Lectures: Sociological Theory Since 1945. New York: Columbia University Press, 1987.

Barber, Bernard. "Theory and Fact in the Work of Talcott Parsons," in Samuel Klausner and Victor Lidz, eds., *The Nationalization of the Social Sciences*. Philadelphia: University of Pennsylvania Press, 1986, pp. 123–130.

Black, Max. *The Social Theories of Talcott Parsons*. London/Amsterdam: Feffer & Simons, 1976; originally, 1961.

Bourricaud, Francois. *The Sociology of Talcott Parsons*. Translated by Arthur Goldhammer. Chicago: University of Chicago Press, 1981.

Brick, Howard. *The Reformist Dimension of Talcott Parsons' Early Social Theory*. University of Oregon, Eugene, 1991, mimeo.

Gerhardt, Uta. "Models of Illness and the Theory of Society: Talcott Parsons' Contribution to the Early History of Medical Sociology." *International Sociology* 5 (1990): 337–355.

"Talcott Parsons and the Transformation of German Society from Totalitarianism to Democracy at the End of World War II." *European Sociological Review* 12 (1996): 303–325.

"Die soziologische Erklärung des nationalsozialistischen Antisemitismus in den USA während des Zweiten Weltkrieges." *Jahrbuch für Antisemitismusforschung* 1 (1991): 253–273.

"Normative Integration moderner Gesellschaften als Problem der soziologischen Theorie Talcott Parsons'," *Soziale Systeme* 4 (1998): 281–314.
"Parsons' Analysis of Societal Community," in A. Javier Treviño, ed., *Talcott Parsons Today*. Lanham, Md.: Rowman & Littlefield 2001, pp. 177–222.
Hamilton, Peter. *Talcott Parsons* (London: Tavistock, 1983).
Holton, Robert J., and Bryan S. Turner. *Talcott Parsons on Economy and Society*. London: Routledge and Kegan Paul, 1986.
Johnston, Barry V. "Contemporary Crisis and the Social Relations Department at Harvard: A Case Study in Hegemony and Disintegration." *American Sociologist* 29 (1998): 26–42.
Mitchell, William C. *Sociological Analysis and Politics: The Theories of Talcott Parsons*. Englewood Cliffs, N.J.: Prentice Hall, 1967.
Sociologie et Sociétés, vol. XXI, no. 1, Avril 1989 (entire issue): *Talcott Parsons: Relectures* (realisé par Francois Beland et Guy Rocher).
The American Sociologist, vol. 31, no. 2, Summer 2000 (entire issue on Parsons's connections with Japan, compiled by Lawrence Nichols and William Buxton).
Wearne, Bruce C. *The Theory and Scholarship of Talcott Parsons to 1951*. New York: Cambridge University Press, 1989.

Other Literature

Alexander, Jeffrey C., ed., *Real Civil Societies: Dilemmas of Institutionalization*. London: Sage 1998.
Allport, Gordon W. *The Nature of Prejudice*. Reading, Mass.: Addison Wesley, 1954.
Allport, Gordon W., and Helene R. Veltfort. "Social Psychology and the Civilian War Effort." *Journal of Social Psychology*, S.P.S.S.I. Bulletin 18 (1943): 165–233.
Barber, Bernard. *The Logic and Limits of Trust*. New Brunswick, N.J.: Rutgers University Press, 1983.
   Social Stratification: A Comparative Analysis of Structure and Process. New York: Harcourt, Brace, 1957.
Bell, Daniel, and Irving Kristol, eds., *Confrontation: The Student Rebellion and the Universities*. New York: Basic Books, 1969.
   ed., *The Radical Right: The New American Right Expanded and Updated*. Garden City, N.Y.: Doubleday, 1963.
Bellah, Robert. *Beyond Belief. Essays on Religion in a Post-Traditionalist World*. Berkeley: University of California Press, 1970.
Bendix, Reinhard, and Seymour Martin Lipset, eds., *Class, Status, and Power: Social Stratification in Comparative Perspective*. New York: Free Press, 1953; 2d ed., 1966.
Berelson, Bernard B., Paul F. Lazarsfeld, and William N. McPhee. *Voting: A Study of Opinion Formation in a Presidential Campaign*. Chicago: University of Chicago Press, 1954.
Brickner, Richard. *Report on a Conference on Germany After the War* (no date, no location) November 1944, New York; published: "Germany After the War – Round Table 1945." *American Journal of Orthopsychiatry* 11 (1945): 381–441.
Coser, Lewis. *The Functions of Social Conflict*. New York: The Free Press of Glencoe, 1956.
Cox, Archibald, Mard DeWolfe Howe, and J. R. Wiggins, eds., *Civil Rights, the Constitution, and the Courts*. Cambridge, Mass.: Harvard University Press, 1967.
Cox, Harvey. *The Secular City: Secularization and Urbanization in Theological Perspective*. London: SCM Press, 1967.

Craig, Gordon A. *The Germans*. New York: Meridian, 1991.
Davis, Allison, Burleigh B. Gardner, and Mary R. Gardner. *Deep South: A Social Anthropological Study of Caste and Class.*, 10. impr. Chicago: University of Chicago Press, 1965.
Deutsch, Karl. *The Nerves of Government: Models of Political Communication and Control.* London: Free Press of Glencoe, 1963.
Eckstein, Harry, ed., *Internal War: Basic Problems and Approaches*. New York: Free Press of Glencoe, 1964.
Eisenstadt, S. N. *The Political System of Empires*. London: Free Press of Glencoe/Collier Macmillan, 1963.
Ely, Richard T. *Social Aspects of Christianity*. New York: Thomas Y. Crowell, 1889.
Farago, Ladislas, L. F. Gittler, Gordon W. Allport, John G. Beebe-Center, Edwin G. Boring, Floyd L. Ruch, Stanley S. Stevens, Kimball Young. *German Psychological Warfare. Survey and Bibliography*. New York: Putnam and Sons, 1942.
Friedrich, Carl J. *Constitutional Government and Politics. Nature and Development.* New York: Harper and Brothers, 1937; revised edition, *Constitutional Government and Democracy*. Boston: Little, Brown, 1941.
"Military Government as a Step Toward Self-Rule." *Public Opinion Quarterly* 7 (1943): 527–541.
Friedrich, Carl J. and Associates. *American Experiences in Military Government in World War II*. New York: Rinehart & Co., 1948.
Fromm, Erich. *Escape from Freedom*. New York: Rinehart, Winston and Holt, 1941.
Gerhardt, Uta. "A Hidden Agenda for Recovery: The Psychiatric Conceptualization of Re-education for Germany in the United States during World War II." *German History* 14 (1996): 297–324.
"Charismatische Herrschaft und Massenmord. Eine soziologische These zum Thema der freiwilligen Verbrechen an Juden." *Geschichte und Gesellschaft* 24 (1998): 503–538.
Ideas About Illness: An Intellectual and Political History of Medical Sociology. New York: New York University Press, 1990.
Gerth, Hans. "The Nazi Party: Its Leadership and Composition." *American Journal of Sociology* 45 (1940): 517–541.
Hartshorne, Edward Y., Jr. *The German Universities and National Socialism*. London: Allen and Unwin, 1937.
Herberg, Will. *Protestant-Catholic-Jew: An Essay in American Religious Sociology.* Garden City, N.Y.: Doubleday, 1955.
Heyl, Barbara. "The 'Harvard Pareto Circle.'" *Journal of the History of Behavioral Sciences* 4 (1968): 316–334.
Hilberg, Raul. *The Destruction of the European Jews*. Chicago: Quadrangle, 1961.
Hofstadter, Richard, and Wolfgang Metzger. *The Development of Academic Freedom in the United States*. New York: Columbia University Press, 1955.
The Age of Reform: From Bryan to F.D.R. New York: Vintage, 1956.
Social Darwinism in American Thought. New York: Braziller, 1959; revised edition (originally, 1944).
Hogan, Michael J. *Marshall Plan: America, Britain, and the Reconstruction of Western Europe, 1947–1952*. Cambridge: Cambridge University Press, 1987.
Horkheimer, Max, Erich Fromm, and Herbert Marcuse et al. *Studien über Autorität und Familie*. Paris: Félix Alcan, 1936.
Inkeles, Alex, and David H. Smith. *Becoming Modern: Individual Changes in Six Developing Countries*. Cambridge, Mass.: Harvard University Press, 1974.
Janowitz, Morris. "German Reactions to Nazi Atrocities." *American Sociological Review* 52 (1946): 141–146.

Kaiser, Charles. *1968 in America: Music, Politics, Chaos, Counterculture, and the Shaping of a Generation*. New York: Grove Press, 1988.
Keynes, John Maynard. *The End of Laissez-faire*. London: L. & V. Woolf, 1926; New York: New Republic, 1926.
  General Theory of Employment, Interest, and Money. London: Macmillan, 1936; New York: Harcourt, Brace, 1936.
Kindleberger, Charles P. *Marshall Plan Days*. Boulder, Colo. Westview, 1989.
Klausner, Samuel, and Victor Lidz, eds., *The Nationalization of the Social Sciences*. Philadelphia: University of Pennsylvania Press, 1986.
Kloppenburg, James T. *Uncertain Victory: Social Progressivism in European and American Thought, 1870–1920*. New York: Oxford University Press, 1986.
Kluckhohn, Clyde. "Group Tensions: Analysis of a Case History," in Lyman Bryson, Louis Finckelstein, and Robert MacIver, eds., *Approaches to National Unity*. New York: Harper and Brothers, 1945, pp. 222–231; reprinted in Kluckhohn, Clyde, *Culture and Behavior*. New York: Free Press, 1962, pp. 301–322.
Kogon, Eugen. *Der SS-Staat. Das System der deutschen Konzentrationslager*. Frankfurt: Fischer 1946. Translated: *The Theory and Practice of Hell. The German Concentration Camps and the System Behind Them*. New York: Farrar, Straus & Co., 1950.
Kuntz, Paul G., ed., *The Concept of Order*. Seattle and London: Grinnell College, University of Washington Press, 1968.
Lasswell, Harold. "The Psychology of Hitlerism." *The Political Quarterly* 4 (1933): 373–384.
  World Politics and Personal Insecurity. New York: Macmillan 1934.
Lazarsfeld, Paul F., Bernard Berelson, and Hazel Gaudet. *The People's Choice: How the Voter Makes Up His Mind in a Presidential Campaign*. New York: Columbia University Press, 1948.
Lazarsfeld, Paul F., and Wagner Thielens, Jr., with David Riesman. *The Academic Mind: Social Scientists in a Time of Crisis*. Glencoe, Ill.: The Free Press, 1958.
Leighton, Alexander. *The Governing of Men*. New York: Octagon Books, 1945.
Lewin, Kurt. "The Special Case of Germany." *Public Opinion Quarterly* 7 (1943): 555–566.
Lipset, Seymour M. *The First New Nation: The United States in Historical and Comparative Perspective*. New York: Basic Books, 1963.
Lipset, Seymour Martin, and Neil Smelser. *Sociology: The Progress of a Decade. A Collection*. Englewood Cliffs, N.J.: Prentice Hall, 1961.
Lipset, Seymour Martin, and Theodore Wolin, eds., *The Berkeley Student Revolt: Facts and Interpretations*. Garden City, N.Y.: Anchor (Doubleday), 1965.
MacIver, Robert. *Academic Freedom in Our Time*. New York: Columbia University Press, 1955.
Maier, Norman. *Frustration: The Study of Behavior Without a Goal*. Ann Arbor: University of Michigan Press, 1949.
Marshall, Thomas H. *Class, Citizenship, and Social Development*. With an introduction by Seymour Martin Lipset. Garden City, N.Y.: Doubleday, 1964.
Mayhew, Leon. "Ascription in Modern Societies." *Sociological Inquiry* 38 (1968): 105–120.
Mead, George Herbert. *Mind, Self, and Society: From the Standpoint of a Social Behaviorist*. Chicago: University of Chicago Press, 1934.
Mead, Margaret, and Rhoda Metraux, eds., *The Study of Culture at a Distance*. Chicago: University of Chicago Press, 1953.
Medical Care For the American People, Final Report of the Committee on the Cost of Medical Care. Chicago: University of Chicago Press, 1932.
Meiklejohn, Alexander. *The Liberal College*. Boston: Marshall Jones, 1920.

Merton, Robert K. "Social Structure and Anomie." *American Sociological Review* 3 (1938): 672–682.
Mass Persuasion, with assistance of Marjorie Fiske and Alberta Curtis. New York: Harper and Brothers, 1946.
Social Theory and Social Structure. 2d ed., New York: Free Press, 1957.
Morgenthau, Henry. *Germany Is Our Problem*. New York: Harper and Brothers, 1945.
Mowrer, Edward Ansell. *Germany Puts the Clock Back*. New York: Macmillan, 1933.
Moynihan, Daniel Patrick, ed., *On Understanding Poverty*. New York: Basic Books, 1969.
Myrdal, Gunnar, with Richard Sterner and Arnold Marshall Rose. *An American Dilemma: The Negro Problem and Modern Democracy*. New York: Harper, 1944.
Neumann, Franz. *Behemoth: The Structure and Practice of National Socialism*. 1st ed., New York: Oxford University Press, 1942; 2d edition, 1944.
Poliakov, Leon, and Joseph Wulf. *Das Dritte Reich und seine Denker*. Berlin: Arani, 1957.
Rainwater, Lee. "The Problem of Lower-Class Culture and Poverty War Strategy," in Daniel Patrick Moynihan, ed., *On Understanding Poverty*. New York: Basic Books, 1969.
Rawls, John. "Constitutional Liberty and the Concept of Justice," in Carl J. Friedrich, ed., *Justice* (Nomos VI). New York: Atherton Press, 1963.
Rheinstein, Max, ed., *Max Weber on Law in Economy and Society*. Cambridge, Mass.: Harvard University Press, 1954.
Riesman, David. *The Academic Mind: Social Scientists in a Time of Crisis*. Glencoe, Ill.: Free Press, 1958.
Riesman, David, and Christopher Jencks. "Patterns of Residential Education: A Case Study of Harvard," in: Sanford, Nevitt, ed., *The American College*. New York: Wiley, 1962, pp. 731–773.
Schlesinger, Arthur, Jr. *A Thousand Days: John F. Kennedy in the White House*. Boston: Houghton Mifflin, 1965.
Robert Kennedy and His Times. New York: Ballantine Books, 1978.
Schneider, David. *American Kinship: A Cultural Approach*. Englewood Cliffs, N.J.: Prentice Hall, 1968.
Smith, Richard N. *The Harvard Century: The Making of a University to a Nation*. New York: Simon and Schuster, 1986.
Speier, Hans, and Erich Kähler, eds., *War In Our Time*. New York: Norton, 1939.
Stouffer, Samuel, Edward A. Suchman, L. C. De Vinney, S. A. Star, Robin M. Williams, Jr. *The American Soldier*, 2 volumes. Princeton, N.J.: Princeton University Press, 1949.
Stouffer, Samuel A. *Communism, Conformity, and Civil Liberties: A Cross-Section of the Nation Speaks Its Mind*. Garden City, N.Y.: Doubleday, 1955.
Talcott Parsons on National Socialism, edited and with an introduction by Uta Gerhardt. New York: Aldine de Gruyter, 1993.
Tawney, Richard H. *Religion and the Rise of Capitalism*. New York: Harcourt, Brace & Co., 1926.
Veblen, Thorstein. *Theory of the Leisure Class. An Economic Study of Institutions*. New York: Macmillan, 1899.
Von Schelting, Alexander. *Max Weber's Wissenschaftslehre*. Tübingen: Mohr [Siebeck], 1934.
Warner, W. Lloyd. "American Caste and Class," *American Journal of Sociology*, Vol. 42, 1936, pp. 234–237.
Warner, W. Lloyd, Buford H. Junker, and Walter A. Adams. *Color and Human Nature: Negro Personality Development in a Northern City*. New York: Harper and Row, 1941, reprinted in 1969 on behalf of the American Council of Education, Washington, D.C.

Watson, Goodwin, ed., *Civilian Morale*. Boston: Houghton Mifflin, 1942.
Weber, Max. "Der Sinn der 'Wertfreiheit' der soziologischen und ökonomischen Wissenschaften" (originally 1917), in: *Gesammelte Aufsätze zur Wissenschaftslehre*, 3rd ed., Johannes Winckelmann, ed., Tübingen: Mohr, 1968, pp. 489–540. Translated (abbreviated version), "The Meaning of 'Ethical Neutrality,'" in *The Methodology of the Social Sciences Max Weber*, translated and edited by Edward A. Shils and Henry A. Finch. New York: Free Press, 1949, pp.1–49.

The Theory of Social and Economic Organization, edited with an introduction by Talcott Parsons. New York: Free Press, 1964. (Originally translated by A. M. Henderson and Talcott Parsons, New York: Oxford University Press, 1947.

Wirtschaft und Gesellschaft. Tübingen: Mohr [Siebeck], 1922.

Whitehead, Alfred North. *Science and the Modern World: Lowell Lectures, 1925*. New York: Free Press, 1967.

Name Index

Abel, Theodore, 90–91, 111 n. 222, 134, 136
Academic Assistance Council (Society for the Protection of Science and Learning), 65
Adamic, Louis, 92–93
Adams, Walter A., 262 n. 305, 286
Adorno, Theodor W., 118
Agger, Robert, 188
Alexander, Franz, 111 n. 222/224
Alexander, Jeffrey, x, xiv, 58 n. 1, 70 n. 50, 133, 186, 282, 283
Allport, Gordon W., 75, 79 n. 89/90, 81, 118, 134, 144–146, 283, 284
American Academy of Arts and Sciences, 6, 184, 187, 273–275, 278
American Association for the Advancement of Science, 152, 278
American Association for Public Opinion Research, 204
American Association of University Professors, photo # 6, 182–183, 243, 278
American Jewish Committee, 118
American Journal of Sociology, 1, 188
American Medical Association, 11 n. 38, 64 n. 21
American Orthopsychiatric Association, 110, 203, 243
American Psychiatric Association, 110
American Society for Political and Legal Philosophy, 233
American Society for Research in Psychosomatic Problems, 110
American Sociological Association, photo # 6, 246, 275
Amherst College, xii, 62–64, 69 n. 46, photo # 5, 146, 217 n. 142
Angell, Robert Cooley, 245
Apthorne, R. J., 194 n. 43
Arendt, Hannah, 273
Arensberg, Conrad, 90, 136
Aron, Raymond, photo # 8
Association of Atomic Scientists, 152
Ayres, Clarence, xii, 69

Bales, Robert F., 168 n. 154, 192, 281
Barber, Bernard, x, xiv, 45 n. 195, 153, 155 n. 112, 186 n. 8, 217 n. 142, 279, 281, 282, 283
Baran, Paul, 129
Bateson, Gregory, 75, 135, 147
Bauer, Raymond, 179 n. 201, 254 n. 284
Baum, Rainer, 60
Bavelas, Alex, 107 n. 206
Becker, Howard, 267 n. 233
Beebe-Center, John C., 79 n. 90, 284
Beland, Francois, 283
Bell, Daniel, xiv, 187 n. 9, 217 n. 142, 230 n. 192, 268, 283
Bellah, Robert, 187, 241–242, 283
Bender, Lauretta, 111 n. 222
Bendix, Reinhard, 206 n. 97, 210, 283
Benedict, Ruth, 111 n. 222, 112 n. 226
Bentham, Jeremy, 30, 53

289

Berelson, Bernard R., 191–194, 283, 285
Berkeley (University of California), 267–268
Bernard, Jessie, 83 n. 107
Bettelheim, Bruno, 145
Bibring, Edward, 118
Bierstedt, Robert, 1–2, 3 n. 10, 19 n. 73, 65
Black, Max, x, 185–186 n. 5, 260 n. 302, 282
Blau, Peter, 220
Blumer, Herbert, 211 n. 119
Bock, Gisela, 22 n. 94
Bondy, Curt, 145
Boring, Edwin G., 79 n. 90, 284
Bourricaud, François, 186, 205, 282
Brandt, Karl, 78 n. 85
Breit, William, 69 n. 44
Bretton Woods Conference, 120
Brick, Howard, 11 n. 39, 69 n. 43, 282
Brickner, Richard A., 107–108, 111, 112 n. 227, 113, 114 n. 232, 116, 121, 132 n. 16, 141, 283
Brinton, Crane, 7–8, 12 n. 40, 15 n. 51, 21, 53, 56–57, 131
Britt, Steuart Henderson, 83 n. 107
Brodbeck, Arthur, 191
Brogan, Denis, 273
Bronfenbrenner, Urie, 260 n. 302
Brown, Junius Hagg, 83 n. 107
Bruner, Jerome, 132 n. 14, 134
Bryson, Lyman, 118 n. 251, 133, 148 n. 84
Buck, Paul H., 81 n. 101, 137 n. 41
Bundy, McGeorge, 121 n. 262, 182
Burdick, Eugene, 191
Burke, Kenneth, 273
Burns, Arthur R., 121–122
Bush, Vannevar, 149–151
Buxton, William, 60, 283
Bychowsky, Gustav, 106 n. 202, 111 n. 222

Camic, Charles, x, 2 n. 3, 7 n. 18, 64 n. 20, 69, 70 n. 50
Cannon, Walter, 75
Cantril, Hadley, 75
Carnegie Foundation, 243
Chamberlain, Neville, 74
Chapman, John W., 237 n. 221
Chapple, Eliot D., 75

Chicago University (incl. Chicago approach, etc.), *see* University of Chicago
Child, Irving L., 79 n. 89
Clark, Kenneth B., 237 n. 220, 261 n. 303, 263, 265, 282
Clay, Lucius D., 147
Clayton, Obie, 262 n. 309
Cloward, Richard, 266
Coleman, James, 254–255
Collins, Abigail, xiv
Columbia University, 121 n. 265, 133, 134–135, 179, 191, 231, 268–269
Colm, Gerhard, 78 n. 85
Committee on the Cost of Medical Care, 64, 285
Committee on Un-American Activities, 180–182
Comte, Auguste, 7, 95
Conant, James B., 91, 150, 159
Conference on Science, Philosophy, and Religion in Their Relation with the Democratic Way of Life, 118, 133–134 n. 23, 137–138, 143–144, 147–148, 278
Coon, Carleton Stevens, 83 n. 107
Coordinator of Information Office (COI), 91, 97, 129, 131, 135
Coser, Lewis, 221, 225, 283
Council for Democracy, 75–76, 127, 132–133, 137, 138, 276, 278
Cowan, Thomas A., 235–236
Cox, Archibald, 238–239, 242, 283
Cox, Harvey, 241, 283
Craig, Gordon, 31 n. 131, 85 n. 118, 283
Cromwell, Oliver, 104
Crutchfield, Richard, 111 n. 222
Culbertson, William Patton, 69 n. 44
Curtis, Alberta, 135 n. 29, 156 n. 116
Cutler, Addison T., 64 n. 20

Dahl, Robert A., 194 n. 42
Dahrendorf, Ralf, 191
Darwin, Charles, xii, 13, 15 n. 53, 16–17, 19 n. 73, 29, 52, 222
Davie, Maurice R., 20 n. 81
Davies, Alan, 62 n. 11
Davis, Allison, 262, 284
Davis, Elmer, 75

Davis, Kingsley, 65–66
Deutsch, Karl W., 133, 271, 284
Deutsch, Morton, 201 n. 71, 203, 281
Devereux, George, 65–66
Dewey, John, 255
Dollard, John, 78 n. 86, 118, 262
Doob, Leonard W., 75, 130 n. 5
Drake, St. Clair, 265
Drucker, Peter, 72, 97
Dubcek, Alexander, 210
Duncan, Otis Dudley, 189, 234 n. 203
Durkheim, Émile, ix, xiii, 7, 27, 28, 32–34, 37–45, 49, 52, 80, 166, 222–223, 226, 232, 245 n. 254, 246, 248–249, 255–257, 281

Earle, Edward Mead, 90 n. 137
Eastern Industrial Personnel Security Board, 180, 181
Easton, David, 210 n. 116, 211
Eckstein, Harry, 196 n. 54, 204 n. 84, 282, 284
Edwards, Franklin, 265
Einstein, Albert, 53
Eisenhower, Dwight D., 3 n. 11, 133
Eisenstadt, Shmuel N., 231, 284
Elliott, William Y., 81 n. 101, 233 n. 201
Ellsberg, Dan, 274
Ely, Richard T., 68, 284
Endruweit, Guenter, xiv
Erikson, Erik H., 111 n. 222
Ertman, Thomas, xiv
Etzioni, Amitai, 248
European Recovery Program (Marshall Plan), 158–159
Evan, William E., 201 n. 71, 281

Fainsod, Merle, 179
Farago, Ladislas, 79 n. 90, 133n., 284
Fay, Sidney, 98 n. 178, 134
Feiler, Arthur, 78 n. 45
Finckelstein, Louis, 118 n. 251, 133, 148 n. 84
Fiske, Marjorie, 135 n. 29, 156 n. 116
Ford, Franklin, 272–273
Ford Foundation, 160, 187, 274
Foreign Economic Administration (Enemy Branch), 61, 121–126, 127, 132, 137, 142, 154

Fowler, Henry, 122–123, 126
Fox, Edward, 139
Fox, Renée, 168 n. 154
Frank, Lawrence K., 110 n. 221, 111 n. 223, 118
Franklin, John Hope, 265
Frei, Norbert, 3 n. 11
French, Thomas, 111–112
Freud, Sigmund, 53, 102, 156, 257, 259
Freyer, Hans, 27
Fried, Hans Ernst, 111 n. 222
Friedrich, Carl J., 46 n. 199, 75, 77 n. 81, 78, 83 n. 107, 99, 104, 108, 118, 130 n. 17, 132, 133n., 137 n. 140, 139, 146–147, 180 n. 202, 194, 203, 207n., 211, 233, 234 n. 203, 237 n. 221, 281, 284
Fromm, Erich, 82 n. 103, 106 n. 202, 111 n. 222, 169, 284
Fuller, Lon L., 233 n. 201

Gallup, George, 75, 207 n. 100
Gardner, Burleigh B., 262, 284
Gardner, Mary A., 262, 284
Gaudet, Hazel, 191, 285
de Gaulle, Charles, 210
Geer, Blanche, 267 n. 333
Gerety, Pierce J., 181 n. 205, 182 n. 212
Gerhardt, Uta, x, 11 n. 38, 27 n. 113, 108 n. 210, 121 n. 264, 122 n. 266, 132 n. 16, 186 n. 8, 211 n. 119, 282, 284
German Sociological Society, 21, photo # 3
Gerth, Hans, 134, 284
Gibb, James, 265
Gilbert, Felix, 129 n. 4
Ginzberg, Eli, 72
Gittler, L. F., 79 n. 90, 284
Glazer, Nathan, 267–268, 282
Goldstein, A., 104–105
Gorer, Geoffrey, 75, 112 n. 226
Gould, Mark, xiv
Gouldner, Alvin, 184
Graeber, Isaque, 83–84
Graubard, Stephen, 184
Greece (classic), 89, 232, 258
Green, William, 20 n. 81
Grew, Joseph C., 131 n. 13
Grotjahn, Alfred, 25 n. 105
Gumplowicz, Ludwig, 20

Name Index

Gurian, Waldemar, 86, 133
Gurvitch, Georges, 90, 93, 95 n. 158, 136
Gustavus Adolphus, 113

Habermas, Jürgen, x
Halévy, Elie, 31, 256
Haley, Alex, 250
Halle, Morris, 205 n. 90
Hamilton, Charles, 265
Hamilton, Peter, 58 n. 1
Hamilton, Walton, 64 n. 21, 69
Handlin, Oscar, 90 n. 135
Hartmann, Heinz, 111 n. 222
Hartshorne, Edward Y., 65–66, 81, 91, 93, 110, 130, 131, 132, 134, 136, 284
Harvard University, x, xiv, 6, 9, 33 n. 140, 53, 90, 109, 129–131, 134, 136 n. 36, 149, 177, 179, 180, 184, 213, 238, 243, 268, 271–273, 276–278
   Adams House, 66
   Afro-American Studies Program, 264–266
   Department of Economics, 64
   Department of Social Relations, photo # 7, 149, 158 n. 125, 163 n. 138, 193
   Department of Sociology, 62
   Faculty of Arts and Sciences, 264
   Harvard Defense Group, 80, 81–82, 91, 106, 127, 131, 133, 136 n. 37, 137, 138–139, 145, 154, 278
   Harvard School of Overseas Administration, 108–109, 127, photo # 7, 136–137 n. 40, 145, 147, 148, 154
   Harvard Student Union, 74, 178
   Russian Research Center, 149, 154, 178–180
Hauser, Philip M., 153, 262–263 n. 312
Heidelberg, x, 5, 65 n. 27, 70 n. 50, 124, 256
Hatt, Paul K., 189
Hegel, Georg Wilhelm Friedrich, 256
Heimann, Eduard, 78 n. 85
Heisenberg, Werner, 53
Henderson, Arthur M., 287
Henderson, Lawrence, 255
Herberg, Will, 229, 240–241, 284
Herring, Pendleton, 160–164
Heyl, Barbara, xiv, 131 n. 12, 284

Hilberg, Raul, 61 n. 7, 284
Hobbes, Thomas, 35, 46–47, 60, 104, 255–256 n 288.
Hofstadter, Richard, 17 n. 65, 19–20, 68 n. 38, 266 n. 329, 284
Hogan, Michael, 159 n. 129, 284
Holborn, Hajo, 129 n. 4
Holton, Robert S., x, 186, 283
Hollinger, David A., 250
Homans, George C., 187, 212 n. 124, 220, 254–255, 258
Horkheimer, Max, 82 n. 103, 118, 122 n. 267, 169 n. 158, 284
House, Floyd N., 2–3
Hovland, Carl I., 155 n. 110
Howe, Mard deWolfe, 238 n. 228, 283
Humboldt, Wilhelm von, 63 n. 14
Hughes, Everett C., 267 n. 333

Ingersoll, Ralph, 90 n. 138
Inkeles, Alex, xiv, 179 n. 201, 231 n. 196, 284

Jakobson, Roman, 204–205
Janowitz, Morris, 4 n. 12, 130, 245, 284
Jenks, Christopher, 267 n. 335, 286
Johnson, Lyndon B., 131 n. 13, 187, 242, 263, 271–272
Johnston, Barry V., 158 n. 125, 283
Junker, Buford M., 262 n. 305, 286

Kähler, Erich, 78 n. 85, 286
Kahana, Eva, xiv
Kaiser, Charles, 225, 285
Kaiser, Philip M., 31 n. 131, 122–125, 142 n. 57, 143 n. 59
Kandel, I. L., 106 n. 201, 111 n. 222
Kant, Immanuel, 34, 51, 256
Katz, Barry, 103 n. 197, 118 n. 246, 129 n. 4
Kaysen, Carl, 274
Kekskemeti, Paul, 274
Kennedy, John F., 131 n. 13, 184, 194, 196 n. 56, 203, 223, 240, 241, 242, 258, 261, 278
Kennedy, Joseph P., 74 n. 68
Kennedy, Robert F., 197 n. 56
Keynes, John Maynard, 30, 32, 164, 185, 215, 285

Kindleberger, Charles, 31 n. 131, 126, 129 n. 4, 159 n. 129, 285
King, Martin Luther Jr., 196 n. 56, 264 n. 322
Kissinger, Henry, 274
Klausner, Samuel Z., 85 n. 116, 154 n. 108, 156 n. 114, 160 n. 131, 285
Kloppenburg, James T., 68 n. 38, 285
Kluckhohn, Clyde, 109–110, 118, 133, 136, 147–149, 152, 154, 157, 178–179, 211, 285
Koepping, Klaus-Peter, xiv
Kogon, Eugen, 4 n. 12, 285
Kotschnig, Walter M., 105, 106 n. 201, 111 n. 222
Kris, Ernst, 75, 111 n. 222
Kristol, Irving, 230 n. 192, 268 n. 341, 283
Krohn, Claus-Dieter, 78 n. 85
Krushtshev, Nikita, 203
Kubie, Lawrence S., 111–112
Kuntz, Paul G., 239 n. 233, 285

Labov, William, 266
Landheer, Bartholomew, 90, 135, 199
Langer, William, 129, 131, 182
Larson, Cedric, 133 n. 18
Lasswell, Harold, 38 n. 163, 47 n. 203, 60, 73–74, 99 n. 180, 106 n. 202, 133, 138, 143, 171 n. 172, 190 n. 23, 211, 285
Lazarsfeld, Paul F., 118, 191, 221, 248, 266–267, 283, 285
Lechner, Frank, 60
Lederer, Emil, 78 n. 85
Lee, Albert McClung, 118
Lehman, Edward, xiv
Leighton, Alexander, 149, 152, 157, 285
Leontief, Wassily, 164, 271, 273
Lenin, Vladimir Ilyitch, 176
Lerner, Daniel, 130
Leuba, Clarence, 106 n. 202
Levine, Donald, xiv, 3 n. 10
Levy, David, 75, 157 n. 120
Lewin, Kurt, 75, 107, 111 n. 222, 118, 285
Lickert, Rensis, 118, 135
Lidz, Victor, xiv, 85 n. 116, 154 n. 108, 156 n. 114, 160 n. 131, 180 n. 202, 231 n. 196, 282, 285
Lincoln, Abraham, 223

Lindsay, A. D., 31 n. 131
Linebarger, Paul M. A., 130 n. 5
Lipset, Seymour Martin, 206 n. 97, 210, 228 n. 182, 234 n 203, 259 n. 297, 262, 267–268 n. 340, 283, 285
Locke, John, 35, 46–47, 248
Lodge, John Cabot Jr., 74
Lippitt, Ronald, 107 n. 205
Löwith, Karl, 134
London School of Economics, 70, 121 n. 265, photo # 4
Long, Huey, 73
Lowenthal, Leo, 259 n. 297
Ludwig, Emil, 141
Lynd, Robert, 56

Macchiavelli, Nicoló, 35
MacLeish, Archibald, 99 n. 182
MacIver, Robert, 118 n. 251, 133, 148 n. 84, 233–234, 266
Maier, Charles, xiv
Maier, Norman, 38 n. 163, 285
Malinowski, Bronislaw, 53
Malthus, Thomas, 28, 255
Mann, Klaus, 130 n. 6
Mann, Thomas, 130 n. 6
Mannheim, Karl, 47 n. 205
Marcuse, Herbert, 129 n. 4, 284
Marquardt-Bigman, Petra, 131 n. 10
Marshall, Alfred, 7, 35–36, 45–46, 222–223
Marshall, George C., 159 n. 127
Marshall, Thomas Humphreys, 227, 236, 260, 263, 285
Martin, Albert P., 97 n. 171
Marx, Karl (incl. Marxism), 15 n. 49, 30, 95, 96, 161, 181, 185, 190 n. 23, 222–223, 255
Mason, Edward S., 68, 131
Massachusetts Institute of Technology, 159 n. 129
Maxwell, Robert, 199 n. 66
May, Stacy, 69 n. 46
Mayer, Carl, 83 n. 107
Mayhew, Leon, 217, 285
Mayo, Elton, 81 n. 101
McCarthy, Eugene, 279
McCarthy, Joseph P., 187, 210, 254, 263
McGill University, 228, 249

Name Index

McGraw Hill (Publisher), 8, 71
McNamara, Robert, 272
McPhee, William N., 191, 283
Mead, George Herbert, 48, 53, 102 n. 194, 257, 285
Mead, Margaret, 60, 75, 111 n. 222, 112–113, 115, 117, 123 n. 268, 133, 135, 141, 147–148, 155 n. 111, 222 n. 160, 285
Meiklejohn, Alexander, 63–64, 69, 133, 285
Mellen, Sydney L. W., 108 n. 211
Meredith, James H., 197
Merton, Robert K., xiv, 65, 91, 134–136, 156 n. 116, 168–169, 286
Metzger, Wolfgang, 266 n. 329, 284
Meyer, Adolf, 111 n. 222
Metraux, Alfred, 112 n. 226
Metraux, Rhoda, 111 n. 222, 112 n. 226, 135 n. 31, 285
Michels, Robert, 224
Mielke, Fred, 4 n. 12
Militant Aid to Britain Committee (Campaign), 74, 133 n. 20, 278
Mill, James, 31
Mill, John Stuart, 12 n. 40, 16 n. 59
Miller, Clyde R., 79 n. 89
Millionshcheikov, M. D., 274
Mills, C. Wright, 187–191
Mitchell, William C., x, 283
Mitscherlich, Alexander, 4 n. 12
Moore, Wilbert, 118
Morgenthau, Henry Jr., 120, 121 n. 261, 126, 280, 286
Morot-Sir, Edouard, 221
Moulton, Harold, 20 n. 81
Mowrer, Edgar Ansell, 98 n. 178, 286
Mowrer, O. Hobart, 106–107
Moynihan, Patrick Daniel, 217 n. 146, 263 n. 312, 282, 286
Münch, Richard, 186
Murphy, Gardner, 75, 111 n. 222, 145 n. 70
Murray, Henry A., 75, 81 n. 101, 133, 144, 156
Mussolini, Benito, 224
Myrdal, Gunnar, 120, 262, 286

National Science Foundation, xiii, 149–151, 154
Nelson, Benjamin, 233 n. 201

Neumann, Franz L., 103–104, 122 n. 267, 286
New School for Social Research Graduate Faculty of Political and Social Science, 78 n. 85
Centre D'Études Sociologiques/École Libre des Hautes Études, 90
New York Times, 150–151
Nichols, Lawrence, 283
Nisbet, Robert, 270
Nixon, Richard, 251–254
Nizer, Louis, 118 n. 249
North, Cecil N., 189

O'Connell, Charles Thomas, 178 n. 200
Office of Facts and Figures, 98, 99 n. 182, 135, 156
Office of Scientific Research and Development, 149–151
Office of Strategic Services, 103 n. 197, 129, 131–132, 135, 153, 154 n. 109
Office of War Information, 98 n. 179, 99, 129–130, 131–132, 152, 153, 157
Olds, James, 212 n. 124
Oppenheimer, J. Robert, 133
Overstreet, Harry S., 111 n. 222, 118

Palmore, Joseph R., 178 n. 199
Pareto, Vilfredo, 7, 10, 27, 28, 32–33, 35–36, 39 n. 170, 40–44, 47, 49, 222–223
Parsons, Anne, photo # 3
Parsons, Charles, xiv, photo # 3, 181
Parsons, Charles Edwards, photos #2, # 4
Parsons, Edward Smith, 68 n. 42, 69, photos # 1, # 4
Parsons, Edward Smith Jr., photos #2, #4
Parsons, Elisabeth Ingersoll, photos #2, #4
Parsons, Esther, photos #2, #4
Parsons, Helen Walker, photos # 4, # 10, 177
Parsons, Mary Augusta Ingersoll, photos # 2, #4
Pasteur, Louis, 155
Patterson, Orlando, 266
Penrose, E. H., 120 n. 260
Perry, John, 99, 100 n. 184
Perry, Ralph Barton, 75, 133
Pettigrew, Thomas, 263 n. 312
Peukert, Detlef, 21 n. 91

Name Index 295

Pinson, Koppel, 111 n. 222
Platt, Gerald, 243 n. 245, 270
Ploetz, Alfred, 21–23, 25, 32
Poliakov, Leon, 65 n. 26, 286
Pope, Arthur Upham, 133
Porter, Charles O., 110 n. 220
Postman, Leo, 145 n. 72
Potsdam Conference, 123, 125
Price, Lucien, 63 n. 18
Procter, Robert, 22 n. 94, 26 n. 111
Psychological Warfare Division, 110, 130 n. 6
Putnam, Tracy J., 111 n. 222

Rainwater, Lee, 217, 286
Ratzenhofer, Gustav, 21
Rauschning, Hermann, 86
Rawls, Anne, xiv
Rawls, John, 237 n. 221, 286
Reik, Theodor, 78 n. 86
Reiss, Albert J., 189
Reissman, Leonard, 188
Rheinstein, Max, 237 n. 223, 286
Ricardo, David, 14, 15 n. 49, 30, 31, 255
Riesman, David, 259, 266 n. 331, 267 n. 335, 286
Riley, John W., Jr., 160–164
Robertson, Hector Menteith, 70–71
Rocher, Guy, 283
Rockefeller Foundation, 91, 136 n. 34, 154 n. 109
Roosevelt, Eleanor, 99
Roosevelt, Franklin D., 30, 34 n. 143, 105, 121 n. 263, 150, 151, 191, 207 n. 100, 278
Rose, Arnold Marshall, 286
Rosenau, James A., 201 n. 71, 202 n. 78, 203 n. 81
Rosinski, Herbert, 81–82 n. 103
Rosovsky, Henry, 264–265
Rossi, Peter, 188
Rostow, Walt, 31 n. 131, 159 n. 129
Rousseau, Jean Jacques, 248
Ruch, Floyd L., 79 n. 90, 131, 284
Rumiantsev, Aleksei M., 275

Sacharov, Andrej, 278
Salin, Edgar, 70 n.
Salomon, Gottfried, 21 n. 90
Saturday Review of Literature, 1

Sullivan, Harry Stack, 78
Schaeffle, Adam, 21
Scheler, Max, 47 n. 205
Schelling, Thomas, 274
Schelting, Alexander von, 27 n. 113, 286
Schlesinger, Arthur M., 81 n. 101
Schlesinger, Arthur M., Jr., 81 n. 101, 131, 184, 187 n. 10, 194 n. 44, 286
Schlesinger, Elizabeth, 136
Schmoller, Gustav (von), 68 n. 41
Schneider, David, 250, 286
Schnore, Leo F., 234 n. 203
Schoenbaum David, 65 n. 26
Schrecker, Ellen, 183 n. 214
Schultz, Sigrid, 111 n. 222
Schumann, Frederick L., 90 n. 136
Schumpeter, Joseph, 6–7, 51
Schwab, Gerald, 61 n. 7
Selznick, Philip, 267–268
Seymour, Charles, 20 n. 81
Shils, Edward A., 130, 163 n. 138, 168 n. 154, 245, 287
Shuster, George N., 133
Sills, David, 245 n. 252
Simmel, Georg, 33 n. 140
Sizer, Theodore R., 242 n. 242
Smelser, Neil, xiv, 192, 193, 234 n. 203, 281, 285
Smith, David H., 284
Smith, Dennis, 130 n. 6
Smith, Richard H., 129, 131 n. 13, 149, 286
Snell, John L., 203 n. 80
Social Science Research Council, xiii, 130 n. 7, 153–160, 160–164, 177, 277
Sombart, Werner, 33, 233
Sorokin, Pitirim, 37 n. 153, 53–56, 89
Spann, Othmar, 23–25, 27, 55 n. 235
Special Committee on Un-American Activities, 181, 183
Speier, Hans, 78 n. 85, 203 n. 80, 279, 286
Spencer, Herbert, xiii, 7–8, 12–14, 15 n. 51, 16–18, 30–31, 32, 52, 56, 95, 96, 166, 255, 276
Spengler, Oswald, 53, 54 n. 226/227
Sprague, Theodore W., 96 n. 163
Stammer, Otto, photo # 8
State Department, 131
  Division of German and Austrian Affairs, 126, 159 n. 129
Steel, Richard W., 98 n. 179

Name Index

Stehr, Nico, 7 n. 18
Steinberg, Michael Steven, 65 n. 26
Stern, Bernard J., 20 n. 88
Stern, Fritz, x
Sterner, Richard, 286
Stevens, Stanley S., 79 n. 90, 284
Stimson, Henry A., 121 n. 262
Stonequist, Everett, 83 n. 107
Stouffer, Samual Andrew, 133, 155, 158 n. 125, 180–182, 286
Strauss, Anselm, 267 n. 333
Suchman, Edward A., 155 n. 110, 286
Sumner, William Graham, xii, 12, 17–20, 30, 32, 255
Sutton, Francis X., 274
Sweezy, Paul E., 129

Taeuber, Conrad, 153
Tarde, Gabriel, 192
Tawney, Richard, 70, 286
Taylor, A. J. R. Frazer, 72–74
Taylor, Edmund, 75
Taylor, Harold, 154 n. 109
Thielens, Wagner, 266 n. 351, 285
Thom, Douglas A., 111 n. 222/223
Thomas, Catherine, 110 n. 218
Thomas, William I., 53, 165–166, 211 n. 119
Thompson, Laura, 111 n. 222
Thorp, Williard Long, photo # 5
Toby, Jackson, 231 n. 196
Toennies, Ferdinand, 96, 233
Topitsch, Ernst, photo # 8
Trevino, Xavier, xiv, 283
Trilling, Lionel, 273
Truman, Harry S., 151, 159 n. 128, 191
Turner, Bryan S., x, xiv, 186, 283
Tyriakian, Eward A., xiv

Ulich, Robert, 81 n. 101
Undset, Sigrid, 111 n. 222
United Nations Organization (incl. UNESCO), 106, 124, 154 n. 109, 180, 198–203
United States Army Specialized Training Program (and Civil Affairs Training Program), 136–137, 139–141, 177
United States Strategic Bombing Survey, 135

University of Chicago, 48, 64, 102 n. 194, 130, 136 n. 38, 154 n. 109, 188, 211, 234, 262

Veblen, Thorstein, 19, 286
Veltfort, Helene R., 144 n. 66, 145 n. 67, 146 n. 73, 283
Vernon, P. E., 78–79
Verschuer, Otmar von, 21, 23–26
Vitcha, Elaine, 245 n. 251
Voegelin, Carl F., 273
Voegelin, Eric, 85–86, photo # 10

Waelder, Robert, 93n., 111 n. 222
Wagner, Adolf, 68 n. 41
Wallace, Henry A., 105
Walsh, David I., 74
War Department
  Civil Affairs Division, 136–137, 141, 153
  Information and Education Division, 158
  Marshall Provost General's Office, 113, 132
Ward, Lester, 20
Warner, Lloyd, 118, 206 n. 97, 262, 286
Warren, Earl, 187
Watson, Goodwin, 75, 107 n. 206, 145 n. 70, 287
Wearne, Bruce, x, xiv, 283
Weber, Max, ix, x, xiii, 4, 21, 27 n. 113, 30, 32–34, 37, 39–46, 49, 51–52, 70–71, 87–89, 94, 127, photo # 8, 141, 166, 174, 185, 196, 203, 204 n. 84, 206, 211, 214, 222–224, 232 n. 197, 255–257, 267, 276, 279, 287
Weinberger, Caspar W., 81 n. 101
Wertheimer, Max, 78 n. 85
Winckelmann, Johannes, 287
White, William F., 81 n. 101
White, Winston, 258–259
Whitehead, Alfred N., 52, 255, 287
Wiener, Ron, 178 n. 199
Wiese, Leopold von, photo # 8
Wiggins, J. R., 238 n. 228
Wilbur, Ray Lyman, 64
Wilson, Thomas J., 204 n. 89
Wilson, Woodrow, 223
Williams, Robin M., 153, 155 n. 110, 286

Winckelmann, Johannes, 46 n. 198
Winkler, Allan M., 98 n. 179, 129 n. 2
Winks, Robin W., 129 n. 3
Wirth, Louis, 2, 4 n. 3, 50–51, 133, 279
Wittfogel, Karl August, 80 n. 94
Wolin, Sheldon S., 267 n. 336, 268 n. 340, 285
Woodward, C. Vann, 271
Wright, Quincy William, 133, 201 n. 71, 281
Wrong, Dennis, 180

Wulf, Joseph, 65 n. 26, 286
Wunderlich, Frieda, 78 n. 85

Yale University, 9, 129, 136 n. 38
Yarmolinsky, Adam, 274
Yerkes, Robert, 75, 154
Young, Kimball, 79, 284
Young, Wayland, 199 n. 66

Zelditch, Morris, 221
Ziemke, Earl F., 136 n. 39, 139 n. 46
Znaniecki, Florian, 165–166, 211 n. 119

Subject Index

achievement–ascription, 138, 208, 217, 231–232
    exclusion from achievement chances, 229
    in Nazi and postwar Germany, 87, 114, 122–123
    and science, 172–173
    see also: economy; Germany; modernization; pattern variables, society
action orientation
    anomic, charismatic, ritual, symbolic, 38, 40–41, 43, 169–170
    and deviance, 168–169, 170
    and four-function scheme, 191–194
    and interaction media, 204–206, 210–212, 215–216
    rational, reciprocal, 45, 47, 77, 79, 138
    and science, 172–173
    in societal community, 246, 255–260
    "Unit Act," 50
    see also: anomie; authority; charisma; integration; rationality; social action; society; values
aggression, 46, 120, 169–170
    free-floating, 94, 100, 143–144
    German and Japanese, 58, 85–86, 97–98, 100–103, 105, 124
    re Vietnam War, 271–275
    see also: frustration; insecurity; prejudice
analytical realism, 7, 34, 95, 254–257

anomie, 39, 95–97, 215
    anomic type society, 6, 9–10, 35–45, 216
    coercive social control/alienative action orientation, 101, 168–170, 197–198
    dedifferentiation, deterioration of societal community, 224–225
    vs. integration, 45, 58–59, 186–187, 209–210, 212–215, 249, 251
    supersession, 115–118
    see also: authority; coercion; force; insecurity; social control; social disorganization; society
anti-intellectualism, 28–32, 42, 67–68, 76, 100–101, 138, 218
    see also: discrimination; fundamentalism; insecurity; prejudice
anti-Semitism, 27–28, 61–62, 83–84, 85–86, 119, 134, 140–141, 169–170
    see also: discrimination; Jews; prejudice
atom bomb, 144, 149–153, 164, 177, 203, 271–275
authority, 215–216
    authoritarianism, 50, 61–62, 81–82, 107, 171–172
    change of type, in social change, 121–126, 224–225
    coercive, charismatic, 37, 42, 71–72, 76, 80, 194–198
    fiduciary, 218, 238
    moral, legal, influence, 41, 45–46, 65–66, 206

authority, (cont.)
  types, in action systems, 43–45, 87–89, 185, 195–196
  see also: anomie; "banking;" charisma; coercion; community; four-function scheme; interaction media; modernization; pattern variables; power; professions

"banking," 152, 247
  commitment, 213–215
  differentiation/dedifferentiation in social system(s), 214–215, 224–225, 226
  influence, 206–207, 209–210
  money, 198, 200, 203, 205
  power, 198–203
  and "vicious circles," 216
  see also: democracy; interaction media; modernization
Blacks
  in society, 77, 236–239, 262–266
  in sociology, 120, 187, 226–230
  see also: citizenship; community; discrimination; equality; ethnicity; integration

capitalism, 32, 39, 68–70
  and democratic social order, 46, 115–117, 122–123, 126, 215–216
  and fascism, 87–88
  "spirit" of, 70–72, 214
  see also: Communism; economy; power; professions
change, see revolution, social change
charisma, 62, 71
  and "banking," 247
  in McCarthyism, 192
  in Nazi regime, 42, 86–87, 88–89, 117–118
  and ritual/anomie, as type of authority, 40–43, 43–44, 66, 174–177
  and social change, 212–215, 216, 224–225
  see also: action orientation; authority; fundamentalism; "Führer" principle; power; society
choice, freedom of, 41, 47, 199, 204, 213, 227, 240–241
  see also: individual; integration; voluntarism

Christianity, 11, 36, 62, 71, 86, 98, 117, 119, 140, 240–242
  see also: Protestantism; religion; values
"Civics," 6, 51, 71, 240
civil liberties, 98–99, 101
  in American society, 76, 79, 138, 261–265
  and citizenship, 218, 226–228
  and civil rights, civil religion, 185, 242–245
  denial of, in anomie, 87, 212–215
  see also: community democracy, legality; Rechtsstaat
citizenship, 161, 214
  basis of social system in the nation, 113
  historic changes, agendas, 185, 261–275
  and inclusion, pluralism, 212–215, 218, 226–228, 236–239, 249–251
  see also: community; equality; integration; legality; legitimation; society; sociology
classes, see social class (stratification), see also: citizenship; equality, society
coercion
  anomic pole in interaction media system(s), 196–198, 208–209
  vs. influence (persuasion), 47, 66, 215
  and jurisdiction, 235
  as type of social control, 101–102, 104–105, 158, 174–177
  see also: anomie; authority; dictatorship; force; fundamentalism; power; totalitarianism
commitment
  vs. conformity, in democracy, 48, 76, 99–100, 168–169, 196–198, 202, 218
  and cultural meaning construction, 218, 223, 249–251
  as interaction medium, 210–214, 216
  loss, in "inflation/deflation," 101, 215, 229
  and value integration, pattern maintenance, community, 101, 210, 233–236
  see also: "banking"; four-function scheme; influence; institution; interaction media; power; voluntarism

Subject Index

Communism, 6, 73, 77, 170, 172, 180, 181–182, 199, 209–210, 210, 225
community, 35, 68, 185
   and "disinterestedness," 45
   and evolution of society (modernization), 229, 231–233
   Nazi folk community (anomic type, pseudo-community), 43, 76, 170–172
   societal community
      integrated type society, 46–48, 117, 209, 214
      integrative subsystem, 236–245, 251–254
   and world order, 200–202, 209–210
   see also: anomie; culture; integration; professionals; society
conflict
   vs. consensus, 192–193, 201, 228–231
   anti- "conflict theory," 186–187, 225
   strain in social structure(s), 119, 170–171, 185, 244
   and system type change, 212–215
   Vietnam war, 271–275
   see also: aggression; pattern variables; system; utilitarianism; "vicious circle"
"conscience collective," 40, 232, 248, 257
constitution(alism), 46, 77–78,
   in American democracy, 79, 138, 223, 228
   and power, influence structure in polity, 191–194, 207, 209
   and societal community, 236–239
   see also: legality; legitimacy; rationality
control, *see* social control
criminality, 168–171
   and charismatic authority, 42–43
   tolerance of,
      as coercive, 47, 197
      in Nazi Germany, 88, 101, 105
   and utilitarian action orientation (anomie), 38–39, 40
   see also: deviance; force; insecurity
crisis
   and change of types of systems, interaction media dynamics, 209–210, 212–215
   responsibility of social science (scientist), in times of, 74–75, 86–89, 103, 165
culture
   cultural pessimism, xi–xii, 36–37, 53–57, 89, 230
   as (fourth) functional system, 220, 246
   and meaning, social order, 107, 222, 232, 257
   and ressentiment, 218
   reconstruction (Germany), 107, 110–113
   research, 109–110, 112–113, 131–132, 166–167
   and value-commitments, 211–212
   see also: commitment; community; four-function scheme; interaction media; research; society; universities; values
"cybernetics"
   "evolutionary-cybernetic" theory, 246–248
   hierarchy of control, 210, 216, 223, 233
   re interaction media, two-pronged, 209, 209–210, 207–208, 214–215
   vs. "Rational choice" theory, 254
   societal progress, 222

Darwinism (including social Darwinism), 5, 7, 12, 13–32, 50–52, 221–222
   see also: heredity and environment; positivism; utilitarianism
democracy
   vs. anomie, fascism type social system, 32, 46, 51–52, 58, 75–80, 87, 102, 119–120, 170–172, 174–176, 215–216
   re interaction media, two-pronged functional system variation, 186–187, 195, 196–198, 204, 223
   Germany, pre-Nazi vs. postwar structures, 93–95, 97–98, 105–106, 108, 123–124, 141–142
   knowledge interest of social sciences, ix–x, 155–160, 161–162, 243–245
   re societal community, 226–230, 236–239, 240–241, 243–245
   U.S. democracy, structural features 1940s, "strategy of truth," 76–77, 99–100, 138

democracy, (*cont.*)
  see also: community; differentiation; four-function scheme; interaction media; integration; modernization; morality; pattern variables; politics; society; welfare state
deviance
  in democratic society, as non-community prone action, 217, 238–239, 246
  as type of social action system, 101–102, 120, 168–170, 196–198, 215–216, 227
  see also: criminality; social control, "vicious circle"
dictatorship
  charismatic, based on force, insecurity, 10f., 42, 73, 87, 100, 103, 196–198
  and destruction of university, 244
  and ethics, 224
  in terms of interaction media dynamics, 215–216
  see also: charisma; coercion; force; totalitarianism
differentiation
  and dedifferentiation, regression, 88, 185, 199, 215–216, 224–225, 246–247
  of functions in government, division of power, non-zero sum, 77–78, 101, 121–126, 191–193
  and pluralism, inclusion, 185, 226–228
  see also: "banking"; democracy; four-function scheme; interaction media; modernization
discrimination
  danger zone in democracy, 77, 144, 168–170
  inclusion/exclusion in societal community, 228–230
  in non-democratic regimes, 88, 118–120, 140–141, 197
  protection from, 239
  see also: anti-intellectualism; anti-Semitism; deviance; emotion; prejudice
"disinterestedness," 45, 48, 102, 165–166, 173, 207
  see also: medical practice; pattern variables
disorganization, see social disorganization

economy
  and charismatic, non-democratic regime(s), 42, 88, 106, 119
  and democratic change, regime(s), 116, 117, 121, 122–126, 141–142, 195, 199
economics
  economic individualism, 8–9
  institutional, 69–71
  Keynesian, modern, 30–31, 33, 46, 68–69
  vis-à-vis political science, sociology, 50, 166
  industrial revolution, 231
  money interaction medium system type, 216
  "postindustrial" society, 247
  relative to four-function scheme, 185, 193
  see also: "banking"; capitalism; industrialization; politics; society
education
  denigration of, 17, 19, 89
  exclusion from, 229
  higher, liberal learning, Western civilization, 63–68, 105–106, 124, 136–137, 139–141, 141–142
  modern society, educational revolution, 187, 201, 230–231, 247, 249
  university unrest, 266–271
  "vicious circle," upgrading, 120, 240, 243–245
  see also: citizenship; culture; modernization; reeducation; revolution; universities
"effort," 20, 41, 100, 129–149, 153–160
emotion
  negative, as "tabloid thinking," 94–95, 115, 119, 125, 192–193, 196
  positive, as interpersonal "affect," 259
  see also: discrimination; institution; integration; values
equality
  and inclusion/exclusion re pattern variables, interaction media, 77, 88, 209, 216–219, 228–230
  of opportunity, 76, 117, 138, 209, 217
  and political ideas, authority structures, 96, 123–124, 187, 195, 201

and "secondary" inequality in
    "postindustrial" society, 217,
    249–251
  see also: constitution(alism);
    community; economy; ethnicity;
    individual; interaction media;
    pattern variables; social class
    (stratification); society
ethics
  "Gesinnungsethik" vs.
    "Verantwortungsethik," 71, 89, 211,
    224
  see also: charisma; democracy;
    morality; *Wertfreiheit*
ethnicity
  and citizenship, 217, 249–251, 262–266
  and polarization, inclusion/exclusion in
    "postindustrial" society, 226–230,
    247
  see also: Blacks; citizenship; equality;
    Jews
Europe
  European science, standpoint, xi, 12–13,
    32–33, 40, 51, 255–256
  racism, pessimism, 21–26, 36–37
  war and postwar reconstruction, 79–80,
    90–92, 98–99, 108, 109, 120, 121,
    123, 124–126, 160, 158–160
  see also: economy; reeducation; values
exchange
  coercion, in anomic type society, 66, 89,
    204, 212–215
  vs. "exchange theory," 185, 220–221,
    254–255
  reciprocity, in integrated type society,
    47–48, 66, 116, 204, 212–215, 227
  see also: freedom of choice; interaction
    media; rationality; reciprocity;
    utilitarianism

family, 109–110, 123, 136, 143, 197, 217,
    240
fiduciary, 200, 212–215, 218, 249
  see also: authority; "banking";
    community; differentiation;
    medical practice; professions
force
  and anomic social order, 10, 35–37,
    37–38, 38–39, 42–44, 46, 47, 48,
    88–89

and interaction media "gold-standard"
    fundamentalist pole, 208–209,
    234–235
  and responsible social-science analytical
    impetus, 151, 155–160
  and two-pronged functional systems,
    196–198
  see also: anomie; coercion; Darwinism;
    insecurity; National Socialism;
    totalitarianism; "War of All Against
    All"
frustration, 38, 143
  see also: aggression; insecurity
four-function scheme
  AGIL-scheme, 185
    explaining action, voting, 191–194
    and LIGA-scheme, for social control/
      socialization, 257
    and societal community, 232–233,
      245–246
    and two-pronged structure(s) of
      subsystems, 195–198, 210, 214,
      216
  functional institutions, 219
  see also: institution; social action;
    society
fundamentalism, 76–77, 95–97, 114,
    123–126, 140, 185, 196–197, 209,
    214–215, 251
  see also: anti-intellectualism;
    anti-Semitism; insecurity;
    militarism; National Socialism;
    McCarthyism; politics; prejudice;
    religion
"Führer" principle, 10, 34, 42, 65–55, 76,
    87, 195, 214–215
  see also: authority; charisma; National
    Socialism; universalism-
    particularism

Germany, 5, 59, 60–61, 222
  pre-Nazi, Weimar, 82–83, 93–95
  Nazi, 21–26, 34, 36, 86–89, 96, 176
  postwar, 61, 97–98, 105–106, 108–110,
    110–118, 121–126, 141–142, 147,
    179–180
  see also: achievement-ascription;
    Europe; National Socialism;
    racism; reeducation;
    universalism-particularism

Subject Index

heredity and environment, 27, 48–49, 52, 220–221, 222
  see also: Darwinism
history, 3, 39, 185–187, 221, 251–254, 261–275
  see also: modernization; social change; society; theory

ideal type, 27, 50, 52, 212–213, 216
individual
  in democratic-type society, 200, 201, 215–216, 218
  negated in anomic-type society, 38, 48, 87–89, 115–118, 123–124, 196–198
  in societal community, 232–233, 236–239, 258–259
  see also: freedom of choice; community; equality; four-function scheme; institution; integration; interaction media; pattern variables; social action; theory
industrialization, 226, 256
  industrial revolution, 230–231, 249
  rapid, 74
  rational-legal type society, 94, 113–118, 121–126, 132, 185–187
  see also: "banking"; economy; insecurity; modernization
influence
  and societal community, 218, 236, 238
  in two-pronged structure(s) of function(s), 145, 185, 197, 203–204, 205, 206, 207–208, 215–216
  types of, 65–66, 66–67, 101, 207
  see also: "cybernetics," four-function scheme; interaction media; persuasion; power
information
  in authoritarian vs. democratic society, 99, 120, 226
  in societal community, 243–244
  two-pronged structure(s) of media, 185, 195–198, 204–205, 210–212, 212–215
  see also: citizenship; interaction media; institution; universities

insecurity, 38, 73–74
  in isolationism, 73, 75
  and prejudice, 72, 94–95, 96–97, 120, 140–141, 143–144
  vs. security, 46–47, 116, 123
  system pathology, 212–215, 216
  see also: aggression; anomie; coercion; deviance; fundamentalism; industrialization; modernization; social disorganization; totalitarianism
institution
  controlled social change, 117–118, 125–126, 141–142
  and institutionalization in societal community, 204, 218, 226, 229
  and internalization of values, 212, 214–215, 257–260
  and legitimacy, in democratic social order, 43, 48, 75–77, 102–103, 114, 116, 170, 195
  see also: commitment; individual; integration; legality; legitimacy; values; voluntarism
integration
  vs. anomie, coercion, 38–39, 45, 51–52, 59, 196–198, 215–216
  in bipolar function systems, 191–194, 195–196, 209–210, 212–215, 215–216
  democratic social order, 45–48, 50, 102–103, 114–118, 123–126, 166, 170, 172
  loss of, in anomie, dedifferentiation, 39, 224–225
  per diversity, differentiation, 230, 247, 249
  "partial" vs. modern, 51–52, 120, 171–172, 202
  in/through societal community, 186–187, 214, 225–233, 236–245, 245–246, 249, 254–260
  see also: authority; freedom of choice; community; differentiation; institution; profession; society; values
interaction media
  beyond "zero sum," 194–198, 203–208, 212–215, 219

integrative vs. anomic bipolar structure, 212–215, 215–216
language analogy, 204–205
in societal community, "postindustrial" society, 226, 234–235, 236–239, 245–246
see also: action orientation; "banking"; commitment; "cybernetics"; differentiation; influence; power; society; symbolization; values

interests
anomie vs. democracy, 39, 45, 47, 77
and pluralism, 202, 223
"vested interests," 105, 114, 125, 143–144, 174, 202
see also: "disinterestedness;" individual; liberalism; pattern variables; situation; utilitarianism

Jews, 10, 65, 72, 77, 88, 101, 119, 140, 169–170, 228, 251
see also: anti-Semitism; ethnicity; fundamentalism; prejudice
Japan, 135, 148–149, 152–153

legality
and authority, 46, 48, 76, 196
law as baseline for civil rights (equality), 187, 218, 227, 229, 261
law and deviance, 170
loss of independent judiciary, Nazi Germany, 88, 94, 104, 115–116
and justification, procedural rules, 79, 204
science legislation, 150–153, 154–160
see also: citizenship; community; democracy; institution; integration; legitimacy

legitimacy, legitimation
as basis for societal community, 213, 215–216, 228–230
in democratic vs. authoritarian regimes, 42–43, 44, 45, 46, 48, 71–72, 94–95, 115–117, 171–172
in relation to interaction media structure(s), 191–194, 195, 204, 209
see also: authority; charisma; legality; rationality

liberalism
liberal-democratic society in United States, Europe, 76, 79–80, 93, 116, 123–126, 170, 184–185
liberal learning, 63–68, 243–245
"Manchester" liberalism, 18, 35, 38–39, 170, 175, 209
see also: anomie; democracy; Europe; economy; utilitarianism; "War of All Against All"; welfare state

McCarthyism, ix, 178–180, 180–183, 185, 187, 190, 192, 208, 209, 254, 260
see also: fundamentalism; modernization
medical practice, 11, 64, 67–68
physician-patient social system, 103, 112, 161–162, 167–168
and "professional complex," 207, 219
see also: "disinterestedness"; professions; sociology
militarism, 76–77, 81–82, 94, 98, 115, 121–126, 214–215
modernization
and anomie, 39, 75–76, 86–89
of modern society, 48, 115–118, 121–126, 174, 184–185, 225–226, 246–247
reversal, regression, 174–175, 215, 268–270
two-pronged media process dynamics, 193, 213–214, 246–247
see also: community; "cybernetics"; differentiation; insecurity; social change
morale, 81–83, 104–105, 135
morality, xii, 69
in anomie-democracy divide, 27, 39, 40, 41, 45–46, 46–47, 48
and interaction media structures, 197–198, 209–210
morale-demoralization-amorality, 70–72, 74, 78–79, 88, 94, 97–98
moral resource of the nation, moral leadership, 139, 214–215, 229
value generalization, "postindustrial" society, 239, 247

Subject Index

morality, *(cont.)*
  see also: community; democracy; ethics; integratiaon; normative systm; social control; social order; system; values

nationalism, 10, 76, 88, 97–98, 105, 123, 131, 151, 171, 197, 202, 209, 229
National Socialism, 9–11, 27–28, 36, 61
  anomie, atrocities, 3, 6, 10, 51, 61–61, 73–74, 102
  overcome, 97–98, 105–118, 121–126
  as "partial" social order, 138, 202, 227, 229
  in *The Social System*, 167, 169–170, 171–172, 175–176
  as type society, 61–71, 65–66, 67–68, 72, 75–80, 81, 86–89, 138
  type structural elements, 59, 80, 93–95
  see also: anti-Semitism; Germany; coercion; insecurity; pattern variables; prejudice; ritualism; society; totalitarianism; utilitarianism
New Deal, ix, 11, 29–30, 34, 45–48, 51
"Nordic" man, 27
normative system
  in civic society (societal community systems), 218, 226–228, 233–236, 236–239, 239–242
  and system type changes, 121–126, 174
  and two-pronged media structure(s), 194–198, 204, 215–216
  voluntarism vs. heredity and environment, 45–48, 49, 102–103
  see also: community; democracy; fiduciary; integration; morality; professions; society; values; voluntarism

office
  breakdown of idea of office, in Nazi regime, 11, 80, 88, 126
  as typical for democratic-type society, 66, 96, 170, 192–193, 195, 204, 207, 232
  see also: democracy; influence; pattern variables; society

paranoia, 10, 101, 107, 108, 118, 124, 143–144, 169–170
  see also: anti-Semitism; deviance; prejudice; reeducation
pattern variables
  achievement replaced by ascription, ascription by achievement, in Germany, 87, 122–123
  "disinterestedness," as collectivity orientation, 45, 48
  ethical particularism, Nazi "Führer" principle, 76, 80
  ethical universalism, in religion, American society, 62, 68, 79
  and interaction media structures, societal community, 214, 215–216, 217, 257
  non-democratic vs. democratic poles, 114
  particularism replaced by universalism, in Germany, 141
  tensions, mechanisms in social system, 170–172
  see also: achievement-ascription; commitment; situation; social action; society; system; universalism-particularism; values
permissiveness, 116, 125, 141, 167–168, 253
persuasion, 47, 48, 99, 100, 172–173, 204, 214–215
  see also: freedom of choice; influence
politics
  anomic totalitarian type, xi, 43, 73, 93–95, 196–197
  democratic type, 3–12, 46–48, 75–78, 113–115, 121–126, 195–196, 203–204
  distinct from economy, society, 50, 170–172, 190, 192
  national, international, 83, 86–89, 144, 158, 160
  political science, 108, 231
  varying between "gold standard" -and "credit" -type structure, 212–215
  see also: anomie; democracy; economy; fundamentalism; influence; power; society

positivism, 255–257
  anti-positivism, 1930s-1950s, 5, 7,
    27–32, 95, 165–166, 190–191
  in Homans, Coleman, 220–221, 254–255
  "pseudo-realistic theorizing," 203, 208,
    211
  vs. science in social system, 170–172
  see also: Darwinism; utilitarianism,
    Wertfreiheit
power, polity
  change of type, 97–98, 123, 174
  democratic, integrated, 48, 66, 99–100
  force and fraud, ritualistic/charismatic,
    11, 42, 65, 76, 86–89, 96–97, 104
  in "postindustrial" society (societal
    community), 218, 226, 247
  non-"zero sum" concept and
    phenomenon, 190–191, 197–198,
    199–203, 208–210, 213–215,
    215–216
  see also: anomie; authority;
    commitment; "cybernetics";
    democracy; economy; influence;
    politics; society
prejudice
  and coercion, murder, 120, 169–170,
    197
  and differentiation, social change, 124,
    227–228
  vs. professional science, 172–173
  and "relative deprivation," 217–218
  "tabloid thinking," "scapegoating," 114,
    118, 119, 148
  see also: aggression;
    anti-intellectualism; anti-Semitism;
    discrimination; fundamentalism;
    insecurity; racism
professions, professionalism
  between capitalism and socialism, "third
    model," "educational revolution,"
    60, 249
  "learned professions" as experts through
    influence, 66, 102–103, 126, 138,
    207–208
  fiduciary authority, 218, 219, 243–245
  negated in Nazi regime, 87
  promoted in industrial revolution,
    modernization, 96, 163

sociologists, 103, 161–162
  in universities, 172–173, 213
  see also: community; education;
    influence; legality; medical;
    rationality; science; society;
    sociology; universities
propaganda, 65–67, 94, 98–103, 117, 131,
  172, 197
  types of (democratic, anti-democratic),
    78–79, 101–103, 117
  vis-à-vis public opinion (pluralism),
    214–215
  see also: public opinion
Protestantism, 70–71, 85–86, 113, 214,
  227–228, 240–242
  see also: capitalism; Christianity;
    religion
psychology
  "German Social Structure and National
    Psychology," 82, 93, 97–98, 107,
    111–112, 122–124
  practicing theoretically orientated
    research, 166–167
  psychological warfare, disarmament,
    98–100, 126
  see also: sociology
psychoanalysis, 102, 111–113, 119,
  167–168
  see also: Germany; medical practice;
    prejudice
psychiatry, 108, 110–114, 157
  see also: Germany; reeducation;
    sociology
public opinion
  and citizenship in democratic society,
    207, 214, 235–236, 238
  and "strategy of truth," (social) science,
    98–100, 173
  see also: influence; politics; society

race, racism
  re integration of Blacks ("Unity and
    Conflict"), 228, 229–230
  pre-Nazi, Nazi, post-Nazi Germany,
    21–26, 61–62, 86–88, 97–98, 104,
    118–120, 123–124
  universalism-ascription mechanism,
    171–172, 197

race, racism, (*cont.*)
see also: anti-Semitism; Blacks; citizenship; ethnicity; equality; fundamentalism; prejudice; society
rationality
denied in Nazism, Europe, 86–89, 96–99
ir- and non-rationality (ritualism) vs. means-end rationality, 33, 38, 40–41, 44, 47–48
"learned professions" vs. utilitarian thought, 60, 66
opposed to force, pathology in social process, 215–216
in societal community, academic system, 244, 252–254
in U.S. society, postwar German society, 77, 79, 94–95, 121–126, 138, 173–177, 194–195
see also: authority; democracy; legality; professions; reciprocity; science
Rechtsstaat, xiii, 4, 46, 88, 115–116, 194–195, 234
see also: citizenship; constitutionalism; legality
reciprocity
denied, in prejudice, 169–170
in rational, democratic type relations, society, 47, 102–103, 191–194, 195–196, 226–227, 255–256
see also: "disinterestedness"; rationality; social action; voluntarism
reeducation, 97–98, 105–108, 121–126, 141–142, 272
see also: Germany; social change
religion
civil religion, pluralist and integrative, 187, 223, 228–230, 237, 239–242
in rational action, democratic authority, 44, 47–48
reestablished, in postwar Germany, 117
in ritual action, charismatic authority, 33, 40–41, 42, 47–48
source of inequality, 217
threat to universalist religion, liberal economy, in Nazism, 62, 68–72, 77, 83–86, 118–120, 127
see also: authority; economy; society

research
agendas, 162, 163
as basic national resource, national resource, 153, 155–160, 160–167
"theory-oriented," 163, 165–166, 172–173, 191–194
see also: science; sociology; theory; *Wertfreiheit*
revolution
charismatic type takeover, 42, 61–62, 71–72, 115, 121–126, 174–175, 185, 198, 214–215
and differentiation, moderization, 227
industrial, political, educational, 230–231, 249
intellectual, 29–30
and media dynamics, dedifferentiation, 198, 216, 224
see also: social change
ritualism
in anomic type society, 8, 39, 40–43, 71
as deviant motivation, 169
in Nazi type regime, 71, 80, 86–89
replaced by rationality, 115, 121–126
see also: ethics; National Socialism; totalitarianism
Russia, xiii, 6, 73, 92, 110, 115, 149, 167, 172, 176–177, 189, 202, 221
see also: charisma; Communism

science
expertise, characteristic in democracy, modernization, 65–66, 75, 77, 96, 97–98, 109–110, 126
corrupted in Nazi Germany, 62, 66–67, 80
vs. quasi-science, pseudo-science, 11, 27–28, 52, 47
social sciences,
equal to natural sciences, 129–130, 134, 149–153, 155–160, 160–167
research based, 256
scientific professionalism, 172–173, 218, 222
understanding contemporary society, 9, 191–194, 215–216, 230
see also: education; morality; professions; rationality; research; sociology; theory

situation (definition of the situation), 100–102, 114, 119, 125, 165–166, 172–173, 195, 202
  see also: interests; pattern variables; social action
social action
  change of type, 121–126, 173–177
  charismatic-ritualistic vs. democratic-integrated, 40–43, 45–48
  four-function scheme, 185, 191–194
  interaction media dynamics, 215–216
  per societal community; 236–243
  U.S. society, vs. Nazi society, 79–80
  Weberian theory, 167, 168–169, 173–177
  see also: action orientation; anomie; community; democracy; four-function scheme; integration; interaction media; pattern variables; rationality; reciprocity; religion; society
social change
  controlled institutional change, 115–118, 121–126
  different from social process, 225–226
  through differentiation, inclusion, 224–225, 228–230, 242–245
  through inflation-deflation, media dedifferentiation, 214–215, 215–216
  regressive, 87, 198
  sources of anomie in modernization, 96, 258
  three types, Weberian perspective, in *The Social System*, 173–177
  in U.S. society, 1960s, 184–185
  see also: differentiation; insecurity; modernization; revolution; social control; "vicious circle"
social class (stratification), 47, 77, 116, 171, 189, 195, 217, 226, 240, 247, 249–251
  see also: citizenship; differentiation; discrimination; equality; insecurity; society
social control
  and differentiation, pluralism, civil society, 224–225, 239–242

four types, as action incentive, 197–198
  and reeducation, 102–103, 141–142
  types, re change, 115–117, 173–177
  two types, coercive vs. voluntary, 101–103
  and types of society, "cybernetic" hierarchy of media, 210, 215–216, 233
  see also: action orientation; "banking"; coercion; "cybernetics"; interaction media; pattern variables; permissiveness; social action; social change; values; voluntarism
social disorganization
  in anomie, dictatorship 10, 39, 45, 50
  controlled by authority, property, 195, 216
  controlled post–World War II in Germany, Europe, 110, 125
  per dedifferentiation, 224–225
  not necessarily desintegration, 102
  see also: anomie; force; insecurity; social control, "War of All Against All"
"Social Gospel," 68
social order
  American vs. European, 75–77, 123–126
  anomic (totalitarian) vs. integrated (democracy), 35–48, 77, 202
  and atom bomb, 152
  and interaction media conceptualization of society, 191–194, 199–202
  plus system function and type variation, 215–216
  focus societal community, 232–233, 234, 236–239
  and pattern variable conceptualization of society, 170–173
  see also: anomie; coercion; democracy; four-function scheme; interaction media; integration; legitimation; morality; nationalism; pattern variables; society; "War of All Against All"
socialization, 103, 111–112, 185
  see also: four-function scheme; reeducation
society
  American, elements and principles, 62, 75–77, 79

society, (*cont.*)
  evolutionary universals, 231–233
  pre-Nazi, Nazi, and postwar German, elements and principles, 82–83, 86–89, 93–95, 124–126
  and societal community, "postindustrial" society, 233–245, 247
  as subject of sociological analysis, 8–9, 50, 79, 161–162, 163, 187, 191–194
  two-pronged model(s) of analysis for empirical society, 8–9, 34–35, 35–48, 59, 114, 195–198, 212–215, 215–216, 219–223, 260–261
  variation in empirical societies, relative to types of social order, 114–115, 170–171
  Western, democratic, integrated, 6, 103, 114, 124
  see also: economy; four-function scheme; interaction media; pattern variables; politics; social action; science; sociology
sociology
  analyzing new agenda 1960s, theory per interaction media dynamics, civil society, 187, 191–194, 203, 208, 210, 211, 231, 243–245, 246–248, 257, 260–261
  analyzing political crisis, societies, policy options, World War II, 84, 86–89, 97, 110–115, 117, 120–126
  distinct from economics, politics, re empirical analysis, 2, 34–35, 49–51
  profession, basic science, national resource, 103, 151–152, 153, 160–162, 172–173
  see also: research; science; society; *Wertfreiheit*
symbol, symbolization
  representation of tension in society, through ressentiment, 120, 123, 144
  and science, 168–170
  in societal community, 232–233, 233–239
  symbolic media of interaction/interchange, 185, 198–203, 204–205
  and system dynamics, 215–216
  see also: "banking"; differentiation; interaction media; prejudice; religion; science; society
system
  "cybernetic" hierarchy, societal subsystems, 223
  dynamics, four-function scheme, 185
  dynamics, interaction media, 219–223
  dynamics, political subsystem, 191–194, 194–203, 215–216
  integrative subsystem societal community, 245–246
  see also: action orientation; morality; normative system; social order; society; sociology; *The Structure of Social Action*; *The Social System*; values
The Structure of Social Action, 3–5, 32–48, 51, 101–102, 128, 170–172, 177, 187, 219, 255–260
The Social System, 163, 167–177, 192, 210, 215–216, 219

theory
  and empirical society, 8–9, 164–167, 185–186, 191–194, 215–216, 260
  in science, 172–173, 255–257
    non- "elementary," 220–221
    non- "pseudo-realistic," 203, 208, 211
  see also: research; politics; science; society; sociology; *Wertfreiheit*
totalitarianism
  vs. democracy, 75–77, 79, 80–83, 99–100, 196–198, 212–216
  opposed to freedom of research, social science, 65, 161–162, 173
  supersession, 114–118, 121–126
  see also: anomie; coercion; force; militarism; power; ritualism; system
traditionalism, 44, 47, 71–72, 80, 86, 88–89, 93–95, 115–118, 126, 176–177, 197, 216
  see also: authority; insecurity; social change; society

universalism–particularism
  competence, fiduciary authority, 219

decrease of universalism, in Nazi type
society, 10, 68–72, 76, 87, 138,
169
increase of universalism, in democratic
type society, 79, 114, 121–126,
231–232
institutions in "postindustrial" society,
247
and types of social control, 114, 197–198
see also: ethics; "Führer" principle;
fiduciary; Germany; modernization;
pattern variables; prejudice; racism;
social control; values
universities, 63–65, 67–68, 103, 124,
136–137, 172–173, 210, 218, 230,
243–245, 252–254, 266–271
see also: anti-intellectualism;
community; democracy; education;
National Socialism; professions;
science; sociology
utilitarianism, 5, 7, 13–20, 27–29, 35–36,
38, 40, 45, 47–48, 96, 131,
165–166, 185, 203, 208, 211,
220–221, 246–248, 254–255,
255–257
see also: Darwinism; force; heredity and
environment; positivism

values
in anomic society (lack of value
integration), 10, 11, 38–39, 45
in civil society, focus societal
community, 223, 231–233, 247
commitment, an interaction medium,
210–215
in fascist society, 95–97, 120, 169–170
in integrated order, 48
reestablished, through reeducation,
117, 126
of sociologist (*Wertfreiheit*), 50, 51
in "theory centered research," 165–167,
172–173
and two-pronged structure(s), 196–198,
201–202, 215–216

see also: authority; commitment;
constitution(alism); four-function
scheme; interaction media;
institution; integration; morality;
normative system; pattern
variables; society; theory
"vicious circle," 120, 125, 175, 198,
214–215, 216
see also: conflict; deviance;
discrimination; prejudice;
revolution; social change; social
control
voluntarism
criminalized in Nazi Germany, denied in
coercion, 88, 102, 174, 197
as democratic, integrative element in
system(s) of modern society,
102–103, 115–118, 121–126, 138
increase in modernization, 231–233
as one side in two-pronged structure(s)
of action, 197, 212–215, 216
promoted by social sciences, 161–162
in *The Structure of Social Action*, 1–2, 6,
8–9, 12, 32, 41, 45–48, 51
see also: freedom of choice; influence;
institution; integration; persuasion;
reciprocity; science; sociology;
values

"War of All Against All," 30, 39, 40, 47,
51, 55, 209, 216, 257
see also: anomie; force; insecurity;
power; utilitarianism;
totalitarianism
welfare state, 6, 11–12, 16–19, 30–31, 34,
47–48, 222
see also: democracy; economy;
equality; integration;
modernization; New Deal; society
Wertfreiheit, xi, 4, 46, 51, 103, 161–162,
270
see also: science; sociology; universities
women, 94, 105, 113, 123, 227
see also: citizenship; Germany

Stafford Library
Columbia College
1001 Rogers Street
Columbia, Missouri 65216